Western Water Rights and
the U.S. Supreme Court

Western Water Rights and the U.S. Supreme Court

JAMES H. DAVENPORT

McFarland & Company, Inc., Publishers
Jefferson, North Carolina

This book has undergone peer review.

Library of Congress Cataloguing-in-Publication Data

Names: Davenport, James H., author.
Title: Western water rights and the U.S. Supreme Court / James H. Davenport.
Description: Jefferson, North Carolina : McFarland & Company, Inc., Publishers, 2020 | Includes bibliographical references and index.
Identifiers: LCCN 2020040770 | ISBN 9781476681207 (paperback) ♾
ISBN 9781476641478 (ebook)
Subjects: LCSH: Water rights—West (U.S.)—History. | Water resources development—Law and legislation—West (U.S.)—History. | Water-supply—West (U.S.)—History. | United States. Supreme Court—Decision making—History.
Classification: LCC KF5569 .D38 2020 | DDC 346.7304/32—dc23
LC record available at https://lccn.loc.gov/2020040770

British Library cataloguing data are available

ISBN (print) 978-1-4766-8120-7
ISBN (ebook) 978-1-4766-4147-8

Printed in the United States of America

McFarland & Company, Inc., Publishers
Box 611, Jefferson, North Carolina 28640
www.mcfarlandpub.com

Just as no man is allowed to be a judge in his own cause, similar fears of bias can arise when—without the consent of the other parties—a man chooses the judge in his own cause.

—*Caperton v. A.T. Massey Coal Co.*,
556 U.S. 868, 870 (2009)

The hubris of men led them to believe they could disregard even nature itself.

—Erik Larson, *Isaac's Storm*, Crown Publishers (1999)

Table of Contents

Prologue: Of Water, Men and the Law

Shall we still live in the Gilded Age, an age premised on unlimited potential, while aware of limited resources? Shall we still organize our affairs by rules built to enrich ourselves, while to do so is to diminish the potential of others? Perhaps these questions are too difficult to ask in a society now thoroughly founded on consumerism aided by technology.

The story below is fundamentally about the natural resource of water in the American West. Its setting, however, is the political and judicial realm, particularly the U.S. Supreme Court. It is about the effect of the case of *Wyoming v. Colorado* and the man Willis Van Devanter[1] upon future policy decisions affecting an important natural resource: water. The reasonableness and integrity of the man who wrote the opinion, in the context of the times, is a necessary ancillary study. It focuses also on the social, economic and legal history of the times. It raises the issues of judicial bias, recusal and political preferment for judicial appointment. In 1968, Professor M. Paul Holsinger suggested deferring the difficult-to-answer question whether the "at times herculean efforts made to get [Justice Van Devanter] appointed [to the Supreme Court] were justified" "until his career on the Court is assessed in proper historical perspective."[2] Hopefully this work will answer that question.

The U.S. Supreme Court is generally regarded as the final arbiter of legal controversy in the United States. Most Americans think first of the Court's role in sorting out controversies involving the meaning of the Constitution. But the Court also addresses a much broader band of legal questions, raised to it from the lesser federal and state courts. One aspect of that broader judicial practice is its role in solving conflicts between individual states, under the Court's "original jurisdiction." It is within this jurisdiction that the Court typically influences state powers, boundaries and natural resource policy.

The American people accord the Court great credence and trust. It is generally regarded, perhaps naively, as an institution above politics, an institution sorely needed in our modern fractionated society, where remote political extremes are wedged apart by the artisans of partisan politics and media-generated profits. But Americans have grown more wary of late, what with the spectacle of *Bush v. Gore*,[3] the atrocious consequence and strained reasoning of *Citizens United*,[4] and the divisive effect of the Patient Protection and Affordable Care Act and the Court's split decision in *National Federation of Independent Business, et al., v. Sebilius*.[5] It is now commonly argued by both of America's majority political parties that the prime reason to vote for its presidential candidate is that he or she will nominate jurists to the Court who will perpetuate the political thinking of that party. The history of the Court is indeed a history of its individual judges.

Is the Court a legal or a political institution? Is the answer derived from the Constitution itself—or from history and action? Should the Court's primary deference be to its historical situation, making its object the perpetuation of the views and mores of the founding fathers? Or should the Court's loyalty be to social justice, making its objective to find and perpetuate rational social relationships in a modern society? Can it balance and integrate these apparently competing objectives?

Americans' general expectation is that judges will be inspired by motives above the political. That whereas politicians might pontificate themselves "above the law," jurists will behave and admonish the society "within the law." Is a political judiciary consistent with that notion, or contrary to it? It is facile to espouse the latter, but more realistic, albeit difficult, to acknowledge the former.

Normally, public expectations of politicians' behavior can accommodate expediency, but rarely will they tolerate the same in jurists' behavior. Where a politician's self-serving actions might be accepted as normal, a jurist's will not. Where the debate regarding the functional relationship between the ends and means, the means and ends, may be appropriate for the politician, it would not be so for the jurist. And for the Supreme Court jurist, it would not be so in spades.

In truth, the United States Supreme Court has, throughout its checkered history, acted the political counterfoil of the Congress. Its authority, partially but scantly enumerated in the Constitution itself, is more largely assumed and self-defined by judicial fiat, accommodating federal legislation, and political acquiescence by the other of the three constitutional branches, and the public. The Court's members, the justices seated at the nation's highest bench, have been arrayed as broadly in the spectrum of political suasion as the members of Congress and the President. Historically, most justices who have served have risen from the political realm, rather than from the judicial. Their reason to rule in any given case cannot, therefore, be attributable necessarily to the legal merits of the cases presented to them, but rather to the political and social consequence of their decision. Characterization of the Court as "political" cannot of course stand as a generic truth. Exceptions, even large exceptions, abound.

An important area of law which popular court-watchers tend to overlook, an area where the wedge-makers tend to be looking the other direction, but an area where the Court's actions are no less political and its decisions consequential, is the Court's lawmaking pertaining to the ownership and use of the nation's natural resources: its forests and fisheries, its oil, gas and water supplies. The Court's natural resource cases, and particularly its water cases, make for a fascinating historical specimen of the Court's political behavior. And the political acumen of particular justices in this field is revealed in the now little-remembered Supreme Court practitioner and jurist, Associate Justice Willis Van Devanter.

This work focuses on the Supreme Court case of *Wyoming v. Colorado*,[6] the role that decision played in the development of U.S. western water policy, and its effect upon the best future policy decisions affecting the important natural resource of water. This decision involving the Laramie River was published in June 1922, a few months before the seven Colorado River basin states agreed upon the Colorado River Compact at Bishop's Lodge in Santa Fe, New Mexico. It addressed the interstate implications of the principle that was by then guiding the intrastate allocation of water, the prior appropriations doctrine, as well as the federal/state jurisdiction issue. The case is now vaguely remembered by westerners as the case that expanded the influence of the prior appropriation doctrine, further distinguishing it from the equity-oriented approach elsewhere predominant, holding it applicable to interstate water supplies, thereby giving impetus to the interstate compact device by which numerous interstate rivers have since been apportioned between states, and as one basis of state jurisdiction.

In the United States, surface water supplies are apportioned between surface water users by two basic principles. Eastern states utilize the "reasonable use" aspect of the "riparian" doctrine, balancing one use against another. States west of the 100th meridian primarily use the "prior appropriation doctrine," a doctrine arising from America's Gilded Age, which recognizes an absolute right, one against the other, based on who got there first. California uses both. The U.S. Supreme Court's principles, predilections and practices played a role typical of Gilded Age opportunism in the development of the western doctrine.

You will find a discussion of the history and effect of the Supreme Court case of *Wyoming v. Colorado* in Parts III and IV of this book. A better understanding of that case and its author will be found by first digesting Parts I and II about the times and man responsible for it.

The Laramie River rises in Colorado, descends into Wyoming, crosses the Laramie Plain northeast to reach the North Platte, at Fort Laramie, and then proceeds to the Missouri. The Wyoming plaintiffs objected to a project in Colorado called the Laramie-Poudre tunnel, a project that would have diverted water from the Laramie in Colorado and moved it into the Cache-La Poudre drainage.

Counsel for the Cache-La Poudre district was one Adelphus "Delph" Carpenter, later the primary advocate for the interstate compact paradigm. Carpenter was committed to the agriculturist culture and American hard work ethic common to the Cache la Poudre Valley, and the settlement of Greeley, that had its origins in Pennsylvania and Ohio, from which Carpenter's father had emigrated. Carpenter ultimately lost his health and the case, as he was totally "home-towned" by Justice Van Devanter, who awarded his old clients in Wyoming 272,500 acre-feet of Laramie River water and Carpenter's clients only 15,500 acre-feet. Justice Van Devanter's judicial bias and secretive control of the litigation is here set forth.

Although the State of Wyoming was the putative plaintiff in *Wyoming v. Colorado*, the real movers were the cattle interests in the Laramie Plain which Van Devanter had represented while in Wyoming. The counsel team for Wyoming included John W. Lacey, Van Devanter's brother-in-law, with whom the Justice had practiced law. The case was heard on original testimony before the Supreme Court, with three oral arguments following between 1914 and 1918. The case transitioned through three Chief Justices (White, Taft and Hughes) and was finally decided

The Laramie Plain rises above the Laramie River in eastern Wyoming (author's photograph).

eleven years after filing, in 1922. Wyoming's U.S. Senators, who obtained Van Devanter's position on the Supreme Court, were the primary beneficiaries of the Court's decision. Van Devanter acted alone. There is no evidence that any other justice of the Court, save Chief Justices William H. Taft and Edward D. White, were even aware that the case was before the Court at all, nor that any other justice, except Chief Justice Taft, reviewed the decision in the case before its publication on June 5, 1922. In the end, Van Devanter, a meticulous, careful, smart, dogmatic and self-serving man of his times, ruled in favor of his old clients, never recusing himself, and no one then or later accused him of any violation of judicial ethics.

One must consider the reasonableness of the case's author and the integrity of his actions in the context of his times: the social, economic and legal context, including nineteenth century economic recessions, politics of the Reclamation movement, anti-trust and the Sherman Act, the progressive ("insurgent") movement, agrarianism, World War I, westward expansion, constitutional amendment (income tax, direct election of senators, women's suffrage), the labor movement, and the interstate compacts movement of the 1920s to 1940s. Van Devanter's personal story epitomizes the American colonial and predecessor British notions of "preferment" (promotion) and "interest" (connections). Van Devanter seeks and manipulates both. Issues of judicial bias, recusal and political preferment for judicial appointment raise their heads.

After some twenty years working in water law, I was surprised upon rereading the Laramie River case to see that the opinion's author was a judge whose name I didn't even recall. Since then, I have polled a large number of "in-the-know" water lawyers and Supreme Court aficionados and have discovered that they don't remember Associate Justice Willis Van Devanter either. I decided to do some reading and encountered an amazing story.

The Laramie River where it meets the Platte at Fort Laramie today, looking east at sunrise (author's photograph).

The Laramie and Platte rivers meet at Fort Laramie. Drawing contained in *Book of the Governors,* 1926 Governors' Convention, Cheyenne, Wyoming, July 26–28 (courtesy Wyoming State Library).

The Laramie River, running north to the North Platte River in Wyoming, and the Cache La Poudre River, running southeast to the South Platte River in Colorado, are only about eight miles apart as they leave the Medicine Bow Mountains. The Laramie-La Poudre Tunnel, subject of the litigation in *Wyoming v. Colorado,* was proposed to divert water from the Laramie into the Cahce La Poudre (author's map, 2020).

Justice Van Devanter was appointed to the U.S. Supreme Court in 1911 by President William Howard Taft, whom Van Devanter had followed at law school at the University of Cincinnati. Van Devanter was the son of a lawyer, who, after law school and brief law practice in Indiana with his father and one John W. Lacey, followed the same Lacey to Wyoming, where Lacey had been appointed chief justice of the Wyoming territorial supreme court by President Chester Arthur. Van Devanter began to practice law, became city attorney for the town of Cheyenne, and quickly became the "go-to guy" for Wyoming politicians. One of those politicians was stockman Francis Warren, who later became Wyoming's U.S. Senator and author of the "Warren Act" (which still today ostensibly limits the use of Bureau of Reclamation reservoirs to agricultural purposes while urban users need them). Van Devanter was within the inner circle of drafters of the Wyoming constitution, together with later (1923) Reclamation Commissioner Elwood Mead (think Lake Mead behind Hoover Dam on the Colorado River)[7] and later (1922) Majority Leader of the U.S. House of Representatives Frank W. Mondell.

There at Wyoming statehood in 1890, Van Devanter became chairman of the Wyoming Republican party, allegedly "rigged" local precinct voting to secure Warren's election to the U.S. Senate (this was before direct election of U.S. senators), and defended an out-of-state gang of hired guns alleged to have murdered "rustlers" in Wyoming's notorious "Johnson County War" and the Union Pacific Railroad who brought them there. While attorney for the town of Cheyenne, Van Devanter simultaneously represented the Union Pacific in negotiation of land development agreements with the town. Supreme Court historians remember mostly Van Devanter's representation of the Union Pacific and his "pen paralysis."

With sponsors in the U.S. Senate, President William McKinley appointed Van Devanter to the default position of Deputy Attorney General serving the Department of the Interior. With similar sponsorship, President Theodore Roosevelt appointed Van Devanter to a new seat on the Eighth Circuit Court of Appeals, a seat created for him by his Senate sponsors. Upon Van Devanter's appointment to the U.S. Supreme Court by President Taft in 1911, the State of Wyoming sued the State of Colorado in the that Court, seeking its original jurisdiction.

Wyoming v. Colorado is noteworthy because of its role in the controversy over whether water in the west belongs to the United States or to the States. Colorado advocated the latter, resting on the Harmon Doctrine. The U.S. had relied upon the same (then retreated) *vis à vis* Mexico prior to its 1906 Rio Grande Treaty with Mexico. Now, the State of Colorado argued it was the sovereign entity entitled to control all the water originating within its borders. Justice Van Devanter unilaterally called the U.S. Attorney General into the Laramie River case, whereby to give voice to the otherwise unraised issue of federal ownership, and ultimately ruled in favor of Wyoming on a theory, which he claimed founded in equity, but which can only be characterized as *federal* common law.

Ten years after Justice Van Devanter's decision in *Wyoming v. Colorado*, he took on a new fight, with Franklin Delano Roosevelt, in the historic "Constitutional crisis" over Roosevelt's "court-packing plan." A constant conservative throughout his twenty-six years on the Supreme Court, Van Devanter was again an "inside man" in organizing and persuading the Court's conservative coalition (including the "Four Horsemen" and Justice Owen Roberts) in undermining the New Deal programs and legislation FDR had secured in the Democratic congress elected in 1936. The crisis resolved when Justice Van Devanter managed to secure a golden parachute from Congress (full Supreme Court justice salary for life with no income tax imposed) with the help of his old western Senator friends then in power in the Congress.

In retrospect, Justice Van Devanter is alternatively considered as the "foremost intellectual conservative on the court during his twenty-six-year tenure," and the least productive writer with "pen paralysis." He was cherished by Chief Justice Taft as the silent partner who carried the day in conference, convincing more recalcitrant judges to join the majority and not dissent, being "good fellows" on a collaborative, chummy, club-like Court. Van Devanter died in 1941.

Wyoming v. Colorado bears the imprint of no other justices, but for the reference in Daniel Tyler's biography of Adelphus Carpenter about Chief Justice White having been present at one hearing. One wonders what Justice Holmes was thinking, sitting on the Court together with Justices John Marshall Harlan, Joseph McKenna, William R. Day, Horace Harmon Lurton, Charles Evans Hughes, J.R. Lamar, and Mahlon Pitney, at the outset. Justices J.C. McReynolds and Justice Louis Brandeis joined the Court in 1914 and 1916 while the case was pending. What might the intellectual Brandeis have thought, had he known of the compromised behavior of his colleague Willis Van Devanter?

Van Devanter's personal story carries the backdrop of parental erudition and ethics, classical undergraduate and law school education characteristic of the rising professional wealth class, western expansion (cowboys, railroads, rustlers, political muscle), congressional and Supreme Court politics, a little bit of racism, association with some great minds (e.g., Charles Evans Hughes, Oliver Wendell Holmes, Jr., Louis Brandeis) and some lesser ones (e.g., the irascible racist James Clark McReynolds, "one of the most unpleasant men ever to sit on the Court," in particular). It coincides with the major congressional enactments driving development of the west, through the Homestead Acts of the 1860s, the Desert Land Act of 1877 and the Reclamation Act of 1902. It coincides with the 1864 grant of 2 million acres of western real estate to the Union Pacific Railroad and other generous support of western opportunism. It encompasses the economic failures of agriculture in the west due to "rushing" and risky investment in the cattle industry in Wyoming (1887), overexuberant wheat farming in Oklahoma (1925), pursued by the same Herbert Hoover, then Secretary of Commerce, who returned from European reconstruction after World War I and presided as well over formation of the seven Colorado River basin states' interstate compact under the cloud of the Supreme Court's decision in *Wyoming v. Colorado.*

Proponents of the interstate compact approach to resolving competing claims to interstate waters often cite the platitudes of the Colorado River Compact of 1922, signed by governors' representatives of the seven Colorado River Basin states at Bishop's Lodge, outside Santa Fe, New Mexico, in November 1922. But attention is rarely paid to the judicial and political events leading to that signing. On June 22 of that year, the U.S. Supreme Court issued two interstate water cases, *Wyoming v.*

Colorado and *Adelbert A. Weiland, as State Engineer of Colorado, et al. v. Pioneer Irrigation Company*[8] (sometimes known as *Nebraska v. Colorado*). Both cases were reported with an opinion signed by a single Justice. In the first, *Wyoming v. Colorado,* which distributed the waters of the Laramie River, that Justice was Associate Justice Van Devanter. Although the second opinion was attributed to Associate Justice Clarke, it was more likely also authored by the same Van Devanter.

Part I

The Times

1

The Nation Moves West (1830–1880)

Fur trapper and wanderer Jacques La Ramie got himself lost, killed, or forgotten somewhere in the 1830s, and somewhere in the low-lying mountains today called the Medicine Bow, in what is now eastern Wyoming. Jim Bridger, known as "Old Gabe" to his fellow Mountain Men, beginning his career as a trapper in 1822, traveled the West extensively, including the Powder River Country where the Bozeman Trail ran.[1] His knowledge of the land and Indians proved valuable to the Army on the Bozeman Trail, first with the Connor Expedition in 1865, and later for the fort garrisons of 1866–1868. Bridger's advice was usually sound. But it sometimes went unheeded, with tragic consequences such as the Fetterman disaster.

Begun in 1834 as Fort William, Fort Laramie became an Army post in 1849. Significant Oregon-bound traffic passed through Fort Laramie, a safe re-provisioning post on the Oregon Trail where wagon trains rested before heading over the Rocky Mountains at South Pass or Bridger Pass. In the summer nine years later, General Grenville Dodge surveyed and platted a town which he named "Cheyenne," after the native American nation "Shay-an-nah," a prominent Great Plains tribe closely allied with the Arapaho.

During the 1840s, speculators from Council Bluffs, Iowa, from which the "Mormon Trail" emanated, ferried across the Missouri north of the Platte River's confluence to settle in Indian country, trespassing within the lands of the Omaha Tribe, the tribe itself having been pushed west from the Ohio Valley a century before. The Mormons and other westward pioneers passed through, but American settlement of the great plains had begun. A treaty between the Omaha Tribe and the United States, together with Congress' adoption of the Kansas-Nebraska Act of 1854, permitted formation of the Nebraska Territory and the founding of Omaha City that year, and the admission of Kansas and Nebraska as U.S. states in 1861 and 1867, respectively. The Act was proposed initially by Congressman, then Senator, Stephen A. Douglas of Illinois. Fueled by his commitment to the development of a transcontinental railroad, Douglas ultimately won the battle, but lost the war, as the slavery/abolition issue exacerbated by the enactment of the Kansas-Nebraska Act became the grist of Douglas' debates with then Illinois Congressman Abraham Lincoln, debates which propelled Lincoln to the presidency which Douglas also sought.

When Congress established the Nebraska Territory in 1854, it included that portion of the Wyoming Territory north of the 42nd parallel and east of the continental divide, which had been acquired by the United States in the 1803 Louisiana Purchase. The northern half of the Nebraska Territory, including the northeastern portion of future Wyoming Territory, became part of the Dakota Territory in 1861. That southern portion of the Wyoming Territory, south of the 42nd parallel, had become part of the United States with the 1848 Mexican Cession following the 1846 Mexican War. That portion, which included Cheyenne, remained in the Nebraska Territory until 1864. In 1861, Congress created the Idaho Territory which included all of the modern states of Idaho and Montana plus most of modern Wyoming (notwithstanding the 42nd parallel) minus the southwest corner. In 1864, Congress partitioned the Idaho Territory, carved out the Montana Territory, and placed the remainder, including Cheyenne, in the Dakota Territory.

By 1859, prospectors, miners, cattlemen, farmers, and emigrants were making a thriving trade for the merchants of the bustling towns of St. Louis, at the confluence of the Mississippi and the Missouri rivers. Having spent their money, they pushed up the Missouri to Independence, where the Kansas River meets the Missouri, to St. Joseph, and past the mouth of the Platte to Council Bluffs and Omaha, from which the Mormon Trail departed, crossed the plain, and reached the Platte where it heads north and west toward the Dakotas.

Following on the gold fever of the Pike's Peak Gold Rush of 1858–1861, a rush that brought the first large concentration of white settlement to the mountain west region, Congress authorized the Colorado Territory, south of the Dakota Territory, on February 28, 1861. The new territory's boundaries followed those still in effect today for the State of Colorado, as Congress carved out the rectangle from portions of the Nebraska, Kansas, Utah, and New Mexico territories. But Colorado would be off to a shaky start.

By 1865, the Colorado Territorial Legislature voted for statehood, and Congress passed an Enabling Act. But President Andrew Johnson vetoed it on the grounds that the territory had not legally fulfilled the Enabling Act. He replaced Governor Evans and the territorial judges with an unqualified set of absentee political office-fillers, like those carpetbaggers who plagued the deep South. Several federal officials were caught moving public funds to their private benefit. Congress again passed an act authorizing Colorado's statehood in 1867. President Johnson vetoed it again, this time on the pretext that Colorado had insufficient population. Congress' effort to override the veto was unsuccessful. Congress tried again in 1867, but the votes were not there. Statehood would not come for Colorado until 1876.

The dream of transcontinental rail service had been extant since the 1830s. But now it was in full flower. Frederick A. Cleveland and Fred Wilber Powell's 1909 railroad history, *Railroad Promotion and Capitalization in the United States*, attributes the first suggestion of a rail line to the Pacific Coast to the "anonymous author of 'Something New,' an editorial which appeared February 6, 1832, in the *Emigrant* of Ann Arbor. This writer, who it is supposed was Judge S.W. Dexter, publisher and one of the editors of the paper, after apologizing for suggesting a plan which might be thought visionary, proposed a railroad from New York along the south shores of Lake Erie and Lake Michigan, across the Missouri near the mouth of the Platte, through the Rocky Mountains near the source of the Missouri, and thence by the Lewis and Columbia rivers to the Pacific."[2]

America's wealthy class, residing primarily in the Northeast, Pennsylvania, and Ohio, utilizing the vehicle of the increasingly robust model of the American corporation, prompted Congress to subsidize railroad development through the land grant process. Nearly 200,000,000 acres of public land would be made available to seventy-nine land grant railroads, twenty-one of which were subsidized directly by Congress, mostly between 1862 and 1864.

Thirty years after the first mention of intercontinental rail service, Congress chartered the Union Pacific Railroad. The Pacific Railway Act of 1862 authorized the incorporation of the Union Pacific Railroad. It issued 100,000 shares at $1,000 each, capitalizing the corporation at $100 million. It was to be built west from Omaha essentially along the 42nd parallel. The 1862 Act granted the Union Pacific five alternating sections (6,400 acres) of public land per mile on each side of the track, totaling 2 million acres of western real estate, much of it in Wyoming. The land could be maintained, sold or encumbered at the corporation's will.[3]

The same year, Congress passed the Homestead Act,[4] expanding on the Preemption Act of 1841, which had been applicable in the states of Ohio, Indiana, Illinois, Alabama, Missouri, Mississippi, Louisiana, Arkansas, and Michigan, when they became states. The Act offered 160 acres of arid land to homesteaders who would farm them. People and goods began to move west by rail.

When Congress approved the Pacific Railroad Act in 1862, it had finally decided on a route following the Platte River Valley. Two railroad companies were chartered. The Union Pacific would track westward from Omaha while the Central Pacific would lay track eastward from Sacramento. Beginning nearly 1,800 miles apart, they would meet somewhere between. Land grants to the railroads were a major incentive as they were based on miles of track laid. Not until late 1865, however, did workers lay the first rail in Omaha, there then being a shortage of money, materials and men due to the U.S. Civil War.

In 1867, the Union Pacific's chief engineer General Greenville M. Dodge and his survey party reached Cheyenne to locate a base or "division point" for the railroad. Dodge decided that the point where the line would cross Crow Creek was ideal in that here began the "gangplank," the gradual slope of the prairie that meets the steepening grades of the Laramie Mountains. This slow grade allowed for a reasonable crossing of the mountains at Sherman Pass, named for Civil War General Sherman. Dodge intended that Cheyenne would become the locus of massive railroad shops and facilities built later to maintain the railroad's equipment.

Railroad construction was now in full vogue. Dreams of transcontinental movement of goods perpetuated railroad construction pushing across the Nebraska/Dakota plain. The Union Pacific began to chart its route further west. The rail line could extend west along the Platte River to the town of North Platte, and then northwest along the North Platte River to Fort Laramie, the route of the Oregon Trail. From there the line could follow the South Platte as far as Julesburg, Colorado, where Lodge Pole Creek meets the South Platte River. From there, the line could run up Lodge Pole Creek to Cheyenne, Wyoming, and on to Laramie. From Laramie, the rail route could follow the Overland Trail to Utah. The other alternative was a more direct route to Denver, Colorado, and across the Rocky Mountains there.

By November 1866, the Union Pacific had decided that the Colorado Rockies were too formidable to cross. It would be better to lay its track due west through Wyoming. This northern route unfortunately missed the business potential to be found had the rail reached Denver directly, rather than later by north-south spur. It was a regrettable, but necessary decision for the Union Pacific. Denver's business potential was estimated as far greater than anything foreseeable on the Wyoming route. But as John Charles Frémont had found in the 1840s, there was no open course by which to move directly west from Denver. And the railroad's course through the southern border of Wyoming would afford a faster route with which to deliver emigrants and commerce to the Pacific Coast and quick transportation of cattle as the railroad returned to the east. A spur line south from Cheyenne to Denver would have to suffice.[5]

The Union Pacific's decision to cross the Rockies due west through Wyoming also defined the interest of the developers of the Central Pacific, operating out of California. Frederick A. Cleveland and Fred Wilber Powell's 1909 railroad history accounts it well.

> Work was begun on the Central Pacific ... in 1864, and on the Union Pacific in 1865, and when the lines met at Promontory Point, May 10, 1869, the Central pacific had built 689 miles from Sacramento and the Union Pacific 1086 miles from Omaha. These results were brought about by the activities of two groups of men whose names have been inseparably linked with whatever of credit or of odium has attached itself to the achievement, and to the methods by which it was effected. Upon the Union Pacific was the "irrepressible George Francis Train," Thomas C. Durant, Sidney Dillon, and the brothers Oakes and Oliver Ames, and in charge of the work of the Central Pacific was that remarkably efficient quartet made up of Collis P. Huntingdon, Leland Stanford, Charles Crocker, and Mark Hopkins.[6]

The prospect of crossing the continent by train via the Union Pacific and Central Pacific railroads fired corporate entrepreneurs' expectations with dreams of access to Asia and abroad, and chagrinned Atlantic ocean liner operators whose vessels stood significantly unreserved while transcontinental railroad construction was underway.

The Union Pacific reached Cheyenne, now within the Dakota Territory, in November 1867. The region's population began to grow steadily. More than 4,000 people had been attracted to the new town, speculating on the construction of the Union Pacific and the prosperity it would bring. Discoveries of gold placers along the Sweetwater River further west that year spiked the speculation even higher. South Pass City was soon populated with 700 people and the consequent hotels, markets, law firms and saloons. A year later, South Pass City was home to 4,000 people. Ten years later, it was largely abandoned.

The Union Pacific Railroad's extension west would define growth on the plains throughout the 1870s and 1880s. For the immediate future after the railroad's arrival, however, its influence manifested itself in what its construction left behind. Gamblers, saloon owners, thieves, opportunists, displaced cowboys, miners, transient railroad gangs, proper business men, soldiers from "Camp Cheyenne" (later named Fort D.A. Russell, now F.E. Warren Air Force Base) all hung on in Cheyenne after the railroad moved west toward Promontory Summit, where it was destined to meet the Central Pacific and form the transcontinental railroad.

As the Union Pacific headed west, it traversed the west slope of the Laramie Mountains, reaching the settlement of Laramie, on the bank of the Laramie River in 1868. Laramie had been a provisioning site for stage companies, freighters and emigrants heading south from the Oregon Trail on the Overland Trail into Colorado. First a tent town of 500, primarily to shelter the transients who moved with the train west from Cheyenne, Laramie became a "board town" built hurriedly to accommodate the influx of the westward-moving population. The presence of the railroad, the consistent movement of people through Laramie, caused the Dakota Territorial Legislature to declare Laramie the county seat of a new county, Albany County, in 1868. But it was a hectic year for the flash-in-the-pan county seat. The general transience of the place induced lawlessness, causing the same Dakota Territorial Legislature to soon dissolve Laramie's government and place it under the jurisdiction of the federal courts.

When the transcontinental railroad opened, those tourists who formerly pursued the Grand Tour of Europe turned west rather than east, seeking the other coast in George Pullman's comfortable "palace cars." The far-west's mining and ranching regions were now open to eastern financiers. Travel from New York to San Francisco took six days instead of six months. Railroad track mileage would triple between 1860 and 1880, and then double again by 1920. Formerly isolated areas would be connected with larger markets. Commercial farming, ranching and mining would be possible, suggesting visions of a truly national marketplace. And the steel needed to join the now-tracked nation induced American steel production, surpassing that of Britain, Germany, and France combined. European financial capitals invested in both the railroad boom and the consequent steel production through the New York securities market.

A 1908 General Land Office report, showing land grants made by Congress to aid in the construction of railroads reported that Congress ultimately granted one-fourth of Minnesota and Washington, one-fifth of Wisconsin, Iowa, Kansas, North Dakota, and Montana, one-seventh of Nebraska, one-eighth of California, and one-ninth of Louisiana to various railroads. It also reported that the Northern Pacific railroad had been granted 44,000,000 acres, the Southern Pacific system 20,000,000 acres, the Santa Fe system 17,000,000 acres, the Illinois Central system over 2,500,000 acres, and the Mobile and Ohio system over 1,000,000 acres. In the name of efficiency, the railroads introduced a standardized time system. At noon on November 18, 1883, the railroads began a system of new time zones. The centuries old method in which each town set its own time according to the position of the sun in the sky would be curtailed. The railroads also switched to a standard rail gauge of 4' 8.5" in the interests of efficiency. Competing railroads could not use the same equipment.

Congress also subsidized the railroad growth through loans. The United States treasury issued bonds, in the amount of $64,623,512, thus allowing the companies to enjoy the benefit of credit against which they could also seek private funding. The

Union Pacific received $27,236,512, the Central Pacific $25,885,120, the Kansas Pacific $6,303,000, the Western Pacific $1,970,560, the Central Branch Union Pacific $1,600,000, and the Sioux City and Pacific $1,628,320. These bonds would mature between 1895 and 1899. Repayment of the loans was not, unfortunately, as easy as their extension. Payment of interest on the loans created the largest controversy. Later, in 1890, Congress would pass a general statute providing that lands along portions of railroads not completed would be forfeit.

* * *

Back in Marion Indiana, Young Willis had been only nine years old when Congress created the Wyoming Territory, severing it from the Dakota Territory and designated Cheyenne the Wyoming territorial capital. Congressman J.M. Ashley of Ohio introduced the Organic Act of Wyoming to Congress on July 25, 1868, to provide a "temporary government for the territory of Wyoming." Congress now designated Cheyenne the Wyoming territorial capital. U.S. Senator Simon Cameron, of Pennsylvania, moved the bill in the Senate. His son, James D. Cameron, was then president of the Northern Central Railway, which extended south from Pennsylvania into Maryland and Washington, and west at least as far as Springfield, Illinois, to which it had carried Lincoln's remains to Springfield in 1865.

Senator Cameron had been partial to the historic name "Wyoming" in Pennsylvania. He had been a candidate for President in the same Republican convention in which Congressman Abraham Lincoln had prevailed. Upon winning the national election, Lincoln named Cameron Secretary of War. Ineffective in that role, Lincoln named Cameron minister to Russia. By 1868, Cameron had returned to the Senate. Later that year, Ulysses Simpson Grant had been elected President. Originally from Point Pleasant, Ohio, Grant fit the expectations of the corporate interests of New York and Ohio and was, of course, a military man.

The same year that Congress created the Wyoming Territory, a 24-year-old Civil War veteran went to Wyoming to seek his fortune. He was Francis Emroy Warren, born in Hinsdale, Massachusetts, on June 20, 1844. He had served as a private and non-commissioned Union officer with the 49th Volunteers of Massachusetts during the Civil War and earned a Medal of Honor. He had farmed and raised stock for a short time in Massachusetts before heading west in 1868. When he arrived, he worked first as a railroad hand.

Apparently confident of his economic future, Francis Warren took a bride, Helen M. Smith, also from Hinsdale, who joined him in Cheyenne. It would become their life-time home. Cheyenne's mercantilists outfitted prospectors going to the Black Hills and provided them with stage transportation. Warren's wealth would grow as he became owner of a hardware and mercantile store, a merchant outfitter of other men's expeditions to satisfy their own wealth dreams, a model already perfected in the 1850s on bigger terms by Californians Leland Stanford and Edward Harriman.

The nation's beef industry had burgeoned in the 1860s. Plentiful grasses on the western plains, newly available for fattening beef cattle due to wholesale extermination of the buffalo herds that had previously grazed the western plain, coincided with the advent of a hungry Union army to stimulate the American beef industry. Herds of Texas cattle had been moved north, first to Kansas and Nebraska, then to Wyoming over the westernmost Goodnight-Loving Trail. When fattened in Wyoming, they would be transported east for consumption. The public domain's free fodder and the government's subsidy of railroad construction made Wyoming, and Cheyenne as its economic center, a golden opportunity for personal and corporate interests.

In the 1870s, stockgrowers discovered that cattle could winter over on the northern plains. Texas Longhorns, newly arrived from Texas, were soon interbred with shorter-horned varieties, several of which were imported east from Oregon and Idaho through Utah and over the Rocky Mountains into Wyoming. The Montana and Wyoming cattle industry began to flourish.

Most of the land was in the public domain, in Wyoming's early days, open to stock raising as open range. But things began to change in 1870, when the first homestead entry in Wyoming was accomplished. Thus began a period of inexorable conflict between the open range approach of the large scale corporate cattle

Cowboy logo from *Book of the Governors*, 1926 Governors' Convention, Cheyenne, Wyoming, July 26–28 (courtesy Wyoming State Library).

The Phoenix Building, built by F.E. Warren in 1882. Warren sold the building in 1887 to the Chicago, Burlington and Quincy Railroad (CB&Q) for use as a depot for their Cheyenne and Burlington rail line (author's photograph, 2019).

industry, which relied upon open government property, and the nation's concept of Jeffersonian agrarianism and westward expansion of the American population.

Francis Warren arrived in Cheyenne in 1868 while it was still within Dakota territory. He was instrumental in promoting the first electric lighting system and served as a member of the city council in 1872–74. He would serve as member and president of the territorial council in 1873 and 1884, territorial treasurer in 1876–77 and 1879–1885, and mayor of Cheyenne in 1885 from which he would be appointed that year by President Chester A. Arthur to become the Wyoming Territory's fifth governor.

Francis Warren's successful mercantile business, first serving Dakota miners, now began to serve the growing cattle industry. He would become, himself, a cattleman, where he would invest in real estate and make his fortune as owner of the Warren Land and Livestock Company.

In the midst of the Panic of 1873, Francis Warren became a member of the Cheyenne City Council and was elected to the Council of the Territorial Assembly the same year. He would be elected president of the Council and thereafter be appointed to three terms as Territorial Treasurer of Wyoming. Willis Van Devanter, now 14, was still in grammar school back in Marion, Indiana. President Grant was reelected President. The Republican post-war establishment was now clearly established. In Wyoming, the would-be Republican establishment was well under construction.

Notwithstanding the economic stress suffered generally in the mid 1870s, the West was now beginning to come of age in the American establishment. Congress granted statehood to Colorado in 1876, and passed the Desert Land Act the following year, authorizing settlement on arid lands in the West, an action that would dramatically affect the development of the American West. The Act, together with the onslaught of cattle from Texas and the Pacific significantly affected the ratio of cows to people. By 1879, there were 450,000 cattle in Wyoming. In 1880, the population of Cheyenne, Wyoming, was less than 3,500. Only 20,789 people lived in all of Wyoming Territory.

2

Herbert Spencer and Social Darwinism (1859–1938)

The American society which greeted Willis Van Devanter was changing rapidly, attaining modicums of success for the most aggressive and definitionally "principled." The "Gilded Age," generally thought to have commenced about the time of Ulysses Grant's 1868 election, and bearing the moniker derived from Mark Twain and Charles Dudley Warner's 1873 satire "The Gilded Age: A Tale of Today," was in its teens. Rapid economic and population growth was burgeoning in the United States.

Charles Darwin published his now famous treatise, *On the Origin of Species*, in 1859, the year Willis was born. All species had, according to Darwin, descended over time from common ancestors. Different modern species "evolved," so goes the theory, due to a constant struggle for survival. Those with stronger survival characteristics pass their traits down through their genetic descendants. Each modern species' unique survival attribute could reckon back to the particular survivalist trait of some parent, perhaps common, species.

Five years after Darwin's seminal publication, English political theorist, sociologist and anthropologist Herbert Spencer took Darwin's thesis a step further in his acclaimed *Principles of Biology*, coining the phrase "survival of the fittest," later to be dubbed "social Darwinism." Spencer posited that the structure of modern society reflected that those who possessed the greatest wealth had inherited, or at least currently practiced, behavioral skills that perpetuated their greater survival—those with lesser means possessed weaker survival skills. In its extreme also a later justification for racism (eugenics posited that genetic development created one race genetically superior to others), Spencer's theory provided a rationalization and justification for wealth accumulation at the same time that America's industry and business were metamorphosing due to the inventive American spirit.[1]

The Supreme Court's historian and Chief Justice William Rehnquist observed, in 1987, that "Social Darwinism taught that the notion of 'survival of the fittest' enunciated in Charles Darwin's *Origin of Species* as an explanation for the evolution of life on the planet could be transposed to the world of social and political philosophy."[2]

Both Darwin's and Spencer's theories were posited in the context of environment. Survival skills were important because the environment was otherwise limiting and cruel. Without them the species, later the entrepreneur, could not survive. Through generations, those with the better skills *vis a vis* the environment would spawn better progeny. But American social Darwinism added a complimentary component, that the constraints of the environment should be minimized or removed altogether, thereby permitting the thriving entrepreneur's progeny to "evolve" at an accelerated rate without environmental, i.e., regulatory, interference. Regulatory interference with wealth accumulation should not be countenanced at all, because those who accumulated it were genetically disposed to the skills of that accumulation. The consequential notion, that assistance to the poor actually weakens their ability to survive in society, a notion still espoused, was voiced in 1884 by Yale University professor William Graham Summer in his *What Social Classes Owe to Each Other*.[3] Government, it was advocated, should not interfere with "natural selection." In its lesser manifestation social Darwinism thus corroborated the Ben Franklin–type inclination toward self-improvement and upward mobility. In its greater manifestation Social Darwinism thus justified stratification of wealth and the abuse of corporate power, merger and market control which would prevail by the height of the Gilded Age.

Spencer's concept of the origins of social order was premised on the existence of a new American "industrialized" society in which interpersonal relationships were contractually assumed, entered voluntarily through social choice. By comparison the old world's "militant" society was structured by a power-based hierarchy. Because relationships were now consensual, free to be had or shunned at will, the environment for exercise of stronger social survival skills was open and the "fittest" could attain the higher rungs of the societal ladder. In order that the consensual model of interpersonal relationship be permitted to thrive, government must *let it be*, hence "laissez faire," ultimately both a governmental regulatory philosophy and a social ethic.

Purely stated, the principle of laissez faire economics is that governmental interference disturbs the natural and equitable forces of economic development. Those forces should therefore be left to work themselves out with maximum freedom and minimal government interference.

Spencer's premise of social organization was eschewed by established religious organizations, as "theologically corrupt." It is no wonder, as the church had manned the "power-based hierarchy" of the "militant" society. But both Spencer and the church overlooked the fact that social relationships can also be organized on the basis of broad, societally based principles, like honesty, transparency, courtesy and equity. Social Darwinism merely threw these babies out with the bathwater.

3

Economic Fortunes and Misfortunes (1860–1875)

Marion, Indiana, was remote from the major population centers of New York and Pennsylvania when Willis Van Devanter was growing up. Marion was not New York, where its Fifth Avenue above 50th Street, bordering new Central Park, would be the high point of the Age. But Willis certainly would have been aware of the changes taking place in American economics and society. His father would have carried home the significant events of the day, due to his political involvement in Indianapolis. Newspapers were prevalent, and Willis was certainly a reader, perhaps even an early reader. He would collect newspapers all his life. Whether he may have recognized the crony capitalism, extreme inequalities in wealth and income, ostentatious spending and wage depression prevalent with the age, we can certainly guess. His education, his upbringing, his environment, his later life, all suggest that he took the principles of social Darwinism for granted.

The economic milieu in which Willis Van Devanter was reared saw post-war economic malaise and misfortune, thence inventive and industrial building, economic growth, and eventual market control and excess. During the antebellum period "common law doctrines had been transformed to create immunities from legal liability and thereby to provide substantial subsides for those who undertook schemes of economic development."[1]

"This pattern of subsidization raises several important questions concerning the relationship between legal and economic change in the period. Was legal subsidization socially efficient? Did it encourage investment in areas in which, as the welfare economist would put it, social benefits exceeded social costs even through private costs were greater than private benefits? Or did it in fact promote over-investment in technology, which might be inferred from the strikingly low contribution to the gross national product?"[2] Throughout, political realignment prevailed. A nascent, then establishment, Republican Party and eventual political standoff would lead to a new century.

The nation had grown quickly. Growth in the period was primarily due to manufacturing—in 1869, Willis a mere ten at the time, the manufacturing sector of the economy generated $3 billion, and would grow to $13 billion by 1900. Urban populations grew twice as fast as rural populations. The number of manufacturing workers tripled to 4.5 million and factory output multiplied by eleven times as the U.S. became the world's leading industrial power. America's labor force increased from

13 to 19 million people. Its population grew from 35.7 million to over 77.5 million people, many of them immigrants, between 1865 and 1901.

Booms and busts have been inevitable hallmarks of America's economic history. And economic panic and depression have followed swarthy economic expansion more than once. The government's financial needs during the Civil War had led to a variety of taxes, including the first income tax, enacted in August 1861, imposing a 3 percent tax on incomes over $800. By 1865, 20 percent of federal receipts were collected through the income tax. But as the money supply was still short, the treasury issued $500 million in paper money ("greenbacks") not backed by gold or silver. As the Union's economic fortunes flickered, so did the value of paper money, sometimes falling as low as 35 cents to the dollar.

In England in the 1850s and 60s, Carl Wilhelm Siemens, Pierre Emile Martin and Henry Bessemer of Sheffield had invented open hearth and blast furnace processes that would greatly facilitate steelmaking. Alexander Holly licensed the Bessemer furnace in America in 1865 and the steel industry took off. Inflation followed the Civil War, softening earlier more robust economic conditions. Between 1866 and 1873, fifty-six thousand miles of track were laid across the nation driven in significant part by government subsidies and land grants. Speculation in the railroad industry caused abnormal growth in factories, warehouses and other industrial activities, as well as in railroads, some of which offered no immediate return on investment. It would all lead to financial panic and depression.

Meanwhile, new technologies proceeded to enhance industrial and agricultural production. An emerging industrial economy quickly was expanding to meet new market demands. From 1869, Willis then ten years old, to 1879, Willis then twenty, the U.S. economy would grow at an accelerated rate (3.8 percent per year), holding through the 1880s. The Gross Domestic Product would double, but not without trouble.

The United States had financed the American Civil War in part with Civil War bonds promoted significantly by one Jay Cooke (1821–1905), who advertised and sold over $1.6 billion of the bonds. Hundreds of thousands of American citizens bought them. Upon the War's completion, Cooke began to sell bonds to finance construction of the Northern Pacific Railroad, a railroad projected to run from Duluth, Minnesota, to the Puget Sound.

As America has learned again in more recent times, unbridled exercise of unchecked power leads necessarily to economic trouble. Willis Van Devanter was ten years old when on "Black Friday," September 24, 1869, gold fell in price, bankrupting many local banks. The cause was laid at the feet of President Ulysses S. Grant. Speculation and insider trading by Jay Gould and Jim Fisk, railroad men who tried to corner the market on gold, and later attempted to bribe President Grant's staff, challenged Grant's presidential integrity.

Two years later, the Crédit Mobelia scandal surfaced. Crédit Mobelia had been organized by President Lincoln's designee Congressman Oaks Ames and his brother Oliver, to be the primary construction contractor for the Union Pacific Railroad. Through a disguised method of overpricing of the actual construction cost to the Railroad corporation, the Ames brothers raked the government-subsidized venture and distributed the railroad's profits to Crédit Mobelia shareholders, including themselves and congressmen, leaving the Union Pacific Corporation $10,000,000 in debt. The firm's 1868 distribution, in the form of stocks, bonds and dividends in the value of 280 times investment went public in the *New York Sun*. The Ames brothers were ensured. The congressmen raised their own salaries. Uninitiated public investors in the Union Pacific took the hit.

Economic dislocation in Europe due to the 1870–1871 Franco-Prussian War began to take its toll on the U.S. economy. The 1871 fire in Chicago and 1872 fire in Boston caused property losses and worsened investors' fears. Rampant speculative railroad investment, stimulated by government land grants and subsidies, exacerbated the situation.

Notwithstanding the economic malaise, President Grant was re-elected in November 1872, the Republican Party again prevailing. Grant shortly signed the Coinage Act of 1873,[3] sometimes called the Mint Act, into law. The Act generally revised the laws relating to the U.S. Mint, but more notably abolished the right of holders of silver bullion to strike their metal into coinage. "Bimetallism," the concurrent tender of currency minted from gold and silver was thus terminated. U.S. currency would now rely exclusively on the "gold standard." Although the law had been debated in Congress over the prior three years, it came as somewhat of a surprise to Western silver mining interests, who were obviously destabilized. The Act immediately affected silver prices and reduced the nation's money supply. Interest rates went up. Bank reserves were at risk of depletion. Farmers and others typically bearing heavy debt loads, and faith in financial institutions and long-term obligations, crumbled, undercutting railroad financing.

In the summer, financial failures began in Vienna and spread to most of Europe and North America. By then, Cooke's bank owned $7 million in Northern Pacific debt. When the Northern Pacific couldn't meet its obligations and could no longer convince the public to buy its bonds, Cooke suspended operations at the bank, setting off a panic to withdraw funds from competitor banks. By September, the "Panic of 1873" hit the stock market. It was forced to close for ten days to protect against a precipitous collapse. In New York City, bank reserves dropped from $50 million to $17 million during September and October. Consequently, almost 5,000 banks, brokers and commercial houses went bankrupt.

By November 1873, some 55 of the nation's railroads had failed, and another 60 would follow in the coming year. Some 6,000 businesses, employing over 500,000 people, are estimated to have failed. The Panic's effects would endure throughout most of the balance of the decade in America. At least five years of economic depression ensued. The Northern Pacific would declare bankruptcy in 1875, a bankruptcy which would take eight years to untangle. Eighty-nine of the country's 364 railroads would go bankrupt as well. As in most recessions, businesses hoarded money, not knowing whether the worst was yet to come. It would be called the "Great Depression," at least until the crash of the U.S. stock market in 1929.

Midst President Grant's second term, things did not improve. One John D. Sanborn was hired in 1874 to collect outstanding debts for the IRS. He kicked back revenues into Republican campaign funds. A year later, Secretary of the Interior

Columbus Delano was forced to resign for taking bribes and paying his son for surveying work that was never done. The "Whiskey Ring Scandal" surfaced. It was another conspiracy, this time between tax officials and distillery owners, to defraud the government of $1.2 million in taxes—much of which was funneled into Grant's 1872 re-election campaign. In 1876, Grant's Secretary of War, William Belknap was forced to resign after it was revealed that he had taken thousands of dollars in bribes in exchange for prime trading posts in Indian territory. What lessons in honor, honesty and stratagem might young Willis have learned?

As the industrial economy of the late nineteenth century was constructed, the corporation became perfected as the prime business model, the strongest engine of economic concentration since the Civil War. William Rehnquist later related that 65 percent of the goods manufactured in the country were turned out by corporations by 1890, 79 percent by 1900, and that the corporation had by then become "the dominant form of industrial organization in the United States."

Throughout the 1870s, flour miller Charles Pillsbury (1842–1899) had revolutionized the milling industry, competing with General Mills' founder Cadwallader Washburn (1818–1882). New milling technologies that produced inexpensive high-quality flour to American families brought growing agricultural and industrial wealth to the Middle West. The output of wheat would increase by 256 percent, corn by 222 percent, between 1865 and 1898. In 1876, Thomas Edison exhibited the multiplex telegraph and Alexander Graham Bell exhibited the telephone at the Centennial International Exhibition in Philadelphia. The 45-foot-tall Corliss steam engine also on display touted a 1,400 horse-power engine that could power 800 machines. The same year, Alexander Graham Bell's telephone revolutionized business communication. Edison was back at it the next year, patenting the phonograph, and the two years later, patenting the incandescent lamp. Urban homes were soon electrified. Factories got electric power. General commercial establishments were lit up. Cities saw electric streetcars and streetlamps by the 1880s.[4]

Innovations in manufacturing and engineering, improvements in structural steel, elevators, refrigerator cars, air brakes, stock tickers, punch car tabulators, and wireless telegraph all came into play in that fast-moving decade. Thick national networks for transportation and communication were created. The corporation became the dominant form of business organization, and a managerial revolution transformed business operations. And, the United States surpassed Britain as the leader in industrialization. The nation was rapidly growing its economy premised on heavy industry like factories, railroads, and coal mining.

Urban demand, consequent of growing population in cities, grew markets. Industrial businesses demanded better-trained workers. Rail transportation improved, allowing products to reach more distant markets. Financial innovations more efficiently allocated capital to creative endeavor. Individual personal savings grew. A variety of new financial institutions were born. Commercial banks, savings banks, and insurance companies all provided new means for capturing and making available those savings to business borrowers, thereby providing the capital needed to fuel America's economic growth.

In the business context, Scottish philosopher Adam Smith (1723–1790) had espoused that market forces determine success or failure. With no regulatory parameters on market forces and a laissez faire social ethic prevailing, more ruthless and cutthroat business practices had their permission—and their rewards. Removal of competition, even utilizing corrupt practices, was warranted, as the exercise of bolder, stronger, "fitter" men. In the governmental context, however, regulation was not the only relevant governmental practice. Politically approved franchise, opportunity and subsidy also ensued from government. Access, suasion, even bribery, were thus also seen as appropriate tools of the "fittest" business interests.

Many successful capitalists of the Gilded Age, not the least including nineteenth century entrepreneurs such as Cornelius Vanderbilt (1794–1877), Andrew Carnegie (1835–1919),[5] J. Pierpont Morgan (1837–1913),[6] John D. Rockefeller (1839–1937),[7] James J. Hill (1838–1916), Andrew Mellon (1855–1937), embraced Herbert Spencer's Darwinism. These industrial luminaries used his words to oppose social reform and government intervention. As Spencer said, these would interfere with the natural law of survival, a law beneficial in that it would improve and perfect societal quality overall. These magnates of American economic history all deferred to "let-it-be" social organization—easier for them to do as they had already ascended the ladder of wealth and station. Willis could hardly have failed to observe their rise to wealth.

Railroad financing was "creative" and "speculative." Newly capitalized railroad corporations could issue stock. The four investors in the Central Pacific Railroad (Leland Stanford, Mark Hopkins, Collis Huntinton, Charles Crocker), for example, initially invested less than $200,000 and sold railroad stock in the corporation worth $8.5 million. A state legislature or congress could grant a charter and land grant to a railroad corporation. The land would collateralize a bond issue. Revenue generated through bond sales would repay the land grant and establish a route which could be marketed to other rail lines. Once incorporated and financed, the original investors could create an independent construction company to do the actual railroad construction. In the case of the Central Pacific Railroad, corporate principals of the construction company later burned the financial records to frustrate accounting of their inter-corporate billing practices.

Public ownership of large corporations had by now become broadly accepted in American society, but the communication between the broadly spread stockholders and corporate management permitted corporate operation without daily oversight by shareholders. A class of corporate managers developed to manage the new corporate organism which manifested its own personality in the absence of consultation with, or advance authorization by, shareholders. Their guide was thus their trained image of themselves as masters of the principles ingrained in them by their antebellum educations. The excess corporate profit, and the ostentatious display of wealth, which ensued would be worthy of Twain's satire.

As one might guess, the business-political alliance often did not serve the public interest well. In some cases, those depending on railways for business purposes, particularly farmers, were met with uneven and often unfair shipping rates, especially where the essential rail link had no competitive line, or where railways owned strategically-placed grain silos and storage facilities. Large corporations like Carnegie Steel or Standard Oil could pressure rail companies to give them favorable rates and rebates, sometimes under the table. In some instances, "drawbacks," payments for shipment of even competitors' goods, were exacted.

The courts, unfortunately, were not much help. The laissez faire philosophy was translated by the courts into a set of practical rules that enabled businesses to operate with even greater autonomy. During the 1880s and '90s the courts strengthened rules increasing the sanctity of the contract. State laws that attempted to regulate the workplace, such as restrictions on work hours and safety requirements, were repeatedly struck down by state courts with the argument that they violated the rights of employers and employees to enter into contracts freely.

Unskilled workers in industrial factories mostly did not share in Gilded Age prosperity. Hours were long, wages were low, conditions were dangerous. Many workers lived in miserable urban slums. Courts increasingly applied the "fellow servant" rule, relieving employers of responsibility for workplace injury if the negligence of another employee could be identified as a contributing cause. And the courts weakened labor unions, finding that employers had a right to replace striking workers and holding that strikers had no right to organize boycotts.

Economic development witnessed unbridled competition, excessive greed, manipulation of markets and political corruption. Government officials made land grants, established tariffs, and proffered political favors in exchange for campaign contributions, cheap stock, free goods and services, and even outright bribes. The Gilded Age saw a new class of business owners, collectively to become known as "robber barons," a term first used to describe railroad owners who controlled shipping routes and could dictate exorbitant rates and fees to farmers shipping their produce to market, but then extended to wealthy industrialists generally.

The standard view of entrepreneurial America was, of course, that governmental interference should be rejected. Even so, businessmen understood the time-honored tradition that access to political support was an essential component of the laissez faire business environment. In order to keep the government close to business' objectives, railroads offered free passage to congressman and other government officials. Sometimes complimentary shares of stock in building corporations found themselves available to political friends of business.

The realignment of politics in the decade before the Civil War and the political requirements of reconstruction left the political parties and Congress preoccupied with issues that had little to do with the daily affairs of working people. As we have seen, huge changes occurred in American economic and social conditions between the end of the Civil War and 1900. The movers and shakers of the era were all in business. Some of those made profitable use of their financial prowess to buy their way into high office, including state governorships and the United States Senate.

Intense competition between the major political parties generated close elections throughout the Gilded Age. Presidential elections between the two major parties were so aggressively contested that a minor incident could shift the electoral outcome.

The Civil War's aftermath drove loyalties that largely defined the political parties. The Republican Party held a slight edge in national politics, based significantly on their blaming the Civil War on the Democrats, waving the "Bloody Shirt." Union veterans gravitated to the Republican Party, the Grand Army of the Republic becoming a GOP auxiliary. Republicans were also known as the party of business, as they supported protective tariffs, transportation improvements and a tight money policy. Their philosophy, derived from the fact that the party was dominated by business, was that what was good for business was good for everyone else, including workers.

The Democratic Party base, often led by Irish Catholics, was made of Catholics, poorer farmers, traditional party members and resentful southerners. Chided by their treatment in, and outcome of, the Civil War, southerners were attracted to the Democratic Party, away from the more economically successful Republican Party in northern states. After the end of Reconstruction in 1877, competition in the south took place mainly within the Democratic Party. And, the gradual disenfranchisement of Afro-Americans in the south diminished Republican influence there.

Union veterans, businessmen, professionals, craftsmen and larger farmers supported the Republican Party, which consistently carried the north in presidential elections. The Party included northern Protestants and Americans descended from older generations. Ethnically they were supported by Scandinavians, German Lutherans, English Methodists and Anglicans. They were shunned by Catholics because of their opposition to parochial schools. Immigrants sometimes disagreed with their policy that all teaching in schools must be in English.

The controlling factor defining the more general American political system between 1875 and 1900 was that the parties would be evenly divided. Republicans and Democrats fought over control of offices, which were the rewards for party activists, as well as major economic issues. Voter turnout was high, sometimes exceeding 80 or 90 percent, particularly where political parties drilled their loyal members in army fashion. After 1900, voter turnout nationwide would recede sharply.

Rapid population growth in major metropolitan centers caused an increase in governmental, public service contracting and public sector jobs. These made worthy preferments for political friends. The term "spoils system" is oft attributed to New York Senator William L. Marcy, who said, "To the victor belong the spoils." It was hardly a new concept, as Herbert Spencer had established it in 1859. Following his victory in the election of 1828, President Andrew Jackson had argued that the awarding of government positions to loyal political supporters enhanced the democratic process. Jackson believed that any average, intelligent citizen should be able to perform government's mundane tasks. However, the awarding of government jobs increasingly became viewed as a source of corruption. Political machines' gaining more control over partisan activities exacerbated the opprobrium. A desire to reduce political corruption would ultimately induce the movement for civil service reform.

Both political parties used "political machines" to sway elections, the winning party distributing the spoils of the election to friends and party regulars. The most famous of these was, of course, the Democratic Party's, and Boss Tweed's, Tammany Hall. The New York machine provided more services to the poor than any city government before it, but a lot of public money went into private pockets. Tweed was said to have enriched himself in the strikingly broad estimate of $30 to $200 million before he was prosecuted in 1873.

Beginning with General Grant, Republicans would nominate former Civil War officers for President in every election through 1900, except in 1884, again cashing in on the legacy of the War. Congress suffered political stalemate. Very little serious legislation was passed. Between 1875 and 1896 only five major bills passed Congress and were signed by the president. Even discussion of the graduated income tax, by any definition a revolutionary measure, failed to arouse much interest or public debate. Even so, voters turned out in large numbers. But important issues created by the influx of immigrants, industrialization, and urbanization, were only passively and confusedly addressed.

The major political issues of the Gilded Age included tariff and currency reform, obviously of interest to businessmen, and civil service reform. Business lobbied and spent freely to gain support for favorable tariff legislation and business-friendly monetary policy. Civil service reform was a broad reaction to the widespread political corruption throughout the post–Civil War era. Meanwhile, the controversy between "silverites" and "goldbugs" would not go away.

4

The Prior Appropriation Doctrine (1840s–Present)

In the course of human history, water supplies have been shared or commandeered, allocated or appropriated. In by far the majority of cases, sharing and reasoned allocation of water has been the rule. The prior appropriation doctrine is, however, in the minority, a virtual anomaly when considered in the broad set of societies from ancient to modern history, from the Thames to the Indus, the Mississippi to the Chesapeake.

Early American water law, and the English tradition from which it derived, was initially "fact driven," that is developed at the common law by judges rather than by legislatures. The earliest English water law about which we are aware arose in the Middle Ages in actions brought primarily by monopolistic mill owners whose mills had devolved from manorial operations. These actions involved the defense of rights, rather than their origin or source. They sounded in the law of *nuisance* (*nocumentum*),[1] i.e., actions addressing the wrongful disturbance of enjoyment of property where there was no interference with or encumbrance on title, no dispossession of the landholder, nor any direct physical or trespassory injury to the land.

The water-powered mills of the English feudal period had been operated since before the memory of those now living ("time out of mind," *time immemorial*).[2] When upstream water uses affected mill operation, "disturbance of enjoyment" or "nuisance" was alleged to have occurred against a *praedial servitude*,[3] a claimed property right in upstream water supply appurtenant to the thirteenth century English mill owner's downstream mill site.[4] One defense to that claim was that the upstream owner possessed his own right to water flowing in the stream, a right premised on *user* or *servitude*. The principle that each riparian owner was entitled to some share of the natural resource was yet to evolve.[5] Prescription of incorporeal rights would not lie as a means to divest titles held by feudal right.[6] The defense to nuisance was in fact that each riparian owner had a right to a reasonable use of the water's supply.

Notwithstanding the English common law tradition, one eighteenth century English legal treatise writer, Sir William Blackstone,[7] built a theory of water right from Roman law and Roman-derived civil-law concepts of common goods and the natural rights of ownership. Blackstone's views were heavily influenced by his belief in unlimited legislative power in Parliament.[8]

Roman law, as published in Justinian's *Institutes*, divided public property into three classes, all of which were incapable of private ownership: property belonging to the common (*res communes*), to the state (*res publicae*), or to the corporate body (*res universitatus*).[9] Running water fell within the first classification, *res communes.* "The things which are naturally everbody's are air, flowing water, the sea, and the sea shore."[10] Justinian also distinguished between things that are *corporeal,* physical things (the *corpus*) the ownership of which could be fragmented, and things that are *incorporeal,* or incapable of partition of ownership. Running water was incorporeal. At least since Justinian's sixth century BCE review of Roman law, if not before, it has been understood that there are natural things, like water, which are incapable of partition and should be held in common.

On the other hand, "private law," that relevant to private property, was deduced in Roman law from natural law, "the *jus gentium* of all peoples." Private law and the civil laws and customs of established states included three main categories: persons, things (*res*), and actions. The second category (*res*) had two subcategories: those things capable of ownership and those things incapable of ownership. Possession was the basis of the right of ownership ("*dominium*"). Real property (*terra firma*) could be possessed. *Dominium* was essentially an economic or commercial right.[11] But, as flowing water could not be possessed, and continuance of its flow to serve Rome's municipalities was essential, *dominium* did not extend to water. In the late eighteenth century, Blackstone attempted to justify dominium over water by arguing that it too can be possessed—it could therefore be "appropriated."

Blackstone thus ignored what English Philosopher John Locke had better said in his 1689 *Two Treatises of Government*:

> Though the Water running in the Fountain be every ones, yet who can doubt, but that in the Pitcher is his only who drew it out? His *labour* hath taken it out of the hands of Nature, where it was common, and belon'ed equally to all her Children, and *hath* therefore appropriated it to himself....
>
> Nor was this *appropriation* of any parcel of *Land,* by improving it, any prejudice to any other Man, since there was still enough, and as good left; and more than the yet unprovided could use. So that in effect, there was never the less left for others because of his enclosure for himself. For he that leaves as much as another can make use of, does as good as take nothing at all. No Body could think himself injur'd by the drinking of another Man, though he took a good Draught, who had a whole River of the same Water left him to quench his thirst. And the Case of Land and Water, where there is enough of both, is perfectly the same.[12]

Blackstone contended that the origin of rights was nature—the "natural law" theory.[13] "Like many natural lawyers before him he began with Scriptural assertions of the basis of property and title."[14] With respect to the ownership of property, he basically adopted the Roman law notion related to land ownership. As expressed by Justinian: "Ownership" is acquired either through original acquisition (such as by occupation, possession) or "causa" (e.g., grant from another).[15]

The water sharing proposition in most of the world's cultures has been based on the Latin "*allocara,*" as distinguished from the Latin "*appropriare,*" "to make one's own." The distinction between the two words is in the actor and direction of the action. With *allocare,* meaning "to place" or "to locate," the action is directed from a first person to a third person. With *appropriare,* meaning "to take" or "to personalize," the action is directed from a first person to the same first person. Appropriation is based upon notions of capture and empire rather than principles of equity, economic or social (including environmental) value.

Notwithstanding Blackstone "from 1750 the [British] common-law courts developed a large but unstable body of legal doctrine, specifying strong property rights in flowing water attached to riparian possession, and also limited rights to surface and underground waters."[16]

Historians debate the influence of Blackstone on America's founding lawyers.[17] By the time that Blackstone wrote his treatise, the water law of the American colonies had long adopted the British common law of water, which provided for water's reasonable use in the context of the use of others. *Sic utere tuo, ut non alienum lædas.* The portion of Blackstone's writing that would have pertained to the American founders was that related to British government,[18] not that related to property ownership, and the former was disregarded by the authors of *The Federalist* (1787–1788), while the Constitution was under debate, as failing to recognize individual liberty.[19]

In 1827, the United States Supreme Court defined American riparianism, adopting the time honored principles of English common law, notwithstanding Blackstone.[20] John Quincy Adams was in the White House. Chief Justice John Marshall led the Court. Justice Joseph Story wrote for the Court in *Tyler v. Wilkinson.*[21] By virtue of a landowner's ownership of riparian land, the Justice wrote,

> ...he has a right to the use of the water flowing over it in its natural current, without diminution or obstruction. But he has no property in the water itself.
>
> Every proprietor may use the water as it flows, according to his pleasure, if the use be not to the prejudice of any other proprietor.
>
> This is the necessary result of the perfect equality of right among all the proprietors of that, which is common to all.
>
> When I speak of this common right, I do not mean to be understood, as holding the doctrine, that there can be no diminution whatsoever, and no obstruction or impediment whatsoever, by a riparian proprietor, in the use of the water as it flows; for that would be to deny any valuable use of it. There may be, and there must be allowed of that, which is common to all, a reasonable use.
>
> The law here, as in many other cases, acts with a reasonable reference to public convenience and general good, and it is not betrayed into a narrow strictness, subversive of common sense, nor into an extravagant looseness, which would destroy private rights. The maxim is applied, "*Sic utere tuo, ut non alienum lædas*."

But such time-honored, equitable notions would not prevail in the American west, whose settlement was proceeding under the influence of eastern American industrialization, Social Darwinism, and the imperialist paradigm of England's growing world empire. The Pike's Peak Gold Rush of 1858 in the Western Kansas Territory gave rise not only to the territory and state of Colorado, by 1861. It also perpetuated the need for a synthesizing principle of water management in the West. In the 1840s, California gold miners had spontaneously adopted the principle that those who claimed the water first, just as the gold ore itself, were entitled to a better claim to its use than were those who claimed and used it later. In order to be recognized as legal rights, however, they had to put the water to a "beneficial use." Even today, in the Wyoming Supreme Court's Judicial Learning Center it is stated:

"Prior appropriation means that if someone takes water for himself before anyone else does, that person's right to it is stronger than the right of anyone who may come along later."[22]

The acquisition of a water right by appropriation of the water has no origin in the customary or "common law" of England, the Roman water law of the second century, the Spanish Law of the twelfth century, or even the Spanish-Mexican law of the properties, including California, appropriated from Mexico by the United States

A SIMPLE QUESTION OF PRIORITY.

"A Simple Question of Priority," Robert E. Strahorn (aka "Alter Ego"), *The Hand-Book of Wyoming and Some of the Black Hills and Big Horn Regions for Citizen, Emigrant and Tourist*, Cheyenne, Wyoming, 1877 (courtesy Wyoming State Library).

in the Mexican War, a fact corroborated by Wells Hutchins in his *Water Laws of the Nineteen Western States*. Shop lifters do it. Horse thieves do it. Nations do it, as did Putin with the Crimean Peninsula. America's gunboat diplomacy in the nineteenth century did a lot of it. In the Middle Ages in England, ecclesiastical law, developed as custom in monasteries, justified appropriation of portions of benefices intended for local vicars, that is, a raking of the till on its way to charity.

"Appropriation" was the guiding principle of the United States' foreign policy in the early nineteenth century. The U.S. had appropriated the Spanish Florida territory through Andrew Jackson's campaign leading to the 1821 Onis-Adams Treaty. Through the Treaty of Guadalupe Hidalgo winding up the 1846–48 Mexican War, the U.S. had appropriated the ports of Los Angeles and San Diego and all else north of the 39th parallel from Mexico (the Mexican War was premised on the pretext of Mexican attack on General Zachary Taylor's forces venturing into Mexico's claimed territory). And in its domestic policy through its Indian treaties and Homestead Acts, the American Congress had appropriated the wide-ranging homelands of North America's indigenous peoples in the 1820s–1870s.

The law of prior appropriation is argued to be valuable in the arid American west because it supposedly accounts for the problem of scarcity, of drought. It is supposed to tell with certainty who gets the water when there is not enough of it. Whereas that certainty may have been thought to be an essential commodity in the nineteenth century, it may now be a social cost encumbering the flexibility of a more adaptive notion, that of reasonableness, in today's climate changing world.

5

Equitable Apportionment (1902–Present)

Natural systems, particularly including surface and ground water systems, do not abide solely within political boundaries. Rather, river and groundwater basins are the modern consequence of hydrogeologic events that predate the hubris of humankind (and its political representatives) by thousands, if not millions, of years—witness the Colorado (Green, San Juan), Columbia (Snake), Mississippi (Missouri, Ohio, Arkansas, Tennessee/Cumberland) and other interstate rivers and the Oglalla Aquifer. The United States' Geological Survey's second director, one-armed John Wesley Powell, had recommended that the nation's water resources be managed by unified hydrological basins, but political pressures and the interests of "statehood" carried the day, establishing political boundaries that would corner resources for in-state interests.

The first Supreme Court case involving conflicts over interstate water supplies was filed in 1901, when Kansas sued Colorado for diverting too much water from the Arkansas River.[1] The most recent case, involving claims to the Yellowstone River, was filed by the State of Montana against the State of Wyoming.[2] Other cases are pending.[3]

Congress became increasingly involved in the potential for developing water supplies in the western territories and new states during the close of the nineteenth century and opening of the twentieth century. A primary legal question was whether those water supplies, particularly including those surface water supplies that ran through or between multiple states, should fall within the regulatory jurisdiction of individual states or the United States.

In an equitable apportionment case, the Supreme Court has said that the plaintiff state must prove injury.[4] Without injury to a plaintiff state, there is no original jurisdiction.

The substantive law of equitable apportionment seeks to find a fair allocation of economic opportunity. "Equitability" is not the right to a precisely equal share of a system's water, but the right to its equitable utilization. Competing states claiming a portion of a common interstate resource are entitled to a reasonable share, not unlike the reasonableness standard of intrastate riparian thinking. In the case of an interstate river, the Court's primary objective is to make an "equitable apportionment of benefits between the ... States resulting from the flow of the river." The Court applies federal common law to determine each state's share.[5] Local law is not determinative:

In more recent equitable apportionment decisions the Court has considered comparison of harm and benefit,[6] the feasibility of means to improve water use efficiency and enhance water supplies, and the protection of existing economies dependent on water.[7] The Court may also consider relevant population and economic demand. In the event the Court were to further fashion its enquiry after that of riparianism's reasonableness it might also consider how the economic and social needs of one riparian state may be fulfilled without substantial injury to another, past and present utilization, availability and costs of alternative resources, geography, climate, hydrology, and practicability of compensation, each factor having some comparative weight *vis a vis* the others. Neither the location of an interstate waterbody's origin nor the timing of its waters use is relevant to equitable apportionment.

6

Interstate Compacts (1922–Present)

Today there are 38 interstate river compacts addressing water supply, water allocation, planning, flood prevention, pollution control, fisheries, species protection, power production, and commerce. Many of the nation's major interstate rivers, including the Animas-LaPlata, Arkansas, Bear, Belle Fourche, Canadian, Colorado, Connecticut, Costilla, Delaware, Kansas-Nebraska Big Blue, Klamath, Merrimack, Missouri, Ohio, Pecos, Potomac, Red, Republican, Rio Grande, Sabine, Snake, South Platte, Susquehanna, Thames, Vermejo, Wabash, Wheeling and Yellowstone, are the subject of interstate compacts. In the southeast United States, interstate conflict over the Apalachicola-Chattahoochee-Flint River system has provoked now-expired compacts, federal legislation and federal litigation.[1] The Alabama-Coosa-Tallapoosa River system is similarly challenged.

Although compacts between states are intra-sovereign contracts, they are nevertheless federal law, as they are authorized by the U.S. Constitution's "Compact Clause."[2] In the case of the Colorado River Compact, for example, the 67th Congress authorized the Colorado River basin states to negotiate a compromise on the Colorado River providing for "equitable division and apportionment ... of the water supply of the Colorado River and of the streams tributary thereto."[3] Congress' subsequent approval of the Compact subjects the rights of the United States in the waters of the Colorado River to the Colorado River Compact.[4]

Part II

The Man

7

Young Willis Van Devanter

Born in Marion, Indiana, Willis Van Devanter moved to Cheyenne, Wyoming, then to Washington, D.C., back to Cheyenne, back to Washington, and ultimately retired to Parry Sound, Quebec, Canada. Marion, Indiana, had been a frontier town, rested from the Miami Indians by William Henry Harrison in the 1812 Battle of Mississinewa. Its pioneer homes had been built of logs, heated by the same fire that cooked the evening meal. Travel was by horseback, wagon or foot, at least until the railroad reached the town. Travel time over good roads by wagon was roughly 20 miles a day. Roads were mostly "corduroy," logs covered with dirt, which made rough riding. Winters were quiet, without many visitors, as roadways were near impassable in winter snows or muddy spring warmings. Where the roads crossed creeks, the creek would undermine the log-based crossings and riders would avoid the road, creating unpassable bogs. If then needed, travel went cross country. In the summer, when roads were passable, church services were held in the schoolhouse, usually convened by a preacher riding circuit, and arriving no more than bi-weekly.

Parenting was straightforward. Children obeyed or went hungry. Students attending the log schoolhouse with grease paper-covered window holes would sit on backless benches made of split logs, tiring by day's end. A single writing desk, composed of a large box at the rear of the room, also served as storage box for books that remained at school. The three month "school year" occupied only a portion of the teacher's time, and he farmed the balance of the year to make ends meet.

People raised buckwheat, corn, oats, wheat, and rye. Tied wheat, oats and corn were stored in the barn. Summer and fall were for hunting and preserving. Deer, bears, opossums, foxes, raccoons, porcupines, rabbits and squirrels were fair game. Common work was recreation. In winter, the neighbors would gather and shuck the corn and thresh the oats and wheat. Threshing was first by flails, later by horse, then by steam engine, and finally by better machines.

By 1850, the frontier town of Marion, named after the General Francis Marion, the "Old Red Fox" of South Carolina, was the county seat of Grant County, having been designated thus by the Indiana General Assembly in 1824. Willis Van Devanter was born there on April 17, 1859, at the turning of an era, the beginning of the "Antebellum Period." President Lincoln would be elected and the Civil War begun the following year. Two years before, the U.S. Supreme Court had offered its decision in the *Dred Scott Case*.[1] There, under the leadership of Chief Justice

Roger Taney, the Court had declared that Congress had a constitutional obligation to protect slavery in the territories and no power to ban it. The decision would be repudiated nine years later in the adoption of the Fourteenth and Fifteenth Amendments to the U.S. Constitution. Chief Justice William Rehnquist much later quoted prior Chief Justice Charles Evans Hughes' characterization of Taney's opinion as America's "self-inflicted wound."[2] Supreme Court historian Jeffrey Rosen points out, with a wry smile, that two years after the constitutional amendments, Justice Harlan wrote his dissent in the *Civil Rights Cases,* reversing *Dred Scott,* using ink from the same inkwell that Chief Justice Roger Taney had used to write his majority opinion in the first place.[3]

Willis' great-grandfather, Peter, had been a gunpowder manufacturer in Pennsylvania during the American Revolution. His grandfather, Jacob, had been a captain in the War of 1812. His father, Isaac, was an Indiana lawyer and abolitionist. Isaac was provost marshal of his Indiana congressional district during the Civil War. He moved west to Indiana in 1850.

Isaac Van Devanter had been born in Delaware County, Ohio, on May 28, 1821. Isaac's parents, derived from "toiling, liberty loving Hollanders" and the "Scotch-Irish," migrated to La Grange County, Indiana, where Isaac secured his "common school" education. He entered Lagrange Collegiate Institute at sixteen and the White Pigeon branch of the Michigan University at nineteen. He thereafter read the law with attorney Joseph Lomax, of Valparaiso, Indiana, and under the direction of Judge Nathaniel Bacon, of Niles, Michigan, before attending lectures at the Cincinnati Law School, from which he graduated in the spring of 1848. He began professional law practice in Marion in 1850, together with Andrew J. Harlan, later a congressman.

In 1855, Isaac entered another law partnership with Hon. James F. McDowell, married the daughter of a prominent Marion citizen, one Violetta M. Spencer, with whom he would have 8 children, Willis being the first, and became a member of the Methodist Episcopal Church in Marion.[4]

The following year, Isaac was elected state Senator from the counties of Grant, Delaware, and Blackford, Indiana. He served four years in electoral Republican politics, during which time he was certainly acquainted with Indiana's future favorite son, Benjamin Harrison. In 1856, the Republican Party had supported its first bona fide presidential candidate, John Frémont, the ultimate western frontiersman, who had wandered back and forth across the mountain west and promoted himself as defender of U.S. interests at Sacramento, in the Mexican War of 1846.

Isaac became a provost marshal of his Indiana congressional district during the Civil War. During the Antebellum Period, America's social and legal environment had begun to shift, a shift which Isaac's son, Willis, would later opportune to his advantage. Willis' birth in April 1859 and young years, not to mention his adult years, would parallel the birth and young years of the America's rampant industrial growth, urbanization, westward expansion, and wealth accumulation.

At the outset of the Civil War, the federal government's capability to meet the extraordinary needs of an army of over one million men was severely tested. Once over, the demand subsided. But post-war events presented new arenas of federal responsibility, stretching the resources of government. Growth of industrial facilities in eastern states burgeoned westward. Railroad projects went boom and bust. Thirty-five thousand miles of track in America's 1865 rail network would become 242,000 by 1900. The nation returned to peacetime activities—farming, manufacturing, railroad building, and all the advances stimulated the arrival of a second Industrial Revolution. America's expanding infrastructure would bring new goods to a growing population.

Willis' young years would also parallel the birth, growth and predominance of the Republican Party in America. Little mention is now made of the importance of exploration of the American West, and expansion of U.S. dominance into it, in the history of the nascent Republican Party. In 1861, Abraham Lincoln had observed that he favored the parceling of the American west, thereby to make available a landed home for America's poor. The Homestead Act of 1862[5] would make 160 acres of public land available to each man and woman who could afford the ten-dollar fee.

The era of expansion had already begun. Isaac's move to Indiana had been typical of a significant shift of population from Pennsylvania to Ohio to Indiana in the early nineteenth century. Willis' later move further west would mark the next generation's expansion. Isaac died at 78, in Marion, on November 26, 1898.

Isaac's son Willis likely attended a typical Indiana grammar school, as had father Isaac at Lagrange Collegiate Institute a generation before, teaching the precursors of the courses later taught in the post-war college where Willis would attend: language (Greek and Latin, composition, rhetoric), the physical sciences (anatomy, chemistry, mineralogy, geology), and the nineteenth-century version of the social sciences (philosophy of rhetoric, mind, and politics, political history, natural history, political economy), and the moral order (natural theology, evidence of revelation)—in short a course of study in the denial of the recrimination with which the nation was infected as a natural reaction to the long and terrible civil war.

Judicial historian Mark Warren Bailey described the elements of the typical Antebellum education in moral order, taught under the rubric of "natural theology," in his study of the legal philosophy of the Supreme Court during the period 1860–1910. The academic regimen proselytized the fundamental principle that the universe was God's creation and was therefore orderly and moral. Its order proved God's intention that nature benefit man and encourage his progress toward moral and material perfection. The first invariable law of nature, exemplified by the history of the United States, was "progress." God rewards virtue and punishes sin. "Progress" is a reward of virtuous life. "Economic virtue such as industry and frugality and the material rewards that resulted from them were blessed by God, whereas idleness and sloth merited divine punishment in the form of poverty and misery." The outcome of success thus defined the morality of the actions taken to realize it. A man is Christian, moral, and civically virtuous because of what he attains, not because of how he attains it. The ends justify the means.[6] The theology fit well with the more scientific-sounding social Darwinism.

And so would it be with Willis Van Devanter. Earnest, justified in his own sense of what is "moral" and "right." Virtuous, justified by the reality of his "progress" or "success." Willis would go on to attend Indiana Asbury University, later DePauw, in Greencastle, Indiana, where he would graduate, according to Professors Alexander Bickel and Benno Schmidt, with "an almost perfect record" in history, mathematics, Greek, Latin, and deportment. Undoubtedly infused with the "moral philosophy" of the Methodist institution, he would have further assimilated the principle that natural theology justifies the natural, social and economic order, and that the "hand of Providence at work in the natural order" taken together with the "belief that reason or an innate moral sense" permits an educated individual to perceive "the dictates of natural and absolute justice."[7]

Knowing justice from within, rather than from the facts or a societal sense of common good and fairness, Van Devanter would be prepared to pronounce the law, notwithstanding the circumstances. Upon graduation, Willis returned to Marion to assist in family support, due to his father's physical frailty. He wouldn't stay long. Young Van Devanter, now 20 in 1879, headed for University of Cincinnati Law School, his father's alma mater.

Circumstantial evidence strongly suggests that young Benjamin Harrison (later, 23rd President of the United States) and Willis Van Devanter's father Isaac were acquainted, and politically affiliated, a factor that would be important to Willis' young adult life to come in Wyoming. Harrison would play an instrumental part in Young Willis' legal and political career. Benjamin Harrison was born on August 20, 1833, in North Bend, Hamilton County, Ohio, as the second of eight children. His father was John Scott Harrison, a U.S. Congressman from Ohio. His grandfather was William Henry Harrison, 9th President of the United States. His great grandfather was Benjamin Harrison, revolutionary leader and governor of Virginia. President Benjamin Harrison attended a one-room schoolhouse near his home in Oxford, Ohio, and was later tutored in preparation for college. Benjamin enrolled in Farmer's College near Cincinnati, Ohio, in 1847, attending for two years, but graduated from Miami University in Oxford, Ohio, 1852.

Both Isaac Van Devanter and Benjamin Harrison had followed the path from Pennsylvania, through Ohio, to Indiana in several generations. Isaac reached Indiana with his parents earlier, in the 1830s, and made his home at Marion, Indiana. Harrison reached Indiana in 1854, two years after his graduation from Miami University, six years after Isaac Van Devanter had finished law school at the University of Cincinnati Law School (in Harrison's home county of Hamilton), and four years after Van Devanter took up law practice in Marion.

In 1856, bachelor Isaac Van Devanter was elected to the Indiana State Senate, sitting in Indianapolis, representing Grant, Delaware, and Blackford Counties. He would serve four years, during which time he was a member of the Judiciary Committee, and the Committee on Organization of Courts, and on Elections, according to the Proceedings of the Twenty Second Annual Meeting of the American Bar Association, held at Buffalo, New York, in 1899. When Harrison reached Indianapolis, he became admitted to the bar, took up law practice and became a crier for the federal court. A fourth-generation politician, he can hardly not have noticed the lawyer member of the state senate's legal committees, twelve years his senior. Nor would Van Devanter likely have failed to notice the grandson of the former President Harrison who had followed the same path west. Harrison ran successfully for Indianapolis city attorney in 1856, the same year the Republican party organized around the presidency of John C. Frémont, whom Harrison supported.

The two lawyers, together in the young capital city, must certainly have found time to commiserate on the developing Republican Party platform. In his first pursuit of elective office, Harrison was the successful candidate for the nonpartisan position of reporter of the Indiana Supreme Court in 1860. Harrison was nevertheless an active supporter of the Republican Party platform, which he advocated in debate against Democrat Thomas Hendricks, candidate for Indiana governor and later Vice President of the United States.

Both Isaac and Benjamin had served in the Civil War, Van Devanter as provost marshal of what was then the 11th Congressional District, Harrison first as an officer of the 70th Indiana Infantry, which joined General Sherman's Atlanta Campaign in 1864.[8] Ultimately promoted to Brigadier General in 1865, he returned to his position as reporter of the Indiana Supreme Court in Indianapolis in the summer. He had been reelected in absentia in 1864.

Harrison and Van Devanter pursued their respective law practices in Indiana throughout the post-war years. They must certainly have remained acquainted, as the clients they represented in their law practices were notable. The older Van Devanter represented railroad corporations, including what became the Pennsylvania Railroad, and was admitted to practice in the Supreme Court in 1871. Harrison's law practice was also notable. He received a commission from President Ulysses Grant to represent the federal government in a civil claim based on a wartime conviction for treason, which had been reversed by the Supreme Court, and helped to mediate between the workers and management and to preserve public order, when the Great Railroad Strike of 1877 reached Indianapolis. While Van Devanter's upstate political activity was less noticeable, Harrison would run for the Republican Party nomination for Indiana governor in 1872, and despite the Panic of 1873 would build a grand home in Indianapolis in 1874.

Harrison's political activism drew attention from the Republican establishment, as would later happen for young Willis Van Devanter. President Rutherford Hayes, who hailed from Delaware County, Ohio, the very same county to which Isaac Van Devanter's parents had initially moved from Pennsylvania after the War of 1812, would appoint Benjamin Harrison to the Mississippi River Commission in 1879, which would be founded to facilitate internal improvements on that river. And Harrison would become a delegate from Indiana to the 1880 Republican National Convention in Chicago, which nominated James Garfield for President. Later, in 1888, he would be nominated and narrowly elected to become the one-term President of the United States.

In spring of 1930, Willis returned to Marion to reminisce as a United States Supreme Court Associate Justice, his speech later republished in the *Indiana Law Journal*:

> Marion, where you meet, is my birthplace and was the theatre of most of my activities until I was twenty-five. It was here that I came to the Bar and entered the practice. It was here that my father came to the Bar 33 years before and pursued his professional work for fifty years.

> It is here that my mother, always to me a guardian angel and an inspiration, is now enjoying an unusual span of life. And it was on the spot where you now are meeting that my maternal grandparents lived and always made me more than welcome. Thus the surroundings have a special appeal to me.[9]

Little may young Willis have anticipated that later in his adulthood, he would sit on the Nation's highest court and act in such a way, as we shall see, so as to let the air out of the tires of the Sherman Act, to compromise the Congress' earlier effort to constrain the power of the corporate engine, to stand in the way of the reconstruction of the nation's economy through FDR's New Deal legislation, to give away its water supplies to his political cronies, and by the way to endorse the appropriative model of cornering public resources for the private interest. Van Devanter is remembered by the legal establishment now, if at all, for his conservatism, paucity of written opinions, situational constitutionalism, and a fight with Franklin Roosevelt.

8

Cincinnatus (1833–1885)

When the University of Cincinnati Law School, where Willis matriculated, was founded in 1833 there had been only three or four other law schools in existence. The Cincinnati Law School was a school of the traditional style. Lectures were provided in a large, barnlike room in the old Mercantile Library Building in the heart of the city heated only by an iron stove. Several hours of lectures each day in real property, evidence, civil procedure, torts and contracts, equity jurisprudence and criminal law were provided by a small faculty, probably including Dean Rufus King and professors George Hoadley, Henry A. Morrill, Manning F. Force and Jacob Cox. Political economist William Graham Sumner lectured as well. The case system prevalent in law classrooms today was not used, as "precedent" had not yet taken root as a basis for judicial decision making. Law school seniors were required to participate in moot court.

Supreme Court historians Friedman and Israel describe the pedagogical approach of an antebellum law school as primarily professorial lecture about broad, sweeping philosophies of the law. No practical training or case analysis was involved.[1] The philosophy of the law espoused by the school's professors certainly included the principles of moral philosophy with which Willis would have been familiar, having been inculcated in him by the antebellum college curriculum of the times. There is no evidence that the post war law school had changed its philosophy from the antebellum. That philosophy was well-summarized by historian Mark Bailey:

> Americans in the late nineteenth century possessed a view of society drawn originally from the moderate Enlightenment. That view rested upon faith in a unified and regular natural and social order of providential design, in the close connection between the improvement of knowledge and the moral and material progress of society, and in the benefits of a republican democracy giving the greatest practical freedom to the operation of the fundamental values of moral voluntarism and individual accountability. That faith reflected a synthetic vision of society that would shortly succumb to new conceptions of the nature and purpose of creation, philosophy, human nature, and society but that remained an integral part of American jurisprudential thought well into the early years of the twentieth century.

Translated, from today's perspective, this meant that those possessing wealth, power, station, or favored race, could justify their station through the notion that God had established their priority, that the "natural system" in which men find themselves justifies aberrance of power where necessary to accumulate more of it. Economic success therefore defines morality. The law school's lessons mirrored the accepted principles of Gilded Age politics, economics and station: in short, social Darwinism.

American historian Doris Kearns Goodwin notes in her biography of Theodore Roosevelt and William Howard Taft that Willis Van Devanter's fellow Cincinnati Law student, Taft, "remembered one professor above all, the political economist William Graham Sumner, who, he said 'had more to do with stimulating my mental activities than anyone under whom I studied during my entire course.' Considered one of the most gifted educators of his generation, Sumner lectured to classes packed not only with eager students but with professors from various universities 'seeking the secret of his success.'"

Goodwin describes Sumner as "an impassioned advocate of laissez-faire and social Darwinism, of property rights and economic freedom, ... an apostle for the gospel of wealth, the reigning philosophy of the Industrial Revolution and the Gilded Age that followed the Civil War." Willis would likely have heard the same lectures as Taft and imputed the same message. "Will [Taft] absorbed Sumner's central teaching—that property rights demanded protection against the onslaught of radical theories and socialist ideals."

The social infrastructure from which American colonists had earlier come raised and lowered gentlemen by propertied family position. But a perhaps more important factor following the urbanization of England in the fifteenth and sixteenth centuries and the commercial expansion of the seventeenth was the ascendency of bright and capable men, unfortunately not women, who were drawn up into the more influential ranks through their connections with other, elder men of wealth or station, a practice generally called "patronage." The younger was "preferred," his connection with the elder gentleman was his "interest." The younger sucked up to the elder for his eventual station. Some element of the younger's eventual performance should inure beneficially to the elder.

There is no record that, while at law school, young Willis and future President and Supreme Court Chief Justice Taft were acquainted, allies, opponents or anything else. Taft preceded Van Devanter by two years.[2] But both of their later lives prove out the essential factor of their law school instruction. Taft's later history certainly indicates his understanding of preferment and interest. "Meanwhile the famine years for young men with Republican leanings were beginning."[3] And so would Willis' yet-to-be lifelong relationship with patron and client Francis E. Warren.

Willis served as librarian and worked with the arrangements committee for commencement ceremonies. He would have had significant opportunity to consider the school's lessons, as he likely worked his way while sitting for lectures at the law school. Early morning, late afternoon or evening lectures at the law school would have accommodated his work ethic, and most of his classmates were also so engaged. Van Devanter graduated second in his class of sixty-five in 1881, receiving his law degree.[4]

9

Watching the Court (1870s, 1880s)

Upon the death of U.S Supreme Court Chief Justice Chase in 1873, the year of the Panic, President Grant immediately moved to appoint a successor. His approach was to select someone from his friends and political allies. It would take four tries. Grant's first choice to succeed Chase would be his political ally, U.S. Senator Roscoe Conkling of New York. Conkling was indeed a lawyer, but his only objective qualification was that he was a Republican Party leader with control of a political machine built primarily from federal patronage.

On the merits, Conkling advocated reliance on the Fourteenth Amendment to protect corporations and business interests from state regulation. Conkling's nomination tanked in the Senate. Grant next named his Attorney General, Oregon's George H. Williams, whose judicial credentials were also questionable. The Senate rejected Williams due to corruption unearthed during Senate confirmation. Grant then nominated Caleb Cushing, prior member of the Massachusetts supreme judicial court and Attorney General of the United States, but now seventy-four years old. Again, the Senate said no, criticizing Cushing for lack of principle and conscience. Grant withdrew Cushing's nomination.

Then, seeking a nominee the Senate would not reject, Grant named Morrison R. Waite to be Chief Justice. Little known outside Ohio, and like Grant's other nominees, Waite had little judicial experience. He had served one term in the Ohio legislature and had chaired the state's constitutional convention. As a lawyer, he had represented banks, insurance companies and railroads, and participated in corporate management when not litigating their cases. Grant had earlier appointed Waite to represent the United States at Geneva in connection with the arbitration of British claims arising from the outfitting of Confederate vessels in the American Civil War. Waite's primary attribute was that he was associated with no scandal. The Senate approved his appointment 63 to 6. He would remain Chief Justice of the Supreme Court until his death in March 1888, most notably voiding state commerce laws on the grounds of federal preemption.

Aspiring law students and young lawyers pay attention to the economic fortunes of the markets they aspire to serve, their technological improvements and political process. They also watch the U.S. Supreme Court. As a younger lad, Willis' lawyer father Isaac had certainly apprised him of the 1858 decision in *Dred Scott v. Sandford*[1] in which Justice Taney applied the due process provision of the Fifth

Amendment to a law enacted by Congress, in the Compromise of 1820, holding that by prohibiting slavery in the territories Congress had unconstitutionally deprived slave owners of their property without due process of law. Slaves were property. When Willis was 12, the Court had decided *Collector v. Day*,[2] where the Court found that Congress was without power to impose a tax on state officials. When he was 14, the Court had decided the *Slaughterhouse Cases*,[3] ruling that the Constitution's privileges and immunities clause[4] applied only to federally created rights, not state-created ones.

When Willis was 16, the Court declared a section of the Civil Rights Enforcement Act of 1870 unconstitutional in *United States v. Reese*.[5] Two Kentucky election inspectors had been indicted under the 1870 law for refusing to count votes cast by Negroes in a municipal election. The Court found the statute unconstitutional because it did not specifically say that its provisions were limited to denials to vote on account of race, color or previous condition of servitude. In the Court's view, that was the only type of denial that the Fifteenth Amendment prohibited. And in *United States v. Cruikshank*,[6] the Court reversed the conviction of a mob of Ku Kluxers, under the Anti-Ku Klux Klan or Civil Rights Enforcement Act of 1870. There, Chief Justice Waite said for the Court that the federal government had no power to punish violence against Negroes as private persons. The Fourteenth Amendment, he said, prohibits only states from depriving persons of life, liberty or property without due process of laws, and does not prohibit private individuals from doing so. Only states have the responsibility to punish such crimes.

When Willis was 18, the Court decided *Hall v. DeCuir*.[7] There, the Court held unconstitutional an act passed by Louisiana's Reconstruction legislature forbidding railroads to discriminate against passengers because of race or color, because that legislation interfered with interstate commerce.

The constitutionality of state laws setting maximum rates for railroads, grain warehouses and elevators, as espoused by the Grangers, was challenged in a number of cases which would collectively become known as the "Granger cases." The most important of them was *Munn v. Illinois*.

In the 1870s, Midwest states passed tough laws curbing abuses by railroads, such as arbitrary rates and land-grant frauds. The pressure for action came from new farm groups, especially the National Grange of the Patrons of Husbandry. Oliver H. Kelley, an official of the Department of Agriculture, had organized the National Grange in 1867, ostensibly for social and educational purposes. Its local units would be called "granges." The Panic of 1873 changed and expanded their interests. Soon the granges became forums for farmer protests against manufacturers of farm machinery, grain warehousemen and railroads. With nearly a million members, the Grangers now controlled the legislatures in several states, such as Illinois and Minnesota. They secured the passage of what became known as the "Granger laws," setting maximum rates for railroads, grain warehouses and elevators, establishing railroad commissions empowered to set maximum rates, end discrimination, and enforce their orders.

The railroads' corporate influence persisted nationally and was pervasive of governmental thinking. Of the 73 men who served as cabinet officers between 1868 and 1896, 48 had either served railroad clients, lobbied for railroads, sat on railroad boards, or had relatives connected to railroads. The railroads and grain elevator operators argued that the Granger-dominated legislatures' refusal to allow them to charge as much as the traffic would bear violated the Contract Clause, the Commerce Clause and deprived them of the liberty and property preserved to them under the Fourteenth Amendment.

The general constitutional complaint was reduced to specific facts in the *Munn* case. There, a Chicago grain operator's overreaching of farmers and merchants inspired the Illinois' legislature to impose licensing and inspection regulations on grain elevators. Munn refused to comply. The Illinois Supreme Court ruled that the state could regulate all matters involving "the public welfare." Munn appealed to the U.S. Supreme Court.

In 1876, Rutherford B. Hayes, a Republican lawyer and prior Ohio Governor from Cincinnati, Ohio, became President, having been selected by the Republican convention held in his hometown. Hayes' mandate was circumscribed by the close election, where he was said to have "stolen the office" from Democrat Samuel Tilden. Tilden had received more popular votes (50.9 percent) in the 1876 election than had Hayes (47.9 percent). Tilden initially won 184 electoral votes; Hayes won 165. But 20 more electoral votes were disputed. In Florida, Louisiana, and South Carolina, both parties declared that their candidate had won the election. Congress passed a law creating a commission to investigate and resolve the impasse. When its report was published, Senate Democrats promised a filibuster of Senatorial approval, thus determining the occupation of the White House. The filibuster was ultimately called down by Senatorial compromise in the "compromise of 1877," wherein southern democratic senators obtained a presidential commitment to withdraw federal troops from southern states. Hayes would win the 1876 election with 185 electoral votes, one more than Tilden.

The Court finally heard argument in the Munn case in January 1876 and rendered its decision on March 1, 1877.[8] The majority opinion was authored by Chief Justice Waite, with a dissenting opinion by Associate Justice Field. As with the more current *Citizens v. United* case, the Waite Court assumed that the railroad and elevator corporations were "persons" entitled to the benefits of the Amendment. Even so, the plaintiffs lost the battle but won the war. The Court found the laws constitutional, holding that the regulated property had been dedicated to a public use, thus the states did have the right to regulate them. Once dedicated to public use, the properties were subject to governmental regulation. Notwithstanding the narrow holding, the necessary precedent that the due process clause was available to corporations would have a long-term impact on wealth accumulation.

Chief Justice Waite had assigned the writing of the Court's opinion to himself. He wrote that an owner who devotes his property to a use in which the public has an interest has, in effect, granted the public an interest in that use, and must submit to be controlled by the public for the common good. Waite also found that all the other challenged rate regulations did not affect interstate commerce or impair contract rights. It had taken the Waite Court four years to consider the "Granger Cases," but for the Grangers, the outcome had been worth the wait.

The excesses of the wealth class in the Gilded Age frustrated workers, transforming the labor movement into a vigorous, sometimes violent, force. The depression of the mid 1870s had made it easier for management to break unions. Some three million unemployed and desperate workers on the sidelines, it was difficult for unions to keep their members united. But the labor movement would grow. By 1877, three national unions existed. By 1880, there would be eighteen. Labor's bargaining chip was the value of its own labor. Strikes were its available tool. The media were generally sympathetic to railroads and industry. Industrialists began taking a harder line against unions, inducing growth in the labor movement.

The railroad unions were on strike, stopping transportation in Pennsylvania and Chicago. President Rutherford B. Hayes' effort to break the strike with federal troops brought injury and death, rather than peace and resolution. The economic condition tumbled further as a crash in the lumber market dragged lumber enterprises down in Michigan and California.

Four months after the Supreme Court's decision in *Munn v. Illinois*, railroad unions started a strike at a key B&O railroad junction at Martinsburg, West Virginia, protesting that railroad's cutting of workers' wages. It would grow into the explosive Great Railroad Strike of 1877. Rail shipping in Maryland, Mississippi, Kansas, Iowa, Nebraska, and California was ultimately halted. General supportive strikes erupted in Buffalo, Baltimore, St. Louis, Louisville, Cleveland, Columbus, Pittsburg, Scranton, and Cairo.

In Baltimore, the state militia fired on strikers, killing 11 and wounding 40. Thirty protesters were killed in Chicago. In Philadelphia, strikers fought local militia. Before federal troops could intercede, much of the downtown area burned. But the railroad's wage reductions were not reversed. The War Department created the national guard to put down future disturbances.

The nation's management class would be aggravated by violent labor strikes and riots throughout the balance of the nineteenth century. By 1879 a broad sense of unrest and potential uprising against wealth and authority had matured. Some ten thousand strikes and lockouts would happen in the 1880s, nearly 700,000 workers striking in 1886 alone.

President Hayes had announced early on that he would not run for reelection, making him a lame duck from the beginning. He was said to have been aloof, maintaining a forbidding presence based upon his sense of moral rectitude. Mrs. Hayes had refused to serve alcohol in the White House and become known as "Lemonade Lucy." The President was apparently not enamored of the Court's determination in *Munn* that corporations were persons. According to Mark Wahlgren Summers, Hayes wrote in his diary, "This is a government of the people, by the people, and for the people no longer. It is a government of corporations, by corporations, and for corporations." Hayes issued executive orders forbidding government officeholders' management of political organizations. And, he forbade the practice of demanding that government employees make political contributions. But he was unsuccessful in convincing Congress to support comprehensive civil service reform, perhaps due to his stubbornness with congressional bosses, particularly including New York Republican Senator Roscoe Conkling.

These cases certainly would have been within young Willis Van Devanter's field of attention during his impressionable youthful years. His lawyer father's son, the law school directed student, he would have followed the Court's judicial progress and product. While at law school in Cincinnati, Willis would certainly have taken notice of developing Republican politics, much of which emanated from Hamilton County, Ohio, President Rutherford Hayes' home, and from Indiana. Hayes would serve as President until 1881.

Isaac Van Devanter's colleague Benjamin Harrison led the Republican delegation from Indiana to the National Convention in 1880, Harrison also again mentioned as a possible Senate candidate, where he spoke in favor of James Garfield in Indiana and New York, further raising his profile in the party. He would have to deal with New York State's Republican machine run by Roscoe Conkling.

James Garfield, Cuyahoga County, Ohio-born Republican lawyer and Ohio senator, would be elected President of the United States on March 4, 1881, the spring of the year Willis graduated law school. Garfield had been elected unanimously to the U.S. Senate by the Ohio legislature and later nominated to the Republican presidential ticket at the Republican convention in Chicago. Garfield and Chester Alan Arthur, chosen to run as Garfield's running mate so as to mollify the New York delegation, were elected President and Vice President by a very narrow popular vote, beating Democratic presidential candidate Hancock by a slim margin of 9,464 votes out of the total 8,999, 368 votes cast. Garfield offered Harrison a cabinet position, but Harrison declined it in order to join the U.S Senate, where he served from March 4, 1881, until March 4, 1887.

But Garfield didn't last that long. He was shot four months after inauguration by Charles J. Guiteau on July 2. He would linger until September 19, 1881. Willis, just graduating from law school, would surely have noticed. The assassin Guiteau was a disgruntled office seeker who had been trying to get a position in Garfield's administration. New York lawyer Chester A. Arthur succeeded Garfield to the presidency the next day on September 20. He would serve until March 3, 1885.

Garfield had seemed promising to the civil service reform movement before his assassination. After his death, support for civil service reform grew significantly. The reason behind the assassination attempt, along with evidence of fraud in government, especially in the Bureau of Indian Affairs and in railroad supervision, would lead to founding of the National Civil Service Reform League later in 1881. By 1883 Congress had passed the Pendleton Civil Service Reform Act, which President Arthur signed. The act took on the spoils system by classifying certain administrative positions, eliminating patronage—at least for those positions. In conjunction, the United States Civil Service Commission was established to build a system that would hire prospective employees on the basis of merit rather than on political connections. But President Arthur was himself a creature of the spoils system and would make appointments, one very significant to Willis Van Devanter, before the Reform Act went into effect.

Chester Arthur is unfortunately now remembered as a "hack" politician with a shadowy record in the dregs of Roscoe Conkling's New York Republican machine. Issues of corruption in the New York Customs House had dogged his reputation at the 1880 Chicago convention. Notwithstanding his early political problems, Arthur turned out to be a better President than the reputation that preceded him, the Pendleton Act being a major factor in his later reputation.

After earning his law degree in Cincinnati, Willis had returned to Marion, where he joined his father and his brother-in-law in 1882 in the firm of Lacey and Van Devanter. While Willis had been in law school, Grant County's tax base had reached the point that a new county courthouse was possible. Marion's legal and fraternal establishment gathered on June 1, 1881, to lay the cornerstone for the new courthouse. The town was decked out in red, white and blue. The Indian Band, and Jonesboro Silver Band played. The county commissioners officiated. All the bigwigs of the fraternal establishments of the Odd Fellows, Masons and Knights Templar attended and approved.

In the midst of the economic malaise following the Panic of 1873, Isaac Van Devanter had formed a partnership with his son-in-law, John W. Lacey. Born in Indiana in 1848, Lacey joined the Union Army in 1863 at the age of fifteen and served two years. According to M. Paul Holsinger, Wyoming lawyer and historian, Lacey began reading the law under Isaac Van Devanter in 1871 and became admitted to the bar of Indiana in 1875. Lacey, who was eleven years older than Willis, married

President Chester A. Arthur and party in the Yellowstone. Sitting, left to right: Montana Governor Schuyler Crosley, General P.H. Sheridan, President Arthur, Secretary of War Robert T. Lincoln, Senator George C. Vest. Standing, left to right: Col. Mike Sheridan, Gen. Anson Stager, Capt. Philo Clark, and two unidentified men. President Arthur appointed John W. Lacey as Chief Justice of the Wyoming Territory in 1884 and Francis Warren as the fifth territorial governor of Wyoming on February 28, 1885. He was notified of his appointment on that day by telegram from H.M. Teller, Secretary of the Interior. John W. Lacey, chief justice of Wyoming territory, administered the oath of office to the new governor. Photograph by J.E. Haynes, St. Paul. *Book of the Governors*, 1926 Governors' Convention, Cheyenne, Wyoming, July 26–28 (courtesy Wyoming State Library).

Willis' sister Elizabeth in 1878. The law partnership would last seven years, during which Congress continued to implement its western land development policy, notwithstanding the prevailing economic condition.

The nation's ethnic complexion was changing. Willis' ancestors had emigrated to the American continent the century before. Now more emigrants from England, Ireland, Germany and Scandinavia approached the eastern seaboard of the United States. Where the nation had been populated with scantly more than 31 million people in 1860, it would attain 76 million by 1900, 14 million of them having immigrated from abroad since 1870 (14.5 million more would emigrate to the United States before 1915). Some pressed on west. Others were "facilitated" west, at least from the historical perspective of Supreme Court historian and Chief Justice Rehnquist, by political notions seeking to preserve American cities against unwanted factionalism of emigrant Italians, Slavs and Jews fleeing threat of persecution in Russia and Austria-Hungary.

In 1883, President Arthur travelled to Yellowstone National Park, returning to Washington refreshed after two months of travel. He would appoint one John W. Lacey to become a judge in the Wyoming Territory.

In 1884, Willis married Dellice "Dollie" Burhans of Ionia, Michigan. Dellice Burhans, now also of Marion, was a close friend of Willis' sister, now Mrs. John W. Lacey.

10

Willis Goes West (1883)

Willis Van Devanter's father Isaac was now ready to retire from practicing law. Isaac's son-in-law and law partner, John W. Lacey, had by 1883 secured an appointment from the Republican President Chester A. Arthur to serve as the chief justice of the Wyoming territorial supreme court. Lacey grabbed the opportunity and moved his family from Marion, Indiana, to Cheyenne, Wyoming. The firm of Lacey and Van Devanter dissolved. Isaac retired from practicing law and moved to his farm adjoining the City of Marion and overlooking the Mississinewa River. Remembered for his moral character, his fine address and appearance, and his literary and scientific knowledge, he would end his days in Marion. Twenty-five-year-old Willis had a choice: remain in Marion, inherit and succeed to his father's law practice, handling it alone, or follow Lacey and the tide of young men seeking opportunity and head west.

Willis' choice of where to make his career may have seemed obvious. The economic prowess of the Wyoming cattle industry was well known. His father and brother-in-law would not be available to teach him the ropes of law practice in Marion. And his brother-in-law Lacey could be counted on as a "friend in power" in Cheyenne. Willis chose Wyoming. His wife's friendship with his sister, Lacey's wife, may have sealed the choice. Although some U.S. Supreme Court historians attribute young Willis' preference for the "raw and boisterous frontier life," we shall see that the indoor, political life would be more Willis' cup of tea.[1]

Although Holsinger suggests that the Willis Van Devanters may have first considered Arizona[2] and southern California, the familial connection in Cheyenne probably turned the tide. They arrived in Cheyenne in July 1884, while President Arthur was still in the White House. Cheyenne was still a quiet town of nine thousand people. But in the surrounding territory there would be found cattle-rustlers, horse thieves, contentious cattle barons, and Indians quarreling with white settlers over public lands.

Although touted in the East as part of the untamed wild west, Cheyenne now possessed some of the creature comforts Willis and Dollie would find accommodating: ready access to the Union Pacific and its eastern connections, large, well-stocked mercantile houses like that operated by Francis E. Warren, later to be Governor and United States Senator, not to mention electric lights, running tap water, telephones and a municipal opera house (built by Francis Warren).

The economic success of the cattle industry in the West generally, and Wyoming in particular, reached its peak just as Lacey and Van Devanter arrived in Cheyenne. Favorable rains falling all over the West made excellent pasturage, and the cattle bubble swelled with the grazing opportunity.

Stories of the rich Laramie Plains had reached the East, and wealthy Englishmen had begun to purchase choice ranches in the area, build mansions in Laramie, and organize social clubs. Large numbers of cattle were turned loose in the open range by these large ranches, who would hold spring roundups where the cows and calves belonging to each ranch were separated and branded. Before the roundup, calves, including orphan or stray calves, were sometimes surreptitiously branded. The large ranches defended against cattle rustling often by forbidding their employees from owning cattle and by lynching suspected rustlers—or at least threatening to do so. Property and use rights were usually respected among big and small ranches based on the size of the herd and who was first to settle the land, not unlike the doctrine of prior appropriation in the water context. And large ranching outfits would sometimes band together, using their combined power to monopolize large swaths of range land, preventing newcomers from settling the area.

Cheyenne had by now become the capital of a vast cattle-ranching region. Cattle men had lobbied the Wyoming territorial government, and befriended John A. Campbell, the first territorial governor of Wyoming (1869 to 1875). In May 1871, Governor Campbell had sponsored the first organization of cattlemen in the territory and become the president of the Wyoming Stock Grazers' Association. When the second territorial legislature met in Cheyenne in November 1871, Governor Campbell had called a simultaneous meeting of the stock growers and the legislature. A joint session was held in the hall of the House of Representatives. The Governor's cattle organization soon disbanded. But on November 29, 1873, a new group called the Laramie County Stock Association was formed by some of its former members and became the nucleus of the Wyoming Stock Grower's Association. The WSGA would become a significant player in Wyoming and regional politics. Its members would include some of the state's wealthiest and most popular citizens.

The WSGA's approach to organization of the cattle industry was to centralize the scheduling of roundups and cattle shipments. They secured legislation purporting to extend governmental power to their management of private interests. They tracked cattle brands and established a plan to eliminate the competition of lesser ranching interests, identifying that competition as "cattle rustling." In order to achieve this last objective, the WSGA hired professional heavies whose job as "detectives" was to prevent and punish cattle thieves.

The WSGA gathered socially as the Cheyenne Club in Cheyenne. Founded primarily by young men from prominent east coast, British, and European families, it settled in to the premises at what is now 17th Street and Warren Avenue in Cheyenne. As the cattle industry thrived in the 1870s and 1880s, the Club would lavishly entertain the socialites, celebrities, and foreign dignitaries who visited Cheyenne. Its membership was instrumental in fashioning the state's early political, economic and social infrastructure as the Cheyenne Club became one of the wealthiest and most exclusive establishments on the frontier.

Situated on the main transcontinental line between Omaha and Salt Lake City,

Cheyenne was now the only city of any consequence in the cattle empire. It had become the seat of the stockyards where cattle would be loaded onto the Union Pacific Railroad. The cattle industry, managed from the Cheyenne Club, of which WSGA members comprised the primary core, became the centroid of political power and would hold that place through the late 1800s. During these years, the WSGA held an essentially quasi-governmental status, exercising its will through political representation by members who were governors and members of Congress.[3] A majority of the state's early legislators were members of the association. Many of the WSGA's rules and regulations became state laws. While often accused of secrecy and heavy-handedness, the WSGA nonetheless kept extremely detailed records, paperwork, minutes of meetings, and preserved nearly all correspondence to and from the association.

One of the WSGA's chairmen was John Clay, a tough, wealth-oriented Scotchman. A businessman, he had little understanding of cattle, the range, or the nature of the cowboys. Clay disparaged the cowboys in particular, declaring them illiterate, uncivilized, drunkard, criminal, and loyal to their own. Clay would later become founder of the Chicago commission house of Clay, Robinson and Company.

Another significant member of the WSGA was the Swan Land & Cattle Company, a large cattle ranching operation. In the early 1880s, Alexander Swan and his brother Thomas had begun buying grazing land outside Cheyenne. By the end of the nineteenth century and the beginning of the twentieth, the Swan Company would become the epitome of the large corporate cattle company. Its ranches were at one time as large as the state of Connecticut. Its principal range ran along the Chug and Suybille creeks and over the mountains to the Laramie Plains. The Swan Company's initial ranches were established in the Chugwater Valley. The original ranch house and barn on the ranch there had been built in 1876 by Thomas A. Maxwell, and purchased from Maxwell's widow by the Swan and Frank Live-Stock Company, owned by Alexander Hamilton Swan (1831–1905) and Joseph Frank, in 1882. It would later serve as a hotel and stage station prior to the coming of the Colorado and Southern Railway to Chugwater in 1887. The home ranch in Chugwater was connected to company headquarters in Cheyenne by a telephone line that cost the company £1,000 to install. The company maintained its own hotel in Cheyenne for personnel visiting the headquarters.

In November 1882, Swan, along with James Converse, Joseph Frank and Godfrey Syndacker, sold three cattle companies, Swan & Frank Live-Stock Company, National Cattle Company, and the Swan, Frank & Anthony Cattle Company, to James Wilson of Edinburgh, Scotland. The transaction had closed in March 1883, for $2,553,825. The Swan Land & Cattle Company, Limited, was established as a British limited liability company with an initial capital position of $3 million. The transaction included the purchase of "all and singular the lands and tenements, water rights, improvements upon lands, houses, barns, stables, corrals, and other improvements and grazing privileges; also all live stock, consisting of meat cattle, horses and mules, belonging to the said three Wyoming corporations, or any or either of them; also all live stock, brands, tools, implements, wagons, harness, ranch, camp, and round-up outfits, and branding irons."

The now-British cattle company, sitting on the Chugwater in the Laramie River plain, was one of the largest in the nation and one of several best-known foreign companies that engaged in the cattle business in the United States. It ranged from Fort Fred Steele in Wyoming in the west to Ogallala, Nebraska, in the east, and from the Union Pacific Railroad on the north to the Platte River on the south. In 1884, with combined American and British support, the new company was capitalized at $3,750,000 and in July, the same month that young Willis Van Devanter arrived in Cheyenne, the new concern announced the purchase of 550,000 acres of land from the Union Pacific for $2,300,000, giving it control over 3.25 million acres. Cheyenne newspapers declared this the largest purchase of its kind ever made. The owner of more than 130,000 head of cattle, under 100 brands, the Swan Land and Cattle Company was required to publish a brand book just so that its foremen could keep track of the company's brands.[4] The company took advantage of the federal government's acquiescence in the company's free use of public lands, enabling its grazing territory to run 100 miles east to west.

Alexander Swan had ridden the wave of expansion in the Wyoming cattle industry, and sold when the market was high. His wealth expansion was the model, a model broadcast throughout the eastern business establishment and across the ocean into European financial markets. James Sanks Brisbin's 1881 book *The Beef Bonanza, or, How to Get Rich on the Plains* and J.S. Tait's brochure *The Cattlefields of the Far West* both speculated that investors could earn as much as 33 to 66 percent in profit. For several years prior to 1882, the price of beef had grown steadily in New York and Chicago, reaching an all-time high in eastern markets. Wyoming historian Morris observed, perhaps too circumspectly, "The men who had ventured in to the business were richly rewarded for their enterprise."[5] The message would not be lost on a young Indiana lawyer seeking the key to fame and fortune.

"The cattle boom in the Great Plains continued until the mid-eighties and in its later years attracted large amounts of foreign capital. Range cattle worth only $7 or $8 a head in 1878 were fetching the peak price of $30 to $35 in 1882."[6] But the bubble wasn't all real. As a result of high cattle prices in 1882, cattle "drives increased and the northern range became overstocked. In view of this glut, the Chicago packers slashed the prices they offered, and cattle were back to $8 per head in 1885."[7] And some overrepresentation of assets to absentee shareholders and purchasers also came to light.[8] Alexander Swan, for example, had represented to his purchasers in 1883, when he sold his companies to the British syndicate, that there were 89,167 cattle in the company's herd books. Swan stayed on as general manager of the Swan companies at a salary of $10,000.00 a year. He swore that the books were accurate, a fact that his British buyers would dispute.

Now in Wyoming at a bristling young 24 years, Willis may have read the Supreme Court's opinion in *United States v. Harris*.[9] There, on January 22, 1883, the Court had held the key provision of the Anti-Klan Act unconstitutional. Twenty members of a Tennessee lynch mob had seized four Negro prisoners held by a state deputy sheriff and beat them severely, killing one. They were indicted under a provision of the Anti-Klan Act prohibiting a conspiracy by two or more persons to deprive others of their civil rights. The Court found the section unconstitutional, based on the view that the Fourteenth Amendment applied only to deprivations by states, and does not authorize Congress to enact any law making it a federal crime for private persons to lynch Negroes or otherwise deprive them of their civil rights.

The case was followed later in the year by the *Civil Rights Cases*.[10] There, on October 15, 1883, the Court found the Civil Rights Law unconstitutional. A number of individuals had been prosecuted under the Civil Rights Law of 1875 for denying San Francisco hotel and New York theater accommodations to Negroes because of their race. A Tennessee railroad had also been indicted for refusing to allow a Negro woman to ride in a railroad car. The Court's logic was that the Fourteenth Amendment only invalidates state laws and actions that deny equal protection of the law and authorizes Congress to enact legislation to implement that invalidation. It did not authorize Congress, so said the Court, to affirmatively legislate penalties for breach of equal protection by states. In both cases, the Court was not at all moved by the policy of the Fourteenth Amendment—that racial discrimination was wrong. Indeed, the moral philosophy of social Darwinism sanctioned it. That philosophy was permissive of aggressive behavior toward the less opportune.

Within the year of Willis Van Devanter's arrival in Wyoming, he offered his support to the territorial governor, Francis E. Warren, now prospering as hardware store owner, cattleman and owner of the Warren Land and Livestock Company. It would be the beginning of a life-long political relationship for both men, Warren building a political machine with the objectives of self-enrichment and Wyoming development, and Van Devanter acting as counsel, confidant, political advisor, political figure in his own right, free to pursue his own ambitions.

11

The Warren Machine (1884–1890)

In May of 1885, Willis wrote to a friend that Cheyenne was a "lively, busy and substantial city with a population something in excess of 8,000." The cattle population in Wyoming Territory was approaching 1,500,000.[1] The bubble had not yet burst. Van Devanter began to seek political position, becoming elected as Cheyenne City Attorney by 1887,[2] the town now over nine thousand people. Willis' primary client had by now become the town of Cheyenne's mayor, merchant and cattleman Francis E. Warren.

Van Devanter associated immediately with the Warren political machine. Warren had formed a business partnership with A.R. Converse in general merchandising and succeeded to the firm's ownership in 1878, had been elected again to the Territorial Council in 1884, and was elected Mayor of Cheyenne in 1885.[3] As one of his last acts prior to President Elect Cleveland's first-term inauguration, President Arthur appointed Warren to fill the unexpired term of non-resident Territorial Governor William Hale. Warren, the first Wyoming resident to be appointed to the office of Territorial Governor, had been generally approved by both political parties in Wyoming. His inexperience in matters legal, however, created a void which a young, aspiring eastern lawyer could readily fill. The relationship was immediately co-dependent, Warren relying upon Van Devanter for legal knowledge, the younger Van Devanter relying on Warren for political connection with the Republican organization controlled by Warren and Joseph M. Carey. Van Devanter "connected immediately with the political machine of Governor Francis Warren."[4]

"Warren [had] built his political machine for two reasons: to enrich himself and to further the development of Wyoming. In Warren's mind, and at times in fact, these two aims were identical."[5] Van Devanter would ultimately occupy a preeminent place among now Governor Warren's friends in Cheyenne.[6] And Van Devanter's connection with the Territory's Republican Party would become essential in making him most influential in Wyoming's public affairs and ultimately buy him a ticket to the U.S. Supreme Court.

It was only natural that Willis join the Republican establishment in Wyoming. He had learned the political system at his father's knee in the midst and atmosphere of Midwest Republicanism.[7] His legal training and sense of entitlement had reinforced it.

By the fall of 1884, the American electorate had, however, begun shifting left in reaction perhaps to the pro-business, pro-railroad policy of the Republican administrations up to and including the Arthur administration. "Mugwump" Republicans (reformers unhappy with the high level of corruption in government) were shifting their support to Democrat Grover Cleveland, then governor of New York. Cleveland also opposed "free silver." In November Cleveland was elected in one of the muddiest elections of U.S. history, his margin of victory only 25,000 votes out of 10 million cast and 37 electoral votes out of 401. He would serve until 1889, be unseated by Benjamin Harrison in 1893, and return to the Presidency in 1897. Although honest, courageous, and displaying integrity, Cleveland was a rigid, self-righteous, sometimes haughty man, failing to inspire much public affection. He had fought the New York City Tammany Hall machine and had become famous as the "veto mayor" of Buffalo and later the "veto governor" of New York. His stalwartness was both a blessing and a shortcoming once he was in office.

Republican Warren was allowed to govern Wyoming Territory for the first twenty-one months after Democrat Grover Cleveland's inauguration in March 1885. Meanwhile, Van Devanter pursued his political associations. Quick-rising Willis was elected to the Wyoming Territorial Legislature and served as a member and leader of the Republican Party in the Territorial legislative session which convened in January 1886.[8] He sponsored bills to begin construction of the Wyoming Capitol in Cheyenne and the University of Wyoming at Laramie, which would be signed into law by Governor Warren in March 1886. He served as chairman of the resolutions committee at the territorial convention and also on a commission to revise and compile Wyoming's territorial statutes. He was all of 27.

Young Willis Van Devanter, member of the 10th Legislative Session of the Wyoming Territory (1888), enlarged inset taken from the composite group photograph of members of that legislative session (courtesy American Heritage Center, University of Wyoming, from the Willis Van Devanter Papers).

Several days after the legislature adjourned, in March 1886, Warren appointed Van Devanter to serve on the Wyoming Territory Statutory Revision Commission, charged with revising the laws and statutes of the Territory. Working with him were two other prominent Republicans, Isaac P. Caldwell and J.W. Blake. The laws, when finished, were patterned after the statutes of the state of Ohio which Van Devanter had studied at Cincinnati Law School six years before. When the Daily Sun Steam Printing House, of Cheyenne, published the Revised Statutes of Wyoming, in force January 1, 1887, including the Declaration of Independence, the Articles of Confederation, the Constitution of the United States, the Organic Act of Wyoming, and all laws of Congress affecting the territorial government, the text was prepared and edited by the same three commissioners.

Outside Wyoming, back in the East and Midwest, 1886 was a tumultuous year. Labor anxiety and accumulation of wealth in interstate corporations were colliding. Massive uprisings of whole communities joined in resistance to the power of coal mine, railroad and industrial wealth. It would be called the Great Uprising of 1886. Three hundred forty thousand workers stopped work at 12,000 companies nationwide, seeking reduction of the standard workday from twelve to eight hours. A bomb exploded in Chicago's Haymarket Square where police were trying to break up a large labor meeting. A police officer was killed. Police fired into the crowd. One striker went down, many more wounded. As a result of the melee, four labor organizers were ultimately hanged.

But 1886 was also a year of significant construction in Cheyenne. Handsome houses, including the Whipple House, at 300 East 17th Street, an Italianate brick

Whipple House at 300 East 17th Street, Cheyenne, home of John W. Lacey. Lacey and Francis Warren lived across the street from each other for the entire pendency of *Wyoming v. Colorado* in the U.S. Supreme Court (author's photograph, 2019).

residence built in 1883 by Ithimar C. Whipple, Cheyenne merchant, financier and cattleman, would later become home to Judge John Lacey. The Territorial Legislature authorized $150,000 for construction of the first phase of the Wyoming State Capitol, at 24th & Capitol Avenue. It would become one of ten gold domed U.S. state capitols. Across House Avenue from the Whipple mansion, grocer Erasmus Nagle,[9] a commissioner of the Capital Building Committee, built a mansion at 222 East 17th Street with the unused stone from the Capital, utilizing the Capital architect.[10] Completed in 1888, it would become by 1892 the home of Francis E. Warren.[11]

Construction simultaneously began at the Union Pacific's new Depot at 121 West 15th Street, at the bottom of Capitol Street, where a Romanesque clock tower would become a prominent landmark for railroad travelers approaching Cheyenne by the turn of the century

The heavy hand of the railroads and management won again on October 25, 1886, when the U.S. Supreme Court decided *Wabash Railway Company v. Illinois*,[12] finding that states had no direct right to regulate interstate commerce, as the

The house at 222 East 17th Street, Cheyenne, across House Street from the Whipple House, was built by Erasmus Nagle in 1888, with indoor plumbing, electric lights and a full *en suite* bathroom in the master bedroom (rounded room at front in the center of photograph). Senator F.E. Warren purchased this home in 1910 and lived here until his death in 1929 (author's photograph, 2019).

Constitution reserved that power to Congress. Now, ten years after Chief Justice Waite's opinion in the *Munn* case, hundreds of small rail lines were bankrupt or going there. Huge lines had taken over, and the nation essentially had an interstate rail system. The *Wabash* majority now prohibited states from regulating the rates charged by any railroad linked to an interstate network, even in those cases where the regulation affected only trips within the state. The Granger cases were essentially erased.

In Wyoming, on November 5, 1886, Warren was suspended from gubernatorial office, accused by the Cleveland Administration of having illegally fenced the public lands.[13] President Cleveland now appointed George W. Baxter, a young Democratic cattleman, to succeed Warren. Accusations soon reached Washington charging Baxter with the same offenses as Warren. Although Baxter was exonerated before the end of his second month in office, Cleveland was forced to ask for his resignation as well.

Upon Governor Baxter's resignation at year's end 1886, and in a departure from his announced policy of appointing residents of a territory as governor, President Cleveland named Col. Thomas Moonlight, a Kansas Granger, to become Wyoming's territorial Governor on January 24, 1887.[14]

Previously Kansas' Secretary of State, Moonlight had been at the time serving as Kansas State Senator. Born a Scot, Moonlight had emigrated to the United States alone at age twelve. Working first on eastern farms, he enlisted in the 4th U.S. Artillery regiment at age twenty. He raised a company of artillery for the 4th Kansas Infantry during the War, but the regiment never got organized. Moonlight moved up through the ranks of Kansas military, serving as captain of the 1st Kansas Battery, lieutenant colonel of the 11th Kansas Infantry, colonel of the 11th Kansas Cavalry, leading his troops primarily against bushwhackers and border guerrillas. Moonlight pursued William C. Quantrill's raiders following the Lawrence Massacre, and in 1864 commanded the 3rd Sub-district in the District of South Kansas. At War's end, Moonlight campaigned against Indians on the plains as commander of the District of Colorado. In 1865, he had received a brevet promotion to brigadier general.

Now, Moonlight committed himself to breaking "the stranglehold of the cattle kings" on Wyoming affairs and constantly antagonized the Republican leadership, principals in Wyoming's cattle industry, throughout the year 1887. The Cleveland administration also now removed John Lacey from his appointment as Chief Justice of the Wyoming Territorial Supreme Court and replaced him with William L. Macginnis, an Ohio Democrat.

Warren's and Lacey's sacking must have chagrinned young lawyer Willis. He certainly would have sided with Cheyenne's more established, cattle interests. In 1887 Congress reacted to the Court's earlier *Wabash* decision and passed the Interstate Commerce Act, requiring "reasonable and just pricing" in interstate transportation of passengers or property and prohibiting rebates and drawbacks, a first step in governmental regulation of commercial activities. The Act created the Interstate Commerce Commission.

But shift of control of the Presidency to the Democrats, and its consequence to territorial appointees, was not Wyoming Republicans' only problem. In Wyoming Territory, the winters of 1885–86 and 1886–87 burst the cattle bubble. The force of nature essentially broke the unnatural growth of the cattle economy in the northern plains.[15] Unfortunately for Wyoming, for the prowess of the cattle industry, for eastern and foreign investors, and even for the family fortunes of the Van Devanters, the weather turned against them. Millions of cattle died in those winters in the ranges and ranches of Wyoming, Montana, the Dakotas and Nebraska.

In the summer before the first of the two cold winters, when the tally of Wyoming stock had reached 8,000,000 head, roaming freely on the range, Van Devanter had negotiated the purchase of a one-third interest in a new venture of the Swan Cattle Company for the sum of $20,000 of Mrs. Burhan's, his wife's mother's, money. The investment appeared sound at the time. The directors of the parent company had paid a nine percent dividend in 1883, ten percent in 1884.[16] A large return on investment seemed certain. But the ensuing winters changed that.

After the sudden death of Willis' father-in-law, the family affairs in the Wyoming Territory had fallen to Willis. With his mother-in-law's permission, he traded the family's stock to Alexander Swan in September 1886 in exchange for $24,000 of Swan's promissory notes. Swan was a big man, influential in the Territory, prominent in financial circles. But Van Devanter naively accepted the notes without security against their performance. Perhaps Willis assumed that the up-side prospects of the cattle industry were so good that no security was required. Perhaps he found Swan's wealth so impressive that he felt no security was required. But the winter of 1886–1887 turned out even worse than the year before. After an extremely hot and dry summer in 1886, a severe blizzard hit the plains in late January, stranding thousands of cattle in frozen, foodless terrain. Temperatures dropped to 40–50 below zero. Cowboys were forced off the range for the season. Some cattle companies lost the majority of their herds. Although perhaps only a bit more than 15 percent of the total cattle population was lost across the Territory, the 1886–1887 "die-off" was too much for many companies. Some cattle companies never recovered from the two cold winters of 1886 and 1887.[17] The "cattle kingdom" in Wyoming, which had existed on borrowed capital for years, came to an abrupt end.[18] Companies with questionable management and some self aggrandizement would be victims.

Economic conditions plummeted. The price of prime beef cattle dropped to under $2 per hundred pounds in Chicago. A twelve-hundred-pound steer might bring only $5, when shipping and other expenses were taken into account. Cattle herds diminished by 30 to 100 percent. Crops were poor in the Corn Belt. Demand for feeder cattle fell off. Some cattle companies would never recover from what had once been almost valueless beasts, roaming the Nueces valley twenty-five years earlier, then had become premium commodities in eastern markets, had now become worthless again. An era in the history of the American frontier had come to an end in a generation.[19]

Following the "die off" of the winter of 1886–1887, the Swan Company declared bankruptcy on May 28, 1887, having suffered losses that Holsinger estimates were over $100,000 in 1886. The Niobra Company of Nebraska followed suit. The position Van Devanter had established for the Burhan family in the Swan Company, now reduced to unsecured promissory notes, was now worthless. The evening that the Swan cattle company declared itself bankrupt in May 1887, "in an effort to save his mother-in-law's interest," Van Devanter posted a $100,000 bond, endorsed by Francis E. Warren as surety, and had himself appointed receiver for the firm. For over a year he worked unsuccessfully to straighten out the complex legal and financial affairs of the Swan Company. Holsinger recounts, "Instead of money, however, Van Devanter received from the company only the books and one empty fireproof safe. Finally acknowledging his inability to recover the family's losses, he resigned his post in June, 1888." "Despite his failure, however, Van Devanter's role as receiver as well as his legal dealings with many of the smaller companies in the Territory went far toward making him known throughout all of Wyoming. With his background as a stepping stone it was far easier to climb in prestige in the following years."[20]

In the bankruptcy proceeding, the Swan Company and its British shareholders contended that the herd books that Alexander Swan had supplied to them had been falsified, that the actual number of cattle was at least 30,000 less than represented, and that the Company had been cheated out of more than $800,000. Swan was fired as general manager and replaced by John Clay, a member of the Wyoming Stock Growers Association who had managed other British-owned ranches. Clay reduced the Swan Land and Cattle Company's capital and, by 1893, cut the Company's herd to 40,000.

During this intrepid period, in 1887–1888, Willis served as city attorney for Cheyenne, during which, according to Friedman and Israel, he helped wage a vigorous campaign against prostitutes.[21] In January 1888, the first horse-drawn trolley service ran on light rail and operated out of the Abney Livery Stables—16th Street between Capitol Avenue and Central Avenue (then Ransom Street), near Warren's Phoenix Block completed in 1882 by Warren for a mere $35,000, at the southwest corner of 16th Street & Capitol Avenue, where it boasted three stories and a complete plumbing system with water and gas.[22]

Unfortunately, the authoritarian hand of Thomas Moonlight was ill-equipped to contend with the social and economic dynamic occurring in Wyoming and throughout the American West. And the vacillating electorate in the upcoming national elections of 1890 and 1894 would be no help. Since the early 1880s, a surge of settlement had been coming into Wyoming answering Congress' inducement under the homestead laws. The often-uneasy relationship between larger, wealthier ranches and smaller ranch settlers became steadily worse after the miserable winter of 1887–1888. Newcomers' newly built wire fences interfered with the free range of cattle on the public land in which cattle owners claimed a virtual property interest. The same fences stood in the way of cattle moving toward natural shelter in storms and water holes when water was scarce.

The cattlemen characterized the farmer import from the East and the Midwest as "nesters." In fact, the "nesters" problem was probably a scapegoat, as cattle companies had been ignoring several other important operational and economic factors. Prices paid for cattle had become artificially inflated, as compared with their inherent value. Some grazing land was overstocked, with forage rapidly depleting.[23] The loss of thousands of cattle during the severe Wyoming winters inspired apprehension and a defense anxiety in the managers of the large cattle companies, who began to appropriate land and control the flow and supply of water. Some forced settlers off their land and set fire to settlers' buildings. The cattle owner syndicate, represented in the WSGA, also tried to exclude smaller ranchers from participating in the annual roundup. Justification for these excesses on once public, now private, land was premised on the catch-all allegation of rustling. Ultimately the justification would lead to murder and political consequences in Wyoming in 1892.

Desiring to upgrade the quality of his clientele beyond the "horse thieves" who were occasionally the clients of his solo practice,[24] Van Devanter formed a new law partnership in 1887. He chose Charles N. Potter, a former Cheyenne city attorney, as partner, a choice with some political significance. The affiliation may have been at the suggestion of Francis Warren or otherwise to secure his approbation. Potter's reputation as an "influential Republican," cannot have been lost on Van Devanter. Friedman and Israel report that the newly established firm soon touted the Burlington Railroad as a client.[25] Van Devanter also sought out and represented the many growing cattle companies around Cheyenne and, of course, pursued the protection of his family's investment in Wyoming's major livestock concern, the Swan Land and Cattle Company. The Potter-Van Devanter partnership would last until 1889, and proved to be remunerative. Wallace Johnson says he suspected that Willis was "a very capable lawyer" based on the fact that "the economic interests in Wyoming all turned to Van Devanter to represent them. He represented the Union Pacific and the Burlington railroads. He represented the Wyoming Stockgrowers and most of the powerful and sizable stock ranches in the state."[26]

Business increased to the point where Van Devanter could write to a friend in Ohio, "I should say that there is but one firm in Wyoming having a better practice than ours." By January 1888, Cheyenne's newspaper, the *Cheyenne Weekly Leader*, as quoted by Holsinger, saw Van Devanter on the upward swing to political position, appearing "smiling and composed, speaking in his usual suave tones."[27] "Mr. Van Devanter ... is a young man of smooth address, with no false modesty about asserting his own claims to recognition, and a well-defined purpose of shoving himself ahead in the world."[28] His acumen for articulating truth in convenient terms would serve well in his future years.

By the spring of 1888, Van Devanter would report to another friend on his rapid rise, on his widening professional experience, and on the flavor of the community that was shaping him. In a letter quoted by Alexander Bickel and Benno Schmidt, Willis said:

> In our office we have all the business we can attend to and it yields us a fair return for the labor expended.
>
> The experience acquired in some of the positions I have held there has been of benefit to me. I have been the City Attorney of Cheyenne at a salary of $750, and was a member of the Commission which prepared the revised statutes of the Territory (compensation $1,000) and I was a member of the legislative assembly, which but recently adjourned.... As a rule, lawyers

work much harder here, and get better fees accordingly. There are no really old practitioners in Wyoming, but what is lacking in experience is more than made up by constant study and application....

Our lawyers usually have good libraries. I have all the Reports of Ohio, New York, Michigan, and Wisconsin, and the American and English railroad cases, and also a large and well selected list of text books. My partner has about the same number ... making in all a fair library.

....

Litigation at Cheyenne often involves very large amounts, which make the fees here good.... W. Van Devanter letter to A.A. Frazier, April 9, 1888.[29]

For whatever reason, Willis didn't mention his election to the Republican controlled territorial legislature. The fortunes of the Territory's Republican party prior to the legislative session of 1888 had not fared as well, however, as Van Devanter's private practice. Van Devanter remained politically active all the while, and he was now elected to the 1888 Territorial Legislature. Larson recounts, "In the forefront of the Republican leadership was the twenty-eight-year-old representative from Laramie County, Willis Van Devanter."[30] Convening in 1888, under Van Devanter's leadership as Chairman of the Judiciary Committee, as reported by the February 2 *Cheyenne Weekly Leader*,[31] the Legislature battled Governor Moonlight with the objective of laying the ground for Wyoming statehood as a state that could be controlled by elected Republican leadership. Illuminated by the prospect of political success and future prospects, Van Devanter got more politically active and involved in the statehood movement. Wyoming Republicans organized and convened a second constitutional convention,[32] the first, to which Willis had not been a delegate, having been organized unsuccessfully in 1887.[33] Van Devanter secured himself a seat as a Wyoming delegate to the Republican National Convention to be held in Chicago in 1888.[34]

When the Republican convention organized in Chicago, James G. Blaine, who had been the Republican flag-bearer in 1884, refused to accept a second nomination. In his stead, the convention chose Indiana's prior U.S. Senator, Benjamin Harrison.[35] Harrison, great-grandson of Benjamin Harrison, a signer of the Declaration of Independence, grandson of Whig President William Henry Harrison, son of Ohio Congressman John Scott Harrison, had a name worthy of party intentions seeking to re-secure the White House. New York and Indiana were swing states capable of determining the outcome of Presidential elections. And his political success in Indiana must certainly have been attractive to Republican delegate Van Devanter, particularly given the likely association of Harrison and Willis' father Isaac, still living in Indiana. As Indiana's Democratic legislature had previously defeated Harrison's re-election to the U.S. Senate, his presidential nomination must certainly have felt like a vindication.

As Harrison hailed from Indiana and was member of the same state Republican Party to which Van Devanter's father was loyal, the political coincidences of Van Devanter's situation must have seemed obvious, and opportune, to him. Harrison had been Indiana's U.S. Senator while Van Devanter studied law in Cincinnati and had served as chairman of the Senate Committee on Transportation Routes to the Seaboard in the 47th Congress (March 4, 1881, March 4, 1883), and chairman of the Senate Committee on Territories in the 48th and 49th Congresses in 1883–1885 and 1885–1887, respectively. There he advocated the admission of new western states in the anticipation that they would provide more Republican representation in Congress.

Wyoming's Republicans hoped that a Republican victory in 1888 would likely return Republican leadership to the Wyoming Territory and bring statehood. But, as a territory, Wyoming voters couldn't vote in the national election. Nevertheless, Van Devanter touted Republican performance and deprecated Democrats. Both as a delegate to the Republican Territorial Convention and as a campaigner, Van Devanter pursued election victory for in-state Republicans.

The outcome of the national election depended on Harrison's and Van Devanter's home state of Indiana, as well as New York, New Jersey, and Connecticut. Wyoming Republicans hoped that a victory for Harrison would regain their control of territorial administration after March 1889. Even Democratic newspapers conceded this and pushed Francis Warren's reappointment as territorial governor. The *Cheyenne Daily Leader* commented in late December, "We've had enough [of the Moonlight administration].... We could wish Wyoming no better Xmas [sic] gift than the assurance of Governor Moonlight's immediate and precipitate removal." Twenty-four of the twenty-seven newspapers in the Territory either openly or tacitly supported Warren's return.[36]

Political conditions in the United States were now in a state of "political equipoise."[37] Democrats and Republicans were nearly equal in their political strength nationwide. Republicans generally supported governmental activism, fostering economic development, and welcomed burgeoning industrialization. They felt that government should assist the wealth-making process. Democrats, on the other hand, retained the Jeffersonian notion of small government and states' rights. Primarily southern and agrarian, they opposed tariff protectionism.

The fall general election campaign was relatively calm, Harrison giving "front porch speeches" from his home and incumbent Grover Cleveland declining to campaign actively at all. In November, Cleveland won the popular election by 100,000 votes. But Harrison won the election in the electoral college.[38] Harrison's victory was tarnished by allegations of voter fraud in Indiana, a matter that would particularly have drawn the attention of Willis Van Devanter, whose own star was rising. The fraud was uncovered by the testimony of a railroad employee who alleged that "blocks of five" electors were solicited to sell their votes to the Republican Party.

President Harrison took office on March 4, 1889, when he was sworn into office by Chief Justice Melville Fuller.[39] He would serve only one full term (1889–1893) before being unseated by Cleveland's re-election. Three weeks after his inauguration, on March 29, 1889, President Harrison reappointed Warren to the post of territorial governor. He had pledged in his presidential campaign to support home rule, which Warren also advocated.[40] Governor Moonlight's quixotic term as territorial governor was done.

President Benjamin Harrison isn't noted for great contributions to the nation's history. Constitutional lawyer and Supreme Court advocate Laurence Tribe characterized Harrison as "a typical Midwestern Republican politician of the times, devoted to large business interests and willing to allow the party hierarchy to run his administration for him."[41] Although historians generally consider Harrison to have been a mediocre President, he is nevertheless remembered for managing the admission of several Republican states, including Wyoming, into the Union and authorizing pensions for Civil War veterans, even though that severely stressed the U.S. treasury.

Wyoming Republicans now encouraged Willis Van Devanter to assume the position of Chief Justice of the Wyoming Territory, if they could get Cleveland appointee William L. Macginnis to resign and President Harrison to appoint him. But Macginnis was not predisposed to voluntarily vacate the position. Van Devanter lobbied for the post. His correspondence revealed a faux sincerity and tone of self-sacrifice to do that which he had, himself, probably proposed. This was the tone of false modesty that the would-be Supreme Court Justice would employ repeatedly in his rise to station. In an April 4, 1889, letter to Alfred A. Bright, quoted by Holsinger, "My practice is such that it will be a sacrifice for me to take the Chief Justiceship, but the position being a highly honorable one, and furnishing, as it does, ample opportunity to develop one's best ability, I shall be especially pleased if the appointment is given to me."[42] As we shall see, Willis' loyalty to public service was merely convenient as he would serve a term only satisfying his personal needs.

The situation was ripe for Wyoming's statehood. In early April 1889, newly appointed Governor Warren had urged Wyoming residents to begin to prepare for it. Five months later a constitutional convention was called. The convention remained in session from September 2 to September 30, with the Republicans holding a slim majority. As Chief Justice, Van Devanter was not a delegate, but a pass to the floor of the meeting remains in his papers, and it is not unrealistic to assume that he also played an important behind-the-scenes role in drawing up the state constitution. T.A. Larson documents that one convention member, W.E. Chaplin, remembers that Van Devanter was one of "an invisible delegation of extraordinary power," along with then Wyoming Territorial Governor Francis E. Warren, and Elwood Mead (later engineer of the U.S. Bureau of Reclamation and namesake of Lake Mead which holds water behind Hoover Dam).

Van Devanter was indeed in an excellent position to advise and direct the course of the convention, as it adopted those statutes which had been drafted by the Statutory Revision Commission to which Territorial Governor Warren had appointed him in March 1886. The Commission's draft had been formally adopted in 1888 by the Territorial Legislature, of which Van Devanter was then a member and Judiciary Committee chairman. The three commissioners, Van Devanter, Isaac P. Caldwell and J.W. Blake, all Republicans, knew them well. These revised statutes were then used by the Constitutional Convention of 1889, most probably at Van Devanter's behest, in formulating the new constitution and laws for the State of Wyoming.

President Harrison was now certainly partial to Wyoming's admission to the Union. For more than ten years no new states had been admitted. Congressional Democrats had stood in the way of the Republican agenda, as they presumed that the new Western states would elect Republican legislatures that would send Republican Senators to Congress. The mandate of the electorate in the 1888 election was marginally Democratic, but the White House was now occupied by a Republican. The 50th Congress (1887–1889) ended in a lame duck session, one which would be beneficial to the Republican Party. When the lame duck was done, North Dakota, South Dakota, Montana, became states on November 2, 1889, and Washington did the same on November 11. Wyoming did not. At the first election following their statehood, congressional representatives from the four other states were Republicans.

President Harrison's biographer, Charles Calhoun has said that President Harrison had a "problem of office-hungry Hoosiers" when he took office.[43] Willis Van Devanter was likely one of them. While the applicant or the messenger to Harrison is unknown, young Van Devanter's acumen at exploiting the political situation is not. On August 31, 1889, President Harrison rewarded Wyoming's Territorial Republicans for their loyalty in the 1888 election, appointing their youthful party lieutenant, Territorial Legislature Judiciary Committee Chairman Van Devanter, as chief judge of the Wyoming Territorial Supreme Court with Warren's support. Willis was only 30. The position would pay $3,000 per year. He would travel over the state to hear what Friedman and Israel describe as "dull local cases."[44]

Civil Service reform had become a prominent issue following Harrison's election. Harrison had campaigned as a supporter of the merit system, as opposed to the spoils system. Although the origin of the spoils system is attributed to Democratic President Andrew Jackson, the system of repayment for political loyalty had been enhanced dramatically by Abraham Lincoln as a means to support the Republican Party and the Union's Civil War effort. But by the late 1860s, reformers began demanding a civil service system.

Congress had passed the Pendleton Act in 1883, creating a bipartisan Civil Service Commission to evaluate job candidates on a nonpartisan merit basis. The Act, however, had little breadth of application, covering a relatively few administrative positions, and allowed the President to transfer political appointments into the merit system, thereby creating permanent positions filled by party loyalists.

The reach of the Pendleton Act had thus become a political football by the time of the 1888 election. At least until 1896, each successive president had used the terms of the Pendleton Act to maintain his party's loyalists in office during his successor's term, undermining the successor's potential to implement those programs upon which he had campaigned. Even though some of the civil servants Harrison found in place when he took office had been classified under the Pendleton Act by previous administrations, he dedicated his first efforts to deciding upon political appointments, and the appointment of judges at all levels would become a major concern of Harrison's Presidency.

The Wyoming Territorial Supreme Court was a court with general jurisdiction but acted, according to Larson, predominantly in criminal matters.[45] Willis remained in the position through the state constitutional convention which would take place in September that year and congressional consideration of Wyoming statehood in the spring of 1890.

On November 5, 1889, the Wyoming constitution, having been submitted to the people, was approved by a popular vote of 6,272 to 1,923, a majority of slightly more than three to one. This vote, nevertheless, presented problems for the Territory. Idaho, which was also seeking admission as a state, had just voted in favor of its new constitution by a majority of eight to one; Montana had approved its constitution by twenty to one, South Dakota's by twenty-three to one. According to Holsinger, many Congressmen in Washington consequently argued that the people of Wyoming really didn't want statehood, since the percentage favoring the constitution seemed slim in comparison with that of other territories.[46]

Although the 50th Congress' lame duck session hadn't produced statehood for Wyoming, the new 51st Congress convening in 1890 would do so. Wyoming secured statehood a week after Idaho in the summer of 1890, becoming the forty-fourth state. President Benjamin Harrison signed the Wyoming statehood bill on July 10, 1890. Both states' first congressional delegations were solidly Republican.

Statehood now in hand, elections for state officers would be forthcoming and Warren's and Van Devanter's terms as political appointees of the Harrison Administration would soon lapse. Several years after Van Devanter left the Wyoming bench, he characterized the merits of his own judicial experience as territorial Chief Justice. His self-evaluation was probably offered in the context of his later seeking a federal appointment from President McKinley, an agenda that would be pursued by then Senator Warren on Willis' behalf. In a January 21, 1897, letter to Francis Warren, quoted by Holsinger, Willis said:

> When Chief Justice of the Territory, I by virtue of that position also held the District Courts in the First District. During that time many important civil and criminal cases were tried before me and no appeal from my decision was ever taken in a criminal case, although I sentenced a great many offenders from murder down. In civil cases there were perhaps a dozen appeals, but my decision was affirmed in every case.... In this respect my record is better than that of any Territorial Judge, not even excepting Lacey.[47]

Van Devanter's claims of the volume of his judicial activity are a bit suspect, given that he served less than a year, from August 31, 1889, to July 10, 1890, and that during that time he was engaged in significant political activity. Holsinger says, "During the period of Van Devanter's Chief Justiceship, his most important role was nonjudicial. A leading Republican politician as well as a judge, Van Devanter played an active part in the drive of the G.O.P. to achieve statehood for Wyoming."[48] And the events intervening between his initial judicial service and his misrepresentation of it seven years later undercuts any claim Van Devanter may have thought he had to station in the ranks of ethical jurists. But his political skills are well remembered in Wyoming. Gould says:

> This activity enabled him to win a greater and greater measure of Warren's confidence. Thirty-one years old in 1890, Van Devanter possessed limitless ambition, an immense capacity for hard work, and a never-failing commitment to Warren's cause. In him, Warren found the perfect lieutenant—discreet, loyal, and knowledgeable. Behind Van Devanter's thin face and neat moustache was an alert and perceptive mind, equally adroit at drafting bills, arguing election contests in court, supervising legislatures, or running political campaigns.[49]

Willis Van Devanter's photo of the period bears out Gould's description.

Wyoming was growing rapidly, particularly near the state's now-primary communication artery, the Union Pacific Railroad. According to Gould, "Of Wyoming's

Willis Van Devanter about 1895. After Wyoming became a state, he became elected Justice of the new state Supreme Court, a position from which he resigned four days later to return to private law practice (courtesy Wyoming State Archives).

sixty-two thousand residents in 1890, forty-four thousand lived in the five southern counties along the line of the railroad. Cheyenne, with eleven thousand inhabitants, and Laramie, with six thousand, were the largest towns, followed by Rock Springs, Rawlins, and Evanston; significantly, all five towns were seats of the Union Pacific counties."[50]

Five days after Congress granted Wyoming's statehood, Governor Warren announced that the first general state election would be held on September 11. A period of no more than thirty days would be allowed for campaigning. The Republican State Central Committee met on August 14 in Cheyenne to nominate candidates. Francis E. Warren was named by the Republicans as their gubernatorial candidate. Though he was not present, Van Devanter was selected together with H.V.B. Groesbeck and Arthur Conaway, to run for the three justiceships on the now state Supreme Court. The Democrats nominated ex-justice Samuel Corn, P. Gad Bryan, and Henry S. Elliott for Supreme Court justices.

In September, Warren was easily elected governor. Van Devanter won a seat on the Wyoming Supreme Court, so situated as to become the state's first Chief Justice. Their Republican running mates, candidates for state offices, won as well.[51] In the state Senate, thirteen of the sixteen members elected were Republicans. In the House of Representatives, twenty-six out of thirty-three of the members elected were Republicans. The *Cheyenne Democratic Leader* dejectedly reported the election as a "landslide, clean sweep, snow storm or soup festival" for the Republicans.

Early on the morning of October 11, 1890, one month after the election, the votes were canvassed. Supreme Court justice candidate Van Devanter served as a member of the canvassing board certifying his own election. When the board officially announced that the Republicans had made a clean sweep of all the state administrative offices, Van Devanter and his fellow justices drew lots to decide the length of their terms as provided for by the new state constitution. The terms of the justices were to be staggered, one for four years, one for six, and one for eight. The justice who drew the short term would become the Chief Justice. Van Devanter found himself the holder of the four-year term and thus the new Chief Justice of the state. A few minutes before midnight, he, his associates on the state Supreme Court, and other Republican leaders met Warren, who had been out of town, at the railroad depot, rushed him to the capitol, and with him all were inaugurated.

Four days later, with his political ducks in line, and with no advance warning, Van Devanter resigned his elected position as Chief Justice of the Wyoming Supreme Court, ostensibly "in order to return to his very lucrative law practice."[52]

Governor Warren, empowered by the new Wyoming Constitution to appoint a justice to replace Van Devanter until the new general election, appointed another Republican, Homer S. Merrill, to succeed Van Devanter. Justice Groesbeck would succeed Van Devanter as Chief Justice.

The reason for Van Devanter's sudden resignation cannot be specifically determined. Bickel and Schmidt suggest "[t]he Chief Justiceship of Wyoming had evidently not been satisfying."[53] Hardly had Willis had time to be dissatisfied in his four days in office. The Swan bankruptcy in his recent memory, and his family's financial loss three years before, may have caused private practice to be his only viable choice. The Chief Justice's annual salary would have been only $3,000. But he probably also realized that if he wished to advance quickly, the better hope for the future lay in open participation in political activities from which he should be barred as a member of the Supreme Court. The fact that he resigned so quickly would also seem to indicate that he had determined that he would do so prior to the election, and that his name, an important drawing card, had been used simply to guarantee a complete Republican victory in the voting. If this is true, it will probably never be verified since many of Van Devanter's papers pertaining to his Wyoming political activities were destroyed at his orders some years later after his elevation to the United States Supreme Court.

But Van Devanter's resignation should not be viewed as a dislike of judicial station. Bickel and Schmidt suggest "judicial office became henceforth a fixed ambition" for Van Devanter. Citing Willis' February 28, and March 1, 1891, letters to Francis Warren, Bickel and Schmidt identify Van Devanter's unsuccessful attempt to gain appointment to a newly-created federal Circuit Court of Appeals position, and in the alternative, "virtually any other available federal court."

A month after Van Devanter's resignation from the Wyoming Supreme Court, on November 18, 1890, Wyoming's first legislature as a state met in special session to elect Wyoming's two United States Senators. Joseph M. Carey was elected quickly. The legislature's choice of its second Senator[54] took more time, however. Morris reports that, after seven ballots, the Republican-dominated legislature finally also selected Governor Warren to be the second Senator. Warren had repeatedly vowed during the prior gubernatorial election that he would not seek the Senate seat. Democrats had charged that he should not be trusted not to do so and that Republican interests were expected to elect Warren to the Senate. Notwithstanding his prior vows to the contrary, Warren resigned his office as Governor and accepted the Senatorship. Warren's decision to become Senator was to be highly advantageous for Van Devanter, who now became the recognized resident head of the Republican Party in Wyoming.

The next few years were to be vitally important to Wyoming's development but even more so for Van Devanter's drive for preferment.[55] Warren's departure to Washington would not diminish the relationship which Warren and Van Devanter had formed. Professor Gould accurately characterized the relationship in his 1966 PhD thesis: "From 1890 to 1897, the team of Warren and Van Devanter functioned with efficiency, and Warren owed much of his success to the contributions of his faithful aide."[56] As it turned out, both were partial to political convenience, and neither partial to keeping his promise. Between the two, one was the more powerful, the other the more wily.

The new Wyoming constitution provided that the vacancy in the gubernatorial position created by Warren's resignation would be filled by the duly elected Secretary of State, serving as an acting governor until the next possible election. Dr. Amos W. Barber, a Republican also elected in the Republican sweep of the state's September 1890 elections, was Secretary of State. Born April 26, 1861, in Doylestown, Bucks County, Pennsylvania, Barber had moved to Wyoming in 1885 to take a position as surgeon in charge of the military hospital at Fort Fetterman. Having worked as a staff physician at the Pennsylvania Hospital, he was promoted to acting U.S. Army surgeon and accompanied General Crook's expedition to Arizona, the later assigned to Fort D.A. Russell near Cheyenne.

After resigning the military, Barber opened a medical practice in Cheyenne, joined the Republican Party, and ran for Secretary of State in September 1890. While he "acted" as governor during the vacancy in the governor's office, he remained Secretary of State, later continuing that service until 1895, as John E. Osborne became governor on January 2, 1893.

Van Devanter was by now in control of Republican Party apparatus as chairman of the state party and was now regarded, in the retrospective view of Holsinger and Hall, as the unofficial Republican spokesman in the absence of Senators Warren and Carey.[57] But Wallace Johnson probably has it most correct, that it was the corporate interests behind the scenes who really called the shots: "Some would suggest, not without some support, that the railroad and the cattle interests 'ran' the state [of Wyoming] a century ago. The lawyer for those powerful interests was Willis Van Devanter, and Van Devanter was very much at the center of cultural, political and economic Wyoming."[58]

When Willis went back to private practice in October 1890, it was a practice which Bickel and Schmidt said "prospered and was varied, including some substantial railroad clients." David Schutz called it a "return to his very lucrative law practice."

Willis had practiced briefly with his brother-in-law earlier (1881–1883) back in Marion, Indiana. Lacey, who had been appointed chief justice of Wyoming on July 5, 1884[59] by President Arthur, and who had held that post for three years before his being replaced on November 8, 1886, by the Cleveland administration, had then organized a law firm under the name Corlett, Lacey, and Riner, the latter representing the Union Pacific. On September 22, 1890, John Alton Riner was appointed the United States District Judge for Wyoming by President Harrison.[60] William Wellington Corlett, who had come to Wyoming in 1867 and who had been John Clay's attorney died in 1890. Clay was now president of the Wyoming Stock Growers Association. Willis now joined partnership with Lacey.[61] At the first term of the U.S. District Court for Wyoming after statehood, Charles Potter and Willis Van Devanter were the first attorneys sworn to practice before the court.

The new firm to which young Van Devanter turned, Lacey and Van Devanter, uniquely offered the services of two former Chief Justices of the territorial or state Supreme Courts, and the practice was successful. The partnership became Wyoming's prominent law firm, Lacey and Van Devanter managing to obtain the business of many of Wyoming's leading personalities. The business of representing the Union Pacific which had eluded Van Devanter four years earlier now became his and for the next six years Van Devanter was the railroad's counsel,[62] defending the company in numerous court cases.

Friedman and Israel mention casually that attorney Van Devanter "was kept quite busy by the Union Pacific."[63] By this time, the Union Pacific had been many years under investigation by the Federal Land Office and congressional committees. Fraudulent land surveys in Wyoming and Montana and appropriations of valuable coal lands and exclusion of actual settlers from land along streams under the Desert Land Act had given rise to criminal charges that the company desired be supported or contested.

In one prior instance, Willis had worked on the development of contracts between the Union Pacific and the City of Cheyenne, for whom he was then acting as city attorney, regarding facilities, property transfer and maintenance.[64] Morris mentions the contract taking effect in January 1889. But to his frustration, Willis had learned that the railroad company preferred to deal only with large and established firms. Now, the legal business of the Union Pacific Railroad, who could boast of 901 miles of track in Wyoming by 1890, would be his. Notably, he would represent

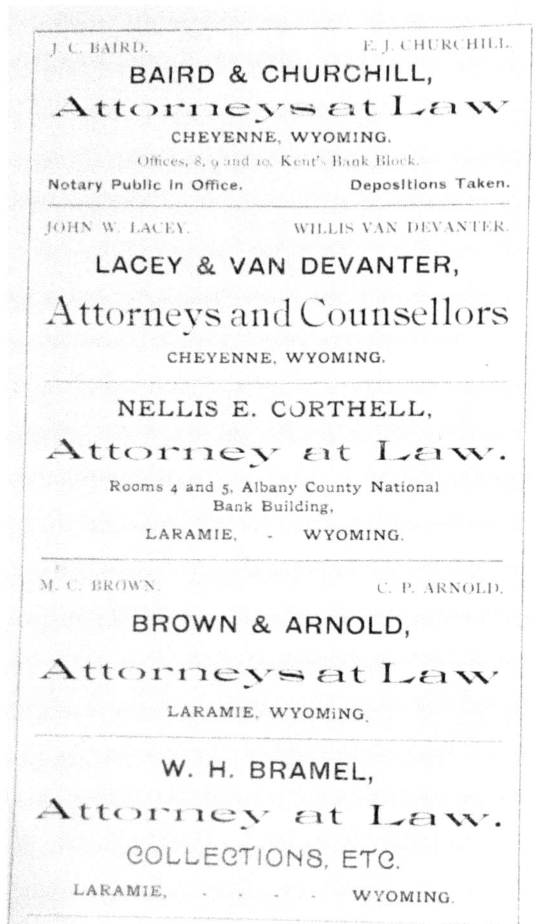

Attorney advertising in Souvenir Program, First Annual Commencement, University of Wyoming, Laramie, Wyoming, June 10, 1891 (courtesy Wyoming State Library).

the Railroad in *Redman v. Union Pacific Railway Co.*[65]; *Schenck v. Union Pacific Railway Co.*[66]; *White et al. v. Hinton et al.*[67]; and *Link v. Union Pacific Railway Co.*[68] He represented other railroads, and cattle companies as well.

Friedman and Israel have it that the new "firm of Lacey and Van Devanter handled Union Pacific Railroad business, including efforts to prevent injured workers from obtaining compensation." They also describe Willis' continued work for Francis Warren during these early years of the 1890s, exerting pressures on the Wyoming legislature on Warren's behalf.[69]

Both politically and professionally, Willis Van Devanter's welfare had improved throughout the decade. Consistent with the premise that success corroborates station, young Van Devanter fulfilled the ethic he had been taught at school. Wyoming was now Willis' oyster.

12

Willis and the "Johnson County War" (1890–1892)

In 1890, when Willis Van Devanter rejoined John Lacey in private law practice, Lacey had likely inherited Corlett's representation of cattle interests, including John Clay and the WSGA. As that work would have been political as well as strictly legal, Van Devanter would be involved in that representation. According to Holsinger, as a lawyer, Van Devanter devoted proportionally more of his time to cases dealing with political matters than with any other topic.[1] Van Devanter and Lacey were thus situated to be called upon to defend the interests of Republican cattle barons which might arise from their excessive exercise of arrogant power. The partnership would continue until 1898.

Van Devanter's most widely publicized, and certainly most sensational, case as a lawyer in private practice after departing his elected position on the state Supreme Court, was his defense of the cattlemen leaders of the so-called "Johnson County War" of 1892, the name given to the Wyoming Stock Grower's Association's unsuccessful effort to eradicate the "nesters" in northern Wyoming.[2] Those farmers and small cattle ranchers who relied on the federal statutory device of homestead had organized themselves into a nascent and competitive cattle growers' association. The homestead approach and the competitive association interfered with the free-ranging of cattle permitted by the cattle barons' loose management and accounting practices. The disloyal and self-serving practice of large ranch employees exacerbated the problem.[3]

Van Devanter's role in the violence, by his complicity and legal defense, is usually overlooked. Johnson says only that "the persona of Willis Van Devanter only emerges when he is considered in the context of the historic and turbulent times during territorial Wyoming and its early statehood before the turn of the last century."

The "War" was a classic case of Garret Hardin's "tragedy of the commons," those commons being public grasslands and "maverick" (unbranded) cattle. In retrospect, at least one historian, William H. Kittrel, in his Foreword to Mercer's *The Banditti of the Plains or The Cattlemen's Invasion of Wyoming in 1892 [The Crowning Infamy of the Ages]*, attempted to view it objectively:

> In attempting to assay the motives of the invaders and the settlers, to determine accurately the proportion of good and evil in each, there seems to be a tendency toward a balance. The theft of hard-earned chattels from the honest herdsman is an evil, an injustice that demands to be righted. The hazing of the rustler and granger, ranging from warnings, burnings, and quasi-legal seizing of his cattle, on up to hanging and dry-gulching, cries out for justice and retribution. You can see in it facets of the age-old question of human rights versus property rights, of the distinction between crimes against person and crimes against property.[4]

But the likelihood of Willis Van Devanter's objectivity regarding such issues of theoretical justice, given his political and client loyalties, as well as his attraction to wealth and power, is slim.

The illegal exploits of an organized group of bona fide rustling outfits in the Wyoming-Montana region was becoming well publicized in the late 1880s. Much of which is known about at least one extreme case of cattle owner reaction is due to the reporting of Asa Shinn Mercer.[5] Although his account of what he learned and saw is discredited by Lawrence Woods[6] because of treatment he later received from Wyoming's wealth and political establishment, Mercer's reportage stands as the most complete and documented version of the sordid affair.[7]

Well-armed bands of horse and cattle rustlers roamed across various portions of Wyoming and Montana. Montana cattle interests had declared "War on the Rustlers" in 1889. Wyoming cattle interests did so a year later. In Johnson County, Wyoming, with emotions running high, agents of the larger ranches killed several alleged rustlers from smaller ranches. Many were killed on dubious evidence or were simply found dead while the killers remained anonymous. Frank M. Canton, sheriff of Johnson County in the early 1880s (also reported by E.S. Osgood in *The Day of the Cattlemen* as a United States marshal for Wyoming)[8] and better known as a detective for the WSGA, and who later used the names Joe Horner and Tom Horn, was rumored to be behind many of the deaths.

In the summer following Van Devanter's return to private practice and Senator Warren's departure for Washington, a number of dubious lynchings of alleged rustlers occurred. Journalist Asa S. Mercer observed that one lynching victim, Jim Averill, "was given to writing letters to near-by newspapers, criticizing what he viewed as the excesses of the big cattlemen and prophesying their ultimate downfall," and that of another's, Cattle Kate's, "popularity there can be no doubt, as her increasing cattle herd visibly attested it. It seems the lonely cowhands evidenced their high regard for her by tendering her slicks and doggies to which her brand was subsequently affixed. When her herd had grown to number fifty to eighty calves, the cattlemen from whose herds these calves had obviously come served notice on Cattle Kate to abandon her evil ways or take the consequences."[9] "Kate, who was known as the Queen of the Sweetwater, defied the order and continued her operations. Averill, likewise, kept on writing printable pieces for the papers, espousing the cause of the homesteader and challenging the ranchers, whose anger rose as the settlers increased." "The cattlemen, practical if not prosaic, decided that it would be simpler to hang Kate [than hang the cowboys who brought her stray calves], thus avenging their losses and preventing further thefts."[10] Other lynchings occurred near Newcastle, Wyoming.[11]

By early 1892, depression was threatening. Wyoming's economic development had lagged for several years following the devastating winter of 1886–1887. As with any depression, the public charged the incumbent political party and its leaders with responsibility for causing, or not curing, the problem. In March, Senator Warren voiced his concern in a letter to his party lieutenant. In a March 19, 1892, letter Warren asked Van Devanter who he thought should run for office in the state. Warren added with some foreboding that "it seems to me we have many unfortunate features to overcome" before the election.[12] By now both Van Devanter and Warren were certainly aware of the brewing plan being implemented by the WSGA, a plan that would ultimately exacerbate the loss of public distrust engendered by the general economic conditions. Growing populism fed the fire.

During the winter following the organization of NWFSGA[13] and the lynchings and ambushes in northern Wyoming, three of the members of the Board of Livestock Commissioners[14] met in Cheyenne. They were joined by Frank Wolcott, a large North Platte cattle rancher and member of WSGA from Glenrock, Wyoming, who would become the field marshal of the operation. The group met in Acting Governor Barber's office, in the Commercial Block adjacent to the Cheyenne Club, and met frequently, according to Mercer, with acting Governor Barber. Governor Barber later denied this. U.S. Senator Joseph M. Carey was reportedly a contributor to the cause. U.S. Senator Francis Warren was also reported by Mercer to be in the know.

The "war" that would ensue from the Livestock Commission's meeting involved a plot to invade Johnson County, assassinate its new county sheriff and expropriate its cattle. It culminated in a lengthy shootout between local ranchers, a band of hired killers, and a sheriff's posse, with the final intervention of the U.S. Cavalry. The plot's first order of business was the distribution of disinformation intended to color public opinion in favor of the cattlemen's future plan. The second was to secure the armed force necessary to eradicate the purported threat. That force was centered around the gunmen, including Frank Canton, who were hired directly by the WSGA and euphemistically called "stock detectives." Twenty-three gunmen from Paris, Texas, were recruited to work with the WSGA's four "cattle detectives." This notwithstanding Article XIX, Section 1, of the so-recently adopted Wyoming Constitution, which prohibited bringing any "armed police force, or detective agency, or armed body of men" into Wyoming. Ranch hands from Idaho and Montana were also recruited, one of whom, Idaho ranch hand George Dunning, later gave his revealing confession in the face of prosecution. The armed force would deal with the "tormenters"—those "rustlers" who collected "maverick" cattle into their own herds. It would kill specific individuals identified on a "dead list," including then-sitting Sheriff Angus of Johnson County.[15] The shock and awe of the plan would induce other settlers to abandon Wyoming, leaving their smaller cattle herds to be appropriated by the larger, open-range ranchers.

Complicit state and federal support were also secured. Acting Governor Barber said, "I am willing to give all the assistance possible to any body of men which will attempt to exterminate the rustlers,"[16] suggesting federal intervention in support of moneyed interests if county law enforcement were to interfere. On March

23, 1892, U.S. Adjutant General Frank Stitzer's General Order No. 4 advised Colonel De Forest Richards of the Wyoming National Guards that he should advise company commanders that they should follow *only* those commands received from Stitzer. The admonition was executed pursuant to "the order of the Governor and Commander in Chief."[17] If Governor Barber had in fact so ordered, the order was inconsistent with Wyoming law, as the law in effect at the time[18] authorized the governor, any county sheriff, mayor or judge to call upon any "commanding officer of any regiment, battalion, company, troop or battery" "to act in aid of the civil authority" if there is "reasonable anticipation of" a "tumult, riot, mob or any body of men acting together with intent to commit a felony, or to do or offer violence to person or property, or by force or violence to break or resist the laws of the territory." Barber's order would thus acquiesce to federal military intervention in state criminal law—and would protect law offenders against the intervention of state law enforcement officers—like Sheriff Angus. Mercer observed later that Barber's "closest personal friends with whom he had been in intercourse most of [5 April 1892], joined the gang at the depot, and it was simply impossible, under the circumstances, for him not to have known of the violation of the constitution being perpetrated."[19]

What Asa Mercer said of Governor Barber could also have been said about Willis Van Devanter. The Commander in Chief was the same Republican President Harrison whom Van Devanter had supported at the Chicago convention that nominated Harrison to the Republican ticket.

When the expedition launched in April 1892, a number of WSGA and Wyoming dignitaries followed along. A total of over 50 men were organized for the armed incursion. Frank Canton was designated its leader. The group led by Canton became alternatively known as "The Invaders," "Wolcott's Regulators" or just "The Regulators." Canton's gripsack was later found to contain a list of dozens of rustlers to be either shot or hanged and a contract to pay the Texans $5 a day plus a bonus of $50 for every rustler killed.

State Senator Bob Tisdale, state water commissioner W.J. Clarke, and W.C. Irvine and Hubert Teshemacher, both instrumental in promoting and organizing Wyoming statehood, rode along. Dr. Charles Penrose, a surgeon and colleague of Dr. (Governor) Barber also accompanied the group, carrying Governor Barber's surgical instruments case.[20] Asa Mercer went along for the reporting.

The group organized in Cheyenne, where they accumulated the Texas contingent delivered by train through Denver, and rode a specially hired train to Casper, Wyoming. There, they mounted up and rode toward Johnson County, cutting telegraph lines north of Douglas, Wyoming, so as to prevent reports of their action. Canton and the Texas gunmen traveled ahead. Walcott and the WSGA officials followed a safe distance behind.

The first target of the WSGA's gang was Nate Champion at the KC Ranch, near the modern town of Kaycee, Wyoming. In the night of Friday, April 8, the cattlemen's armed force quietly surrounded Champion's ranch buildings and waited for daybreak.[21] Champion kept a record in his journal as the mob burned his house. After the siege, the journal was found in Champion's pocket. Champion had written: "Boys, I feel pretty lonesome just now. I wish there was someone here with me so we could watch all sides at once." The last journal entry read: "Well, they have just got through shelling the house like hail. I heard them splitting wood. I guess they are going to fire the house tonight. I think I will make a break when night comes, if alive. Shooting again. It's not night yet. The house is all fired. Goodbye, boys, if I never see you again." Champion ran out the back door while the house was on fire. Four men shot him dead.[22]

Two eyewitnesses notified local rancher Jack Flagg who rode to Buffalo, the Johnson County seat, to alert the authorities. Within 24 hours, Johnson County's Sheriff Angus raised a posse of 200 men. The cattlemen's armed gang had headed north toward Buffalo the day before in a show of force. The Johnson County posse set out for the KC Ranch on Sunday night, April 10, and caught up with the MGA's men at the TA Ranch on Crazy Woman Creek on early Monday morning, April 11, where they discovered that they outnumbered the WSCA's hirelings four to one.

The cattlemen's force took refuge in a log barn. Ten of them tried to escape the barn but the posse beat them back, killing three. One of the cattlemen apparently escaped and made contact with acting Governor Barber on April 12, who was, according to Mercer, at the time together with WSGA Secretary H.B. Ijams in Denver.[23] A late night telegram over the Governor's signature was sent to President Harrison pleading for help to protect the prominent cattlemen against Sheriff Angus' posse. The telegram, the full text of which was printed on the front page of the *New York Times* on April 14, read:

> About sixty-one owners of livestock are reported to have made an armed expedition into Johnson County for the purpose of protecting their live stock and preventing unlawful roundups by rustlers. They are at "T.A." Ranch, thirteen miles from Fort McKinney, and are besieged by Sheriff and posse and by rustlers from that section of the country, said to be two or three hundred in number. The wagons of stockmen were captured and taken away from them and it is reported a battle took place yesterday, during which a number of men were killed. Great excitement prevails. Both parties are very determined and it is feared that if successful will show no mercy to the persons captured. The civil authorities are unable to prevent violence. The situation is serious and immediate assistance will probably prevent great loss of life.[24]

President Harrison, apparently relying on Article IV, Section 4, Clause 2 of the U.S. Constitution that authorizes the use of U.S. forces under the President's orders for "protection from invasion and domestic violence," immediately ordered U.S. Secretary of War Stephen B. Elkins to take action. Elkins ordered the Sixth Cavalry from Fort McKinney near Buffalo to proceed immediately to the TA ranch, protect the cattlemen's armed forces from the sheriff's posse and take the cattlemen into custody. The Cavalry left Fort McKinney at 2 a.m. on April 13. Dunning said later that the invaders knew they were coming to rescue them.[25] When the Cavalry reached the TA ranch at 6:45 a.m., the besieged gunmen surrendered immediately to the Cavalry, saving themselves from the imminent attack of Sheriff Angus' posse, which was planning to burn the log barn where they were besieged.

The cattlemen and their hired Texans were placed in custody in Buffalo.[26] Among the captured cattlemen, according to Osgood and Holsinger, were W.C. Irvine, later president of the Stockgrowers Association and a member of the State Board of Livestock Commissioners; H.W. Davis, former president of the Associa-

The TA Ranch in Johnson County, Wyoming, where the invaders took refuge while they waited for the U.S. Cavalry, but were nearly burned out by the Johnson County posse. Gun ports cut in the siding are still visible (author's photograph, 2019).

tion and a member of the legislature; W.J. Clarke, state water commissioner; Frank Canton, deputy United States marshal for Wyoming; and H.E. Teschmacher, long-time member of the executive committee of the Association.

There is no direct evidence of Van Devanter's complicity in the planning of the crimes that would follow in April 1892. But there is substantial circumstantial evidence of his foreknowledge and participation in these criminal events. The young attorney certainly knew the players. The earlier cattlemen's attack on Champion and others in 1891 must have been known to Van Devanter. If it was, his actions constituted knowing anticipation of felonious behavior, a behavior hopefully disparaged by prior judicial officers. Although an officer of the law and prior chief justice of the Wyoming Territory, albeit short lived, he sought no sanctions against the perpetrators. He did not call out their actions as "above the law." Rather, he merely accepted their actions as within the realm of the law defined by raw power rather than legitimate, democratic confirmation of power. He apparently found it legitimate to act unlawfully and autocratically to control public resources in the face of a weaker, disenfranchised interference with raw power.

It is impossible that Van Devanter was unaware of the WSGA's intentions regarding the Johnson County invasion. The incursion's planning was conducted under the auspices of the Cheyenne Club, of which John Clay was then President.

Van Devanter clearly knew Clay well. Although Wallace Johnson has Clay "conveniently out of the country during the 'invasion,'"[27] and later denied the accusation, he was suspected of playing a major role in its planning.[28] Clay, a prominent Wyoming businessman, had been the general manager of the Swan Cattle Company after Alexander Swan was fired in 1886 and saw the company through bankruptcy during the period that Van Devanter served as receiver for the firm in May 1887. Clay was a client of Van Devanter's partner and brother-in-law John Lacey, inherited from law-partner Corlett, and a constructive, if not direct, attorney-client relationship existed between Van Devanter and Clay. Van Devanter would more than likely have been aware of Clay's involvement in the planning.

Van Devanter also knew Frank Canton. Canton had earlier been the sheriff of Johnson County while Van Devanter was chief justice of the Wyoming Territory. Sitting in that position, Van Devanter would have known all the local sheriffs. And Van Devanter at some point apparently represented Canton's alias, Tom Horn. Horn, according to Wallace Johnson "was ultimately indicted, convicted and then hanged for murder!"[29]

The invasion plan was also developed with full knowledge of the leadership of the Republican Party in Cheyenne and Washington, D.C., of which Van Devanter was at the time state Party Chairman and in-state spokesman. Planning for the incursion took over a year according to Dunning, including fund raising, and was broadly discussed within the WSGA.[30] Van Devanter was acquainted with many of its members, including intimately with Francis Warren, if not a member of the Cheyenne Club himself. And certainly, the grist at the Cheyenne Club would have carried the message to Van Devanter, if he had not heard it otherwise.

Governor Barber, a physician, his physician friend Dr. Penrose, who accompanied the mob likely at Barber's request, and Van Devanter represented the small collection of educated and professional men extant in Cheyenne at the time. Van Devanter was well acquainted with Amos Barber, likely recruiting or helping him to win election as Secretary of State in 1890 and transitioning him to governor as Warren's lieutenant. And Barber and Van Devanter were on the same Republican electoral slate in the 1890 general election, when Van Devanter ran for the state Supreme Court. Surely they would have shared the information regarding the WSGA's plot.

Dr. Barber's April 12 telegram to President Harrison rings of a lawyer's draftsmanship, not a physician's. Van Devanter, as Warren's aide, who had been involved in the 1890 election, and certainly counseled Barber as well, may have drafted the telegram. The telegram spun the news of the cattlemen's "protection" of their livestock and the "unlawful roundups by rustlers" in precisely the fashion that characterizes Willis Van Devanter's other writing. The predicate that the Governor's friends were "besieged by Sheriff and posse and by rustlers from that section of the country, said to be two or three hundred in number" and that "the civil authorities are unable to prevent violence" satisfied the condition established by General Stitzer's March 23, 1892, communication to Colonel De Forest Richards which would require state law enforcement officials to stand down in deference to federal action. The lawyer's mind is at work in these allegations, not the physician's. The convenient, well-chosen words of the telegram permit both the intended untruth and the plausible deniability of Van Devanter's and the Governor's own involvement and culpability.

And the WSGA's plan had not been hidden under a bushel basket. Recruitment for armed assistance was multi-state, broadcast by word of mouth through cattlemen of prominence in Wyoming, Montana, Idaho, Colorado, and Texas. The Texas mercenaries (primarily previous deputy U.S. Marshals) who were recruited by Tom Smith were moved by train to Denver, then to Cheyenne, and ultimately to Casper, Wyoming, at the expense of WSGA. They were carried on a special train arranged through the Union Pacific. Van Devanter represented the Union Pacific and other railroads during 1892 and has been reported by T.A. Larson to have been "privy to the plan"[31] of the Union Pacific officials to furnish their special train.

General hearsay knowledge of the plan was prevalent in Cheyenne, and particularly to the WSGA's stock detectives in advance of the invasion. According to Dunning, the individual perpetrators of the prior (1891) assaults in Johnson County were known, as was the intention of the WSGA to seek the removal by murder of all of the witnesses of the prior year's events.[32] It was generally known by April 3, 1892, that Governor Barber "had the running of the soldiers" and "would not let them molest the mob,"[33] a fact which had been corroborated by the order of the U.S. Adjutant General to Wyoming law enforcement officials earlier on March 23. And the WSGA's outfitting of gunfighters was occurring openly in Cheyenne city streets and stores by April 5, 1892.[34]

Van Devanter was an astute observer of public affairs who read the local newspaper daily. He collected past issues, published even before his arrival in Cheyenne, as an informational data base. Later, he would donate 34 volumes of the *Cheyenne Daily Leader* (1867–1895) and two volumes of the *Cheyenne Weekly Leader* (1869 & 1882–83) to the state historical society.[35] The WSGA's plan to assault and murder civilians and law enforcement officers cannot have passed him by. Van Devanter's March 19, 1892, correspondence with Senator Warren, as reported by Holsinger, also suggests his awareness.[36] Warren was also claimed by Dunning to have been aware of the plan. Dunning quoted WSGA general manager Ijams to the effect that "the stock association had approved of the general plan of the campaign of his [Ijams]," that "the other two officers of the stock association had charge of the arrangements for recruiting the mob and of the general plan of killing the rustlers," that "the mob would get along nicely; that every man that was a member of the Wyoming Stock Growers' Association was backing up the movement; that Governor Barber, Judge Blake, the United States marshal and nearly all the state officials were on the side of the stock association, and would stay with the mob through thick and thin." Last, he quoted that Ijams "said the mob had some very influential friends in Congress and the United States Senate, among whom he said were Senators Carey and Warren, whom he said were men of great influence and wealth." When Dunning asked Ijams if he thought the mob might not be arrested at Fort Russell on the way to Casper, Ijams apparently said, "there was no danger; that Governor Barber and Senators Warren and Carey would manipulate the troops; that the troops could not be called out except for the protection of the mob, and that the mob would be able to take care of itself, and that the officers at Fort Russell were friends of the stockmen."[37]

And Van Devanter cannot be said to have been ignorant of the laws being broken. His prior service on the Wyoming Territory Statutory Revision Commission, to which then Territorial Governor Warren had appointed him in 1886, his behind-the-scenes drafting at the constitutional convention of 1889, in which the legislation drafted by the Statutory Revision Commission was adopted, and his prior service as a sitting judge on the territory's and state's highest courts, charged him with at least constructive, if not actual, knowledge of the law. The component of the plan that called for the assassination of a sitting sheriff should have been especially offensive to Van Devanter, an officer of the law himself.

With respect to U.S. Adjutant General Stitzer's order to Wyoming's law enforcement officers, Van Devanter was in a position to know precisely what exemptions from state law would be required to shield WSGA invaders against intervention by local law enforcement, a protection afforded by federal military action.

Van Devanter should have known better. It was clearly a capital crime to premeditatedly plan to exterminate the operators of small ranches and cattle herds, just by characterizing them as "rustlers." It was an obvious crime to plan to expropriate their property in order to cover the costs of their other capital offense. And the intention to murder a county sheriff is so clearly against the law that it should have made Van Devanter blush. His breach of professional duty is remarkable. Officers of the law, and of the court, have a duty to act in accordance with the law. Van Devanter must either have learned nothing while a student of legal philosophy, judiciary committee chairman or judge. Otherwise, he had no conscience or was totally acquiescent to apparent power and wealth.

Van Devanter, Lacey, and eight other attorneys were retained to defend the vigilante cattlemen and the "purported Texan 'thugs,' hired by the cattleman's association to intimidate the small ranchers in Johnson County."[38] The date of their retention is unknown, but it may have merely been a continuance of ongoing representation. Van Devanter soon took the lead lawyer role. On April 15, from Washington, Senator Warren wrote Van Devanter, in a letter found by Holsinger in Senator Warren's papers, anticipating the political ramifications of the nationally reported case:

> I have worried much over the situation and am quaking now with apprehension, not knowing how this matter is to end or what will be its result. The worst feature is the cattle contention creeping into politics, with primaries, conventions, etc., adopting platforms for or against.... It will be harder to eradicate the evil and to secure peace and good government [now]....[39]

It would be a difficult defense for Van Devanter, in the face of contemporaneous deathbed statements written by the victim in the course of the killing. The presence of several eye witnesses, including one Will Walker, one of the abducted witnesses to the killing of Champion and Ray,[40] and the written confession of one of the perpetrators—Dunning—sworn in front of two county clerks,[41] incriminating other defendants, wouldn't help. Within days of the altercation, on April 20, attorney Van Devanter began to fight the public relations war, seeking to revise the facts of the case in a letter to Francis Warren. Van Devanter wrote:

> You have doubtless read the sensational reports in various newspapers and even in those at Cheyenne, concerning the war in Johnson County. So far as I have observed fully ninety percent of the telegrams appearing in the press are either entirely false or so much so as to give a grossly inaccurate impression of the expedition which went North and the results which attended it.... There is no question but that the expedition was either poorly managed or committed many grievous errors; none, however, so grievous as the error of going at all. However, it is true in this case as in others that public opinion largely goes with the successful party and had the expedition been successful in the purpose which is attributed to it by the press, it is probable that the present opinion would be somewhat modified.[42]

Attorney Van Devanter would ultimately be credited with saving the cattlemen's lives on a "procedural technicality."[43] As the Johnson County prosecuting attorney began to gather evidence for the prosecution case, the details of the WSGA's plan emerged. Canton's gripsack was found and disgorged. The invaders' plans reportedly included eventually murdering people as far away as Casper and Douglas. *The Times* reported on April 23, "The evidence is said to implicate more than twenty prominent stockmen of Cheyenne whose names have not been mentioned heretofore, also several wealthy stockmen of Omaha, as well as to compromise men high in authority in the State of Wyoming. They will all be charged with aiding and abetting the invasion, and warrants will be issued for the arrest of all of them."

The U.S. Cavalry moved the defendant cattlemen, along with their Texas mercenaries, to the Laramie County jail in Cheyenne, on the basis, perhaps pretext, that it was necessary to protect them from local reprisal. But, as the Laramie county jail was unable to hold that many prisoners, the better-moneyed WSGA stockmen were taken to be held at the barracks of Fort D.A. Russell in Cheyenne. Notwithstanding pending charges of murder, they there received preferential treatment and were allowed freedom from the base by day, provided they agreed to return to the fort at night. Johnson County officials complained that the group should have been kept at more local Fort McKinney. The general in charge of the 6th Cavalry believed, however, that tensions were too high for the prisoners to remain in the area, hundreds of armed locals sympathetic to both sides of the conflict apparently having gone to Fort McKinney over the next few days under the mistaken impression the invaders were being held there.

When pressure developed to return the defendants to Johnson County, attorney Van Devanter opposed it and sought a change of venue. On June 27, he advised Senator Joseph Carey of his intentions:

> [S]o long as I have anything to do with the defense I do not propose to see their necks put into the noose by having them tried in some county where there will be a certain conviction, unless the jury is bought, and neither do I expect to have anything to do with, nor will I permit, the buying of a jury. It is all nonsense to say that these men can be tried in any county. The most favorable one will undoubtedly prove a dangerous place.[44]

Van Devanter's motion was successful and the murder trial was reset for August 7, 1892, at Cheyenne. Meanwhile, the defendants enjoyed the comfort and benefits of their preferential confinement. Holsinger reports "throughout the summer the prisoners had enjoyed all the comforts of home in the Laramie County jail; in fact, several of the men had been allowed to go home when they chose and others had even taken a business trip to Denver. Many persons began to say openly that considering their influence, the cattlemen would never be tried."[45]

At someone's suggestion, perhaps Attorney Van Devanter's, the Laramie County sheriff asked the presiding judge in Cheyenne County that Laramie County be relieved of the responsibility of jailing the prisoners at county expense, or that Johnson County be required to pay the Laramie County jailer's costs. The costs of housing the men at Fort D.A. Russell were said to exceed $18,000; the Laramie County jailer's bill is unknown. Sparsely populated Johnson County would be unable to pay. Wallace Johnson lists one of Van Devanter's "successes as a frontier lawyer" as "running Johnson County financially 'ragged' to the benefit of the large cattle interests who brought the 'heavies' up from Texas to hassle the small ranchers."[46] The only remaining alternative was that the prisoners be released on bail. The hired Texas gunmen fled to Texas and were not seen again. Trial was rescheduled for January 1893.

In the midst of growing negative public opinion regarding Republican-led vigilante justice in Wyoming, Senator Warren was seeking re-election to his U.S. Senate seat. Things looked bleak for Republican candidates in the upcoming congressional elections. Nationally, support was ebbing for the re-election of President Harrison. He had cooperated with congressional Republicans on legislation, but his unanimous re-nomination for a second term as President was not certain. Until Blaine's announcement in February 1892 that he would again remove his name from the competition for the Presidential nomination, party regulars complained significantly about Harrison. At the Republican convention in Minneapolis that year, Harrison ultimately prevailed on the first ballot, but only over the resistance of significant opposition.

Wyoming Republicans elected Van Devanter as state party chairman at their convention in Laramie on September 14, and the other party leaders were initially untroubled by the move. They nominated a "strong" ticket of Edward Ivinson, a pioneer Laramie banker, for governor and Clarence D. Clark, the incumbent, for Congress. In an effort to keep Wyoming "in the Republican column where it belongs," Van Devanter and the state central committee set to work to push their candidates.[47]

Although many of the leaders of the WSGA's compensated gunmen, such as W.C. Irvine, were Democrats, the ranchers who had hired the group were tied to the Republican Party and their opponents were mostly Democrats. Many viewed the rescue of the WSGA group at the order of Republican President Harrison and the failure of the courts to prosecute them a serious political scandal with overtones of class war. Faith in the leadership of the Republican Party was further undermined by the fact that the treasury surplus had evaporated under the Harrison Administration, as the nation's economic health was worsening with the approach of the conditions that would lead to the Panic of 1893.

The Populist Party (sometimes the "Peoples' Party," essentially a coalition of "Grangers" and "Greenbacks"), which had gained momentum by early 1892, also capitalized on the situation. At its first national convention in 1892 in Omaha, Nebraska, the party passed a resolution, reported by Edward Stanwood in his *History of the Presidency*, condemning "the recent invasion of the Territory of Wyoming by the hired assassins of plutocracy, assisted by federal officials."[48] By the time of the Wyoming Populist Party's nominating convention in September, the Populists had gained enough strength to be on bargaining terms with the Democrats. After some political maneuvering, the two parties worked out a "fusion" ticket, similar to those being formed in Colorado, Idaho, Kansas, and North Dakota. The Wyoming Populists agreed to support the Democratic state candidates, John Osborne, the mayor of Rawlins, who had been nominated for governor, and Henry A. Coffeen, a Sheridan banker nominated for United States Congressman, in return for Democratic support of the Populist presidential electors in the state who were pledged to General James B. Weaver.

Although the Republican administration had been aware of the impending effect of the "war" and the defense of cattle interests identified with the Republican Party, nothing had been done to ameliorate the effect. Republicans protested, denying any knowledge of, or connection with, the cattlemen's action, but Democratic charges of complicity were hard to refute, especially since most of the cattlemen were leaders in the Republican party, as was their lawyer Willis Van Devanter.

Despite Van Devanter's argument on behalf of the Republicans, that "the result of the present election not only affects our State government, but also that of the National government," it soon became apparent that the combined Democratic-Populist Party, with its attacks on alleged Republican corruption and inefficiency, was cutting sharply into Republican ranks. The Democratic candidate for governor, John Osborne, traveled the state, picking up support wherever he went. In contrast to Ivinson, a lackluster campaigner, Osborne was an active and dynamic speaker and his work, and the increasing unrest over the ineffectual prosecution of the cattlemen invaders who still had not been brought to trial, began to show.

On April 9, 1892, Van Devanter wrote to Senator Warren suggesting, "It is time to quietly consider the selection of a chairman of Wyoming's State Republican Central Committee." Quiet consideration obviously succeeded, as Willis was selected for the position, where he would lead the state Republican Committee for the next four years, managing three campaigns. Bickel and Schmidt characterize Van Devanter as "informal counsel and one-man drafting service to the state legislature, at least so long as it was under Republican control." Friedman and Israel characterize his service as Republican State Committee chairman as evidence of his aspiration for national office.[49] According to Holsinger, "The two men communicated endlessly by code on matters concerning the state, and Warren began to rely increasingly on the younger man's help."

The Democrats re-nominated former President Cleveland in 1892, making the upcoming election a rematch of the one four years earlier. The issue of the tariff had worked to the Republicans' advantage in 1888, but the revisions of the past four years had made imported goods so expensive that now many voters shifted to the reform position. Many westerners, traditionally Republican voters, defected to General Weaver, who promised free silver, generous veterans' pensions, and an eight-hour workday.

During the political season leading to elections, tensions in Johnson County Wyoming remained high. The 6th Cavalry was said to be ineffectual under the local political and social pressures and were unable to keep the peace. The 9th Cavalry, the "Buffalo Soldiers," was ordered to Fort McKinney to replace the 6th. In a fortnight they moved from Nebraska to the rail town of Suggs, Wyoming, where they created "Camp Bettens" to quell pressure from the local population. One Buffalo Soldier was killed and two wounded in gun battles with locals. The 9th Cavalry remained in Wyoming through the election in November.

The 1892 Republican national convention was held in Omaha, Nebraska. By then, the Populist Party was at its zenith, supporting James B Weaver for President. Whether it was populism or fatigue, the voter turnout for the 1892 election was the lowest since 1872. In November, Pennsylvania Democrat and prior incumbent Grover Cleveland won the election and returned to the White House after four years' absence. Weaver's 22 electoral votes were not enough to affect the outcome of the election. The Presidency returned to the Democratic Party's hands. The election of 1892 thus ended the political career of President Benjamin Harrison, notwithstanding that he carried the day in Wyoming, now voting in its first presidential election. Harrison returned to Indianapolis to practice law. Cleveland would serve from March 4, 1893, until March 3, 1897, and his term would not be rosy, as panic and depression in 1893–94, again the consequence of over-construction of railroads based on shaky financing, brought widespread unemployment and the worst labor conflicts in the country's history.

Warren's re-election to the U.S. Senate depended upon the outcome of state legislative elections. The Wyoming Senate would vote in January after the outcome of legislative elections was known. Both Warren and Van Devanter could feel the effect that the Republican cattlemen's autocratic misbehavior would have on electoral outcomes. They knew it in the fall before the elections. In order to counteract movement in the Democratic direction, state Republican chairman Van Devanter offered to send "subscriptions" of $100 to newspapers in Buffalo, Saratoga, Lander, Casper, and elsewhere, if the local papers would guarantee consistently strong Republican editorials supporting Warren. Holsinger cites Van Devanter correspondence to Gertrude Huntington (*The* [Saratoga] *Lyre*), October 7, 1892; to John H. Lott (*The Buffalo Bulletin*), October 7, 1892; to W.A. Deniecke (*The Natrona Tribune*), October 8, 1892; to Matt Borland (*The* [Lander] *Wyoming State Journal*), October 8, 1892.[50] Van Devanter justified the "subscriptions" device as a means to provide funding to allow the newspapers' to send free copies of their newspapers to non-subscribers. The funds came directly from Republican campaign funds. Van Devanter distinguished his unsolicited gifts to the newspapers in return for their favorable editorial comment, arguing they were not bribery, on the basis of the donative aspect of the "subscriptions."

Friedman and Israel politely say that Van Devanter "excelled as chairman of the Republican state campaign" even though Warren was unsuccessful, and that Van Devanter's "methods were sometimes unorthodox.[51] Since the fifteen to twenty thousand voters were spread out across the large state, he paid subsidies to newspapers and concentrated on using the written word to reach voters, though he also traveled about the state by horseback and buckboard in his party's interests."

Notwithstanding Van Devanter's "subscription" strategy, when the local elections came, they went against the Republicans. In Hanna, Wyoming, voters chose Democrats as their representatives to the Wyoming legislature. Van Devanter sued, on behalf of the Republican party, seeking invalidation of the election on a technicality. Failing, the Democratic legislators were seated.

In January following the election, Francis E. Warren sought re-election to the U.S. Senate in the Wyoming Senate. In the first ballot, Warren won 8 of 25 votes. On February 11, with no one, including Warren, receiving the requisite number of votes, Van Devanter's name was placed in nomination. When the vote was taken, even he, Warren's surrogate, fell three votes short, gathering 22 of the necessary 25 votes. On February 19, after thirty-one ballots, the state Senate gave up. Governor Osborne appointed A.C. Beckwith of Evanston, but the U.S. Senate refused to seat him. Wyoming thus had only one U.S. Senator, Carey, in the 1893–1894 period.[52] Notwithstanding his failure to retain his Senate seat, Congress awarded Warren a Medal of Honor for brave action in the Civil War thirty years before.[53]

Emotions continued high for many years after 1892, as some regarded the large and wealthy ranchers as heroes who took justice into their own hands in order to defend their rights, while others saw the WSGA as heavy-handed vigilantes running roughshod over the law. The Democratic Party became popular in Wyoming for a time as a result of the scandal. A Democratic governor was elected in 1895 and Democrats took control of both houses of the state legislature after the 1892 and 1894 elections. Wyoming voted for the Democrat William Jennings Bryan in the 1896 presidential election.

13

Banditti of the Plains (1893–1896)

Successful in the interim defense of the cattlemen, but not in the 1892 elections, Van Devanter continued his political and legal activities. In 1894, Van Devanter represented the Union Pacific in a noted incident where out-of-work men grabbed a train heading to Washington, D.C., so as to seek federal assistance to address their losses in the Panic of 1893. Ultimately, federal marshals arrested the train grabbers.

On February 20, 1894, Mercer published his eyewitness account of the Johnson County War, which he entitled *The Banditti of the Plains, or the Cattlemen's Invasion of Wyoming in 1892 (The Crowning Infamy of the Ages)*. The "banditti" are, of course, Robin Hood–like characters who use excessive strategies at the expense of the more privileged class (in this case the profligate cattle barons), to the advantage of the peasant (settler) class. As Mercer had witnessed the aggressive exercise of power by corporate cattle interests and their clearly overreaching treatment of individual ranchers, his writing had become more scathingly descriptive of the events unfolding on Wyoming's open range. Mercer's book clearly reflected his, by now, pro-settler view. When the first edition was printed, the WSGA, perhaps represented by Van Devanter and Lacey, sued to enjoin its distribution. The court ordered the first edition destroyed.

While the books were in the court's custody, a number were stolen and smuggled to Denver. A letter from one Philip A. Rollins to the Princeton University Library, dated October 12, 1923, published in the forward to Mercer's *Banditti,* set forth the harrowing backstory:

> There being ways of procuring desirable things, several hundred of the books found themselves one night in a wagon drawn by galloping horses and headed for the Colorado line. The copy handed you herewith was one of those which began the night ride on the wagon. The marks on the back of the last flyleaf represent in part, I am told, the doings of the fire hose that was called into play for a few moments. You will recognize some of the other marks as indicating the course of bullets. I saw these bullets started on their way.... I am also taking the liberty of suggesting that the book be somewhat safeguarded in your Library. Otherwise you very likely will discover some day that it has either disappeared or else been mutilated.[1]

For many years, the WSG Association, their sympathizers, and descendants destroyed every copy that surfaced. The second edition simply disappeared somewhere between Denver and Cheyenne. Mercer's business was ruined, his writing seized in the mail as "obscene material," his printing press burned, ostensibly by arson. He was harassed, arrested and jailed. The plates of his book were destroyed. Mercer ultimately became a successful rancher in Hyattville, Wyoming, where he led a quiet life and died in 1917.

The date of murder trial of the stockmen charged in the Johnson County crimes, still Van Devanter's criminal clients, had been reset again, from August 7, 1892, so as to occur after the election. The case now came on for trial. By this time, however, only twenty-three cattlemen could be found to be tried, the hired Texans having fled the state to escape prosecution. Before lengthy *voir dire* of prospective jurors was complete, an insufficient jury pool was declared. Holsinger reports that Van Devanter held twelve juror challenges per defendant, a total of 276 challenges, whereas the prosecution held only six per defendant, a total of 138 challenges. "On the first day, forty-one men were excused or challenged; the second day, fifty were excused; and, on January 8, 129 more. By January 20, a total of 969 prospective jurors had been dismissed by the court or challenged by either Van Devanter or the prosecution attorney. Questioned about the availability of more men, the Laramie County sheriff admitted that there were not more than 2,100 eligible jurors in the whole county and that to secure many others would mean going miles outside the city."[2]

When the Laramie County prosecuting attorney proposed dismissal of all criminal charges on procedural grounds, Van Devanter opposed the move on the basis that his clients would still be exposed to criminal prosecution in Johnson County. Van Devanter proposed, alternatively, that a special jury be appointed and sworn, that the criminal charges against all defendants, including those Texans who had absented themselves from the court's jurisdiction, be presented and argued, then dismissed with jury approbation, thereby protecting them against subsequent trial in Johnson County under the double jeopardy aspect of the 5th Amendment of the U.S. Constitution. According to Holsinger, Van Devanter later justified the criminal behavior of the defendants whose innocence he had secured on the basis of vigilante justice: that the self-appointed law enforcement was composed of "leading citizens in Wyoming or from fine families," and that the threat of their subsequent attack, without punishment, had the positive effect of dissuading cattle rustling, that viewpoint having been expressed in Van Devanter's April 20, 1892, letter to Francis E. Warren, his June 27, 1892, letter to Joseph M. Carey, and an April 26, 1936, interview with Willis Van Devanter in *The Denver Post*.[3]

14

Willis' Wyoming Politics Go National (1892–1896)

Still chairman of the Wyoming Republicans, Van Devanter nominated Franklin Wheeler Mondell, ex-mayor of Newcastle, Wyoming, for Congressman at the 1894 Republican state convention.[1] Born in St. Louis, Missouri, on November 6, 1860, Mondell was raised in Dickinson County, Iowa. He settled in Wyoming in 1887 and engaged in the development of coal mines and oil property in the vicinity of Newcastle and Cambria and took an active part in the establishment and building of the town of Newcastle, Wyoming. He was elected mayor of Newcastle in 1888 and served until 1895. Mondell had been a member of Wyoming's first state senate in 1890 and served as president of the second senate in 1892. Van Devanter's association with Mondell would serve him well, as Mondell ultimately became majority leader in the U.S. House of Representatives when Van Devanter needed him in U.S. Supreme Court politics.

The admission of four new western states under President Harrison had added several new members of Congress. Congressional pressure in support of silver would likewise grow, simultaneous with the growth of farmers' debts due to overproduction-caused deflation. Their first preference was authorization of free and unlimited coinage in silver, or "Free Silver." In its stead, farmers now urged passage of the Sherman Silver Purchase Act so as to stimulate the economy and cause inflation, permitting payment of existing debts in cheaper dollars. Western mining companies, on the other hand, sought to artificially increase demand for silver through governmental purchasing. Their previous extraction of great quantities of silver had unfortunately caused oversupply and diminishing silver prices. On July 14, 1890, Congress responded with passage of the Sherman Silver Purchase Act requiring the treasury to purchase 4.5 million ounces of silver per month to be converted into coins and silver certificates (paper money backed by and redeemable as silver).

As the 1894 off-year election approached, a rift began to emerge in the Wyoming Republican party regarding the silver standard and the free coinage of silver. Van Devanter took on incumbent Wyoming Senator Joseph Carey. At the 1894 national convention, Republicans had gone on record, as they had in all past elections, in favor of the free coinage of silver. Joseph Carey had been voting differently on the issue in the U.S. Senate. Van Devanter used his wiles to resist Carey's campaigning for Republican candidates within the state of Wyoming, and supported Francis E. Warren and Clarence D. Clark for the U.S. Senate. When it came to voting in the state legislature to elect Wyoming's senators, "Van Devanter arranged free transportation [to Cheyenne] on behalf of Senator Warren for legislators on both the Burlington and the Union Pacific [railroads]." Warren and Clark won.[2] Warren, back in his senate seat, would serve until 1929. Wyoming historian T.A. Larson later observed: "Willis Van Devanter, Cheyenne attorney, was credited with helping to engineer the Warren/Clark elections. He ... and many others who took Warren's side in 1895 were subsequently rewarded with appropriate political appointments."[3]

But Wyoming Senator Joseph Carey was fighting back with ammunition from Congress. On August 18, 1894, he successfully obtained legislation permitting states to designate planned areas where irrigated farming could be pursued, subject to the limitation on the volume of landholding as earlier contemplated by the homestead acts. His accomplishment was the "Carey Act"[4] that would be watered from the Laramie River as facilitated later by Justice Van Devanter's opinion in *Wyoming v. Colorado*. It would provide substantial federal subsidy to the development of irrigated agriculture in the West, particularly in Wyoming.

Van Devanter's affiliations with railroad managers, cattlemen and the Republican Party began to give rise to a treatise of loyalty to political associates, a loyalty that Van Devanter would later find to be a valuable component of the get-along politics of the Supreme Court under the leadership of Chief Justice Taft. Van Devanter wrote in his September 4, 1894, letter to M.C. Barrow, "I always endeavor to be true to my friends, and for the same reason I endeavor to be true to my party."[5] True to his friends, but not true to the law.

15

Cleveland's Second Chance, Senator Warren and the McKinley Administration (1895–1897)

President Cleveland had grown more conservative during the Harrison years. During his second term, he took an anti-imperialist position with regard to events in Hawaii.[1] Cleveland's investigators had uncovered that an American-led insurgency had overthrown Hawaiian Queen Liliuokalani—too much imperialism even for a conservative Democratic president.

On the domestic front, the Cleveland administration was struggling with Mexico to determine boundary issues, particularly as they related to the water supply available from the Rio Grande River. Cleveland's advocate was Judson Harmon, United States Attorney General from 1895 until 1897. Matias Romero, Mexico's Foreign Minister, had written Richard Olney, U.S. Secretary of State, arguing that the 1848 Treaty of Guadalupe Hidalgo, which had created the border between the two countries and guaranteed navigation, required the United States to leave water in the Rio Grande for downstream use by Mexico. Diversions in upstream Colorado and New Mexico in the United States had all but depleted the river when it arrived at the Mexico border near El Paso, Texas, and Ciudad Juarez, Mexico. The Mexican claims to the use of water from the Rio Grande predated the claims of U.S. water users by hundreds of years.

In 1895, Olney asked U.S. Attorney General Judson Harmon to provide his opinion whether the navigation provisions of the 1848 Treaty of Guadalupe Hidalgo were still in force, and whether, in the absence of treaty, the principles of international law permitted Mexico to assert that obstructions and diversions of water on the Rio Grande in the United States entitled Mexico to enjoin their occurrence and receive monetary damages for their prior occurrence. In the "*Harmon Opinion,*" Harmon first noted that Congress had earlier passed a resolution authorizing the U.S. government to negotiate with Mexico "with a view to the remedy of certain difficulties" arising from the "taking of water for irrigation from the Rio Grande."[2] The Secretary of State, acting on behalf of the President, was now in the process of attempting to negotiate a solution. Harmon then answered Olney's first question in the affirmative, concluding that Article VII of the 1848 Treaty "is still in force."

However, Judson also opined that the navigation provisions of the 1848 Treaty (Article VII) applied only to those portions of the river that served as the border between Texas and Mexico. The upstream portions of the river within the United States were not navigable, and reliance on Article VII of the 1848 Treaty was thus moot.

Regarding Olney's second question, Harmon observed: "So it is evident that what is really contended for [by Mexico] is a servitude which makes the lower country [Mexico] dominant and subjects the upper country [the United States] to the burden of arresting its development and denying its inhabitants the use of a provision which nature has supplied entirely within its own territory." It is upon this language that advocates of unlimited U.S. use of water of the Rio Grande relied for their negotiating position—hence the "Harmon Doctrine" ostensibly holding, as Professor Tyler phrased it, that "the United States had 'the right to utilize the total flow of the Rio Grande.'" In 1906, eleven years after the Attorney General's opinion, the United States acquiesced the position to Mexico in the Rio Grande Treaty. As we shall see, the State of Colorado would argue essentially the same theory before the U.S. Supreme Court five years later in the Laramie River litigation, with essentially the same outcome, acquiescence of the position to the State of Wyoming.

President Cleveland, even though a Democrat, was an economic conservative. He would turn out to be the only Democrat to win the Presidency between James Buchanan (1856) and Woodrow Wilson (1916). However, his pro-business, pro-property and anti–Populist views were consistent with those of the Republican administrations that preceded and followed him. Cleveland did have a significant impact on the U.S. Supreme Court. While in office, he appointed four men to the Court: Lucius Lamar, Melville Fuller, Edward White, and Rufus Peckham, thus appointing two future Chief Justices. Their political views would remain true to the same pro-business, pro-property, and anti–Populist outlook that prevailed upon the Court at least until the appointment of Louis Brandeis in 1916.

* * *

In May 1896, Senator Warren headed the Wyoming Republican delegation to St. Louis and carried Van Devanter's proxy, as Van Devanter had now contracted typhoid fever after the Wyoming State Convention. A plight which would last through September, Van Devanter could not attend the National Convention.

Inconsistently, Wyoming first cast its six votes against the currency plank of the national party platform but backed McKinley and the Republican platform of "sound money" nevertheless. Wyoming's support for McKinley was unanimous, while the delegations from Utah, Nevada, and Montana split their support. Colorado and Idaho delegates walked out of the convention over the currency issue. Wyoming's delegates unanimously elected Van Devanter as Wyoming's national committeeman.

The primary issue that faced the Wyoming Republican Party in the 1896 election was the continuing effect of the Panic of 1893, a continuing national depression. It was likely that the incumbent party would suffer the political effect, even though they were associated with railroad success, rather than the railroad speculation and bank failure which had precipitated the Panic, there now being 489 miles of track in Wyoming. According to Holsinger, citing the *Rocky Mountain* (Denver, Colorado) *News*, July 8, 1897, "Governor Richards, Van Devanter (who was accused by some of being both 'political boss' and 'governor de facto'), and other Republicans bore the brunt of the attack. Populism, which had seemed moribund, now revived, and the Democrats, ripe for breaking with their national leader, President Grover Cleveland, gained in strength in Wyoming and the surrounding states. Republicans found themselves in trouble; by the summer of 1896 the outlook was dark for the Wyoming G.O.P."[3]

In the fall elections, Republican candidates fared miserably throughout the West. The national party platform's opposition to free silver had dashed its popularity. "The vote in Wyoming was 10,376 for Bryan, 10,072 for McKinley. In the mountain states as a whole, the Democrats carried 81 percent of the total vote. Wyoming's pro–William Jennings Bryan neighbors all went Democratic. In Montana, Idaho, and Nevada, 80% of the electorate voted Democratic. In Utah, 83% did so. In Colorado, 86%. But in Wyoming, the Democratic majority was much thinner. Congressman Mondell lost his congressional seat to Democrat John Osborne and Republican Supreme Court Justice H.V.B. Groesbeck was defeated by Democrat Samuel Corn. But Wyoming Republicans did manage to hold the Wyoming legislative majority. Van Devanter had come off his sickbed and rallied the Wyoming Republican electorate, only to discover that Wyoming, too, had voted for Bryan."

* * *

Although they found little support in the western states, Republicans and McKinley carried the day in the national elections. McKinley's support for the gold standard had not failed him. He carried the popular vote and took 271 electoral votes, to Bryan's 176. Van Devanter and the Wyoming Republicans characterized their state election as a moral victory. Senator Carey had opposed the entire Republican ticket, but Van Devanter produced a close vote, nevertheless.

Republican William McKinley of Ohio is generally thought the last president of the Gilded Age, although the Darwinism of that Age would persist on the Supreme Court for another thirty-five years. As President, McKinley pursued a conservative, pro-business agenda and was generally responsible for the McKinley Tariff of 1890, and the Dingley Tariff of 1897, the second highest protective tariff in American history. His presidency would be dominated by foreign affairs, most notably including the Spanish-American War—Remember the *Maine*?

McKinley had served on Rutherford B. Hayes' staff. Admitted to the Ohio bar in 1867, McKinley began law practice in Canton, and was elected to Congress that fall, where he served intermittently until 1890. There, he represented the interests of manufacturers, advocating high, protective tariffs. McKinley was elected Ohio Governor in 1891 and reelected two years later.

Premised on the Republicans' narrow loss to Democratic candidates in Wyoming, and the state party's strict loyalty to McKinley at the St. Louis convention, Van Devanter and Warren now worked the new administration for political favor, in the nature of employment opportunities for Van Devanter. Elected, the President and likely cabinet members were hounded by jobseekers and political machine operatives seeking to collect on campaign promises made, as was consistent with the times.

The President first chose Joseph McKenna as his Attorney General. McKenna, sitting on the Ninth Circuit bench would have preferred to stay in California. But McKinley's offer was too persuasive: If McKenna would come to Washington as McKinley's Attorney General, McKinley would appoint him to the U.S. Supreme Court when he first had the opportunity to fill a vacancy.

Joseph McKenna, a small, bearded, birdlike man, who carried himself stiffly erect, was born of Irish immigrant parents in Philadelphia on August 10, 1843. At 11, he migrated with his parents to Benicia, California. He attended St. Joseph's College and studied law at the Benicia Collegiate Institute, graduating in 1865. Serving in the California Assembly beginning in 1879, he ran for Congress three times, being successful on the third, in 1884. On his third term, he was elected a member of the Ways and Means Committee chaired by Congressman William McKinley.

McKenna had acquired the reputation as being connected to Senator Leland Stanford, and therefore as the friend of railroads, as he generally voted favorably, while in the California Assembly and Congress, for railroad issues. With Stanford's support, McKenna was appointed to the Court of Appeals for the Ninth Circuit by President Benjamin Harrison and took his seat in 1892. After five years on the Ninth Circuit, President McKinley's proposition was just too good to refuse. McKenna became the Attorney General.

McKinley also appointed Cornelius Newton Bliss as Secretary of the Interior. He took office in March 1897. The New York firm of Bliss, Fabyan & Co. was one of the largest wholesale dry-goods houses in the country. Bliss was a consistent advocate of the protective tariff and an organizer and president of the American Protective Tariff League. An active Republican, he had been chairman of the New York Republican state committee in 1887 and 1888 and contributed much to the success of the Harrison ticket in New York in 1888. As Bliss had been treasurer of the Republican National Committee since 1892 and was now national committeeman from New York, Van Devanter's Republican activist credentials should now have appealed to Secretary of the Interior Bliss.

Early in 1896, Van Devanter had been acting as Warren's chief lieutenant to secure the Wyoming delegation for William McKinley at the nominating convention to be held later in the year.

At Van Devanter's behest, Warren now began to tout Van Devanter for the Solicitor Generalship of the United States, writing to Mark Hanna, then Republican U.S. Senator from Ohio and a wealthy financier of candidate McKinley's presidential campaign, on April 24, 1896.[4] Holsinger recalls that prior to the St. Louis Convention, "Mark Hanna, the key man in McKinley's campaign, had written local politicians throughout the country that if they would organize their areas for McKinley, they would be consulted after the election with respect to appointments," citing Herbert Croly's *Marcus Alonzo Hanna, His Life and Work.* Warren had conveyed the news of Van Devanter's appointment to the national convention to Hanna by his correspondence of May 15, 1896.[5] He further suggested Van Devanter as a good candidate for Solicitor General or even Attorney General in a new administration. Holsinger, citing Warren's letter to Hanna, characterizes Van Devanter as "altogether and almost exclusively, a technician, a professional, 'forceful, a brilliant and sound lawyer, adroit in politics and thoroughly loyal to his friends.'" Bickel and Schmidt say "His function was more to tell his friends what was feasible and how it should be done than to tell then what to do." Hanna wrote back to Van Devanter on April 29. Mark Hanna would be credited with manufacturing the man that would be elected.

Notwithstanding Wyoming's having gone for William Jennings Bryan, Van Devanter and Warren began audaciously campaigning for McKinley's appointment of Willis as the United States' top lawyer. But the Solicitor Generalship had been promised elsewhere, and Van Devanter would, at last, following an interview in Washington with Attorney General McKenna, reluctantly accept an appointment as Assistant Attorney General assigned to the Department of the Interior. Bickel and Schmidt cite Van Devanter's January 18, 1897, letter to Warren, Warren's January 21, 1897, letter to William McKinley, Van Devanter's January 24, 25, 1897, letter to Warren, Warren's March 12, 1897, letter to Van Devanter, and Van Devanter's April 5, 1897, letter to Warren illustrating the two men's seeking of the solicitorship.

Senator Warren's January 21, 1897, letter to the President-elect played the Republican card: "There is absolutely nothing which will be so kindly received and so thoroughly appreciated by the Republicans of the State of Wyoming, and by my colleague and myself, as this appointment." Additional correspondence cited by Holsinger reveals that Willis had secured additional political support for his appointment to the solicitorship. Letters of recommendation for his appointment dated January 28, 1897, went to President elect McKinley from Senator Clarence Clark and Representative Mondell. All the Senators and members of Congress from Wyoming, Colorado, Utah, and Idaho who were true to the Republican Party during the last campaign also signed a letter. "Wyoming Republican officials from Governor W.A. Richards to the state and federal judges also added their names to the requests."

The Solicitor General appointment didn't come quickly. Months passed and a rumor surfaced that Van Devanter had been engaged in corrupt activities as attorney for the Union Pacific Railroad. Warren's efforts apparently scotched the rumor and McKinley's new Attorney General, Joseph McKenna, and Secretary of the Interior, Cornelius Bliss, asked Warren to get Van Devanter on the train to Washington. Two days later, March 14, Van Devanter was offered the position of Assistant Attorney General assigned to the Department of the Interior. The Senate ratified his nomination four days later.

In fact, Van Devanter's reputation as an apologist for the railroad industry would dog him in years ahead. Holsinger says that "in later years Van Devanter was to be severely criticized for this connection with the railroad by many persons who were afraid that he would make no attempt to be impartial whenever the railroad was concerned. As early as 1897, and then afterward until his appointment to the United States Supreme Court, Van Devanter was continually forced to defend himself against these allegations, as well as from the charge that, as an agent for the company, he was guilty of corruption. Not even the most superficial evidence supported these attacks, but facts were valueless in preventing their constant repetition."[6]

Lewis Gould writes, "On the patronage front, President McKinley was willing to forgive Wyoming's apostasy. Warren's appointments were approved, and in the case of Van Devanter, the Senator [Warren] effected a major coup. His lieutenant wanted to be named solicitor general, but this place had been reserved for an Ohio friend of McKinley."[7] Warren lobbied hard.[8] The Senator had to let Van Devanter down easy regarding his hopes for the Solicitor Generalship. Friedman and Israel have Van Devanter "upon failure," next setting "his sights on being an assistant attorney general."[9] The Senator advised him that obtaining a position as assistant attorney general in the Interior Department might be possible. Holsinger characterizes the sought-after appointment as Willis Van Devanter's "first step up the ladder of preferment."

To Van Devanter, the appointment as Assistant Attorney General was apparently not an end in itself, but what Holsinger describes as a "chance to gain recognition." "He clearly was beginning to focus on the next step to the top." Citing Willis' April 9, 1897, letter to Warren, it appeared to Holsinger that Van Devanter had taken the position "only 'with the intention of earning and deserving a promotion.'"

Friedman and Israel suggest that Willis, when appointed an Assistant Attorney General, would be "entrusted with preparation and conduct of important Supreme Court cases."[10] That, of course, is the role of the Solicitor General. Rather, Van Devanter "was forced to accept a less important position with the same title in the Interior Department." Bickel and Schmidt say, citing Willis' January 31, and March 11, 1897, letters to Warren, that "He would have much preferred to be an Assistant Attorney General in the Department of Justice itself—'headquarters,' as he called it—where he thought he would have not only intrinsically more challenging work, but also greater opportunity to come to the notice of the Attorney General and of other professional dignitaries, such as Supreme Court Justices. He said so to Warren, who replied, somewhat unkindly, that it was a bit early to be thinking of the Supreme Court, and struck a nerve."

Van Devanter went home and wound up his business affairs in Wyoming to head for Washington. But he did not quit his close relationship with Wyoming politics, remaining Wyoming's Republican National Committeeman until 1900, a position from which he continued to seek appointments to national employment for other residents of Wyoming. Cheyenne, now the junction of the main line of the Union Pacific with the Denver Pacific, Fort Worth, Cheyenne and Northern, and Colorado Central railways,[11] continued to grow. Its population had reached 10,000 by 1897. Van Devanter's law partner, John Lacey, continued in practice by himself, becoming, in Holsinger's view, "for the next thirty-two years one of the top lawyers in the West."[12]

16

Assistant Attorney General Van Devanter (1897–1903)

Stephen Johnson Field had been appointed to the U.S. Supreme Court in 1863 by President Abraham Lincoln. He stepped down from the Court at 72 years of age, on December 1, 1897. Keeping his promise, McKinley appointed his Attorney General, Joseph McKenna, of California, to fill the vacancy. He took the bench on January 26, 1898.

Senator Warren had been undeterred in his support for Van Devanter while advocating Willis for Solicitor General. According to Holsinger, "To Francis Warren, any position was possible to obtain if one worked hard enough: A Supreme Court justiceship was no exception." Perhaps in the impendence of the vacancy of Justice Field's seat on the Court and "During the period when he was engaged in securing Van Devanter's appointment, [in the McKinley administration] he wrote the future Justice [Van Devanter] without the slightest touch of humor to warn him that if he accepted the Assistant Attorney Generalship, he 'would not stand a ghost of a show for the Supreme Court Bench for a long while.'" Van Devanter responded in his March 11, 1898, letter to Senator Warren: "I haven't had the slightest idea that I would get on the Supreme Bench if I were even favored with twenty lives." But then, blaming his own "delirium," he admits that he had considered it. "The thing never crossed my mind for a moment excepting when I was deranged with my late illness. You probably wondered how I came to think of it in my delirium if I had never thought of it before, but such is the fact." Thereafter, he admits his ambition: "I realize that I have a good strong ambition ... and in fact I am proud of it ... but my ambition never reached the dizzy heights which might be expected by your letter.... [P]lease don't believe me foolish enough to be attempting to build that kind of ladder."[1]

Ladder it would be. A ladder with a view to the top rung. But now Willis must be content with a lower rung. Van Devanter's assignment within the attorney general's cadre was situated in the Interior Department—actually a well-placed appointment, as it pertained to the great western lands important to his prior railroad clients. Friedman and Israel have Willis simply specializing in "legal matters involving public lands and Indian affairs."[2] Holsinger describes Van Devanter's responsibility in the post as "ruling on all cases involving federal land. Cases growing out of General Land Office rulings, Homestead Act decisions, and disputes over Indian lands found their way to his desk for ultimate adjudication."

Before Van Devanter had been in his new job a year, McKinley had replaced Cornelius Bliss with Ethan Allen Hitchcock,[3] whom McKinley appointed Secretary of the Interior on December 21, 1898. Earlier appointed by McKinley as envoy extraordinary and minister to Russia with the objective of improving American commerce, McKinley raised his status to Ambassador, as the U.S. opened an embassy in Moscow in 1897. Hitchcock was abroad at the time of his appointment as Interior Secretary and did not arrive back to Washington until the following February, two months after the Senate confirmed him. Hitchcock had been president of several railway, mining, and manufacturing concerns, and was certainly sympathetic to the Republican priority of aiding the development of American corporations, a posture with which Willis could certainly agree.

Bickel and Schmidt have Willis heading a busy office. "[T]here is no question but that Van Devanter did a superior job." The Supreme Court historians quote Van Devanter's later, March 10, 1899, letter to one F. Bond:

> Every day more decisions pass over my desk than are decided by the Supreme Court of Wyoming in months. Some of them involve rights to land in the Everglades of Florida, in Alaska, and almost everywhere, including the lake front in Chicago; while others involve matters arising in the U.S. Patent Office and other bureaus of the Interior Department. Some involve the question whether the offspring of a white man and an Indian woman are white or Indian; and quite recently a question arose as to whether a statute affecting marriages between whites and Indians included marriages also between Negroes and Indians; and so it goes. One case involves a desert claim in Arizona, a homestead in Oklahoma, a timber purchase in Minnesota or cash entry in Louisiana. While another involves some mine in Colorado, Utah, California, or Alaska, or many thousands of acres of land under some railroad grant. There is no end to the variety of matters which come and go in quick succession.[4]

Bickel and Schmidt suggest that Van Devanter was fearful "that he would work unknown and without possibility of advancement." However, they posit that he had "sufficient contact with the regular staff in the Department of Justice," and that "he appeared in the Supreme Court."

The *Decisions of the Department of the Interior Related to Public Lands*[5] was first published by the Department in June 1883. Van Devanter's work appears first on March 30, 1897,[6] where he writes on behalf of Secretary Bliss regarding the appeal of one John R. Corry of a decision of the Commissioner of the General Land Office. That and succeeding appeals and correspondence published there deal with homestead entries, desert land entries, Indian lands, status of individual Indians and claims, railroad and wagon road grants, mining claims, timber land, school lands, placer mining. It includes correspondence with other officials within the Department of the Interior, as well as Comptroller of the Treasury, Commissioner of Indian Affairs. One early interesting decision written by Van Devanter established the state boundary between the State of Texas and the "Indian Territory," later the State of Oklahoma. The border's location was uncertain because of the change in the course of the Red River, that being the prior-established boundary. Van Devanter ruled that the boundary didn't move, even though the river did.[7] In another instance, he composed Secretarial correspondence beneficial to Basin City, Wyoming, interests proposing to establish a townsite and sell lots to the public.[8] And he authored a Secretarial opinion facilitating the transfer of desert lands suitable for irrigated agriculture to Wyoming state administrators pursuant to the Carey Act.[9]

But by far, the greatest number of cases Van Devanter reviewed involved conflicts between the railroads and individual homesteaders over particular parcels of land—who had the better right. The railroads often won.

In the fall of 1898, Willis joined the faculty of the Columbian (now George Washington) University Law School, his "colleagues" including Supreme Court Justices Harlan and Brewer. Bickel and Schmidt report that he "soon developed relations of friendship and mutual respect with the two justices," citing Willis' own September 26, 1898, letters to one E.A. Slack, and to one B.L. Whitman. There is no evidence that either Harlan or Brewer corroborated the claim.

From his position as Assistant Attorney General representing the Department of the Interior, Van Devanter would have had a ring-side seat for numerous issues of expansion of American power and influence. "Manifest Destiny" had been the rationale for the American republic's expansion in its early years. The principle, if not the slogan, had justified dislodging the ownership and dominion of then-great nations, Great Britain, France and Russia, from the North American continent. Mexico's sovereignty had also been divested under the banner in the 1846–1848 Mexican War.

Early in 1898, on February 15, the Battleship *Maine* was blown up in Havana Harbor. On March 9, McKinley sent Spain an ultimatum demanding peace in Cuba. A month later, Spain agreed to U.S. demands. But Republicans wanted war to show international prowess and McKinley acquiesced, delivering a message of war to Congress on April 11. On April 25, Congress declared war, on the premise that diplomatic relations between the two nations had broken down on April 21. Congress demanded that Spain cede Puerto Rico, Guam and the Philippines to the U.S. and abandon her sovereignty in Cuba.

After declaration of the Spanish-American War, then U.S. Secretary of State William Rufus Day, with whom Van Devanter would later serve and befriend as Associate Justice on the U.S. Supreme Court, argued that the Spanish colonies, other than Cuba, should be left with Spain. President McKinley, however, believed that the United States should take over control of the Philippines, Puerto Rico, and Guam from Spain, perhaps consequent of his having learned on May 7 of U.S. Asiatic Fleet Commander George Dewey's success at the battle at Cavite on Manila Bay, Philippines, on May 1, 1897, beginning the Philippine-American War. Dewey had been armed pursuant to orders from the Under Secretary of the Navy Theodore Roosevelt. Following orders, Day negotiated peace with Spain on McKinley's harsher terms, leading the United States Peace Commission into Paris and signing the Treaty of Paris (December 10, 1898) which ended the War. U.S. gained possession of the former Spanish colonies of Puerto Rico, Guam and the Philippines, as well as temporary control of Cuba, just as Congress had dictated it wanted.

The Spanish acquisitions were not McKinley's only conquest as he supported an expansionist policy, dubbed "open door," in China. Domestically, Congress under McKinley's support passed the Gold Standard Act in 1900, establishing a single means of redemption for U.S. paper currency. McKinley was re-elected in 1900, now with Theodore Roosevelt as his Vice President, defeating William Jennings Bryan a second time. Unlike the previous election, the McKinley ticket carried in Wyoming

The Spanish-American War, the annexation of Hawaii, and the election of 1900 posed Manifest Destiny and expansionism in a new context—that beyond the continent's natural shores. Expansion of national power and influence, enablement of global commerce and wealth accumulation required new justification and open political support. Unfortunately, the United States' founding documents' romantic notions of derivation of power from popular support and consent of the governed were *inappropos* of the objective. The Constitution said nothing other than to assign the agenda to the President. Colonialism just wasn't yet in the American vocabulary. Now it needed to be, as colonization, rather than direct annexation, of new territory after the Spanish American war was necessary to get control, as for example in the case of Cuba and Hawaii, of their sugar production. These new territories must be annexed without implication of the Constitution's prohibition of tariffs imposed on goods travelling interstate.

Reinaugurated, McKinley was shot at the Pan American Exposition in Buffalo, New York, on September 6, 1901, by Leon Czolgosz, and died eight days later. They remembered him with memorial services in Cheyenne. Roosevelt immediately succeeded him, at 42 the youngest person to have become President, frustrating the "Republican machine" that had tried to bury Roosevelt by naming him candidate for vice-president in the 1900 convention, due to their fear of his progressive ideas.[10] President Roosevelt, although a traditional New York Republican, had a different view of the world than had McKinley, and the Progressive Movement in America was beginning to feel its muscle. We can only wonder whether Willis' views actually meshed with those of young New Yorker Theodore Roosevelt. Later, looking back, the question will be whether Willis' performance within a progressive Department of Interior was merely convenient, notwithstanding his otherwise conservative moralist philosophy.[11]

Willis' view of matters international probably did corroborate Roosevelt's. Theodore Roosevelt would be aggressive in his foreign policy, as well as in his domestic economic battles. Distinguishing between imperialism and expansionism, Roosevelt would contend that the United States would never be imperialistic. To the contrary, mere "expansion" was the same as growth. Growth was "progress." America personified growth as a noble pursuit. Perhaps not so self justifying as the language of exceptionalism, the nobility of the pursuit was its own rationale. Expansion was larger, more noble, than imperialism.

Roosevelt wished to see the United States as the dominant power on the shores of the Pacific Ocean. One aspect of Roosevelt's foreign interests was connection of the two oceans bordering the American continent. In his exhaustive reportage of the construction of the Panama Canal, *The Path Between the Seas: The Creation of the Panama Canal 1870–1914*, David McCullough tells us a lot about the leadership and the society of the United States after the turn of the new century, of the years of the Roosevelt and later Taft presidencies. Comparing Roosevelt with Ferdinand de Lesseps, the French personality extraordinaire responsible for promotion of the Panama Canal after his success on the Suez, McCullough observes that Roosevelt and de Lesseps were both products of cultivated worldly families. Both were raised on the ideal of patriotic service and their heroic exploits of adventurous kinsmen. They had a common love of the out of doors, of shooting, and of horses; the common joy in children, books, theatrics, popular acclaim. "In his boundless love of life, his immensely attractive animal vitality, Theodore Roosevelt might have been direct descendant of Ferdinand de Lesseps."[12]

According to McCullough, Roosevelt drew his inspiration from a gentleman named Alfred Thayer Mahan, a member of the faculty of the Naval War College at Newport, Rhode Island. Mahan's book, *The Influence of Sea Power upon History*, published by Little, Brown, in May 1890, traced the rise and fall of past maritime powers to elucidate the simple theory that national greatness and commercial supremacy were directly related to supremacy at sea. Roosevelt's determination to have a canal between the oceans can be dated to his reading of Mahan's book. With the isthmian barrier broken, the Caribbean would become not simply a prime commercial crossroads, but a vital military highway. The Canal would engender an international, expansionist capability.

Upon McKinley's death, and Roosevelt's succession to the Presidency, Hitchcock stayed on as Secretary of the Interior. Although he would not become one of President Roosevelt's closer advisors, Hitchcock is remembered for maintaining the conservationist principles for which Roosevelt is now revered. As Secretary of the Interior, Hitchcock pursued a vigorous program for the conservation of natural resources and reorganized the administration of Native American affairs, an arcane expertise Van Devanter would carry with him throughout the remainder of his career. Hitchcock resigned his post on March 4, 1907, and died in Washington on April 9, 1909.

Bickel and Schmidt mention two "booms" in Van Devanter's prospects for promotion during the time he served as Assistant Attorney General. The latter of these, in March 1902, involved his purported mention for appointment as Secretary of the Interior. However, they mention no circumstances indicating that the position was then, or would be soon, vacant. In any case, this would have been a wild aspiration when considered in the light of incumbent Hitchcock's qualifications for the same job: prior Ambassador Extraordinary and Minister Plenipotentiary to Russia and first accredited U.S. Ambassador to the Russian court.

From his seat at the Department of the Interior, Van Devanter could closely watch President Roosevelt's Supreme Court appointments. A U.S. Supreme Court vacancy stood pending, due to the anticipated retirement of Justice Horace Gray when McKinley was assassinated. McKinley had intended to fill the vacancy with one Alfred Hemenway, a leading Boston lawyer and law partner of McKinley's Secretary of the Navy. McKinley had promised Hemenway the post. But Roosevelt felt no obligation to Hemenway and appointed Oliver Wendel Holmes to the seat on August 11, 1902.

The Senate unanimously confirmed Holmes' appointment on December 4, and Holmes assumed his seat on December 8, 1902. He had previously succeeded Justice Horace Gray as Chief Justice of the Supreme Judicial Court of Massachusetts in 1889, now he would succeed him on the U.S. Supreme Court. In fact, Holmes already had a twenty-year career on the state bench of Massachusetts.

Born in Boston on March 8, 1841, Holmes was the son of the prominent writer, poet and physician Oliver Wendell Holmes, Sr. Holmes' mother, abolitionist Amelia Lee Jackson, was the daughter of Charles Jackson, Associate Justice of the Supreme Court of Massachusetts. As a young man, Oliver Jr. attended private school, loved literature and supported the abolitionist movement that thrived in Boston society during the 1850s, a society in which the intellectual aristocracy included Ralph Waldo Emerson, Theodore Parker and Wendell Phillips. Holmes attended Latin school, then entered Harvard at age sixteen, was elected to Phi Beta Kappa, and was a member of the Procellian and Hasty Pudding clubs. During his senior year, he enlisted as a private in the Army of the Potomac, and graduated from Harvard in 1861, both as "class poet" and in army uniform.

Holmes' first enlistment in the fourth battalion, Massachusetts militia, led to a commission as first lieutenant in the Twentieth Regiment of Massachusetts Volunteer Infantry. He saw much action, from the Peninsula Campaign to the Wilderness. He was wounded (shot in the chest) at the minor engagement at Ball's Bluff in October 1861; again wounded (shot in the back of the neck) at Antietam on September 17, 1862, and again (shot in the heel) at Chancellorsville (Fredericksburg) in 1863, all according to Chief Justice Rehnquist's wonderful history of the Court. Holmes carried a bullet in his body until his death.

Mustered out of the army in 1864 with the rank of lieutenant-colonel, Holmes entered Harvard Law School, leading to an LL.B. (Bachelor of Laws). He was admitted to the Massachusetts bar in 1866 and began an admiralty and commercial law practice in Boston. In 1870, he returned to Harvard to teach constitutional law, lecture, and write as editor of the *American Law Review*.

The year that Holmes edited a new edition of *Kent's Commentaries on American Law*, and published numerous articles under the title *The Common Law* (1881), he was officially appointed to the Harvard Law School faculty as full professor. Within a year, he was appointed to the Supreme Judicial Court of Massachusetts, where he would remain for 20 years, the last three of which were as Chief Justice. He was now 61 years old.

Within a year after Holmes' appointment to the Court, Associate Justice George Shiras became feeble and then resigned. Roosevelt's first choice to replace him was William H. Taft. But Taft declined, preferring to remain in his position as governor of the Philippines. Next, Roosevelt went to his intimate and loyal friend and advisor—William Rufus Day. Day had been acquainted initially with William McKinley in Ohio politics, where Day's credentials were multigenerational. The Day family had originated in New England—part of a long, strong antislavery tradition. Upon graduation from the University of Michigan, Day read law privately, then suffered a year at the U.M. law school. He was admitted to bar in Canton, Ohio, at 23, after which he maintained a varied trial practice for some twenty-five years. He would become McKinley's intimate in matters legal, personal, and political.

William Day was by now a fourth-generation judge. His father Luther was

Chief Justice of the Supreme Court of Ohio; his grandfather had been a judge of the same court. Day's great-grandfather had been chief judge of Connecticut before that. He had by now served in several capacities in President McKinley's cabinet. McKinley appointed Day to become Assistant Secretary of State under Secretary of State John Sherman, and later replaced Sherman with Day, an appointment that would last throughout the Spanish American War. In 1899, Day had retired his position as Secretary of State, in order to serve McKinley as head of the U.S. Delegation to the peace conference in Paris, which ended the war. When the conference was complete, McKinley named Day to the U.S. Court of Appeals for the Sixth Circuit. On February 19, 1903, following McKinley's death and his having served three years on the Court of Appeals, Roosevelt appointed Day to the U.S. Supreme Court. He took the bench on March 2, 1903.

Although suspicious that Van Devanter had assumed the post in the Interior Department with some disappointment and primarily to position himself for future advancement, Holsinger generally gives Van Devanter good marks for his work. "During the years before 1902, there is little doubt that Van Devanter did indeed earn the respect of his colleagues. Both in and out of court, he was an efficient bureaucrat. Promotion, though, seemed far too slow to satisfy him and for a brief moment he even considered returning to private practice somewhere in the West. When a rumor that Judge Henry C. Caldwell of the Eighth Circuit Court of Appeals might retire began to circulate, however, Van Devanter was soon back on his quest for a Supreme Court appointment, making himself an active candidate for the Circuit post."

It is difficult to presume how Van Devanter played the middle between his loyalty to his political principal and the progressive views of the administration he now served. However, he did so, he was successful, as his future would show.

Roosevelt's view of the appropriate involvement of the government in the preservation and development of the nation's resources had moved away from the heavy consumption approach of the Republican Party since Hayes and Harrison. Just as Van Devanter had conveniently converted his support from silver to gold, securing the support of East Coast McKinley Republicans in 1896, he must now speak the Roosevelt line, such that in retrospect Henry J. Abraham would say that Van Devanter had a reputation as a Progressive, a reputation that "had been a real factor in his appointment to the circuit court by T.R." though little in his history, political associations or career aspirations would verify it. One thing that certainly would not change was his loyalty to his political principal, Senator Warren.

* * *

Associate Supreme Court Justice Henry Billings Brown, who had been nominated by President Benjamin Harrison in 1890 and written the majority opinion giving recognition to the notion of "separate but equal" in *Plessy v. Ferguson* in 1896, resigned from the Court on May 28, 1906, due primarily to failure of his eyesight. Holsinger points out Willis Van Devanter's still-recurring interest in promotion to the higher court: "Opportunity for advancement presented itself in 1906 when Associate Justice Henry B. Brown retired from the Court. Warren immediately sought

Roosevelt's support for Van Devanter." Roosevelt responded that he intended to appoint Secretary of War William Howard Taft.

The President did indeed first offer the position to Secretary Taft, again. Taft declined, again, perhaps now contemplating the presidency for himself. His wife, at least, was by now reputed to have her eye on the White House. Taft actually had his eye on the Chief Justiceship, but Fuller had that seat nailed down. Roosevelt opted next for William H. Moody of Massachusetts, infamous for his prosecution of the Lizzie Borden case ("Lizzie Borden took an axe and gave her mother forty whacks"). Moody also claimed congressional service, and Roosevelt's prior appointments as Secretary of the Navy and Attorney General as worthy credentials.

Professors Bickel and Schmidt tell us that

> Van Devanter's ambition was fixed on an eventual succession to Brewer, and he advised Warren that in the meantime guarded support might be given to the candidacy for any other seat of Van Devanter's senior Eighth Circuit colleagues, including Walter H. Sanborn of Minnesota. At Van Devanter's urging, Warren gave Sanborn such guarded support in 1906, when Justice Brown first resigned. The appointment went to Moody, and that was the end of any withdrawals by Van Devanter in favor of his senior colleague. Henceforth Van Devanter was an active, even relentless, Supreme Court candidate, and he had in Senator Warren the most faithful and effective agent imaginable. But Van Devanter's colleague Sanborn was not aware that his own ambitions were past the point of possible gratification, and so from 1906 on, the two men were obvious, virtually acknowledged, rivals and relations between them were strained.

But Roosevelt's appointment, Moody, would serve only three years on the Supreme Court.

Congress had created the federal circuit courts of appeals in 1891.[13] Chief Justice Rehnquist recounted the history in his *The Supreme Court, How It Was, How It Is*. The U.S. Supreme Court was originally composed of judges representing different portions of the new nation, called "circuits." "By [1854], the Supreme Court consisted of nine members, because Congress created new circuits as states were admitted to the union, and practice dictated that there should be a Supreme Court justice assigned to each circuit."[14] In 1857, the circuits of the Supreme Court were constituted, each Supreme Court justice being responsible to ride circuit in a respective region.[15] These circuits included: 1st Cir. (Maine, New Hampshire, Massachusetts, and Rhode Island); 2nd Cir. (New York, Connecticut, and Vermont); 3^{d} Cir. (Pennsylvania and New Jersey); 4th Cir. (Delaware, Maryland, and Virginia); 5th Cir. (Alabama and Louisiana); 6th Cir. (North Carolina, South Carolina, and Georgia); 7th Cir. (Ohio, Indiana, Illinois, and Michigan); 8th Cir. (Kentucky, Tennessee, and Missouri); 9th Cir. (Mississippi and Arkansas).

But the duties of riding circuit only complicated the Supreme Court's growing calendar as the decades wore on, taking time away from hearing cases in Washington, D.C. "By 1890 it took three and one-half years between the time a case was first docketed in the Supreme Court and the time it was orally argued before the justices. Court congestion is not often a major concern of Congress, but these extreme delays caused the legal profession to rise up in righteous indignation, and in 1891 Congress responded by creating the federal circuit courts of appeals."[16]

As early as 1891, Senator Warren had unsuccessfully proposed Van Devanter's name for one of the newly created Circuit Court of Appeals judgeships. Holsinger later observed in his 1968 article regarding Van Devanter's sanctioned rise to Supreme Court appointment, that "Almost from the moment of Warren's arrival in Washington, he began to promote Van Devanter for an important federal office."

On January 27, 1903, the House of Representatives passed a bill regarding contagious cattle disease, the 57th Congress continuing in "lame duck" session. Two days later the Senate confirmed the vote. Holsinger reports, "Van Devanter was at the time obviously high on everyone's list for appointment" to the circuit court if a new position could be created. Advocated as an "ardent outdoorsman and hunter," even though his bookish history never supported that characterization, Van Devanter was thought "more than acceptable to President Theodore Roosevelt." Justice Harlan had, according to Holsinger, apparently "taken a liking to Van Devanter from their relationship at Columbian Law School" where Van Devanter "had lectured on personal property, domestic relations and conflict of laws in Harlan's law school courses" and personally recommended him to Roosevelt.

On February 2, 1903, Congress passed the Cattle Contagious Disease Act of 1903.[17] Tucked into the legislation was a "private act," so dubbed by the March 9 *New York Times*,[18] authorizing an additional seat on the Eighth Circuit Court of Appeals. Two days later, on February 4, President Theodore Roosevelt nominated Willis Van Devanter to occupy that seat. He was confirmed by the Senate two weeks later on February 18 and received his judicial commission that day. He would join Henry Clay Caldwell, of Arkansas; Walter Henry Sanborn, of Minnesota; and Amos Madden Taylor, of Missouri, then sitting on that Court. The 57th Congress, in which Republicans maintained a significant majority, adjourned two weeks later on March 9, 1903. Wyoming's two senators, Clark and Warren, were 27 and 30 in seniority, respectively, out of 90 sitting Senators. Congressman Frank Mondel, Nevada's sole congressman, hailed from the House. They had picked another plum for their favorite son.

So, Willis Van Devanter became a judge of the U.S. Circuit Court of Appeals for the Eighth Circuit. He resigned not only his professorship of the Columbian Law School but also his post as Republican National Committeeman from Wyoming, which he had held throughout his service at the Interior Department. As the Eighth Circuit included Wyoming, Van Devanter elected to return to Cheyenne to establish his seat.

By now, the Eighth Circuit consisted of Nebraska, Kansas, Missouri, Minnesota, Arkansas, Wyoming, Colorado, New Mexico, Montana, North Dakota, South Dakota, Oklahoma, Arizona territory. Litigation raised against cattle and railroad interests were common in the court's docket. The Union Pacific, Van Devanter's former client, was home-based in Omaha, and its cases would rise under the Eighth Circuit's jurisdiction.

Theodore Roosevelt had campaigned in Wyoming in 1900. Now, less than three years later, after salving Senator Warren's wound, Roosevelt returned to Laramie—on horseback. The Spanish-American War veterans and the Grand Army of the Republic had invited Roosevelt to speak in Cheyenne on Memorial Day 1903. He arrived in Laramie on the Presidential Car pulled by the Union Pacific, joined a

The home in Cheyenne that Eighth Circuit Judge Willis Van Devanter returned to in 1903 (author's photograph, 2019).

group of riders including Senator Warren, and rode the 55 miles over Pole Mountain and Telephone Valley from Laramie to Cheyenne. Once there, speeches concluded, Warren and Roosevelt retired to Warren's Terry Ranch, 13 miles south of Cheyenne for a barbecue supper, and among the hoopla likely mused over the fate of Tom Horn and celebrated their respective accomplishments.[19]

17

Van Devanter's Eighth Circuit Decisions (1903–1911)

Willis would serve seven years on the Eighth Circuit. His opinions as a circuit judge appear in Volumes 126–185 of the *Federal Reporter*. He would be reversed twice and affirmed four times by the U.S. Supreme Court. Friedman and Israel report that Van Devanter found himself dealing with jurisdictional disputes, various railroad cases, land claims, and questions of negligence. His opinions carefully reconstructed the events giving rise to the case's conflicts and described applicable precedent. They opine that his circuit court service came at the height of the progressive era, but, in understatement, that his decisions rarely reflected the social consciousness of the period.[1]

Professors Bickel and Schmidt find that Circuit Judge Van Devanter "was generally rather a hard man to get a judgment for the injured plaintiff in a negligence case, and much wedded to the doctrines of contributory negligence and assumption of risk." The bar to recovery was conveniently sympathetic to the corporate and railroad interests that Van Devanter had served in private practice.

In an early case, Van Devanter ruled in favor of a logging company employer who failed to provide safer tools for its employee, but permitted him to proceed to do dangerous work unbundling a pile of heavy logs, which thereupon rolled and injured him, because the employee had assumed the risk by doing so.[2]

In March 1904, Van Devanter, sitting with Judges Sanford and Thayer, heard a case involving injury to a railroad workman squeezed between two railcars in the rail yard of the Chicago, Minneapolis and St. Paul Railway Co. Van Devanter wrote that the lower court's determination of the company's negligence should be reversed and remanded for retrial because the lower court had not advised the jury that the workman assumed the risk when he worked in a rail yard where he was aware of the company's unsafe workplace practices.[3]

In another 1904 case, sitting with Sanford and Thayer, Circuit Judge Van Devanter found culpable negligence of an injured worker knowingly walking on a railroad crossing in close proximity to an approaching train.[4] On October 6, 1905, sitting with Sanford, he found that a railroad brakeman, who, in the absence of an emergency justifying his action, participated in the risky relocation of a rail car with full knowledge and appreciation of the danger, assumed the risk of injury, although the negligence of other railroad employees was the direct cause of his injury.[5] A week later, on October 13, 1905, sitting with Circuit Judge Hook and District Judge

Lochren, Van Devanter found a plaintiff's wrongful death claim was ameliorated by his own contributory negligence, as he had walked across railroad tracks in front of an unannounced train "without taking the precautions necessary to determine whether he could do so in safety."[6] The railroad company's liability was diminished in all three cases.

Sitting with Circuit Judge Adams and District Judge Philips, Van Devanter found that a plaintiff engineer of a passenger train could not recover damages for his injury because he had "directly contributed" to the cause of his own injury.[7] The same year, 1907, Van Devanter authored an opinion in a case, sitting together with Judges Elmer Adams and U.S. District Court John Riner, upholding the more exculpatory federal liability standard for railroads in lieu of state negligence law in a case charging violation of the Ekins Act, passed by Congress in 1903. The case involved the Great Northern Railway Co.,[8] the same company involved in the *Natural Securities* Case. Great Northern appealed the decision the next year to the U.S. Supreme Court, where it was affirmed.[9]

On September 5, 1908, sitting with Judge Sanborn, Van Devanter found that a pedestrian's contributory negligence, failing to look both ways before crossing, barred recovery based on the negligence of a tramway operator.[10] Within two weeks, on September 21, Judge Van Devanter reversed a decision favoring a worker injured through no fault of his own, but as a result of the company's failure to maintain reasonable safety procedures for operation of machinery.[11] Van Devanter would not question the morality of what he called the "settled rule that as between master and servant, the duty of using a reasonably safe place, of so operating reasonably safe machinery, and of so conforming to an established and reasonably safe method of work, that injury will not be inflicted negligently, is the duty of those to whom the work is entrusted, and is no positive duty of the master."

And, on May 24, 1909, sitting with Judge Sanborn, Van Devanter found that an injured railroad engineer could not recover, notwithstanding the negligence of other railroad employees, due to his own contributory negligence.[12]

In all cases, railroad interests were the beneficiaries of Van Devanter's judgment.

18

Reasonable Rail Rates, the Sherman Act (1890–1911)

In early 1893, as the World's Columbian Exposition opened in Chicago, the National Cordage Company, a hemp rope trust, paid out a 100 percent shareholder dividend. By mid-year the Company was insolvent and declared bankruptcy. The announcement set off frenzied selling of shares of other financially troubled companies, railroads included. Banks closed. The cash supply shrank. Nationally, unemployment in the winter of 1893–94 was almost 20 percent. Farmers lost farms when agricultural prices fell. On May 11, the following year, the Pullman Palace Car Company factory workers walked out, beginning the 1894 Pullman Strike. George Pullman had increased rents in his company town while cutting wages. The Strike went national. Boycotting railways carrying Pullman cars was the strategy. Business characterized the strike as "a coordinated effort to shut down the national railroad system." The strike was led by Eugene V. Debs at and for the American Railway Union. Railroad traffic stalled when the 260,000 workers struck.

Prior to the Pullman car, most rail coaches consisted of rickety wooden boxes, with inadequate springs, that made for a rough ride. The wooden seats or benches were "hard riding." Inadequate heating and ventilation systems barely kept the outside out. Along came Pullman, with his elaborately designed coach—fitted with his own patented folding bed. With carpeted floor, upholstered seats, black walnut paneling, mirror at the back of the car, the Pullman car meant status. No doubt Warren and Willis enjoyed the Pullman car's comforts. The train trip between Cheyenne and Washington could take 7 days, particularly if Chicago had to be negotiated. The Union Pacific's schedule carried three daily arrivals, one each for "passengers," "emigrants," and "freight." The Pullman car's comforts may also have been necessary for the two-man conversation about politics, preferments, station and power. And gentile would be the ride, as within the ornate Pullman Palace sleeping car, not even the Senator nor his judicial lordship were allowed to wear their boots to bed.

The rails were the route to success. But the railroad companies controlled the route. And predatory pricing was inevitable under the circumstances. State railroad commissions dictating reasonable rates rose to address the problem. Their authority soon became the constitutional question. In 1894, in *Reagan v. Farmers' Loan and Trust Company*,[1] Justice Brewer opined that the Supreme Court reserved the power to review whether railroad rates were reasonable, essentially whether rates fixed by a commission or by a legislature violated railroads' or railroad customers' property interests otherwise protected under the due process clause.

Four years later, on March 7, 1898, in *Smythe v. Ames*,[2] the Court, in an opinion involving the Union Pacific Railroad written by Associate Justice John Harlan, found that a railroad is a person within the meaning of the Fourteenth Amendment and that regulation that diminishes the just compensation of a corporation, no matter how small, takes property as prohibited by that Amendment. The Court thus established that due process clause jurisprudence was the means it would use to grant itself the power to review economic measures enacted by the legislative branch. The power to review reasonableness of economic measure was thus reserved to the courts. The case would be essentially overturned in 1944 when Justice William O. Douglas, writing for the Court, found in *Federal Power Commission v. Hope Natural Gas Co.*[3] that the FPC-determined rate was reasonable.

Attorney Willis Van Devanter, still in private law practice in Cheyenne, Wyoming, certainly paid attention to the Supreme Court's railroad cases. Now actively representing the Union Pacific Railroad, and perhaps often visiting its home office in Omaha, Nebraska, he was likely satisfied by the Court's active intervention in Congress' regulatory function.

* * *

In retrospect, Benjamin Harrison had done something that historians tend to overlook. He signed the Sherman Antitrust Act and the Sherman Silver Purchase Act into law, even though he had not actively supported the passage of either bill. The Populist Party had demanded that trusts should be regulated. Opposition had spread through the western states, and state laws with the objective of constraining trust and monopoly began to be passed in the mid–80s. By 1888, both Democratic and Republican parties' platforms contained anti-trust planks. Republicans controlled both houses of Congress. In 1890 Congress unanimously enacted the Sherman Antitrust Act. The Act declared illegal and made a misdemeanor "every contract, combination in the form of trust or otherwise, or conspiracy in restraint of trade or commerce among the several states or with foreign nations."

The Sherman Act would seem to be a major break with the concept of *laissez-faire*. But, as we shall see, the Supreme Court wouldn't let go of the notion so easily. Chief Justice Rehnquist's observation about the ending of the railroad era and beginning of the corporate merger era is succinct: "Three years after it created the Interstate Commerce Commission, Congress in 1890 passed the Sherman Antitrust Act, which forbade monopolization of commerce and conspiracy to restrain trade. A few years earlier the major culprit in the world of big business had seemed to be the railroads, but now the trusts were coming in for their share of public scrutiny and criticism. Congress was getting into the business of economic regulation on a nationwide basis."

Sheer domination of politics by the government-opportuned railroads had persisted while Congress had deliberated the Sherman Antitrust Act. But the merger movement of the late 1890s began to overshadow mere railroad corporate dominance. Abandoning altogether the appearance of competition, industrial leaders simply absorbed their competitors. The movement began in 1897 with a record 69 mergers, and then accelerated. There were 303 mergers in 1898, 1208 in 1899. The Standard Oil Company Copper Trust and the Smelters' Trust were formed that year. The National Sugar Refining Company was organized in 1900. J.P. Morgan organized the United States Steel Corporation combining Carnegie Steel and Federal Steel, in 1901, creating the nation's first billion-dollar corporation.

But a broader opposition to trusts, mergers and monopolies was also growing, partly at the behest of the labor movement. The aggressive and even corrupt practices which accompanied the exercise of corporate power were to some extent tolerated by the "frontier spirit" of the American people. But fear that the natural resources of the country were being exploited and exhausted for private gain nevertheless drove opposition to trusts and monopolies. Growth of the labor movement strengthened the opposition. But the impact of the movement was checked in 1892 by the Homestead Strike. It became a model for combating strikes—stand tough and call in the federal troops, much as had Governor Barber and Willis Van Devanter in April of the same year out in Wyoming to protect the WSGA's vigilantes.

Andrew Carnegie was serious in his efforts to preclude union organization of the industries he controlled. He authorized Henry Frick, his plant manager, to resist the struggling young American Association of Iron and Steel Workers' effort to organize at Carnegie's Homestead steel plant outside Pittsburgh. Steel production and distribution were integral to Carnegie's vertical integration of the steel industry, Carnegie controlling the entire production process from mining, refining, production, fabrication and final manufacturing, in both the rail and steamship industries. Frick had prepared to stand-off the Steel Workers' strike, locking them out and hiring Pinkerton agents to protect the facilities. The Steel Workers' resolve and Frick's stalwart defense strategy led to a shoot out. When the Pinkerton guards surrendered, they were compelled to pass through the striking steelworkers' ranks, where they were ruthlessly beaten, some twenty being severely injured. The Ohio state militia was ultimately called to reclaim the steel mill, which Carnegie reopened with newly hired anti-union personnel.

Five years after the Sherman Act's enactment, Chief Justice Fuller authored an opinion in *United States v. E.C. Knight Company*[4] that would limit the Act's application to interstate commerce. Goods do not become part of interstate commerce, he opined, until they move from one state to another. The merger of sugar companies, that after merger would control over 30 percent of the nation's sugar refining, was not unlawful under the Sherman Act on the basis that sugar was an essential "necessary of life" that should be regulated by states under the police power, rather than by the national government under the Interstate Commerce Clause. President Cleveland's Attorney General Richard Olney took it on the chin. The Sherman Act would have to be modified and tightened by later congresses, but the mere passage of the Act demonstrated that the age of unbridled corporate excess had its limits.

The twentieth century had begun. The United States led the world in industrial production and per capita income, half again that of Britain, and double that of Germany or France. The corporate form was morphing, new business structures were devised that would better support economic growth, hopefully to avoid the volatility, the booms and busts, the overproduction and consequent contraction of individual industries, of the previous century. Initial restructuring began by formation of pools or cartels. These loose associations brought former competitors together as informal partners, in "gentlemen's agreements" with a common goal of smoothing out markets by establishing production levels and agreed prices. These informal alliances evolved into early "trusts" with more formal commitment between several corporate owners. The stock certificates from several companies would be exchanged for trust certificates. A board of trustees of the trust would govern the performance of all of the severally independent companies within the trust. These trusts, sometimes called "holding companies," would theoretically garner the benefits of unified control of complete industries while avoiding state laws forbidding monopolies.

Economic concentration soon festooned many sectors of American industry—a few large corporations dominated the oil, meat, farm machine and sugar industries. The merger that created U.S. Steel in 1901, where Carnegie sold Carnegie Steel Company to J.P. Morgan for $480 million (making Carnegie the richest man in the world) was the signal for things to come. Vertical integration enabled these mega-corporations, now operated under the "trust" model to control all stages of production and distribution of the ultimate product. The profits made possible on the sale of the finished product reflected the costs saved in the production chain, including through access to the raw material from which the product was made. And the strategy made entry by competitors difficult and rare. Lack of competition kept market prices high.

Over the several administrations, prosecution of the Sherman Act against corporate dominance would vary. Only six civil suits and two criminal prosecutions were filed under the Act by the Harrison's administration. Only three civil suits and no criminal prosecutions would be filed by the McKinley administration. Nineteen civil suits and twenty-five criminal prosecutions would be filed under the Sherman Act by the Roosevelt administration. Thirty-five civil suits and forty-five criminal cases would be filed in a single term of the Taft administration. But the Supreme Court's Sherman Act jurisprudence would be political, with judicial prerogatives retained.

In 1897, while Willis was aspiring to federal appointment, the Supreme Court had issued an opinion allowing the Sherman Act to be used against rate-fixing agreements entered into by interstate railroads, and against price-fixing and market-division arrangements by six manufacturers of cast-iron pipe. The dissenting opinion in the case would presage the eventual majority view of the Court on the Sherman Act. In *United States v. Trans-Missouri Freight Association,*[5] Associate Justice White's dissent initiated the cause that would somewhat enfeeble the Sherman Act and empower the Court in the Act's administration. The case was first heard in the Circuit Court for the District of Kansas, First Division.[6] There, District Judge John Riner found that the railroad's agreement was not unreasonable and was therefore not unlawful under the Sherman Act. The Government appealed to the United States Circuit Court of Appeals for the Eighth Circuit. There, after argument, the Circuit Court of Appeals affirmed the lower court's decision in October 1893, Judge Shiras, district judge, dissenting.[7] From that judgment, the government appealed to the Supreme Court.

There, Justice Peckham wrote for the majority, determining that the Sherman Act applied to the interstate railroads. Justice White dissented, together with Justices Field, Gray and Shiras, arguing that only unreasonable restraints of trade were prohibited by the Sherman Act, and that the Sherman Act didn't apply to parties regulated by the prior-enacted Commerce Act (pertaining to railroads).

19

The Supreme Court Turns White (1908–1911)

Sensing as the 1908 election approached that the economic trouble of the October 1907 Bankers' Panic[1] might be his undoing, President Theodore Roosevelt refused to run for a third time. Rather, he endorsed William Howard Taft, his Secretary of War, as a genuine "progressive." Taft had never run for political office, as he had always enjoyed the benefit of political appointment to ever-more responsible positions, including President McKinley's appointment as civil governor of the Philippines in 1900, and President Roosevelt's appointment as Secretary of War in 1904.[2]

Taft's loyalty pleased Roosevelt, who had previously offered Taft a seat on the Supreme Court in October 1902 and 1906.[3] Now Taft sought office for the first time, at age 51, running for President against William Jennings Bryan, who was seeking the Presidency for the third time.[4] Taft won easily. Wyoming voted strongly for Taft.

Taft had risen through Republican political loyalties in Ohio. First a beneficiary and then a repudiator of "Ohio machine politics,"[5] Taft was an "ardent Republican, and therefore conservative in his political and social views."[6] Ultimately, he enjoyed the benefit of his partisan loyalty. He was a "confirmed Republican."[7] Historically it was an era of "machine" politics. Geographically, Ohio was its staunch Republican center.[8]

> "Like every well-trained Ohio man," Taft wrote, "I always had my plate the right side up when offices were falling.... Looking back to your letter, you ask me this—'Will you therefore tell me ... where you get your political pull?' I got my political pull, first, through father's prominence; then through the fact that I was hail-fellow-well-met with all of the political people of the city convention-going type. I also worked in my ward..."[9]

For Taft, loyalty to friends, which was essential, and loyalty to principle were not mutually exclusive. "He [Taft] may, in general, have been willing to forgive the irregularities of his political associates. But when asked to commit irregularities himself, he drew back in stubborn disgust. The distinction is vital; it marked his entire political life."[10]

Once in the White House, Taft soon became frustrated with the aging Supreme Court. In May 1909, he confided to his old Sixth Circuit Court of Appeals associate, Circuit Judge Horace Harmon Lurton, "The condition of the Supreme Court is pitiable, and yet those old fools hold on with a tenacity that is most discouraging,"

"Really the [76-year-old] Chief Justice [Melville W. Fuller] is almost senile; [Associate Justice John M.] Harlan does no work; [Associate Justice David J.] Brewer is so deaf that he cannot hear and has got beyond the point of the commonest accuracy in writing his opinions; Brewer and Harlan sleep almost through all the arguments. I don't know what can be done. It is most discouraging to the active men on the bench."[11] In particular, Taft had little respect for Justice Brewer,[12] author of the 1907 opinion in *Kansas v. Colorado*.[13]

In October, President Taft learned that Associate Justice Rufus Wheeler Peckham was suffering from an acute heart ailment and might die soon. Associate Justice Edward Douglass White sent word to the President that the "condition of the court is such that any vacancy which occurs ought to be filled at the earliest possible moment." Associate Justice Peckham died soon thereafter, on October 24, 1909. Even though Taft had deplored the senility of the highest court only four months before, he proceeded to appoint a rather elderly judge, his friend, the same Horace Lurton[14] to whom he had earlier complained. Lurton was a Democrat and, like Associate Justice White, a prior Confederate soldier. Taft had great respect for his first Supreme Court appointee's legal talents. But their years of association on the bench of the U.S. Court of Appeals was the more likely motivating factor for Taft's appointment of Lurton.[15] This was to be the first of Taft's six Supreme Court appointments.[16]

In April 1910, Associate Justice Brewer died. Willis Van Devanter, then serving on the Eighth Circuit Court of Appeals, had become aware earlier that month that Brewer's position was coming vacant. Wyoming Senators Clark and Warren, the Union Pacific, and Van Devanter immediately began a correspondence campaign proposing Van Devanter's appointment to the Supreme Court. From his desk in Cheyenne, Wyoming, Van Devanter wrote to many of his judicial and political acquaintances, superciliously announcing that he had "acquiesced" in letting his name be mentioned. When Judge Sanborn, who also wanted the job and was more senior on the Eighth Circuit Court bench, opposed Van Devanter's nomination, on the basis that Van Devanter didn't write very many opinions, an opposition apparently shared with Warren by President Taft himself, Van Devanter wrote Senator Warren[17] profusely defending his ardor.[18] It was not the number of cases upon which opinions were written that mattered, Van Devanter argued, but the complexity of the issues and cases. Van Devanter prevailed upon Senator Warren to make his case again to President Taft.[19]

Van Devanter's candidacy was also being supported actively by N.L. Loomis, General Solicitor of the Union Pacific R.R. Co., of Omaha,[20] and Van Devanter's brother-in-law, "Judge" John Lacey.[21] Aware of New York Governor Charles Evans Hughes, Sr.'s lead in Taft's consideration for the open justiceship, Hughes having declined Taft's 1908 offer of the vice-presidential nomination, Van Devanter disparaged it to his colleagues.[22] But Van Devanter pressed on, advocating that Wyoming's senior Senator Clark lobby President Taft,[23] all the while maintaining his ingratiating, unctuously sincere tone and obsequiously humble demeanor.[24] His self-promotion did not cease until the competition, Governor Hughes of New York, had won,[25] whereupon he thanked Senator Warren for his assistance.[26] The President offered the Supreme Court post to Governor Hughes,[27] who accepted the appointment promptly.[28]

Before Hughes could assume the bench,[29] Chief Justice Fuller died,[30] ending the era of the conservative, post–Civil War, Fuller Court. Presented with his third appointment opportunity, Taft deliberated the vacancy, considered appointing now confirmed Associate Justice Hughes as Chief Justice, and ultimately decided to elevate Associate Justice Edward Douglass White to become the new Chief Justice.[31] This would open White's associate justice position for another appointment. White had served on the Court as an associate justice since appointed by Democratic President Grover Cleveland in 1894. White was a Democrat,[32] a Confederate veteran, and a Roman Catholic. Taft's "admiration for him went back to his own days as a judge." In 1894, receiving word that White had been appointed to the federal bench, Circuit Judge Taft had written that he was a "very good man and will make a first-class judge ... he is a man of high courage and ability."[33]

Four weeks after Fuller's death another shoe fell. On July 30, Associate Justice William H. Moody[34] announced his retirement from the Court, due to a serious case of rheumatism.[35] Taft now had the opportunity to make a fourth appointment to the Supreme Court.

Junior Wyoming Senator Warren, and Senior Wyoming Senator Clarence Don Clark, now chairman of the Senate Judiciary Committee, went to bat for Van Devanter once again. They first pressed Taft to appoint Warren's "intimate friend the ultraconservative Willis Van Devanter" to fill Moody's position on the Court.[36] Western Republican senators led by Senator Warren insisted upon Van Devanter's appointment as a successor to White's seat on the Court as *quid pro quo* for their support for Taft's elevation of White, the southern Democrat, to the Chief Justiceship.[37] Taft would need their votes due to the opposition from the populist "insurgent" Republicans in the Senate. After all, Van Devanter had "lobbied for the seat."[38] The deal was cut. Taft appointed Willis Van Devanter to succeed Justice White.[39]

Warren perhaps also reminded Taft that he should remember and be loyal to his old friends: Van Devanter had attended Taft's alma mater, two years behind Taft. Taft had been dean of the Law School from 1897 to 1900, while Van Devanter was working in the Department of the Interior. Taft had become the Secretary of the Interior in 1904. Both Taft and Van Devanter were McKinley and Roosevelt appointees. Had Warren done so, he could not have been more prescient of events eleven years later.

Willis Van Devanter's close friendship and long service of then Governor, now Senator, Warren, a friendship "which was to last until Warren's death in 1929" was clearly "directly responsible ... for Van Devanter's advancement to the United States Supreme Court."[40]

> [T]he simple reason Van Devanter ended up on the U.S. Supreme Court was because of Senator Warren's tenacity. I do not suggest that all members of the Wyoming delegation were not involved. They most certainly were. A prominent Van Devanter client was Union Pacific, and Senator Clarence Clark's brother-in-law was vice president of the Union Pacific Coal Company. But, Warren's correspondence has survived while Clark's has not. So historians are able to

demonstrate Warren's effort and they are unable to demonstrate Clark's. Clark also served as Chairman of the powerful Senate Judiciary Committee, which, of course, reviewed Van Devanter's nomination for the Supreme Court.[41]

The Wyoming U.S. Senate delegation was powerful. Warren was Chairman of the Senate Appropriations Committee and Clarence Clark was Chairman of the Senate Judiciary Committee: One committee controlled the President's purse and the other his access to the Judicial Branch. It is no wonder that, after a fifteen year effort to elevate Van Devanter to high position, his confirmation was routine, and passed through the Senate in a matter of a few days! Nonetheless, getting the nomination was through consistent and persistent, political hard work demonstrably on the part of Senator Warren.[42]

On December 15, 1910, the Senate confirmed Justice Edward D. White's promotion from the position of Associate Justice to that of Chief Justice. The Senate simultaneously confirmed Willis Van Devanter's appointment to fill White's vacated position (leaving Associate Justice Moody's now-vacant seat to be later filled). Although White's promotion was polled out, Van Devanter was confirmed by the Senate the same day by voice vote. Unlike appointments to the modern Supreme Court, where confirmations may be confrontational, Willis Van Devanter's confirmation was brief and apparently non-confrontational. Senate hearings were brief or nil. President Taft's acceptance of western Republican Senators' political price for their endorsement of Associate Justice White to become Chief Justice may also have been abetted by Taft's predilection to help his friends and fellow alums. Van Devanter completed his service at the Eighth Circuit Court of Ap-

The White Court in 1911 after Willis Van Devanter was first seated. Back row from left: Associate Justices Willis Van Devanter, Horace Lurton, Charles Hughes, Joseph Lamar. Front row from left: Associate Justices Oliver Wendell Holmes, John Harlan, Chief Justice Edward Douglas White, Associate Justices Joseph McKenna and William Day (courtesy Wyoming State Archives).

Willis Van Devanter upon appointment to the U.S. Supreme Court, 1911 (courtesy Wyoming State Archives).

peals on December 16, 1910 and immediately became the 65th person appointed to the U.S. Supreme Court.[43]

Associate Justice Moody's position was later filled by Joseph Rucker Lamar.[44] On January 3, 1911, Van Devanter and Lamar took the oath of office together.

The more senior associate justices which Van Devanter and Lamar joined on the new White Court in 1911 were Associate Justices John Marshall Harlan,[45] Joseph McKenna, Oliver Wendell Holmes, William R. Day, Horace Harmon Lurton, and Charles Evans Hughes. Associate Justice J.R. Lamar joined the Court as junior to Van Devanter.

The U.S. Supreme Court which Justice Van Devanter joined on January 3, 1911, was a decidedly conservative[46] court, a Republican court to say the least, a court whose members were largely born before the U.S. Civil War and four of whom had served in either the Confederate[47] or Union[48] armies. The Spanish American War was recent in their memories, as were the upheaval of President McKinley's assassination, the economic depression of the 1890s and 1907, and the fight over the gold standard. The Court Justice Van Devanter joined was still working within the socially constraining assumptions that had been imposed upon American society by the Court's own 1896 decision in the case of *Plessy v. Ferguson*,[49] which upheld southern segregation statutes, and thus both northern and southern segregation practices.[50]

At the time, the Court still occupied the old Senate Chamber in the U.S. Capitol. The justices had no offices, working out of their homes. Their conference room was in the basement of the Capitol. Upon reaching the Court, Justice Van Devanter characterized the Court's library as "imperfect and dilapidated."[51] Van Devanter found suitable accommodations for himself, however, in the three-story walk up apartment on 16th Avenue several blocks up from the White House. Justice Brewer had lived here for years, but upon his death, the living quarters and third floor justice's office had come available.

The "White Court," with the senior members Associate Justice Van Devanter now encountered, together with those members Taft would later add,[52] would remain conservative, and strongly Republican, a "country club GOP,"[53] for years to come. Although perhaps more formally educated, and urbane, in the collegiate sense than the former Fuller Court, the White Court was no less conservative. "It would be difficult, if not impossible, to refute the charge that the United States Supreme Court was a conservative body during the period from 1870 to 1938."[54]

> The foundation of the Court's political theory was based on two main beliefs. God had ordained that man must labor in order to survive. The equally important logical corollary to that proposition was that man acquired property through his labor. These were viewed as axiomatic principles in both moral philosophy and political economy. It should therefore be hardly surprising that American jurists accepted them without question. Similarly man was regarded as a social being. The state, the creation of men living in society, was established in order to promote the safety and advantage of both the individual and the group. It followed from these premises that the primary purpose of the state was the protection of the individual and his property....
>
> In light of the voluntaristic moral setting in which they viewed both the state and individuals, the justices believed that government should protect the fullest extent the autonomy of each individual with the minimum amount of legal apparatus and government interference in private decision making. They believed that, although law may be acknowledged as the "potent force" binding society into a single entity and uniting "the protection of the individual with the efficiency of combined action," that force must be balanced against the demands of man's status as a moral agent. The law must allow for the operation of individual judgment and exercise of free will in order for the individual to reach his full potential and attain his greatest happiness. Within this ethical context, the state became a means to a greater end, the fullest secular development of humanity within an individualistic and voluntaristic ethical framework, rather than an end unto itself.[55]
>
> The moral autonomy of individuals and the dictates of faculty psychology justified the justices' acceptance of legal doctrines emphasizing the importance of protecting property, substantive due process, and freedom of contract. These doctrines were seen as all important in cultivating the highest individual and national character and to promoting and preserving both individual and social happiness and prosperity.[56]

Associate Supreme Court Justice Willis Van Devanter, student in moral philosophy in the ante-bellum grammar school and Cincinnati Law School, apprentice in the law and politics of raw frontier justice, journeyman in the national political machine of the Republican Party, young craftsman in Republican Presidential and judicial administrations, and throughout abiding by the prevailing code of loyalty to his friends, would fit right in.

20

The Sherman Act at the Supreme Court

When the Court opened its proceedings in January 1911, new Justices Van Devanter and Lamar on the bench, two cases rising from the Eighth Circuit were reheard. They involved disputed railroad companies' and homesteaders' claims filed after the railroad had selected lands pursuant to Secretary of Interior action under Congressional land grants statutes. The roads had filed maps and affidavits with the Land Office which the Secretary approved on their strength alone without inspection of the lands in question and issued land patents to the railroads.

In *Weyerhaeuser v. Hoyt*,[1] and *Northern Pacific Ry. Co. v. Wass*,[2] the Eighth Circuit had found in favor of the homesteaders. Both cases were appealed to the Supreme Court on April 27, 28, 1910. No opinion was delivered, but the cases were restored for reargument on December 19, 1910, four days after Van Devanter and Lamar reached the Court. They were reargued on January 19, 20, 1911. The Court's opinion was delivered the same day as reargument. The opinion delivered by now-Chief Justice White in the *Weyerhaeuser* case, reversed Judge Sanborn and found for the railroads. The opinion relied upon the artful device of "relation back," i.e., that the official action of the Commissioner and Secretary related back to the date when the railroad applied for the action, perfecting the railroads' title. Now, Associate Justice Van Devanter, who had been Assistant Attorney General advising both the Commissioner and the Secretary in the years in question, was with the majority. The language of White's opinion for the majority sounds suspiciously like vindication of Van Devanter's prior clients, as well as the Court's prerogative to read into congressional intent as the justices saw fit.[3] Justices Harlan and Day dissented.

Next, the Court relied on its decision in *Weyerhaeuser* to summarily reverse the Eighth Circuit's Judge Sanborn in the *Northern Pacific Ry. Co. v. Wass* case. Harlan and Day dissented again. One cannot but wonder whether Harlan's views had prevailed in the lesser populated Court the year before.

The antitrust issue was still ripe. On the Court, Associate Justice Van Devanter found himself returned to the issue most pre-occupying the American business community: the viability of the Sherman Act in controlling excessive size and power of the corporate entity. As early as 1890, and certainly by the depression of 1893, state court decisions had been disapproving of combinations of business venture that could be technically named "trusts." By the time of the Supreme Court's final consideration of the Standard Oil and American Tobacco cases, the issues of corporate size and concentration of economic power had fully agitated national politics. And the public's fear and anguish about that concentration, together with its desire for its being reined in by the Supreme Court, centered on the Sherman Act. Certainly, the Court would construe the law in a way beneficial to the public.

The Standard Oil case had come up to the Supreme Court as an appeal from the decision of the District Court for Eastern Missouri, on which Judge Van Devanter had participated, back on November 20, 1909.[4] Having been renoted in the circumstance of an insufficient bench to hear the case, it was reargued on January 12, 13, 16, 17, 1911. Once argued, the cases were held for some four months.

The stock market and industrial and commercial world were particularly entranced, awaiting the Court's decision. The outcome was not the issue, but rather an ending to the uncertainty that had slowed business on the street.

Judicial predilections were guarded against public disclosure, the Court taking unusual security precautions. On Saturday May 13, 1911, Chief Justice White's majority opinion in the Standard Oil case was voted on finally in conference. Six justices were definitely with White, apparently including Van Devanter. One unidentified justice, probably Day, was still wavering (he usually wanted to read the opinion before he voted). Harlan was the only dissenter. According to May 14, 1911, correspondence from Van Devanter to his prior Eighth Circuit colleague, Elmer B. Adams, the standard procedure of the opinion writers distributing printed proofs of the draft opinion was modified, the court voting not to send the opinions to the printer, but instead to circulate typewritten copies. Violating the new procedure, Van Devanter prematurely reported out the vote. Over the weekend, the "wavering" Justice joined the majority, making the decision 8–1.

On Monday, May 15, 1911, a standing-room only courtroom heard the Court's decision in the *Standard Oil* case and a written decision was published that day.[5] The Circuit Court's decision would be modified and affirmed. Essentially, the government won the case. Chief Justice White wrote the opinion for the Court. Albeit that Van Devanter had ruled in the case below, he did not recuse himself in the U.S. Supreme Court's decision.

Essentially, the Court had adopted President Taft's rationale, that Standard Oil's practices constituted "unreasonable" restraint of trade, which were precluded by the Sherman Act. Reasonable restraints were impliedly permitted. The distinction would make prosecutions tougher. And the Court's jurisdiction to interpret reasonableness would be reserved. In future, antitrust law would be primarily judicial fiat.

White opined, "the common law abhorred royal monopolies and private contractual restraints of trade because they conferred power to raise prices at will, to limit production, and to lower quality, all to the injury of the public. In America," he reasoned, "royal monopolies were unknown, but in the popular understanding, private actions that restrained trade were seen to have the same purposes and effects, and were condemned as monopolies. Yet the mature common law did not outlaw contracts in restraint of trade," so some restraints, perhaps the "reasonable" ones, should continue to be permissible notwithstanding what Congress had mandated.

The criterion for distinguishing unreasonable and illegal restraints of trade from reasonable and legal ones would be injury to the public.

But at least the academics, and perhaps the public, remembered that in the *Trans-Missouri* and *Joint Traffic* cases of 1897–98, Justice Peckham had held that the Sherman Act rendered all restraints of trade unlawful, rather than merely the "unreasonable" ones. Justice White had in that case argued, in dissent, for a "rule of reason." As he applied it in those cases, the rule seemed to mean that only price-fixing agreements which fixed unreasonably high prices would be held unlawful. By the same token, it was widely assumed, Justice White would think that only unreasonable, or bad, trusts and combinations were unlawful, and not reasonable or good ones. The Court's opinion in the Tobacco case was published the same day.[6]

R. L. Raymond's retrospective article, "The Standard Oil and Tobacco Cases," reported that, when the news hit Wall Street on May 15 that the Supreme Court would likely hand down the decision in the case, the announcement "brought a cheer that echoed in the tower of the Singer Building, so great was the delight of the waiting thousands of bankers, brokers and speculators that the uncertainty that had been hanging over the market like a black cloud was swept away." The Market had closed, with trading virtually suspended, before the result in the case was known. The next day stocks went up.

In short, the Court found that the Sherman Antitrust Act should be construed in the "light of reason" and that it prohibited all contracts and combinations which amount to an unreasonable or undue restraint of trade in interstate commerce. Then it found that the combination of the defendants *was* an unreasonable and undue restraint of trade in petroleum and its products moving in interstate commerce. Given Van Devanter's history, it is surprising that he did not agree with the Company's argument in defense of its actions. Writing for the majority, the Chief Justice summed Standard Oil's position:

> [I]t is insisted that [the facts] demonstrate that the origin and development of the vast business which the defendants control was but the result of lawful competitive methods, guided by economic genius of the highest order, sustained by courage, by a keen insight into commercial situations, resulting in the acquisition of great wealth, but at the same time serving to stimulate and increase production, to widely extend the distribution of the products of petroleum at a cost largely below that which would have otherwise prevailed, thus proving to be, at one and the same time, a benefaction to the general public as well as of enormous advantage to individuals.

It is an argument still heard, even from one candidate for the U.S. Presidency, in defense of artful avoidance of the implications of the modern U.S. tax code. But the Chief Justice's view was consistent with Taft's prior characterization of the import of the Sherman Act.

Professors Bickel and Schmidt express some approbation at now-Supreme Court Associate Justice Van Devanter's premature disclosure of the Court's decision in this publicly attended case.

> This leak of insider court information by a newly sitting Justice is extraordinary. With the stock market sitting in paused anticipation of the outcome of the case, a person with insider knowledge of the outcome would be in a position to buy into a surging market before the surge began. There is no evidence that either Van Devanter or Adams profited on this advance knowledge,

nor is it known how far the information may have spread from Adams. It is also not known who else Van Devanter may have given advanced notice. Certainly Francis Warren may have been so apprised.[7]

Eighth Circuit Judge Elmer B. Adams had been part of the panel who had heard the Standard Oil case in the Eastern District of Missouri. Van Devanter wrote to him again on May 18, 1911, three days after the Court's announcement, this time describing its substance.

White's opinion affirmed the judicial remedy fashioned by the Circuit Court. That decree had required corporate divestiture of holdings in all other companies and forbade future exercise of control over these former subsidiaries, or receipt of dividends from them. It did not, however, require divesture of personal holdings in the subsidiary companies. It did enjoin both the individuals and companies named in the complaint from conspiring to restrain or monopolize trade in the future, prohibiting agreements among themselves. But the White opinion lengthened the period for execution of the divestiture elements of the decree to six months and permitted normal operations until divesture occurred. And the implication of the opinion's holding upon the decree was that, in future, only "unreasonable" combinations need be avoided.

Justice Harlan, one of the more liberal of the justices on the Court Van Devanter had joined, dissented from White's majority opinion. He would have confirmed the entire decree from the Circuit Court without modification, the implication of which was that he saw no reason to limit the statute's application only to that "unreasonable" trust behavior.

In the immediate aftermath of the Court's decision, it was unclear whether the break-up of the Standard Oil trust would have practical meaning to the American consumer public. It did vindicate President Taft's view of the world, and scotch that of the progressives. And it did settle the anxiety of the business community, particularly including Wall Street. When the Court published its decision in American Tobacco case two weeks later, on May 30,[8] Harlan dissenting again, tobacco stocks dramatically dropped in price, but soon recovered.

Professors Bickel and Schmidt report that, during the White Court years there was "an almost unending miscellany of the kind of case that Van Devanter reported when he was Assistant Attorney General assigned to the Department of Interior crossed his desk every day."[9] Otherwise, they say that, on the Court, Van Devanter was quiet, rarely appeared in public, eschewed controversy and "accepted as his own provinces the areas of public law, admiralty law, water rights, Indian controversies, and corporation law." Van Devanter "shone in conferences as a student of judicial procedure." They have him as a "tireless worker," and quote later Justice Brandeis' description of Van Devanter as a "master of formulas that decided cases without creating precedents," and attributed his negotiating skill "much to his experience under Senator Warren."

At least sixty such cases relating to reviews of decisions by the Land Office, of the Department of the Interior, were decided by the Court between 1911 and 1920. In many of those cases, where the Court was, in effect ruling on the validity of determinations made by Van Devanter in his earlier role as Assistant Attorney

General, the Court merely limited the scope of its review, deferring to the earlier determination. In *Ness v. Fisher*,[10] Van Devanter affirmed the decision of the Secretary, holding that the Land Office's construction of the land grant statute, though debatable, should not be reversed by the Supreme Court. He generally found that factual determinations by the Land Office were conclusive unless not plausible.[11]

21

"Good Fellows" Willis and William (1921–1922)

Nearing the end of the Wilson presidency, former President Taft was advocating the selection of judicial personnel as the most important issue. Some things don't change. Taft pointed out that the winner of the upcoming election could appoint four new Supreme Court justices. He advocated the importance of appointing judges that would maintain the Supreme Court as the "bulwark to enforce the guaranty that no man be deprived of his property without due process of law." Alpheus Thomas Mason notes, "He was, of course, not speaking about the protections of undue process, as the more modern Court has defined it, but of the protection of private property rights against any substantive, legislated, governmental interference."

The official portrait of the Court, as composed from 1916 until 1921, is displayed at page 176 of *The Illustrated History of the Supreme Court of the United States.* Willis Van Devanter sits on Justice Holmes' left, his hands folded left over right in his lap. Whereas the shoulders of Holmes' robe are slanted and slack, the shoulders of Van Devanter's appear broadened, perhaps as though to have been padded. Van Devanter's intent gaze to the camera's right looks clean, intent, well managed. Chief Justice White sits in the lower center awkwardly, leaning left with his left shoulder and chin. Puffy faced, his robe open to show his three-button jacket and closed collar, he looks tired. On his immediate left sits Oliver Wendell Holmes, smaller by half than the Chief. Both Civil War veterans, the northerner Holmes appears erect and bright, whereas the southerner White looks resigned. To the Chief's right sit Justices Day and McKenna, both bow-tied. Day, transparently gaunt, looks down, appearing to fidget with his gown. McKenna, also slight and thin, sits more aptly, with the expression of a miner. Behind stand Louis Brandeis, Mahlon Pitney, James Clark McReynolds, and John Hessin Clarke. Brandeis half smiles. The rest appear stalwart or sad.

In May 1921, Chief Justice Edward White began feeling poorly. He notified the Court, and Justice Van Devanter in particular, that he was having difficulty finishing his work. On May 13, he asked Van Devanter to assist him with the writing of several opinions. In a typewritten note the Chief wrote,

> My dear Judge, I have written Mr. Justice Mckenna that I will not be at the next conference and probably not at the final one. By way of explanation I say that this is due to an indisposition which I am sure is of no moment, but which may keep me in for the time stated.

> I inclose [sic] you a list of the cases in my hands for opinion which under these circumstances, if the Court thinks they should be decided this term, ought to be returned to the conference table and be allotted. If not, and they are left standing as they are, I will be able to get them all up by the opening of the next term.
> In looking over the cases the only one which worries me is 4 Original. [Missouri v. Illinois] I ought to have written it long ago, but shortly after I took it my eyesight became affected and I put if off when I ought not to have done so. No. 14 goes with that case, as it involves somewhat the same subject.[1]

The Chief Justice died six days later, on May 19, 1921. Justice Van Devanter was probably very much pleased when he soon learned that none other than his own appointer, past President and fellow Cincinnati Law School alumnus William Howard Taft was in the running, to replace Chief Justice White. The only competition, prior Justice Hughes, was now Secretary of State. But Hughes declined to seek the Chief Justice's position. Taft organized a lobbying campaign to advocate his appointment to Harding. Within a month after White's death, Harding nominated Taft and sent the nomination to the Senate for confirmation. Taft was approved by the Senate in a 60–4 secret ballot on July 11. Taft's lifelong ambition was now to be realized.

Thus the White Court ended, and the Taft Court began. The new Court would be composed of Chief Justice Taft and Associate Justices McKenna, Holmes, Day, Van Devanter, Pitney, McReynolds, Brandeis and Clarke. Returning to Washington, Taft bought a house on Wyoming Avenue at Twenty Third Street and would walk to the Capitol daily. His route down Connecticut Avenue to Dupont Circle, then Massachusetts Avenue to 16th Street would intersect with Willis Van Devanter's walk to the Capitol from several blocks north.

Meanwhile in the Congress, Justice Van Devanter's Wyoming political cronies had also become more senior and powerful, Senator Warren becoming chairman of the Senate Irrigation Committee, and Congressman Mondell becoming House Majority Leader.

Holmes' biographer Sheldon Novick observed, "as Chief Justice, Taft wished to take control and to manage the whole of the judicial branch of government. As president and then as leader of his party, Taft had passed upon the appointments of perhaps one third of the whole federal judiciary. The new President (Harding) and attorney general were political allies and friends. Taft expected to continue influencing appointments to all of the federal courts. He was impatient to see these appointments be made, especially on the Supreme Court itself, where at least three places would be vacant soon. Two of the justices were chronically ill and could not write opinions." In fact, three justices would resign in Taft's first year as Chief Justice.

"More than just naming judges," Novick continues, "Taft wanted to rebuild the antiquated common-law courts. Each of the federal courts was an autonomous barony; there was no coordination among them and little sharing of work. Worst of all, the Supreme Court had little control over its own workload. Most of its time was taken up by cases that it was obliged to hear regardless of their importance. The Court, steadily falling behind its schedule, seemed to spend great energies on numerous minor or frivolous appeals in which the attorneys insisted on their right to talk to the bored justices for two hours each."

Taft's objective, it seems, was to fashion legislation that would reorganize the entire federal judicial system under the chief justice's administration. This would permit the Supreme Court to choose those cases it wanted to hear. In this manner, the Court could act on issues pertaining primarily to national policy—to have effect more similarly to the President and Congress. Taft also wanted Congress to appropriate funds to permit the Court to build its own building, with room for judicial and staff offices.

Although President Harding's appointment of Taft as Chief Justice to succeed White would begin a new era of judicial administration, it would not change the Court's conservative bent. President Warren Harding and ex-president Taft were equally hostile to governmental power in economic regulation and civil rights. The Court's orientation against legislation intended to regulate business and protect workers resurged—the same orientation the Court had exhibited prior to 1908.[2] Peter Irons observed, "By the time of his death in 1930, Taft's tenure and record on the Court, taken together with Chief Justice White's, would extend conservative control of the Chief's post to almost sixty years."[3] A large part of Chief Justice Taft's success on the court, it has been said, was attributable to the congeniality of his colleagues with his conservative views. Indeed, Justices Day, Pitney and Clarke would soon be replaced by judges who were even more conservative.

Although similar in their political orientation, White and Taft were very different people. Unlike the principled southerner White, Taft was an easily manipulated person, evidenced by the extent to which past-president Roosevelt manipulated him during his presidency. Taft's prior correspondence from the Philippines, while serving as Civil Governor, revealed his need to be appreciated.[4] As Secretary of War, Taft was loyal to the Roosevelt agenda, whether he believed it or not. He was acquiescent to Roosevelt, adopting Roosevelt's agenda as his own. Taft's approach was primarily expedience, go along to get along.[5] He was acquiescent to the engineer's opinions in the construction of the Panama Canal, which Roosevelt asked him to supervise, even though he held an independent opinion to the contrary.[6] And, Taft acquiesced and participated in Roosevelt dismissal of the 25th Infantry (a Black regiment), leading to violence in Brownsville, Texas, an acquiescence he later regretted, as Taft needed southern Blacks to support his presidential nomination.[7] In short, Taft failed to initiate individual due diligence when it came to policy, but merely went along with the power group. He was, in the words of Peter Iron, a "yes man," a man equipped with "honeyed words of friendship."[8]

Taft's attributes had been valuable during the Roosevelt presidency. Iron gives him credit:

> Taft, although less forthright than [Roosevelt Secretary of State Elihu] Root, had other qualities of infinite value to a busy president [Roosevelt]. He was a great conciliator. He was an excellent channel through which Roosevelt's opinions and desires could be passed on to others. He was a useful clearing-house for the opinions and desires of others. A confidence reposed in him was as safe as one murmured to a priest in a confessional.[9]

Ten years later, in retrospect of Taft's judicial career, Willis Van Devanter would say of Taft, that "the Supreme Court has had among its members many great jurists, among them the late Chief Justice Taft, who in recent years has been the most loved citizen in the land."

The two men's origins were not all that different. William Howard Taft had been born on September 15, 1857. The Tafts lived at Mt. Auburn, Ohio, an outlying section of Cincinnati. Willis Van Devanter had been born two years later in Marion, Indiana. Like Willis Van Devanter's father Isaac, Taft's father Alfonso Taft was a lawyer, hailing originally from Vermont.[10] His mother derived from Millbury, Massachusetts. Young Taft attended Yale, where his father had also attended, and was tapped for Skull and Bones, his father having been one of the secret society's founders.[11] In 1877, Yale-graduated Taft matriculated at the Cincinnati Law School, sitting in Melodeon Hall.[12]

Taft's personality and personal history made him susceptible to manipulation. And that susceptibility presented the opportunity Van Devanter would need to accomplish his objectives in the Laramie River case. Shortly after Taft's appointment, in the summer following completion of the Court's 1920 term, on July 6, 1921, Justice Van Devanter began ingratiatingly corresponding with soon-to-be Chief Justice Taft. Taft penned a hand-written letter to Van Devanter on the same day the previous term closed. He said,

> Dear Justice Van Devanter, Your kind [correspondence] of congratulations was forwarded by mail to Murray Bay and has just now arrived here. I thank you for sending it. I am glad to come into close personal and official relations with you. You and your colleagues must be patient and forbearing with a neophyte—you must be kind to my rusty shortcomings. I know I am entering a field of incessant labor and great responsibility that you will help me with your long training and experience in the same field.[13]

By September 30, Chief Justice Taft had already begun his administrative duties, sending Van Devanter a notice of an upcoming conference.[14] Soon, according to Sheldon Novick, "The conferences of the Court were no longer acrimonious. Taft presided as if over a seminar, carefully eliciting everyone's views of every case, and Van Devanter, who rarely wrote opinions but whose views were respected by his colleagues, served as Taft's deputy, mediating among the justices and negotiating changes in opinions to secure agreement."

By October, Taft and Van Devanter were together plotting judicial appointments to the Courts of Appeal, including the Eighth Circuit,[15] where Justice Van Devanter remained Circuit Justice. October correspondence contained in Van Devanter's Supreme Court papers include copies of letters from Kansas City solicitors and principles of the Atchison, Topeka, and Santa Fe Railroad, and Union Pacific Railroad, Kansas City Southern and the Pullman and Wells Fargo companies regarding the appointment of District Judge Pollack, Kansas City, to the Eighth Circuit. An October 19, 1921, copy of correspondence from Union Pacific's General Solicitor N.H. Loomis to Sen. Charles Curtis regarding Pollack's appointment; and Taft's letter to Gardiner Lathrop, Kansas City railroad lawyer, also appear there. These copies had apparently been sent by Loomis to Van Devanter under cover of October 29, 1921. "After leaving you [VDV] in Washington, I had in mind Gardiner Lathrop of Chicago and D.W. Mulvane of Topeka as the proper persons to handle the matter we talked about." N.H. Loomis' son, John U. Loomis, would become, by 1931, John W. Lacey's law partner in Cheyenne, Wyoming.

Although Chief Justice Taft had served previously as a state court judge, U.S.

Ambassador, U.S. Solicitor General, and Circuit Court of Appeals Judge, he was not reputed for the excellence of his writing when he reached the Supreme Court. Albeit thorough, Taft was not considered artistic in his drafting and perhaps relied upon others, particularly including Justice Van Devanter, to do his writing for him. Taft's biographer Pringle observed about Taft's writing competence:

> Taft's opinions [as an Ohio Superior Court Judge were] all in all, decidedly dull reading. Their significance, with one or two exceptions, lies in the degree to which they show the early development of traits which later became pronounced. Taft was not, in any sense, a literary craftsman and this, curiously, was despite the fact that he enjoyed writing. [Taft's] letters lacked style or grace, however. They were too verbose and rarely had charm. He had no flair whatever for the turning of a phrase, for brief analysis of a technical subject. The same faults are to be found in his messages as president and in other official documents. They are discernible in the first judicial opinions which he wrote on the Superior Court of Cincinnati. They marked, although to a lesser degree, his decisions as chief justice of the United States.[16]

On the other hand, Willis Van Devanter had now been ghostwriting for others, particularly including Senator Francis Warren, for decades.

By early December, the Chief Justice was cozily forwarding his draft opinions to Van Devanter, seeking "the benefit of your suggestions and corrections before" sending them to the rest of the Court. A typewritten note from Taft to Van Devanter confided:

> I am sending you a tentative opinion in the Arizona Truax case. I wish you would look it over and cut and slash as you think wise. I found on looking into the case that it seemed necessary to take up the due process feature rather more than I had anticipated. I have not sent this to the whole Court, because I want to have the benefit of your suggestions and corrections before doing so. I presume it is too late to expect to get it ready for next Monday, but if you could read it tonight and talk with me in the morning about it, I would be very much obliged. Sincerely yours, Wm. H. Taft.[17]

By late December 1921, other judges familiar with Justice Van Devanter's and the Chief Justice's writing styles, including Eighth Circuit Court Justice Walter Sanborn, who had himself aspired to the judicial position to which Van Devanter had been appointed in 1911, and later in 1922 would aspire to a number of Supreme Court vacancies that would develop, recognized the touch of Van Devanter's hand in the Chief's opinions. On December 19, 1921, the same day that the Court published its opinion *Truax v. Corrigan*[18] Judge Sanborn sent a typewritten letter to Van Devanter,

> I heartily congratulate you and Chief Justice Taft upon the decisions you are handing down, and especially upon those which sustain the constitution of the United States and declare that the means of livelihood of the citizens of the nation are protected thereby, and that they shall not be deprived thereof by violence and robbery.

The *Truax* case involved a strike by union labor against the English Kitchen, a non-union restaurant in Bisbee, Arizona. Their pro-union activity included "inducing [the restaurant's] customers ... to cease to patronize or trade with the plaintiffs. The method of inducing ... included picketing, displaying banners, advertising the strike, denouncing plaintiffs as 'unfair' to the union, and appealing to customers to stay away from" the restaurant. Chief Justice Taft wrote for the majority, overturning the Supreme Court of Arizona. Although there were no physical injuries,

Taft described "the circulation of handbills containing abusive and libelous charges against [the restaurant], their employees, and their patrons, and intimations of injury to future patrons." The English Kitchen's daily revenue was cut in half. An Arizona statute precluded judicial interference with employer-employee disputes. The Arizona Supreme Court had denied the restaurant's claim that the statute "contravened the Fourteenth Amendment to the Constitution of the United States by depriving plaintiffs of their property without due process of law, and by denying to plaintiffs the equal protection of the laws, and was therefore void and of no effect." Taft's opinion essentially repealed the exemption of organized labor from the Clayton Anti-Trust Act. The opinion itself shows Van Devanter's detailed and systematic writing style.

Part III

The Laramie River Litigation

22

Wyoming v. Colorado (1903–1913)

The U.S. Supreme Court's jurisdiction to entertain disputes between states, particularly over interstate water systems, had been well established by Justice Brewer in *Kansas v. Colorado* in 1903. Seizing the opportunity of having a favorite son, Willis Van Devanter, on the U.S. Supreme Court in 1911, Wyoming attorneys filed suit against Colorado in the Supreme Court a mere 146 days after he had been sworn onto the Court. It was coincidentally, the same day that Justice Holmes published his opinion in *Bean v. Morris*, upholding the Ninth Circuit's protection of a senior water right on the Stinking Creek in Wyoming against a junior water right on its tributary Sage Creek in Montana. Chief Justice White witnessed the subpoena to Colorado issued by the Supreme Court on June 10, 1911. The case was entitled *Wyoming v. Colorado*, No. 7 Original.[1] The facts that Van Devanter had once been Chief Justice of the Wyoming Supreme Court, that Wyoming's then sitting U.S. Senators who secured his seat on the Court, Francis E. Warren and Joseph Carey, were principals in the Wyoming corporation that would benefit from Wyoming's success in the litigation, and that the attorney advocates for Wyoming were brother-in-law and nephew of the justice seems little to have mattered. At least then.

Justice Van Devanter would later write, in his 1930 speech published in the *Indiana Law Review*, "The reasons for permitting suits in which a state is a party to be originally brought in the Supreme Court arise out of the fact that it does not comport with the dignity of a state either to subject itself or to be subjected to the jurisdiction of a court of another state. Cases of this class usually present important questions and at times are difficult of solution. But there are not many of them—probably four or five are begun each term. I recall two that were argued three times before a final decision was given." The Justice made no mention of his earlier unprincipled behavior in just such a case.

Most of the irrigation in Wyoming prior to statehood consisted of small private ditches or ditch companies. Wyoming's irrigation interests began growing after the economic catastrophe in the cattle industry following the frigid winters of 1885 and 1886, and water from the Laramie River was seen as essential to the development of Wyoming properties in the otherwise arid Laramie Plain. In the late 1870s the Pioneer Canal Company began the first large-scale canal project, the Pioneer Canal out of the Big Laramie River. The Pioneer Reservoir, built in 1879, was an essential component of the Pioneer Canal Company's irrigation development. The Wyoming cattle industry, once dominant in the 1880s and 90s was now converting its interests to agriculture, depending upon the growth of irrigation facilities like those contemplated in the arising congressional discussion of a national reclamation agency, which would later be accomplished in the 1902 Reclamation Act. Federal fiscal support for economic development, this time federally watered domestic farms and cattle ranches, could replace the same prior support for railroads and access to the open plains for free-range cattle ranching.

The Laramie River rises in the Front Range in Colorado, runs along the east side of the Medicine Bow Mountains of northern Colorado, then flows north toward Wyoming, crossing the state line north of Jelm, Wyoming, after which it descends northeast past Wyoming's Medicine Bow Mountains, through the Laramie Plains to reach the North Platte near historic Fort Laramie. Wyoming's Laramie River water users included the owners of agricultural land on the Laramie Plains, as well as those relatively near the Laramie River itself. In 1883, several of the well-known territorial cattlemen, including U.S. Senator Joseph Carey, Horace Plunkett, William Irvine, and U.S. Senator Francis E. Warren organized as the Wyoming Development Company which then organized the Wheatland Irrigation District, and began construction of a second sizable irrigation project out of the same river system at the Wheatland Colony.

Surveyors completed the initial mapping of the Wheatland project, and the real work of developing it began in the organizational year. The project would have one very large and one comparatively small reservoir for storing water and equalizing flow. The Wheatland Tunnel and Canals No. 1 and No. 2 were completed by 1886. What with the drought, cold and calamity of the winter of 1887–1888, cattle ranching would need to much more greatly rely upon managed production of foodstuffs, for cattle and people, through irrigated farming on the arid Laramie Plain.[2]

The truck farm-to-store economy of pre-teen twentieth-century farming would need to supplant the lost bravado of the cattle range years. Development of economies of scale depended upon corporate ownership and development of the underlying fee and delivery of water, so as to market farmsteads to individual farmers moving west from an Ohio valley experience. Houses and barns could not be pushed up without financial backing from banks that would require secure, clear titles and water supplies. In town, the ice vendor and the dry goods store needed the agricultural economy in order to survive. In the field, haying was done by horse teams, reaping, then hauling hay mows to be lifted into barns by huge winch systems. Horse and man power was essential, even in an era of steam and growing mechanization. After the internal combustion engine came along to make horsepower more efficient, pickups, tractors and harvest equipment could not be purchased without regularized annual crop production to secure bank financing.

James E. Sherow reported, "The 50,000 acre Wheatland tract was a Carey Act development, with Senator Joseph M. Carey and his son involved as company officers."[3] On August 18, 1894, Wyoming's Senator Joseph Carey successfully obtained legislation in the U.S. Congress permitting states to designate planned areas up to a million acres where irrigated farming could be pursued, subject to the modest limitation that at least 20 acres of any 160 acre parcel passed on to would-be farmers

The Laramie River winds its way north toward Wyoming in Colorado's Laramie River valley (author's photograph, 2019).

The Laramie River enters Wyoming north of Jelm. "Birdseye View of Jelm" below Woods Landing, 1901 Directory, Laramie and Albany Counties (courtesy Wyoming State Library).

would be irrigated. Willis Van Devanter, then Assistant Attorney General in the office of the Secretary of the Interior, had authored an opinion in 1897 facilitating the transfer of ownership of federal public domain to the State of Wyoming for Carey Act development.

The Laramie River in Wyoming below Jelm (author's photograph, 2019).

In 1904, Senators Carey and Warren, Wyoming's state engineer Clarence T. Johnston, Wyoming water lawyers, irrigation investors in the Wheatland project, the attorney of the Wyoming Development Company, and others appeared as witnesses for the United States government during the testimony taken in the pending case of *Kansas* v. *Colorado.* They expressed their displeasure at Coloradans' proposed use of Laramie River water. As Sherow pointed out, "The investors in the Wheatland Project needed an undiminished flow of the Laramie River to supply their venture, and they became worried about the effects of a project in the upper reaches of the Laramie Basin in Colorado." They also objected to Colorado's claim, based on state sovereignty over the water originating within Colorado's boundaries and to the tunnel project connecting the Laramie to the Cache la Poudre basin. The witnesses all made special reference to the adverse effects of Coloradans' plans on the development of the Wheatland project.

By 1910 the owners of the Wyoming Development Company had constructed a large storage reservoir on the Laramie River and had opened two additional tracts of land for irrigation in the Wheatland Project.

But growth premised on available water was also occurring in Colorado. The Greely-Poudre Irrigation District contained 125,000 acres of undeveloped land north of Greeley, Colorado, near Nunn. It had been developed by D.A. Camfield in 1909, following on Camfield's other successful Colorado developments. Camfield's plan was to bring water to the development, which would be held in local reservoirs for delivery to properties within the district, thereby making the properties more valuable for resale. The Cache la Poudre River was, however, already overcommitted to existing claims. Camfield's solution was to bring Laramie River water through the mountain ridge prevailing between the Laramie and the Cache la Poudre River via a two-and-one-half-mile tunnel. Once through the tunnel, the water would be delivered by canal to Greeley. Camfield planned to finance the tunnel and canal construction by selling bonds secured by liens on the real property within the district.

By January 3, 1911, Wyoming's Republican and moneyed interests, fully invested in the Wheatland Project, found themselves with their old friend, attorney and political protégé sitting on the United States Supreme Court. Justice Van Devanter's political and personal acquaintance with all the Wyoming Development Company's principals, his knowledge and empathy of the situation occasioned by his having suffered through the failure of the cattle industry, by his prior lawyering on behalf of their legal, and not-so-legal, interests, and by his own efforts to preserve his mother-in-law's assets upon the dissolution of the Swan Cattle Company, certainly would make him sympathetic to Wyoming's growing dependency on the Laramie. And his principal ethic of loyalty to friends and political associates, particularly including those who had put him in the seat he now occupied, could be counted upon.

The Court's jurisdiction to entertain disputes between states, particularly over interstate water systems, had been well established by Justice Brewer in *Kansas v. Colorado* in 1903. But disputes between individual residents of different states arise under federal district courts' "diversity jurisdiction." Citing a July 20, 1911, letter from Delph Carpenter, attorney for Colorado interests in the now-filed Supreme Court litigation, to C.W. Crouter of Wheatland, Wyoming, Colorado Historian Daniel Tyler points out that the Wyoming Senators' intentions were not exclusively directed at Wyoming's general economic interests. "Delph [Carpenter] believed the case was politically motivated and it had been initiated by two men who planned to turn Laramie River water into Lake Hattie near Woods Landing, Wyoming. Knowing their planned project was 'junior' in priority to the Greeley-Poudre Project, they 'started a series of agitations around Laramie City to the effect that the Colorado diverters were about to take *all* of the water of the Laramie River in Colorado and divert it to the Cache la Poudre Valley.' According to Carpenter, they used this threat to gain votes during the most recent political campaign."[4]

Professor Tyler makes the point that the Wyoming Attorney General Douglas A. Preston "would not have considered prosecuting a costly suit of original jurisdiction in the United States Supreme Court had the complaining about Colorado irrigators been limited to small farmers.... A more substantive issue was needed, and the promoters of the Wheatland tract [including Senators Warren and Carey] supplied exactly the stimulus the attorney general required."[5] As original jurisdiction cases are limited to state v. state controversies, the principles in the Wheatland project wouldn't have been able to lodge their complaint before the Court where their go-to judge was sitting, the Supreme Court, without the aid of Wyoming's attorney general, and the complicity of the Court. The case would, rather, have been relegated to the federal district court, as a matter of its diversity jurisdiction.

And better yet, if the cattle, now irrigation, interests could get Wyoming politicians to sue the State of Colorado directly in the Supreme Court, exercising the Court's original jurisdiction, a decision in their favor could not be appealed.

Professor Tyler explains that "even before the farmers and investors of the Wheatland project, others in Wyoming had aired complaints to their attorney general about Colorado water users. 'It appears that our Colorado friends have almost robbed us of Sand Creek,' wrote James M. Hoge, a Wyoming rancher. Coloradans were diverting the flows of this small tributary to the Laramie River through the Divide Ditch, a canal crossing the Continental Divide, and dumping the diversions into Sheep Creek, which flowed eastward and joined the North Fork of the Cache la Poudre River. Hoge requested permission from the Wyoming State Engineer to make alterations to his reservoir system to compensate for his losses in Sand Creek."[6]

"Hoge also wanted to enjoin his 'friends' in Colorado from further water use. He took action against Colorado irrigators, and the decision of the United States District Court for Colorado in *Hoge et al. v. Eaton et al.*,[7] recognized the equal standing of prior appropriation dates on interstate streams. The [Eighth Circuit] Court of Appeals [Van Devanter not sitting], however, reversed this decision in *Eaton* v. *Hoge*,[8] holding in part that Hoge had not shown that he had at least $2,000 [then the prerequisite to establish diversity jurisdiction] in property at stake." "If the small stream of Sand Creek could stir local passions, clearly the specter of trans-mountain diversions from the Laramie Valley to the Platte Valley in Colorado could, and did, focus the attention of farmers all along the Laramie River in Wyoming."

And by February 21, 1911, Wyoming Senator F.E. Warren had accomplished passage of the Warren Act,[9] authorizing the Secretary of the Interior to provide surplus water from federal Reclamation projects to irrigators irrigating land acquired by them under the Carey Act. A win in the Supreme Court on the interstate water issue would guarantee them the certainty which they needed to further develop their project—and it would address another controversy of western water politics: whether water in western rivers was the province of state or federal law.

On May 29, 1911, Douglas Preston, Wyoming Attorney General, filed an Application for Leave to File Original Bill of Complaint, together with the Complaint itself, with the Supreme Court. N.E. Corthell and John W. Lacey joined the Attorney General "of Counsel." N.E. Corthell had handled the *Hoge* case. John W. Lacey was, of course, Justice Van Devanter's brother-in law. Mr. Herbert V. Lacey, Justice Van Devanter's nephew, would become involved in the briefing. The Complaint alleged that the development of a tunnel to deliver water removed from the Laramie River within Colorado into the Cache La Poudre River Basin caused injury to the citizens of Wyoming owning properties riparian to the Laramie and should be enjoined. The initial Complaint stated no injury to the State of Wyoming, but only to the vested property interests of Wyoming business interests, none of them named in the pleadings. The Court issued a subpoena which was served upon John F. Shafroth, Colorado's Governor, and the principals of the Colorado entities on July 7, 1911. The Governor accepted service on August 15, and, the parties having stipulated to an extension of 90 days time for Colorado's response. On October 9 Benjamin Griffith, Colorado's Attorney General, entered his appearance before the Court. Clyde Dawson, Charles D. Hayt and Julius C. Gunter appeared for the Laramie Poudre Reservoirs and Irrigation Company. Gunter appeared as well on behalf of the Greely-Poudre Irrigation District.

The Complaint in the case sought to enjoin use of water from the Laramie River in Colorado by the Greely-Poudre Irrigation District. The Greeley-Poudre Irrigation Company had by now partially completed its tunnel, designed to divert 125,000 acre-feet of water from the Laramie River to the Cache la Poudre River. Once Wyoming filed its lawsuit with the U.S. Supreme Court, potential investors in the Colorado project began to lose courage, diminishing the fiscal strength of the venture. Camfield's unexpected death made things worse. Previously raised funds had been largely dedicated to construction of the tunnel, 60 percent complete in 1911, and few resources remained to build canals and reservoirs, let alone litigate in the U.S. Supreme Court. Unsold bonds from the initial $5 million offering became difficult to sell and bond sales after Wyoming's lawsuit in 1911 all but ceased, the astral alignment of political forces perhaps becoming all too obvious.

Carpenter wrote in a letter to Judge Evan A. Evans, of Chicago, that $2.8 million of $5.1 million bonds were sold as of 1911 when Wyoming sued Colorado. They immediately depreciated by some 25 percent. The project was only 54 percent complete.[10]

On January 9, 1912, the Colorado parties filed a Demurrer to Wyoming's complaint, stating that the complaint was without equity and stated no cause of action entitling Wyoming any relief.[11]

On March 5, Colorado's Attorney General Griffith moved to set Colorado's demurrer for hearing. The Court set the matter for October 15. On September 3, 1912, Wyoming Attorney General Douglas Preston filed a Brief of Complainant on Demurrer for the Wyoming parties. N.E. Corthell and John W. Lacey of Counsel joined him on the brief. When October 15 arrived, Lacey argued the case for Wyoming, he entering his appearance for the State of Wyoming that day. C.D. Hayt and Benjamin Griffith (now "of counsel" to Colorado Attorney General Tew) argued the case for Colorado. On October 21, the Court "overruled" Colorado's demurrer "without prejudice to any question" and authorized Colorado's filing of its answer to Wyoming's complaint within 90 days.

Colorado Attorney General Benjamin Griffith ran for reelection in 1912, but on the Progressive (Bull Moose) ticket, rather than as a Republican. He lost to Democrat Fred Farrar in a five-way race. On January 7, 1913, Farrar entered his appearances on behalf of the State of Colorado and Delph E. Carpenter entered his appearance on behalf of the Greely-Poudre Irrigation District. Carpenter had been elected Republican minority leader of the Colorado State Senate in 1911 and selected as attorney for the Greeley-Poudre Irrigation District, the real party in interest in the litigation, shortly thereafter at an annual salary of $4,000. Carpenter was not disinterested in the case, as his father had been instrumental in the initial settlement of Greeley and its formulation of the irrigated agriculture-oriented western lifestyle, including both Greeley, Colorado, and Wheatland, Wyoming. In response to the Court's order that Colorado answer Wyoming's complaint, Carpenter began to develop and present his theory that Colorado had sovereign claim to the Laramie River, because it rose in Colorado, and therefore had the right to determine where it might be used (the "origin of flow" theory). The case would be distinguishable from *Kansas v. Colorado*, which Associate Justice Brewer had determined five years earlier in 1907, where the domestic water law of the two states differed. Here both states, Colorado and Wyoming, premised their water law on the prior appropriation doctrine.

Carpenter could not resist the thought that the case was politically motivated. He hoped that the Supreme Court would recognize the political context of the case and dismiss it. But there is no evidence of his having brought the political facts to the Court's attention by way of motion seeking Wyoming-based Van Devanter's disqualification.

Colorado's Answer was filed and accepted by the Court on January 8, as was an independent Answer filed by the several irrigation interests. The Answer denied Wyoming's mapping of the conflict area of Laramie River tributaries and headwaters. It argued that Laramie River water use in Colorado pre-dated that of the Wheatland project in Wyoming, and that Colorado's "inherent sovereign power to divert from that section of the Laramie River within Colorado the entire runoff of that section for use within the State of Colorado." "[T]he waters of the said stream and its tributaries within the State of Colorado constitute a part of the natural resources of, and were or are owned by, the State of Colorado, subject to the right of appropriations thereof under her laws." Griffith also argued that there was sufficient water in the Laramie, after taking Colorado diversions into account, to provide adequate water for Wyoming's Laramie River water users. As a matter of affirmative claim, Griffith argued that Colorado was entitled to use all of the water flowing in Colorado's rivers within the state, essentially the same argument as had been initially made by Attorney General Harmon for United States in the case of the Rio Grande:

> This defendant alleges that the jurisdiction and rights of the State of Wyoming, either in its sovereign capacity or as a proprietor of lands, and the rights of the citizens of Wyoming, do not extend into the State of Colorado, and this defendant further alleges that, under the laws and principles of international and interstate law, the sovereign rights of this defendant over the waters of the section of the Laramie River and its tributaries lying within the State of Colorado are not subservient to the sovereignty or rights of the State of Wyoming, and that the State of Wyoming has no dominant estate, rights, or jurisdiction as against this defendant, or its people, in that part of the Laramie River and its tributaries flowing in the State of Colorado, and that the State of Colorado cannot be subjected to the burden of arresting its development, or of denying to its inhabitants the use of an element which nature has supplied entirely within its own territory, and without which, and free use hereof, the lands to which said water is sought to be applied would be uninhabitable.

Colorado further argued that, of the Laramie's length, 25 miles were in Colorado, 150 in Wyoming; of its drainage area, 428 square miles lay in Colorado, 3,865 square miles lay in Wyoming; of the 800,000 acre feet of its annual runoff, 300,000 drained from Colorado, 500,000 drained from Wyoming. The Colorado use sought to be enjoined constituted a mere 75 square miles of Colorado's 428-mile drainage area and 70,000 of Colorado's 300,000 acre feet of runoff.

On April 7, 1913, Douglas Preston, Wyoming Attorney General, together again with N.E. Corthell and John Lacey appearing of counsel, filed a "Replication," or Reply, to the several Answers of the Colorado defendants. The reply merely reaffirmed Wyoming's initial Complaint.

Information is unavailable with which to determine whether the fears of Wyoming irrigators were real and that the prospective irrigation project in Colorado would have actually been preclusive of development within the Wheatland District. Just as the hobgoblin of cattle "rustling" masked the mismanagement of corporate cattle interests in Wyoming in the 1890s and justified felonious actions against unsuspecting agents of Congress' westward expansion policy, now the specter of competitive water demand concealed protection of investor wealth and justified inappropriate exercise of original jurisdiction in the U.S. Supreme Court.

As it ultimately turned out, proof of the volume of prior use or the prospective need for water would never be presented in the litigation. Estimates of normal flow in the Laramie River in Colorado ranged from 188,000 acre-feet to 300,000 acre-feet. The Greeley-Poudre Project is estimated to have taken between one-third and one-half of that flow. But no estimate of Wheatland's need would be presented.

On April 9, Charles D. Hayt and Clyde W. Dawson withdrew their appearances as counsel for the Laramie-Poudre Reservoirs and Irrigation Company. On May 26, 1913, the parties stipulated to terms of the taking of testimony from both parties, naming Clyde M. Watts of Cheyenne, Wyoming, and Newton Garbutt of Denver, Colorado, and that both of them "have the power of Masters in Chancery, as provided by the rules of this Court." The stipulation provided that evidence in the Laramie River case would be taken in two independent segments, each supervised by an independent "special commissioner." Wyoming's evidence would be presented in front of Mr. Watts in Cheyenne. Colorado's evidence would be presented in front of Mr. Garbutt in Denver. By stipulation, neither was authorized to make any findings of fact or conclusions of law. Wyoming Attorney A.C. Campbell of Cheyenne had offered to act as special master and fact finder in the litigation, in a letter now to be found in Van Devanter's personal papers at the Library of Congress. Justice Van Devanter obviously had not accepted the proposal.

In August, attorneys for the two states began developing a factual record in the case, receiving testimony from expert witnesses in Cheyenne, Denver and Greeley, Colorado. According to Professor Tyler, 237 days of testimony were taken.

Eight years later, the Court would find through Justice Van Devanter that there was a true conflict between the competing uses for water from the Laramie system. "The [Wyoming] places of use are in the same watershed [as the supply in Colorado] and relatively near the stream, as is true of the lands on the Laramie Plains served by the greater part of the Wyoming appropriations...."[12] Justice Van Devanter wrote, "But for combined farming and stockraising those [lands] of the Laramie Plains offer opportunities and advantages which are well recognized. It is to this use that they chiefly are devoted. It is a recognized and profitable industry, has been carried on there for many years and is of general economic value. Many of the original ranchmen still are engaged in it,—some on the tracts where they first settled. With the aid of irrigation, native hay of a high quality, alfalfa, oats and other forage are grown for winter feeding, the live stock being grazed most of the year on unirrigated areas and in the neighboring hills and mountains. In this way not only are the irrigated tracts made productive, but the utility and value of the grazing areas are greatly enhanced. The same industry is carried on in the same way in sections of Colorado. In both States this is a purpose for which the right to appropriate water may be exercised, and no discrimination is made between it and other farming."[13]

The October term 1916 Transcript of Record in the case shows Wyoming's expert, M.R. Johnston, brother of Wyoming state engineer Clarence T. Johnston, and superintendent of the Wyoming Development Company from November 1888 to June 1, 1912, testifying that the Company's dams and irrigation canals irrigated 35,000 to 40,000 acres, 3,000–5,000 of those beginning in 1893. He further described the works as including reservoirs No.1 on Company Land and No. 2 on the Laramie River, with a capacity of 126,000 acre feet. Surveying for the latter reservoir began in 1894 or 1895; construction began in 1899 and was completed about 1900.

Tyler reports that Colorado's expert, Louis Carpenter, testified that ample water would remain in the Laramie River to satisfy Wyoming's senior water rights even with an additional diversion of 100,000 acre-feet of water in Colorado.

Eight years later in 1922 when the opinion in *Wyoming v. Colorado* was published, its author, Associate Justice Willis Van Devanter, described the case's procedural history:

> The bill was brought in 1911, the evidence was taken in 1913 and 1914, and the parties put it in condensed and narrative form in 1916 preparatory to the usual printing. The case has been argued at the bar three times. The court directed one reargument because of the novelty and importance of some the questions involved, and the other because of an intervening succession in the office of Chief Justice.[14]

Although it is evident from the Court's opinion that the case was fact-intense, the Court's final opinion made no reference to the evidence adduced pursuant to the parties' stipulation and appointed no special master to consider the evidence, as is the case in more modern interstate Supreme Court cases. Justice Van Devanter's opinion is nevertheless replete with factual findings. Rather, according to Sherow, relying on Delph Carpenter's July 1, 1931, letter to Clarence L. Ireland (now to be found in File Folder L5000.73 "Laramie River," Drawer 11, Denver: Colorado State Engineer's Office), Justice Van Devanter would take Wyoming's expert, one Ralph Meeker, Wyoming's consulting engineer, into his own home office in order to educe the information he needed to reach the conclusion he wanted. No reference was ever made in the final opinion to the factual record made by testimony received in Cheyenne and Greeley earlier in 1913.

23

Who Controls the Water? (1902–1917)

Many conflicts in American Constitutional history devolve into controversy over the locus of authority to regulate—the federal government, state governments, no government, i.e., purely private action protected by the Bill of Rights. A major decision of the United States Supreme Court in March 1917 would address that tension in the context of a controversy between American railroads and the American labor movement. The tension in the U.S. Supreme Court in that case would also cue up the question, swelling in the water law context, as to which governmental interest should control the water resource. Tyler reports, again citing Carpenter's diary, "on February 21, 1917, Carpenter learned that the Court had redocketed *Wyoming v. Colorado* for further argument on certain points and that the Supreme Court had decided to allow the federal government to enter the case." President Wilson's more proactive sense of the power of Congress under the Constitution's Commerce Clause was about to be vindicated in a Supreme Court decision that would be published the following month.[1]

In 1916, two compensation systems defined the earnings of railroad employees. One of those, comprising about 15 percent of workers, provided for an eight-hour day. The railroad employees union petitioned all the railroad companies proposing that the eight-hour work day, with overtime thereafter, apply nationally. The railroad employers refused. President Wilson proposed arbitration. The workers accepted, the railroads declined. A national railroad workers strike ensued.

Wilson, concerned about commercial disaster and public dislocation, asked Congress, first, that the eight-hour standard of work and wages be fixed by law, and second, that an official body be created to observe during a reasonable time the operation of the legislation. He also proposed that, if the eight-hour day increased the cost to railroad employers, the Interstate Commerce Commission be empowered to authorize rate increases. Congress responded.[2] The employers, unwilling to accept Congress' action, challenged its constitutional power. The U.S. District Court for the Western District of Missouri agreed with the employers.

On appeal to the U.S. Supreme Court, in a case argued January 8, 9, 10, 1917, Chief Justice White wrote the majority opinion reversing the District Court. White characterized the matter at issue thus: "did [Congress] have the power, in order to prevent the interruption of interstate commerce, to exert its will to supply the absence of a wage scale resulting from the disagreement as to wages between the employers and employees, and to make its will on that subject controlling for the limited period provided for?" White answered this in the affirmative, particularly given the injury to the public interest consequent of the work stoppage from the wage dispute. The individual rights of employer and employee are compromised, White stated, when the rights they enjoy are invested in activity which directly affects the public interest in *Wilson v. New*.[3] White spoke for the majority that expanded federal power under the commerce clause is needed in an emergency. Four dissenters, Associate Justices Day, Pitney, McReynolds and Van Devanter, took a contrary view.

Justice Day dissented on the basis that Congress' power to regulate interstate commerce was constrained by the due process clause of the Fifth Amendment. The enacted legislation, he argued, imposed upon the employers the cost of providing the same pay for eight hours work that they had previously paid for ten hours work, and that no compensation was proffered therefore. The enacted law did not carry President Wilson's recommendation that the ICC be authorized to raise rates to compensate for increased labor costs.

Justice Pitney dissented on the basis that the Constitution's interstate commerce clause authorized Congress to regulate commerce, but not "the internal affairs of the commerce carriers." In other words, the statute at issue didn't regulate interstate commerce. "This act, in my judgment, usurps the right of the owners of the railroads to manage their own properties, and is an attempt to control and manage the properties, rather than to regulate their use in commerce. In particular, it deprives the carriers of their right to agree with their employees as to the terms of employment." Pitney also found, as had Justice Day, that the law imposed costs uniquely on railroad employers without compensation. Justice Van Devanter concurred in Pitney's dissent. Justice McReynolds also dissented separately.

The majority's view of the Commerce Clause expressed in the *Wilson* case certainly concerned the interest of western states to avoid federal interference in state control of waters moving between states. Conveniently, after argument in January, but before publication of decision in the *Wilson* case, Van Devanter being fully aware of the majority's view with which he did not agree, the Court redocketed the Laramie River case. The Court also moved, on its own motion, to solicit the U.S. Department of the Interior's opinion, through the Justice Department, of the interstate issue in the pending interstate water case.

In the spring of 1917, Wyoming, Colorado, and the United States submitted new briefs in response to the Court's redocketing. Wyoming Attorney General Douglas Preston responded, filing a Supplemental Brief for the Wyoming parties on September 4, 1917. Colorado completed its brief in December and submitted it to the Court in anticipation of a January 1918 argument.

Professor Tyler observes, "What had begun as [Carpenter's] confident assurance that Colorado's geography and history would serve as a valid priority claim became, in Carpenter's mind, a confused mixture of contravening arguments involving state's rights, intrastate priorities, and federal powers. Carpenter began questioning the implications of interstate priorities determined by the Supreme Court, a process that eventually led him to center his thinking on the constitutional meaning of state sovereignty. This conversion emerged gradually during preparation for trial, but his early briefs reveal that he had difficulty breaking away from the priority principle that had so dominated Colorado and the West during the formative years."

The Court's invitation of the Justice Department into the case was peculiar. There is no record of any petition or motion by either of the parties, the Justice Department or the Department of the Interior to seek argument of the position of the United States. Justice Van Devanter had served as an assistant attorney general, representing the Interior Department in the McKinley and Roosevelt Administrations and had watched the federalization of western water interests through Senator Newlands' Reclamation agenda. He certainly understood the long-contested western water issue of federal versus state control of water supplies. The issue had been rampant before, during and after the 1902 adoption of the Reclamation Act.

In June 1897, President McKinley had agreed to a treaty of annexation with representatives of the Republic of Hawaii, and presented the treaty to the Senate for approval (as Cleveland had not), where it failed.[4] It was revived by the "Newlands Resolution," a joint resolution sponsored by then Nevada Congressman Francis G. Newlands and passed by both houses in summer 1898, in which Congress merely resolved to unilaterally "annex" the Republic of Hawaii, a clear and ambitious exercise of American power. Hawaiians acquiesced, accepting U.S. sovereignty.

Francis Griffith Newlands was a congressman, and later a Senator, from Nevada, who became Senator Francis Warren's counterfoil on western water development legislation. Born in Natchez, Adams County, Mississippi, on August 28, 1846, Newlands moved to Missouri, and later Illinois with his parents, who settled in Quincy, Illinois. He was privately tutored, and as a young adult moved to Washington, D.C., with his widowed mother. He attended Yale College and the Columbian College Law School (now George Washington University), Washington, D.C., some twenty years before Willis taught there as an adjunct. Admitted to the bar in 1869, Newlands moved to San Francisco in 1870, practiced law and married the daughter of the owner of the Comstock Lode, then moved to Nevada in 1888, about the time Willis moved to Wyoming. Continuing to practice law, Newlands was elected as a Democrat to the Fifty-third and four succeeding Congresses (March 4, 1893–March 3, 1903). He was elected as a Democrat to the United States Senate in 1902, reelected in 1908 and again in 1914 and served from March 4, 1903, until his death in 1917, while serving as chairman of the Senate Committee on Interstate Commerce.[5]

Theodore Roosevelt had won the 1904 general election in a landslide. He had campaigned throughout the west, notably appearing on May 25, 1903, in North Yakima, Washington, championing the Bureau of Reclamation's forthcoming irrigation project there. His administration was now in full swing. Stressing the nation's right to exercise its international police power, Roosevelt also advocated his Interior policy of conservation and other progressive ideas. Roosevelt relied heavily on his cabinet, including Secretary of War William Howard Taft, with whom Willis Van Devanter would become greatly involved. Roosevelt had earlier appointed Taft Civil Governor of the Philippines following its acquisition by the United States in the Spanish American War, and now relied upon the soft-spoken Taft to implement Roosevelt's "big stick" agenda. Taft's biographer, Henry Pringle, observes that "after the Spanish-American War [regard for Washington, D.C.] was to be different. Through the comic struggle, by the simple expedient of defeating a decrepit nation in an unnecessary war, Uncle Sam was to be accorded almost complete equality in the family of nations."

While expansion was afoot in the international sector, development of America's domestic conquests at the century's ending now also became active. One area of domestic development which would have caught Van Devanter's attention, while sitting at the Department of the Interior, was irrigation of the arid lands. The Western Plains of Van Devanter's experience in Wyoming would surely have come to mind, particularly as his primary political asset, Francis E. Warren was substantially involved, politically and through personal investment. According to William D. Rowley, "There were many irrigation bills afloat in Congressional committees. Senator Francis Warren of Wyoming sponsored many bills and was so vocal that he succeeded in making irrigation the leading western issue from 1899 to 1902, superseding the silver crusade."[6]

The emphasis of Warren's measures was retention of state control of water so as to permit free private enterprise to utilize the resource. This was within the western tradition of local control and private development. But it was also preferential to Warren's Wyoming investments. He, Senator Joseph Carey, Horace Plunkett, and William Irvine had founded the Wyoming Development Company in 1883, which developed the Wheatland Irrigation District, a Carey Act project. His legislative approach would, conveniently, also feather his nest. No doubt, Assistant Attorney General Van Devanter, always Warren's thinker and scribe, assisted in drafting much of Warren's proposed legislation.

But Warren was not the only politician to stake his reputation on irrigation legislation. Nevada's Congressman Francis C. Newlands was no lightweight and he had a different idea. His view, one consistent with that of progressives and originated perhaps by John Wesley Powell, was that interstate water bodies were not manageable by states alone, given their multi-state attributes.[7] The federal government, therefore, would be more capable of managing those interstate water bodies.

Newlands had become interested in development of irrigation even as early as his first election to Congress, in 1892.[8] While McKinley was still in office, Newlands had begun work with Frederick H. Newell, hydrographer of the Geological Survey, developing a national irrigation bill. Under Newlands' approach, public works would be funded from the sale of public lands, without explicit appropriations from Congress, a feature which affronted older, more senior committee chairmen. But upon Roosevelt's matriculation to the presidency, Newlands had a new ally.

Newlands, son-in-law of William Sharon, San Francisco–based principal investor in the Bank of California and the Comstock Lode in Nevada, who reached Congress through favoritism and wealth, had like Van Devanter, vacillated over "free silver" in the prior decade. From the Silver State, his position with the Free Silverites would have been secure if not for his broader view of the question. Their respective views of the West were instilled by somewhat common events. As Van Devanter had watched the bizarre winters of 1885–1887 demolish the Wyoming cattle industry, Newlands had watched what his biographer Rowley recounts as the "bitter 'White Winter' of 1890 that had virtually destroyed the open-range stock industry in Eastern Nevada."[9] Newlands was eleven years' Van Devanter's senior, but like Van Devanter, had argued before the U.S. Supreme Court at a young age, with all the self-recognition that may bring. Newlands, "a skilled lawyer with an eye to fine legal points and methods more characteristic of an administrator than a daring capitalist,"[10] was not altogether different from Van Devanter in style. But their view of the objective differed vastly. According to Rowley, Newlands thought in terms of "statesmanship" instead of "politics." Rowley says:

> When [Newlands] embraced a cause it was not enough that it pertain only to Nevada. He usually attached larger significance to irrigation as a plan for western American development or silver as the salvation of the American economic system. He strove to develop a style that came of age in the Progressive Era. He became comfortable in this new era where every political move and governmental program glowed with the light of idealism.[11]

By contrast, Van Devanter thought purely in terms of "politics," self promotion, and protection of vested interest, as apparently also did his principal, F.E. Warren.

Newlands' irrigation bill incorporating a significant federal involvement was debated in the House on January 30, 1901. Responding to cloaked accusations of failure to loyally represent his Nevada constituents, Newlands responded that the problem was the nature of the West's geography. He argued, as had Powell, that portions of interstate rivers in arid regions reside in several states, those in an adjoining state being beyond the jurisdiction and control of the home state. "Therefore, the national government 'dealing with the entire public domain regardless of state lines, is better equipped to carry out a comprehensive plan than a state....'" Newlands argued, pointing to the Geological Survey, that the national government is the appropriate manager of interstate water resources, as only it possesses the requisite scientific expertise to accomplish necessary projects.

Newlands' bill was stymied in the House by speaker Cannon and referred back to the Committee on Irrigation of Arid Lands on March 1, 1901. A similar bill introduced in the Senate the same day by Senator Henry C. Hansbrough of North Dakota, was also stalled, no doubt by Senatorial advocates of a state and private enterprise water bill. Senator Warren was chairman of the Senate Irrigation Committee. Senator Warren, perhaps on Van Devanter's advice, preferred his version, a sort of "State Engineer's Bill," organized around federal funding of facilities and state control of the water resource. This would allow private ownership of irrigation delivery systems, like the Wheatland Project in which Warren held an interest.

President McKinley had called the U.S. Senate into Special Session on February 23, 1901. It convened on March 4 and adjourned 5 days later. After his death, with Theodore Roosevelt now President, the 57th Congress convened for a "long session" on December 2, 1901. It would not adjourn until July 1 of the following year. The Newlands Reclamation Act[12] would not pass until the very near the end of this long session. Meanwhile, Newlands worked it diligently:

> In late December 1901, Newlands hosted a large dinner at the New Willard Hotel in Washington whose guests included both proponents and opponents of the national irrigation plan. Addresses were delivered by Secretary of Agriculture James Wilson, George H. Maxwell,

> executive chairman of the National Irrigation Association, Gifford Pinchot, head of the Forestry Bureau of the Department of Agriculture, Charles D. Walcott, director of the Geological Survey, and Newlands himself. The Washington *Times* reported that Representative Newlands explained his national approach to the project, but a rival bill, prepared by Senator Warren of Wyoming, provided for irrigation under state control. "A division of forces results upon the issue of Government and State control," reported the Times and concluded, "It is reported that a bill, which will probably be known as the 'compromise bill' is being prepared...."[13]

The following spring, during the long session while the respective irrigation bills were being advocated, Senator Warren was called to his wife's death bed. In his absence, Roosevelt "twisted arms" of western Republicans to accept a bill that, according to Rowley, "pointedly nationalized the building of western irrigation systems,"[14] while securing the support of Midwestern Republicans with the argument that the economic stimulus of agricultural production in western states would not compete with Midwestern farms. The legislation that the President advocated, and that which ultimately passed the Congress in June 1902 with President Roosevelt's endorsement, was structured from Senator Warren's bill but contained many of Newlands' provisions. The Act "passed the House with more nay votes and abstentions than yea votes." "Newlands later pointed out that more Democrats voted for the bill than Republicans, as he tried to make the point that the National Reclamation Act was more strongly supported by the Democratic Party than the Republican. Yet Roosevelt was crucial to its passage because it was he who convinced the key Republicans to switch their votes to the national bill that both he and Newlands supported."[15]

Newlands' approach had been opposed in part by eastern and Midwestern congressmen and senators who feared the development of marginal agricultural properties in the west at a significant cost to the national government. Newlands merely rebutted that making irrigation available to arid western lands continued the governmental policy of administering the public domain as a great trust for the settlement and development of the nation. Newlands won; Warren lost.

Upon completion of the 57th Congress in July 1902, its having adopted the Reclamation Act in June, Newlands headed home to Nevada and to run for the Senate. During the fall campaign, Theodore Roosevelt "trumpeted throughout the West his party's role in achieving national reclamation and his own key efforts." Newlands was elected Senator, and Roosevelt was reelected President. This time, Wyoming voted Republican, for Roosevelt.

Although Francis Warren was thought to have been the "loser in his promotion of greater state control and private enterprise"[16] in the Reclamation Act debate the previous summer, he would exact a consolation prize from President Roosevelt soon thereafter: a seat on the Eighth Circuit Court of Appeals for his preferred and loyal friend, then Assistant Attorney General Willis Van Devanter, created by a "private act" tucked into the Cattle Contagious Disease Act of 1903.[17]

24

Development Under the Reclamation Act and Return to Court (1905–1922)

By summer of 1905, the first projects began to be developed under the Reclamation Act, the first, of course, to be built in now-Senator Newland's home state, on the Truckee River. Rowley tells us that, on Saturday, June 17, 1905, at a consecration/dedication ceremony for the new Derby Dam on the Truckee River, the dam designed to divert water for the irrigation of the desert, "almost 200 from all over the nation, filed from the passenger cars. They included members of the House and Senate Irrigation Committees, the governor of California, local citizens, and Nevada senators Newlands and George S. Nixon, as well as the now retired and aging Senator William M. Stewart. Others among them were Senators Francis E. Warren of Wyoming, Henry C. Hansbrough of North Dakota, Fred Dubois of Idaho, Thomas Kearns of Utah, Charles H. Dietrich of Nebraska, and Charles W. Fulton of Oregon."[1]

> After his speech [that day], Newlands presented Congressman F.W. Mondell of Wyoming, who compared the present occasion to celebrate the diversion of water from the Truckee with a gathering on the banks of the Nile more than six thousand years ago for the dedication of similar works built under governmental auspices that made fertile a valley for a vast population through the ages. The completion of this diversion dam, said Mondell, represented the first fruits of western people to secure the aid of the general government in the construction of works so mighty in their character as to be beyond the possibility of private enterprise. It was appropriate that this first work occurred in Nevada, a state represented by Newlands, "who has always been earnest, faithful, forceful and effective in bringing about the recognition of the national character of this work and in securing the legislation which made this construction possible. Whatever other men have done," Mondell said, "no other man in the country did more than Senator Newlands to make possible these works you find here now."

Senator Warren must have grimaced that his Wyoming crony would praise the new Nevada Senator. Several weeks later, Senator Newlands spoke at a banquet of a Congressional Irrigation Committee in Sheridan, Wyoming, on June 30, 1905. He stressed the Democratic Party's role in passage of the Reclamation bill, but also deferred to Roosevelt's assistance. Senator Warren, Congressman Mondell and then Appeals Court Judge Van Devanter must have bristled, even though now Van Devanter was by then home in Cheyenne, a Roosevelt appointee.

By 1917, Newlands was now proposing a permanent commission to oversee, plan, authorize, and implement river development in aspects of irrigation, dam building, flood control, navigation, forest and soil conservation, and hydroelectric power. This broad proposal would structure significant power in a federally appointed commission. Newlands found significant opposition to the proposal, both from the Corps of Engineers in the War Department and the Reclamation Service in the Interior Department, whose respective authorities would be threatened by centralized water planning and project selection, and also from powerful congressmen who feared loss of their congressional prerogative to select and obtain congressional authorization to fund federal water projects in their states. And even though a Democratic majority now prevailed in Congress, the political notion of strong federal government authority over river systems remained anathema to political constituents in the West. Both the European military theater, and congressional concern for its funding distracted Congress from development of the American interior in any case.

But Newlands accomplished his agenda in an amendment to the Rivers and Harbors Bill of 1917 which Congress adopted in the summer of 1917. Rowley reports that "Newlands took satisfaction in these late years of his life that one of his primary visions might be fulfilled and spoke with great hope for this measure throughout the fall of 1917 as being the key that would link the nation together in a vast web of production, distribution, and efficient use of natural resources...." But Newlands' satisfaction was short lived, as President Wilson never got around to appointing the commission. The central water planning objective had lost its spokesman. Newlands' amendment to the Rivers and Harbors Act would be repealed by the Water Power Act of 1920.

As chairman of the Wyoming G.O.P. back in 1894, Van Devanter had, according to Holsinger, nominated Congressman Mondell, then the ex-mayor of Newcastle, Wyoming, as the Republican candidate for Congress. Congressman Mondell, with whom Van Devanter had worked as early as 1889–90 in development of the Wyoming State Constitution, had advocated a Tenth Amendment basis for state sovereignty over western streams as soon as they were accepted as states in the Republic during the debate on the 1902 Newlands Act, arguing that the congressional enactments acts of July 26, 1866, July 9, 1870, and March 3, 1877, represented definitive congressional recognition of state control over the appropriation and distribution of water, a position consistent with Senator Warren's. The Newlands Act, or Reclamation Act, had now been in place for 15 years, but now Senator Newlands was not strong enough to support it. He died, at 69, in Washington, D.C., on Christmas Eve, 1917.

On March 6, 1917, the Court ordered a re-argument of the cause in Wyoming v. Colorado, requesting that counsel direct their attention specifically to certain matters identified in the Order and to notify the Attorney General of the reargument. On May 18, Colorado Attorney General Hubbard, gave notice to the U.S. Attorney General Thomas W. Gregory that Colorado would move on June 4, 1917, that the case be set down for hearing and fixing a schedule for briefing.

Leslie Hubbard, Attorney General for Colorado, Platt Rogers, and previous Attorney General Fred Farrar, now of Counsel to Colorado, filed two Supplemental

Briefs on behalf of Defendants (Vol. I, "The Law," Vol. II, "The Facts") on October 19, 1917, showing Delph E. Carpenter, attorney for Greeley-Poudre Irrigation District, and Julius Gunter, attorney for Laramie-Poudre Reservoir and Irrigation District.

The United States filed a 174-page Brief for the United States on December 22, 1917. Although originally captioned No. 5 Original, the 5 was overstamped as No. 3 original. The Brief was signed by John W. Davis, Solicitor General, Francis Kearful, Assistant Attorney General, and John F. Truesdell and Ethelbert Ward, Special Assistants to the Attorney General. In the Brief, the United States argued, "Water rights now vested in others derive their existence, like titles to land, from the acts of Congress. All interests in water not so granted necessarily remain in the United States. The acts grant nothing to the States, and the mere creation of a State could not work a change of this ownership or control." The Brief also argued that

> the power of the United States to use the water rights belonging to it or to permit their use by others was not controlled by territorial lines fixed or changing, and is not controlled by State lines. Ownership of a water right necessarily includes the ownership of the right to use water at a particular place, together with the right to have the water flow down to that place uninterfered with by persons above. The Federal Government's grantees of water rights take title to those rights with all their incidents, as vested rights in real property, protected by the Fourteenth Amendment and the laws of Congress. Their rights can only be divested by due process of law and must be respected until so divested. The States, either as the ultimate owners of property within their borders (except that belonging to the United States) or otherwise, own only such water rights as have been granted by the United States to them or to others for use on lands within their borders.

John W. Davis was a conservative Democrat appointed as Solicitor General by Woodrow Wilson in 1913. He would become the Democratic Party's compromise candidate to run against Calvin Coolidge in 1924 and would be resoundingly defeated. Kearful would be drummed out of the Justice Department by Attorney General A. Mitchell Palmer in 1919, Kearful having aggressively prosecuted principals in the Southern Pacific Railroad Company.

On January 5, 1918, Colorado Attorney General Leslie Hubbard filed a Brief in Answer to the Brief of the United States. Delph Carpenter was on the brief as attorney for the Greeley-Poudre Irrigation District, Julius Gunter as attorney for the Laramie-Poudre Reservoir and Irrigation District, and Platt Rogers, Fred Farrar and Ralph Kerwin were of Counsel to the Attorney General. It was captioned for the October term 1917. They argued: "If the Government intends in the carrying out of its reclamation projects or in the use of water on its lands to respect the rights of prior appropriators, it is a matter of no practical importance to it whether the source of title to water by appropriation is the general Government or the State in which the Government plans are carried out or the Government lands may lie." The brief pointed out that the United States hadn't asserted any claim of ownership to interstate streams in the *Kansas v. Colorado* case, and that the States there would have had no justiciable interest in that case were it not for their ownership and jurisdiction over the water at controversy. Then it cited Justice Holmes' decision in *Bean v. Morris* to the effect that the states involved there, including incidentally Wyoming, had "legislative power over" the stream at issue. The brief then relied on the "equal footing doctrine," that all new states come into the union on the same footing as the original thirteen, i.e., owning their water resources. Perhaps offering a sop to Justice Van Devanter, the brief further mentions that the position advocated by the United States had never been proffered by the Land Department of the Department of the Interior, the Colorado Attorney General being fully aware that Van Devanter had served as that agency's Assistant Attorney General. The argument cites a December 1900 case, *New Bear Valley Ir. Co. v. Robert*[2] likely written by Assistant Attorney General Van Devanter, and a Supreme Court decision, *Utah Light & Power Co. v. United States*,[3] written by the same Van Devanter, now a Supreme Court justice, implying the contrary. Ultimately, the brief returned to the choice between relying on equitable apportionment (as had Justices Brewer and White in *Kansas v. Colorado*) or competing several state water appropriations as the basis for resolving interstate water claims.

When arguments were heard in the Laramie River case in January 2018, only the 1907 case of *Kansas v. Colorado* offered any legal foundation for the appropriate consideration of such cases. States operated primarily on a basis of "premeditated self-interest." They assumed that conflicts would end up on the Supreme Court. But no water case had yet been presented where both states claimed the same domestic law of water, in this case the prior appropriation doctrine. At the Supreme Court hearing in Washington on January 9, 1918, Colorado Attorney General Hubbard and his predecessor Fred Farrar argued the facts. The next day, Carpenter argued the law. The hearing did not go well for Colorado. Tyler reports that Carpenter wrote to his diary on January 10 and 11, 1918, that he was "showered with questions" by the justices. He thought that Wyoming's counsel had "grossly misstated the facts." And he became bitter, believing that his argument had become "badly broken." Sherow reports that, after argument was completed, Wyoming's consulting engineer, Ralph Meeker, who had listened to oral argument, stayed in Washington "'as the confidential adviser of Van Devanter' in the areas of hydrology and engineering," citing Delph Carpenter's July 1, 1931, letter to Clarence L. Ireland.[4]

Out West, the League of the Southwest continued to meet. Its purpose was to promote development of irrigated croplands in the southwest, particularly along the Colorado River. After its San Diego meeting, it met again in Tucson, Arizona, in January 1918, and then again in Salt Lake City in January 1919 to consider Secretary of Interior Franklin K. Lane's proposal to reclaim four million acres of land in the Colorado River Basin for World War I veterans and other interested persons. Professor Tyler summarized issues:

> Here, then, was the central issue for the Colorado River basin states. Although still not an official member of the League [of the Southwest], Colorado had called attention [at the Colorado River States Salt Lake City meeting, January 1919] to the threat to future development in the upper basin states if federally constructed works were placed in the lower Colorado River. Because of his experience with Nebraska and Wyoming over the issue of interstate priorities, Carpenter understood how dam construction on the lower Colorado River would obligate Colorado to future water deliveries. He also understood that if the threatened levees broke again on the lower Colorado, the lower basin states would quickly find federal agencies interested in controlling western rivers, regardless of upper basin pleas for equity. For these reasons, he was pleased by the outcome of events that transpired at the Salt Lake City gathering.

At that meeting, the advocates of immediate reservoir construction on the lower reaches of the Colorado River urged a united effort to secure federal aid, but upper basin representatives objected.

When the states met again on August 25–27, 1920, in the Colorado Senate Chambers in Denver, Delph Carpenter proposed the idea of an interstate compact. The idea had first been presented to Colorado's Governor Oliver Shoup, and was proffered to the states by Carpenter at the governor's request. By now, Carpenter was suffering from anticipation about what the Supreme Court might write regarding priorities on the Laramie, and fearing the same on the Colorado.

Nationally, exhaustion from involvement in World War I and the lapse of the progressive momentum laid down an environment where the Republican establishment could regain its control of the White House. The economic stimulus of involvement in war had played out. Wilson's grand strategy of international rationalism through the League of Nations had gone funk. Major strikes in meatpacking and steel industries, race riots in Chicago and terrorist attacks on Wall Street upset the nation. Return to the predictable was imminent. And although President Wilson won the Nobel Prize for Peace in 1919, he suffered a cerebral hemorrhage on September 25, 1919, after a speech in Pueblo, Colorado, never fully recovering, and completing the remaining thirty months of his presidency in convalescence and retirement.

Former President Theodore Roosevelt would have been the probable man for the Republican Party to have turned to in the 1920 election. But his health had failed after his South American excursion to the Amazon in 1918, as described in Candice Millard's *The River of Doubt: Theodore Roosevelt's Darkest Journey*. He died in January the following year. There being no clear Progressive candidate, the Party went for a traditional Ohio Republican, newspaper publisher and U.S. Senator Warren G. Harding, who chose Calvin Coolidge as his running mate. The Democrats also chose a publisher, Governor James M. Cox, as their candidate, who chose New York Governor Franklin D. Roosevelt as his vice-presidential running mate. Harding ran against the Wilson record and won by a landslide. All the Colorado River states voted for Harding. All the northwest and plains states voted for Harding. All the Ohio Valley states voted for Harding. New York and all the New England states voted for Harding. Only Kentucky, Virginia, and the deep south voted for Cox.

The 66th Congress, winding up during the fall 1920 campaign, was held by a Republican majority in both houses of Congress (49 Republican, 47 Democratic in the Senate, 240 Republican, 192 Democratic in the House). The 1920 general election significantly increased the hold of the Republican congressional majority with the new 67th Congress now becoming composed of 59 Republicans and 37 Democrats and the House becoming composed of 302 Republicans and 131 Democrats. Once in office, Harding handed over the keys to the Republican Congress. Harding's victory would significantly affect the history of conservative Supreme Court jurisprudence and sway the development of western water law.

The United States filed a Brief (Reargument 1922) on January 9, 1922. The Brief was captioned "No. 3 Original—In Equity" and was signed by James Beck,

Solicitor General, William D. Riter, Assistant Attorney General, and John F. Truesdell, Special Assistant to the Attorney General. The brief, though extensive, made no new argument. Justice Van Devanter's later, 1922, opinion in *Wyoming v. Colorado* declares that the United States' position was advocated at a 1918 hearing by Solicitor General John William Davis. But Colorado counsel Carpenter reported to his diary on January 10 that the solicitor for the Bureau of Reclamation argued the case for the United States. The lawyer to whom Mr. Carpenter was likely referring may have been Mr. Truesdell, who was not a member of the Justice Department but worked for the Department of the Interior. In his final opinion, Justice Van Devanter also presented that U.S.' arguments were made by Assistant Attorney General William D. Riter. Riter was appointed an Assistant Attorney General on April 5, 1921, by President Harding, serving then under Attorney General Harry Daugherty. Van Devanter also represented that U.S. Solicitor General James M. Beck joined Mr. Riter on the briefs. Mr. Beck was also appointed to his position as Solicitor General in 1921 by President Harding.

By February 1922, Van Devanter was seeking those authorities from the Interior Department that he would need to draft the opinion he wanted, soliciting them from Solicitor Edwin Booth. A typewritten cover letter from the solicitor dated February 13, 1922, rests now in Van Devanter's Supreme Court papers in the Library of Congress' Manuscript Collection, as do the originals of all the following correspondence.

> Dear Mr. Justice, In conformity with my conversation of even date herewith with you over the telephone, I am enclosing the circulars in relation to suggestions to homesteaders and also general reclamation circular. These circulars are the last that have been issued. However, a revision of the circular No. 541 is now in press and will be republished and brought up to date in a very few days at which time I will gladly see that one is mailed to you. Trusting that these comprise the circulars which you desire....[5]

Circular No. 541 (48 L.D. 471) addresses *inter alia* the exemption of irrigable lands from homestead entry.

When Justice Van Devanter later published his opinion on June 5, 1922, he included a phrase alluding to a "possible interest in some of the question" on the part of the United States:

> As the United States appeared to have a possible interest in some of the question, the court also directed that the suit be called to the attention of the Attorney General; and by the court's leave, a representative of the United States participated in the subsequent hearings.[6]

The Justice had again used his position and authority to advance the political interest of his non-judicial colleagues, his family and friends from Wyoming.

Associate Justice Van Devanter never clearly expressed his personal view on this basic question of American federalism, as he played his cards close to his chest. As both a friend, confidant and aide of Senator Warren, Van Devanter may well have assisted in the development of Senator Warren's thinking in preparation of his Reclamation bill. Likewise, his longstanding relationship with Representative Mondell would suggest the same. His service in the legal staff of the Department of the Interior in the Roosevelt administration at the time the bill was under consideration would suggest that his then client loyalty should have caused him to support the federal interest view espoused by Newlands and Roosevelt. Now, he would have a means by which to establish an opposite U.S. Supreme Court view on the pregnant question.

The dispute over Laramie River water, originally juxtaposed between the political power of senior, well placed Wyoming politicians and jurists and weaker Colorado land developers, had now metamorphosed into a policy-determining stratagem within the larger paradigm of the management of western water supplies. Self interest, as manifest in the prior appropriation doctrine, local (state) control and federal subsidy manipulated by congressional seniority, pitted against the public interest, as manifest in equitable apportionment and integrated development. And the unelected man in control of the driving case was awaiting his moment.

More than three years had now transpired since the 1918 oral argument in the Laramie River case with no judicial resolution of the dispute. It is unclear why no judicial action had been taken before now. There is no record of the case having been formally assigned to Justice Van Devanter, nor direct information regarding the means by which cases were assigned, other than the tradition of the Court that the Chief Justice is responsible for naming the author in conference following oral argument. Given Chief Justice White's comments, quoted by Professor Tyler, regarding Carpenter's arguments at the January 1918 oral argument, that Colorado's argument was "one of the most interesting arguments he had heard in many years," it is possible that the then Chief merely wanted to retain the case for himself. He had joined Justice Brewer's opinion in *Kansas v. Colorado* in 1907. The late Chief Justice may have viewed the Laramie River case differently than did Van Devanter. The role of equitable apportionment in interstate water distribution must have appealed to him. It was in a way akin to the reasonableness standard White had fashioned in the Trust Cases. And his perspective may have been substantially different than Van Devanter's. Riparianism's "reasonable use" component would have squared with his reasonable antitrust thinking from the Trust Cases, and the equitable apportionment paradigm implemented in *Kansas v. Colorado*. The water law to which Chief Justice White would have been exposed in his home state of Georgia would have been riparianism, with its reasonable use attribute, not appropriationism. And White's sense of the integral rights of States may have been enhanced by his Civil War experience and his loyalty to the Confederacy.

White must certainly have known of Van Devanter's loyalty to Wyoming and his political affiliations, as Van Devanter's appointment to the Court had been secured by the political exactions of Senate Republicans in the very same political scene in 1911 as had Chief Justice White's Senate confirmation. But Van Devanter knew now that White's view, and knowledge of Van Devanter's biased interest in the case, no longer mattered. Chief Justice White was now gone, replaced by President Harding's appointment, Chief Justice William Taft. It is impossible to know whether Van Devanter intentionally waited White out. More probably Van Devanter had merely waited for an opportunity to present itself when few would be watching him act with so little principle.

Throughout the spring and summer of 1921, the League of the Southwest and California's irrigation districts had pushed the development of irrigated agriculture in the West. On August 19, the strongly Republican 67th Congress passed the bill authorizing the Colorado River basin states to negotiate a compromise on the Colorado River providing for "equitable division and apportionment ... of the water supply of the Colorado River and of the streams tributary thereto."[7]

Colorado's counsel in the Laramie River case, Delph Carpenter, was ready to compromise on the Colorado. According to Professor Tyler, "In light of [Carpenter's] experience with Wyoming, and the forthcoming negotiations with the Colorado River Basin states, the old jurisdiction of origin priority no longer seemed tenable." Van Devanter's old Wyoming contact, Elwood Mead, with whom he had worked in the background of the Wyoming constitutional convention in 1888, was by now substantially involved in the irrigation movement and acknowledged as "an international consultant in irrigation."

In its earlier filed brief, the United States had argued that the case should be decided on the basis of federal law, the law applicable to the United States' grant of statehood to the individual states, not the substantive law of the states. The bases for this contention had included (1) the assertion that the substantive rights involved originated from U.S. sovereignty and only devolved to state administration from the central, national government; (2) the effect of the outcome of the litigation on "the public interests and governmental policies of the United States" (land policy with respect to the "vast areas of land still belonging to the United States," irrigation policy with respect to the aridity of that land and the essentiality of irrigation to give that land value, reclamation policy "which depends upon federal use of both land and water and often upon federal use of interstate streams," and federal Indian policy); and (3) the assertion that federal rights and responsibilities are immune from state regulatory authority. In his 1922 opinion, Associate Justice Van Devanter would dismiss the United States' argument, finding that the United States had acquiesced to the law being practiced in the federal territories when statehood occurred, and recognized the same in later adopted federal statutes. On this basis, Van Devanter applied state law as the basis for his decision and dismissed the United States' interest arising out of its federal land holdings. Without either of the parties having raised the issue, Van Devanter had set up and dismissed the issue of federal interest in water.

> Here the complaining State is not seeking to impose a policy of her choosing on the other State, but to have the common policy which each enforces within her limits applied in determining their relative rights in the interstate stream. Nor is the United States seeking to impose a policy of its choosing on either State. All that it has done has been to recognize and give its sanction to the policy which each has adopted. Whether its land holdings would enable it to go further we need not consider. And here the complaining State is not seeking to interfere with a diversion which has long been practiced and under which much reclamation has been effected, but to prevent a proposed diversion for the benefit of lands as yet unreclaimed.[8]

Justice Van Devanter also found that the Reclamation Act had not changed the substantive law applicable to interstate streams in the West. "Congress was solicitous that all questions respecting interstate streams thought to be involved in that litigation [*Kansas v. Colorado*] should be left to judicial determination unaffected by the act—in other words, that the matter be left just as it was before."[9] The reasons why Justice Van Devanter solicited the United States' view on the Wyoming-Colorado controversy over the Laramie, and then merely dismissed it five years later, would play out in the water politics of the West.

25

Judicial Harmony (1922)

By early January 1922, Justice Van Devanter began to perfect his "affectionate" relationship with Chief Justice Taft, relying on their common background, education, experience, loyalty to the Republican Party, its objectives, and agenda. The Chief Justice asked for Van Devanter's discrete communication regarding "private meetings"[1] and Van Devanter began to instill in the Chief a respect for his own knowledge and expertise about western water. On January 16, 1922, Taft wrote to Justice Van Devanter, "Thank you for sending the fine photographs of instances of dam work done by the National Reclamation Service. I helped to open the Gunnison tunnel, and took a good deal of interest in this kind of work when I was in office. Wm. H. Taft."[2]

On January 25, the Chief again asked for Van Devanter's opinion drafting assistance. "Dear Justice Van Devanter, I am sincerely indebted to you for the trouble you have taken with my opinion."[3] The tone of the Chief's opinion in *Bailey v. Drexel Furniture Company*,[4] published later in the spring, on May 15, suggests Van Devanter's hand. Van Devanter substantively joined Taft for the majority, holding that a federal tax imposed on mines and factories that hired children was unconstitutional, as the protection of workers' health was reserved to the states by the Tenth Amendment. The case would be thought by Progressives as an accumulation of judicial authority to limit the purposes for which Congress may exercise its legislative power. The Court could thus question Congress' legislative motive, as well as Congress' constitutional authorization. Judicial motive could be interposed for Congress' motive. And social problems that had previously been addressed by state legislatures could not be reached by Congress because, in the conservative court's view, the 14th Amendment precluded federal interference with wealth accumulation.[5]

The Chief continued seeking Van Devanter's help and began to espouse his theory of unity on the Court.[6] In 1920, before Taft was appointed to the Court by Harding, a full 30 percent of cases were published with dissenting views, with a full 21 percent in 1921, according to Drew Noble Lanier in his *Of Time and Judicial Behavior: United States Supreme Court Agenda-Setting and Decision-Making, 1888–1997*.[7] Chief Justice Taft disliked dissenting opinions, a dislike that ran even deeper than his dislike for liberal opinions, like those later authored by Justices Holmes, Brandeis or Stone. His December 26, 1921, handwritten note to Justice Van Devanter said,

> Most dissents, elaborated, are a form of egotism. They don't do any good, and only weaken the prestige of the Court. It is much more important what the Court thinks than what any one thinks, not that sense of proportion is not present in the minds of some of our brethren. As to B [Brandeis], that sense is not lacking but his ultimate purpose is to break down the prestige of the Court. Merry Xmas and a Happy New year to you and yours, Sincerely yours, Wm. H. Taft.

According to Pringle, Taft measured potential jurists under the test whether they would agree with other members of the Court.[8] Taft was looking for "good fellows." These were jurists who, in Chief Justice Taft's mind, would not come forward with embarrassing or dissenting views. They aided the Court's stature, Taft conceived, through its unanimity. And they maintained a fairly strict construction of the U.S. Constitution—if it served their conservatism. Van Devanter was clearly a "good fellow."

Taft was convinced that public knowledge of differences among the justices on important constitutional questions would impair the Court's prestige and influence. He considered it the Chief Justice's responsibility to shepherd the justices into unanimous decisions. He would use his personal charm and good humor to accomplish this.

Throughout his administrative career, Taft had been loyal to his old classmates. Pringle says that Cincinnati law students found a warm welcome when they visited a courtroom where Taft later presided.[9] As an Ohio Superior Court Judge, Taft "threw a judicial fee into the lap of his boyhood friend, Rufus B. Smith, by naming him special master to assess the damages" in a case where Taft granted an injunction.[10] When he became Secretary of War, Taft "called upon classmates or other Yale men as assistants. He also got jobs for them on the federal payroll."[11] The Chief Justice had always valued being a member of the power-set, those men who developed and maintained power because of their inclusion in the accepted group. Van Devanter had said likewise to his friend M.C. Barrow, then Chief Clerk of the Wyoming State House of Representatives on September 4, 1894. "I always endeavor to be true to my friends, and for the same reason I endeavor to be true to my party."[12]

Taft and Van Devanter began to work together closely. Taft was just the kind of person, as had been Senator F.E. Warren, with unquestioning loyalty and unsophisticated trust in associates, that Van Devanter had great experience in guiding and manipulating. Henry J. Abraham observed, "The two men became close personal allies on the high bench—Taft regarded him as his favorite colleague—notwithstanding Van Devanter's far more pronounced intellectual conservatism."[13] After having served two years as Chief, Taft would say, "my mainstay in the court is Van Devanter," and nearing the end of his stay at the Court Taft would regard Van Devanter as "an unending joy and comfort."

Van Devanter and Taft had reason to think alike. They had attended the same law school, where Van Devanter trailed by two years. Taft was loyal to his alma mater, and to his law school chums. Given Taft's and Van Devanter's common legal training, Republican Party loyalty, judicial careers, and many years of acquaintance, it is not surprising that the two had a very similar view of the law, a view that permitted them, as educated and privileged members of a judicial aristocracy, to pronounce what the law is. Pringle says "Taft worshipped the law; no understanding of him is possible without appreciation of that fact. The fallacy in his philosophy lies, of course, in the fact that there is no such thing as 'the law.' It is a mass of opinion, formulated by men throughout the centuries, and is constantly being altered. What Taft really did was to revere the law, as he understood it, himself, or as judges with whom he agreed had interpreted it."[14] Taft had appointed Justice Van Devanter to the Court in 1911, perhaps only out of necessity to obtain his primary objective of naming White as chief, and to mollify competing political interests in the Senate, but by now Taft owned the Van Devanter appointment.

Taft's and Van Devanter's political views were much in tandem. A true Republican, Taft was loyal to the corporate structure, even though he was aware of its political ramifications. Although in 1910 Taft had stood a "little to the left of center,"[15] by 1922, he had returned to the true conservatism of his boyhood Ohio upbringing. Van Devanter stood right beside him. Pringle quotes Taft's War Secretary Diaries: "I believe myself to be as conservative as anyone within this company." "I believe that in connection with personal liberty, the right of personal property is the basis of all our material progress in the development of mankind and that any change in our social and political system which impairs the right of private property and materially diminishes the motive for the accumulation of capital by one individual is a blow at our whole civilization."[16] Van Devanter would have certainly agreed. Sumner's lectures back at law school in Cincinnati had forever purchased the political commitments of both gentlemen.

Taft, of course, recognized that it was not always popular to be associated with big money and big corporations. He knew that the voting public did not favor politicians receiving large financial contributions from the corporate and banking sector, and therefore tried to minimize them, within reason given his political needs.[17] As President, he also appreciated the political ramifications of placing too many corporation lawyers in his cabinet—but did so anyway. Pringle quotes Taft's February 23, 1909, letter to William Rockwell Nelson of Kansas City, "I am going to be criticized for putting corporation lawyers into my Cabinet. I think I shall have in the Cabinet five as good lawyers [sic] as there are in the country, and being good first class lawyers they have had a good deal of corporate employment."[18]

Another arena in which Willis Van Devanter was a helpmate to the chief justice was the area of judicial procedure and administration. Alpheus Thomas Mason mentions in his article "William Howard Taft: President by Chance, Chief Justice by Choice" that "also essential to leadership is familiarity with technical matters of procedure and jurisdiction. On this score, Hughes ranks high. Taft on the other hand, confessed inadequacy. In comparison, Justice Van Devanter's knowledge of authorities, procedure and practice made the Chief Justice 'feel quite small.' Van Devanter's assistance was invaluable. Keeping the Court 'consistent with itself' is however, but a single aspect of the job of guiding and directing.'"[19]

Chief Justice Taft also enlisted Associate Justice Van Devanter in his long desired objective of expanding the federal judicial ranks and further limiting the Supreme Court's jurisdiction by greater reliance upon the certiorari writ. The two began to work the congressional wings of the Capitol together, through February and March of 1922, on legislation to accomplish that objective.[20]

Senator Cummins, chairman of the Senate Judiciary Committee, had first requested that Taft become involved, whereupon Taft named Associate Justices Van Devanter, Day, and McReynolds to develop a bill and work the Congress.[21] At the drafting committee's request, Taft also participated. The apolitical tradition of the Court, at least as practiced through the prior century, thus broken, the opportunity for open communication between individual members of the Congress and Court became permissive under Chief Justice Taft's administration. Both institutions being soundly conservative and controlled by the same partisan interests, the power of both was enhanced. For Taft, this all fit with his view of loyalty to party, country and the Court, of which the latter's power and efficiency he wanted to enhance.

As the years had passed, the Supreme Court's docket had become ever more crowded. New Chief Justice Taft believed that the problem could be resolved by greater reliance on the vehicle of *certiorari*,[22] a common law approach used by Van Devanter with some aplomb when writing for Secretary of the Interior Bliss in the late 1890s. That shift would, however, require congressional action to effect it in the case of the Supreme Court. Chief Justice White had been of the opinion that neither he nor his colleagues should petition the Congress. Taft, however, saw no barrier to approaching Congress.

"It was vital," Taft said when he began his legislative agenda on the Supreme Court's jurisdictional changes, "that cases before the court be reduced without limiting the function of pronouncing 'the last word on every important issue under the Constitution and statues of the United States.' A Supreme Court, on the other hand, should not be a tribunal obligated to weigh justice among contesting parties." The Judges' Bill would "limit cases coming from the Circuit Courts of Appeals, the Court of Appeals of the District of Columbia, and all cases from the Court of Claims to only those which the court would accept by certiorari. Only actions from state supreme courts in which the constitutional validity of a state statute had been questioned or sustained would remain as actions 'as of right' in the Supreme Court."

Pringle reports "Taft and his brother justices lobbied vigorously and openly for the bill. Chief Justice Taft reported to his brother later in 1925 when the bill became law that 'Van Devanter, McReynolds and I spent two full days at the Capitol, and Van and I one full day more [in 1922] to get the bill through.'"

While the legislative process moved along, Van Devanter began writing his opinion in *Wyoming v. Colorado* at his home office in Justice Brewer's prior living quarters on 16th Street. The Court was still operating from the cramped quarters in the Old Senate Chamber in the Capitol Building, where it had heard arguments in *Wyoming v. Colorado*. The Court operated from those premises from 1860 until 1935.

It seems a mystery why Colorado counsel had not complained earlier of judicial conflict or bias, or otherwise move the Court to remove Justice Van Devanter from consideration of the case. There are several possible explanations: first, albeit improbable, is that the Coloradans did not know of Van Devanter's prior associations and conflict; second, that there was no alternative but for the Coloradans to go along, given the Court's makeup; third, that Justice Van Devanter was sufficiently discrete, not showing his hand, so that there was no demonstrable basis for seeking that he stand aside; or fourth, that the Coloradans expected that Van Devanter would bend over backward in favor of Defendant Colorado, on the basis of justice

Associate Justice Willis Van Devanter wrote his opinion in *Wyoming v. Colorado* in his third floor study in this 16th Street home in Washington, D.C., previously the home of Justice Brewer, of Kansas, who authored the opinion in *Kansas v. Colorado* in the same study (author's photograph, 2011).

and fairness, as Kansan Brewer had done with respect to his home state in *Kansas v. Colorado* in 1907. Citing Carpenter's July 1, 1931, letter to then Colorado Attorney General Clarence L. Ireland,[23] James Sherow observed:

> The Colorado attorneys knew they could not do much about what surely amounted to a conflict of interest. The problem for them lay in the writing of the *Kansas v. Colorado* decision by Justice Brewer. Brewer was a former Kansan, and he had written a decision in most respects favorable to Colorado interests. Colorado attorneys entertained the notion of requesting that someone else other than Justice Van Devanter write the opinion but felt such a request "bad policy" in light of the precedent established by Justice Brewer. So, from 1917 to 1922, a time which included three arguments before the Court, the Colorado attorneys waited anxiously for the Court's opinion.

Although Associate Justice Van Devanter now lived in Brewer's residence, and wrote from the same third floor library office on 16th Street, the Coloradans unfortunately would not be able to rely on the same judicial deference as Brewer had shown.

26

Natural Resource or Interstate Commerce? (1921–1923)

During the winter of 1921 and spring of 1922, while Justice Van Devanter was writing his opinion in *Wyoming v. Colorado*, he was hearing reargument on another interstate case within the Court's original jurisdiction involving interstate claims, this time to natural gas rather than water. Pennsylvania and Ohio plaintiffs were proprietors of public institutions delivering natural gas to private consumers. West Virginia planned to limit export by pipeline of natural gas harvested and refined within the state to customers in Pennsylvania and Ohio. The case was originally argued on December 8, 9, 1921, and reargued on February 28 and March 1, 1922. It was again reargued on April 20, 1923. Justice Van Devanter issued an opinion in the next term, on June 11, 1923, *Pennsylvania and Ohio v. West Virginia*,[24] finding a justiciable controversy and holding for the plaintiff states relying on the justification that the commerce clause precluded West Virginia's interference with interstate commerce. Justices Holmes, McReynolds and Brandeis dissented. Another reargument was permitted on November 20, 1923, but it had no effect on the earlier, June 11, 1923, decision. The Court's opinion was restated in December 3, 1923. Justices Holmes, McReynolds and Brandeis renewed their dissents.

Although run between states in a pipeline, rather than a natural water course, what Van Devanter had to say about natural gas could well have been said about the Laramie River, although Van Devanter had not. The West Virginia legislature had passed a law giving preference in sale of natural gas to residents of that state, rather than to those of Pennsylvania to which the pipeline ran. Van Devanter ruled that the state law interfered with Congress' unexercised authority to regulate interstate commerce.

> Natural gas is a lawful article of commerce, and its transmission from one state to another for sale and consumption in the latter is interstate commerce. A state law, whether of the state where the gas is produced or that where it is to be sold, which by its necessary operation prevents, obstructs, or burdens such transmission is a regulation of interstate commerce—a prohibited interference.

Not enough resource to go around, to satisfy the economic needs of the respective states. The resource is important to commerce in each of the states. The resource travels between states. Yet water, in the Laramie River case, was the prerogative of states, without regard to the interstate commerce clause. Justice Holmes, dissenting in the natural gas case, makes essentially the same argument as had Colorado counsel initially in *Wyoming v. Colorado:* "The gas is collected under and subject to the law, if valid, and at that moment it is not yet matter of commerce among the states. I think that the products of a state, until they are actually started to a point outside it, may be regulated by the state notwithstanding the commerce clause."

Eighteen months after the Laramie River case, and one week after Van Devanter's final opinion in the West Virginia natural gas case, on December 10, 1923, the Court published its decision in *North Dakota v. Minnesota.*[25] The opinion in that case is attributed to Chief Justice Taft. North Dakota had sued Minnesota for the consequences of flooding in the Mustinka River system, allegedly caused by construction of cut-off ditches and straightening of the Mustinka River in Minnesota, thereby allegedly increasing the speed and volume of its flow into Lake Traverse, and thereby raising the level of the Lake, and causing its outlet, the Bois de Sioux River, to overflow and injure a valuable farming area in North Dakota lying on the west bank of the Bois de Sioux.

Taft's decision first dismissed the claim for damages, arguing that North Dakota only claimed them as a surrogate for damaged farmers, a claim not cognizable under the Court's original jurisdiction in equity (a point well missed in the Laramie River case the year before). As to North Dakota's claim for injunction mandating alteration of the physical conditions allegedly giving rise to the downstream flood, the Court dismissed on the basis that the expert witnesses of the two states were countervailing, that the Court didn't have the expertise to evaluate who was the better expert, and that the Court must therefore "look[s] about for outstanding facts from which the lay mind can safely draw inferences as to the probabilities." This, compounded with an evaluation of the "care and accuracy with which the contrasted experts respectively have determined the data upon which they base their conclusions," permitted the layman fact finder Court (ostensibly Taft himself) to conclude that the artificial modifications of water flow in Minnesota was of "negligible significance," given the significant climatic conditions generally prevailing in the region in the relevant time period.

It is difficult to imagine busy Chief Justice Taft, past President of the United States, a self conscious writer at best, concerned about judicial administration and the role of the court *vis a vis* the Congress, writing such an opinion, particularly since Taft's tenure on the Court only began in May 1921. The facts giving rise to the controversy occurred in 1915–1916, and there is no record that evidentiary proceedings occurred while Taft was on the Court. It is, alternatively, easy to imagine Associate Justice Van Devanter writing it, particularly with the hubris to exercise the expertise necessary to make a lay judgment in the face of countervailing expert engineering testimony. Van Devanter had done the same thing in *Wyoming v. Colorado.* Pringle reports that, shortly after publication of the opinion in *North Dakota v. Minnesota,* Chief Justice Taft characterized Van Devanter as "my mainstay."[26]

Two years later, in December 1926, Taft would praise Van Devanter in a recommendation to Yale University President James B. Angell, again reported by Pringle, that he be awarded an honorary degree by Yale:

> The value of a judge in conference, especially in such a court as ours, never becomes known except to the members of the court. Now I don't hesitate to say that Mr. Justice Van Devanter is far and away the most valuable man in our court in all these qualities. We have other learned and valuable members, with special knowledge in particular subjects, but Van Devanter has knowledge in every subject that comes before us.... Van Devanter exercises more influence, a good deal, than any other member of the court, just because the members of the court know his qualities.

There is no question that Van Devanter was exercising his inside influence. Individual mandates and orders are indeed issued by individual U.S. Supreme Court justices today. But seldom are decisions rendered in cases affecting public policy or significant political issues without much greater collective deliberation and transparency (to the extent that anything at the modern U.S. Supreme Court is transparent). And bias is still not precluded by U.S. Supreme Court rules. It has, however, become much more precluded by practice, perhaps again due to better transparency.

Taking Willis Van Devanter's prior history into account, thinking way back to his education and early exposure to frontier justice following the Johnson County cattle catastrophe, his action in the Laramie River case seems entirely in character. From this hindsight, however, one cannot help but wonder why the balance of the U.S. Supreme Court bench was paying so little attention to Associate Justice Van Devanter's unilateral gift to his prior clients and political friends.

27

Van Devanter's Surreptitious Composition of the Opinion and Decree (1922)

All was not well in Washington in January 1922. Sherow tells us, "there was unusually cold weather and heavy snowfall in Washington , inflation had collapsed, prices and wages were falling, wages more quickly than prices. Five million people were unemployed; there was a new wave of strikes in the coal fields and on the railroads."

Sequestered in Brewer's third floor library office of his 16th Street home, Justice Van Devanter went on quietly working on the Laramie opinion in *Wyoming v. Colorado*. Sweet irony, Justice Brewer had probably written his opinion in *Kansas v. Colorado* in the same study in 1907. It was an opportune time, as the Court was otherwise enfeebled by the absence of at least three other justices.

In March, Van Devanter learned directly from Justice Clarke that which he probably already knew from watching the torrid relationship between Justices McReynolds and Clarke, that Clarke would be resigning his position on the Court soon. "Alas," said Clarke in a March 7, 1922, handwritten note to Justice Van Devanter, "I am passing through waters that are deep and dark and cold. I have always, heretofore, been able to recover resolution sufficient to enable me to meet conditions before me but this is so frustrating that I continue to be overwhelmed by it entirely."[1] Associate Justice Clarke would leave the Court officially on September 17, 1922.[2]

Wyoming counsel may have sensed, perhaps by direct or informal communication, that a decision was imminent in the Laramie River case. Late in March, Wyoming attorney A.C. Campbell, who had unsuccessfully petitioned Justice Van Devanter in 1911 to be appointed to act as magistrate in *Wyoming v. Colorado*, wrote to Justice Van Devanter, inviting him and Chief Justice Taft to a party in Laramie to be held by the Wyoming State Bar Association and the University of Wyoming on the 14th of June, coincidentally when the Supreme Court's term was scheduled to end. The Justice's brother-in-law "Judge" John W. Lacey was now president of the State Bar Association, and Mr. Corthell, Wyoming's co-counsel in the Supreme Court litigation, was running the committee to plan the intended ceremonies.

> Dear Justice Van Devanter, The Wyoming State Bar Association will have its next annual meeting at Laramie beginning Wednesday, June 14th. The University Commencement exercises will

be on the 15th. As you perhaps know Judge Lacey is President of our State Bar Association. Before he left on his vacation trip, he appointed Mr. Corthell, Mr. Mullen and myself a committee to arrange a program for the Bar Association meeting. The Albany county Bar and the University Faculty are working together to make the week referred to one long to be remembered by Laramie city. Said Faculty and said Bar, as also the entire Bar of the State, would feel specially honored, if his Honor Chief Justice Taft and yourself could arrange to be present.... A.C. Campbell[3]

Van Devanter politely declined, deferring to the great amount of work he had to complete, and reminding his Wyoming family of his close association with Chief Justice Taft. On April 12, he wrote to "Hon. A.C. Campbell (State Bar Association) Cheyenne, Wyoming":

Since receiving your letter I have taken up with the Chief Justice several times your request that he be the guest of the Wyoming State Bar Association and of the State University on June 14th and 15th, when the Association has its next annual meeting and the University its commencement exercises. He felt at first and still feels that he cannot adjust his time in such a way as will permit an acceptance of the invitation. I talked with him about it again today, and am quite convinced that while he would like to come he reasonably cannot do so.... As for myself, I would like exceedingly to come, but it is not reasonably possible for me to do so. The present term will continue until June 5th, and possibly for a week longer. We cannot say with any certainty which it will be, and will not know definitely until the time is near at hand. The term has been an exceedingly arduous one and we will all be in need of a very material rest when it is ended.[4]

Van Devanter likewise advised Aven Nelson, President of the University of Wyoming in Laramie. Mr. Campbell stayed in contact, on May 8, 1922, corresponding with Justice Van Devanter regarding the Justice's opinion in *Oklahoma v. Texas*[5] and expressing disappointment with the Justice's having declined the State Bar's invitation. In another interstate case within the Court's aegis under its original jurisdiction, Van Devanter had ruled on May 1 in a case of dispute over the location of a common boundary, the Red River. This was the same controversy that Van Devanter had addressed as an Assistant Attorney General.[6] But now both states as well as the United States claimed the oil and gas beneath the bed of the Red River. The issue ran to the navigability of the Red. Van Devanter held that, consistent with the rule that a river navigable in fact is navigable in law, the Red was not legally navigable. Therefore the bed of the river had not transferred to the State of Oklahoma at statehood, a decision somewhat anathema to Western State interests claiming ownership of rivers, their beds, and the water within them.

In any case, Judge Van Devanter had different plans than heading out to Wyoming at the end of the October 1921 term. Rather, he was headed to Ontario, Canada—to Parry Sound, to do some recreational reading. On May 3, he wrote to the Funk and Wagnalls Co., in New York City.

Gentlemen, referring to your notes of April and May 2d, enclosed herewith, I will thank you to send the set of Kipling's works, cloth-bound, to me at Parry Sound, Ontario, Canada. Please send the books forward about June 7th, because I do not want them to arrive at Parry Sound until about the time I get there. Enclosed is my check for $28.50 to pay for the works. Very sincerely, Willis Van Devanter.[7]

During April, the Justice's nephew Herbert V. Lacey, now also co-counsel in the pending Laramie River case, had kept up a chummy correspondence with his uncle. Van Devanter wrote him in Cheyenne on April 10:

My dear Herbert: I haven't the slightest idea what the package contains which is referred to in the enclosed notice. It may be something which I care nothing about, and, the other hand, I may want it. At some convenient time, please do whatever you think is best about it. Enclosed is a dollar in currency with which to pay the existing postage and also the forwarding postage, if you think the package is one which I want.... With love to all, I am, Your affectionate uncle, Willis Van Devanter.[8]

Young Herbert responded to his "affectionate uncle" three days later, keeping him posted on his mother's and father's vacations.

I am forwarding to you the package which was in the Cheyenne Post Office addressed to you. The package contained a copy of the Legislative manual of the State of New York for the year 1922, with your name stamped upon it. This morning I received a telegram from Father announcing that Mother and he had arrived safely in San Francisco to-day. This completes their cruise. The telegram stated that they are both well and that they have had an excellent trip. Very affectionately, Herbert V. Lacey.[9]

In May "affectionate brother" John W. Lacey corresponded himself to his brother-in-law Willis with an offer to purchase the remaining volumes of the Justice's Wyoming library for the not unpaltry sum in 1922 of $2,094:

the value of books you have here in our library, on the long deferred suggestion that Herbert and I might buy them. We did not run across a good man to make an estimate until during my

A collection of law books, *Federal Reporter* (1890–1912), bearing the names of Van Devanter and Lacey, now found in the Nagler-Warren Mansion in Cheyenne and Wyoming State Library, part of Van Devanter's library purchased by John Lacey in May 1922 (author's photograph, 2019).

absence on my late vacation.... You will note that the total amount which he figures the books worth is $2,094.00. Herbert and I desire to purchase the books and desire to pay you what they are worth. Would be glad if you would state what you think you should receive for them.... In case you sell us the books, it would probably be well and to the interests of all parties if a short bill of sale could be given.... Your affectionate brother, John W. Lacey.[10]

The tendered sum was enough to cover many months of the Washington, D.C., expenses Justice Van Devanter listed in his "Letterbooks" (remaining in the Library of Congress' documents) as paid on June 5: second installment of tax liability for 1921, Messrs Emerson & Orme, Messrs Gait and Bro., Mr. John H. Magruder, Messrs Sherwood & Son, Messrs Woodward & Lothrop, Louise Hand Laundry, Washington Gas Light Co., W.A. Buirdine & Son, American Ice Co., Chestnut Farms Dairy, R.T Weaver, C. Engle's Sons, Chas. H. Fishbaugh & Son, Collins & Co, The Chevy Chase Club, Charles Scribner's Sons, A.N. Fenn, Parry Sound.[11]

Justice Van Devanter responded on May 15, claiming that he was "too engrossed and tired to give it much consideration."[12] The "generosity" of Wyoming lawyers representing Associate Justice Van Devanter's old friends and clients had been manifest before. Professor Tyler mentions Colorado Counsel Delph Carpenter's diary entry for January 11, 1918. Wyoming counsel had engaged in the "tactic of providing gifts in the form of stuffed elk meat to the clerk and to Justice Willis Van Devanter" at the time of January 1918 oral argument in the case.[13] And so had Van Devanter's complicity been manifest in his taking Ralph Meeker, Wyoming's consulting engineer, into his own home office (as reported by Carpenter's 1931 letter) to establish the facts he needed to reach his predetermined outcome.

28

Wyoming v. Colorado, Final Opinion Published (1922)

Chief Justice Taft was now preoccupied with his administrative agenda to reorganize and streamline the Court. In spring 1922, he traveled to England to study the procedural structure of the English courts and learn how they disposed of such a large number of cases in such an expeditious manner. During the trip, King George V and Queen Mary received Taft and his wife as state visitors. Back home, he began to advocate a "Judges Bill." Sheldon Novick posits that the proposed legislation was "drafted by a committee of the justices—fundamentally reforming the jurisdiction of the Supreme Court."

In addition to giving the Court more control over its docket, the legislation Taft would seek, with Van Devanter's assistance, and the Judicial Conference that Taft would organize, would give the Supreme Court and the Chief Justice general supervisory power over the scattered and disorganized federal courts, and also bring the courts of the District of Columbia and of the Territories within the federal judicial system, actually uniting the courts for the first time as an independent third branch of government.

Taft's objective was to shift the Supreme Court's appellate jurisdiction to be exercisable principally on review of petitioning litigants, granting the Court the power to accept or deny an appeal. If the Court accepted the appeal, it could order the court from which the case was being appealed to certify its record to the Supreme Court. This way, Taft reasoned, the Supreme Court would be empowered to give preference to limited cases of national importance. Taft succeeded in pushing his proposed legislation through Congress. He would then be in charge of a national judicial conference, a device through which to "harmonize" the circuit courts by shifting resources where most needed. The "Judges' Bill" would ultimately be adopted by Congress in 1925, as the *Judiciary Act of 1925*.

Over in the U.S. Senate in early March, a "decisive vote" occurred changing a standing Senate rule. A March 8, 1922, article in the *Wyoming State Tribune* reported, "hereafter all general appropriation bills and appropriation matters will be referred to the one committee on appropriations on which Senator Warren is chairman. This important change was brought about after a six days' struggle, which at times was bitter. It marks a distinct victory for Senator Warren."[1]

Busy with thoughts of judicial administration, the Chief Justice kept up his requests that Van Devanter "blue pencil" his work prior to its distribution. On April

20, 1922, the Chief wrote a note to Justice Van Devanter forwarding a draft opinion in the "Stockyards Law case." "I wish you would run over it and give me your views in respect to how it ought to be changed," said the Chief.[2]

On May 12, three days before the opinion in the *Drexel Furniture* case was published, the Chief sent Van Devanter a note[3] asking him to read his draft opinions in "the Chicago Board of Trade case, no. 616,[4] and the Reading case, Nos. 609 and 610"[5] and seek his support at the next day's conference. Eleven days later, as Justice Van Devanter worked away on his opinion in *Wyoming v. Colorado*, he found himself responding to numerous requests for favors from the Chief Justice, and gladly responded, particularly about a favor pertaining to Mr. Robert T. Lincoln's participation in the dedication of the Lincoln Memorial.[6]

Closure of the Supreme Court's October 1921 term was imminent. June 5 would be the last day that opinions could be delivered to the Clerk if they were to be reported in this term. Final opinions would have to be announced by that day. Justice Van Devanter now disclosed his completed opinion in *Wyoming v. Colorado* to the Chief Justice. The Chief Justice sent Van Devanter a handwritten note dated June 3, 1922 (Saturday):

> I have received your opinion in *Wyoming v. Colorado* and have read it with intense satisfaction and greatest pleasure. If as there was a demonstration in Euclid, then your opinion is one. Its simplicity and clearness and compactness make it a model. It must go out on Monday—I doubt if Holmes or Brandeis keep in the face of what you say. It seems easy but one wonders it took the Court so long a time to say it. That, however, indicates not the lack of difficulty presented by the arguments but the mastering of the subject and confident rejection of the opposing opinions' argument.
>
> I congratulate you on your work. It is worth while to exhaust your thought for such a result. Affectionately yours, Wm H. Taft.[7]

The opinion was published with no fanfare on Monday, June 5, 1922. Replete with factual findings determining the flow of the Laramie and the demands upon it, "based" according to Sherow, "almost entirely upon [Wyoming witness] Ralph Meeker's findings," the opinion held, not surprisingly, that Wyoming users of Laramie's flows had a stronger claim to the water than Colorado's users.

Sherow restated Justice Van Devanter's findings:

> [Justice Van Devanter] calculated the available flow for the Laramie Poudre Tunnel project and for all Wyoming appropriations along the Laramie River to and including the Wheatland District at 288,000 acre feet. He came to this figure *after* deducting an average of 22,250 acre feet per year for the gross diversions within Colorado. Next, he attached an appropriation date of October 1909 to the Colorado tunnel, which conveniently postdated the extensions to the Wheatland District. Then he totaled the diversions within Wyoming predating October 1909 and came to a figure of 272,500 acre feet per year. This amount constituted the Wyoming allotment, and the remainder, some 15,500 acre feet, the justice allotted to the tunnel project (Table I). In his computations, then, only the water-right date for the tunnel played a crucial role in the decision.[8]

A Decree signed by Associate Justice Van Devanter accompanied the published opinion. The effect of the Decree was to preserve 80 to 88 percent of the Laramie River's water supply for the Justice's prior clients and political principals in Wyoming. There is no evidence that Justice Van Devanter revealed the Decree, or explained its significance or effect, to the Chief Justice prior to its publication.

Taft's allusion to Euclid's clarity seems urgently sophist. It is reported that Chief Justice Taft was insecure in his self image, as it pertained to his intellectual prowess. Princeton Professor of Jurisprudence Walter Murphy said of Taft, "He thus relied on Van Devanter's 'grasp of the intricacies of the Court's business' and shrewdly utilized Van Devanter's immense learning to improve his own opinions, to supply technical knowledge at conference, and to advise on the numerous political affairs in which the Chief Justice was constantly getting involved."[9] Professor Mason observed that Taft usually assigned land claim cases and Indian litigation to the former Chief Justice of Wyoming, Willis Van Devanter, "perhaps because he distrusted his own knowledge of the same subjects."[10]

Even if the Chief Justice's approval had not been so glowing, it would perhaps not have mattered. In the gentlemen's world in which the Chief lived and operated, Van Devanter had him cold to rights: indebted for Van Devanter's favors, beholden because of his own need for writing assistance, impaled on his own disfavor of dissents, and dependent upon Van Devanter's political access with the Congress, particularly that access to Senator Francis Warren, now chairman of the Senate Appropriations Committee under a new Senate rule dictating that all federal spending be approved by that Committee. Van Devanter's sole, unedited, unreviewed opinion was *fait accomplis*. "It must go out on Monday," said the Chief. And so it was done, with no conference, no circulation among the rest of the Court, and no comment or review on Justice Van Devanter's action of judicial bias, conflict of interest, familial preference or failure to recuse himself.

It must have been a bright day in Laramie, when the State Bar met, Van Devanter's brother-in-law Lacey at the helm, as the news of the decision was received. Van Devanter had certainly communicated it early in the summer to his old political crony and law partner, Charles N. Potter, in Wyoming, the now long-time Chief Justice of the Wyoming Supreme Court.[11] Potter acknowledged receiving it in a September 9, 1922, handwritten note:

> I want to thank you for sending me [a]copy of your opinion [in the] Wyo-Colo. case. Have not read it all yet, as not quite up to that, being still very weak, from my rather serious illness of the summer. Will try and write you later, when I can do so with more ease. I did not see your opinion of course for more than a month after it was rec'd. The date of its mailing was in a week when I had two nurses a day and night nurse and was very sick.[12]

Years later, Professor Paul M. Holsinger would say of Justice Van Devanter: "As he climbed up the ladder of preferment, first as Assistant Attorney General (1897–1903), then as Judge of the Eighth Circuit Court of Appeals (1903–1910), and finally as Associate Justice of the United States Supreme Court (1910–1937), Van Devanter represented the state of Wyoming well."[13]

Justice Van Devanter can hardly be said to have been disinterested in the issues presented in the Laramie River case. Professor James Sherow, historian of the American West, commented:

> Justice Van Devanter, by any account, lacked judicial impartiality. There was far more to his prejudice than simply hailing from Wyoming and having served as a state and federal judge there. He and Judge John W. Lacey, "Wyoming's leading counsel" during the suit, had been former law partners in Cheyenne. In addition, Justice Van Devanter and Judge Lacey were also

brothers-in-law, and according to Delph Carpenter, one of the Colorado attorneys, "were known to entertain the most intimate personal and family relations."[14]

But, Professor Sherow's rebuke is too mild. By 1922, Justice Van Devanter and "Judge" Lacey had been acquainted for over 50 years, he and Senator Warren over 40. Willis Van Devanter had known John Lacey since at least 1871, when young Willis was twelve and John began to read law under Willis' father in Marion, Indiana. Willis had followed John to Wyoming in 1884 and had practiced law with him for several years in Cheyenne.[15] John had been married to Willis' sister since 1878, now 44 years. The clients John Lacey was representing in this litigation were the same clients that now-Associate Justice Van Devanter had previously represented. The two families were certainly intimate. Willis Van Devanter maintained at least monthly personal correspondence with his sister, John Lacey's wife, throughout his complete U.S. Supreme Court career. Many still reside in his papers held by the Library of Congress. Except for his stint in Washington, the Van Devanters and the Laceys lived in the same small town all of Willis Van Devanter's life. Van Devanter's relationship with Senator Warren was longstanding and intimate. The Senator's political power was eminent, as Chairman of the Senate Judiciary Committee. The Senator and Judge Lacey had now lived in worthy mansions across House Street from each other in Cheyenne for some twenty years.

By June 9, Justice Van Devanter had busied his head with plans for his summer at his personal island at Sans Souci, Parry Sound, Canada.[16] His letter of that date to Mr. Hero Hudgin of Parry Sound reminded: "I expect to leave here about the 19th of June." The Justice gave instructions to make the place ready for his arrival. "Sans souci" is, of course, French for "without worry or care." He had had a longstanding invitation out to Judge John Pollock of Kansas City to join him at Parry Sound. Judge Pollock's June 12, 1922, typed letter to Van Devanter acknowledging the invitation also rests in Van Devanter's papers.

Delayed a bit, Willis wrote to his sister, Mrs. John W. Lacey, in Cheyenne on June 17, regarding their sister and their mother. He also wrote to his convalescing wife Dollie on June 19.

> My very dear wife: ... Herbert Lacey came here yesterday and Winslow asked him to come up and have supper with me. He was looking very well. His mother had reached home before he left and had a pretty sore ankle—considerably swollen; Herbert knew but little about it save that waiter was attending to it. I think Herbert left in an hour or so after his mother arrived. Mr. Loomis [Union Pacific general counsel] had sent for him to come to Omaha and then had sent him on here about some matter that I do not know about. Herbert said that the family were all well save his mother's ankle. He did not say how long he would be here, but I gathered it might be two, three or four days.[17]

Nephew Herbert V. Lacey showed up in Washington the day between the two letters. He had supper with the Justice. "He was looking very well." No doubt Lacey's victory, albeit overlong in coming, caused Herbert's happy appearance. The Associate Justice and his nephew also shared another satisfaction: Herbert now also enjoyed the lucrative representation of the Union Pacific.[18]

After the decision, Justice Van Devanter also maintained his acquaintance and correspondence the following winter with Nellis Corthell, his long-time Wyoming friend and the other Wyoming counsel in the Laramie River case. On February 28, 1923, the Justice wrote to attorney Corthell at Laramie. Although it is not clear to whom the letter refers, the Justice's continued familiarity with Mr. Corthell is obvious.[19]

> Dear Mr. Corthell: Enclosed is a document which its author thinks is "profound," unless perchance he is attempting the perpetration of a joke. It occurs to me that you will be diverted for the moment in looking at it. Doubtless its author will be as happy, if not happier, if he does not know that you have seen it. If he is working for you or about you, its contents and general purport will readily suggest to you the uncertainty of his future course and that some advance in his present direction may affect his responsibility. I merely call the matter to your attention so that, if you are not already accurately informed, you can see what the situation is. Of course I do not care to have the document returned. Very sincerely, Willis Van Devanter

Again, on March 26, the Justice wrote to Mr. Corthell: "Dear Mr. Corthell: Your letter of the 23rd instant is along your best lines. To read it is a genuine diversion."

29

Where Was the Balance of the Court on June 5, 1922? (1922)

Where were the other members of the Taft Court on June 5, 1922, when Associate Justice Van Devanter inserted his unreviewed opinion in the Laramie River case in the Court's published reports on the last day of the 1921 Supreme Court Term? Where were Associate Justices Pitney, Day, McKenna, McReynolds, Holmes, and Brandeis, the balance of the Court when excluding Taft, Van Devanter and Clarke, who should, from today's perspective at least, have been aware or concerned about the proper and respectful exercise of Supreme Court power?

We know Justice Clarke's condition and absence. Van Devanter had corresponded with him in his physical deterioration and retirement from the Court.[1] Like Justice Clarke, Justice Mahlon Pitney, the last of William Howard Taft's appointments to the Court, had suffered a stroke and was physically absent in the spring of 1922. He did not return at all for the fall 1922 term of the Court.[2] He died two years later on December 9, 1924. Justice Pitney was a social Darwinist, as we will also see with Justice Holmes, as well as a strong supporter of the Court's substantive due process jurisprudence. It is likely that, if Justice Van Devanter had consulted him regarding the law of the case in *Wyoming v. Colorado*, he would have agreed. There is no indication, however, that Van Devanter ever consulted Pitney regarding the case, nor apprised him of his own compromised situation.

Justice Day was probably not even present in Washington at the close of the Court's year. And he would likely have been no problem for Justice Van Devanter if he had been so. Quite the long-time friend of Van Devanter, they shared very convivial mutual respect and the same April 17 birthday. Justice Day had engaged in regular correspondence with Van Devanter, writing long chummy letters in the summers of 1920 and 1921. Day had visited at Sans Souci, on Parry Sound, from whence he corresponded with Van Devanter in August 1921. He followed up with notes throughout September regarding his intended retirement from the Court.[3] Van Devanter was certainly aware, by the spring of 1922, that Justice Day intended to retire.[4]

Day had served on the Court for nineteen years, throughout the entire period that *Wyoming v. Colorado* was before the Court. But as the case came down, there is no record that he participated in the case in any way, at any time. He would leave the court formally on November 12, 1922.

During the spring of 1922, Taft had dismissed Day as among "the weakest members of the court," along with Justices Mahlon Pitney and Joseph McKenna. Perhaps Van Devanter agreed with Chief Justice Taft, that Day, notwithstanding that he was personally close to Van Devanter, was among "the weak members of the court" along with Justices Mahlon Pitney and Joseph McKenna.[5]

Associate Justice Joseph McKenna was also sitting on the Court at the end of the 1921 term. He had been present when Van Devanter joined it in 1911, having been first appointed on January 25, 1898, by President McKinley. In about 1915, in the midst of the tenure of the case before the Court, Justice McKenna suffered a stroke, limiting his abilities on the bench. Now 79, he was failing badly and largely unable to do his work. He had served throughout the long period that the Laramie River case was before the Court, and would not depart until January 5, 1925,[6] one year before his death on November 21, 1926. There is no evidence that he participated in the case in any way. Chief Justice Taft particularly remarked over McKenna's "inability to do his work."[7] Given his physical condition during the last seven years of his service, the likelihood of his awareness of the case is small. McKenna's political affiliation and loyalty,[8] as well as his rise to the Court, were strikingly similar to Justice Van Devanter's, even though their birth dates placed them in succeeding generations. It is altogether likely that Justice McKenna left the case entirely to Justice Van Devanter (although the outcome would likely have been considered favorable by the political McKenna, its political implications favoring his California constituents).

By the summer of 1922, Associate Justice James McReynolds, had become a solid member of the conservative majority that controlled the Court under Taft, departing from his earlier liberal thinking. Indeed, McReynolds and Van Devanter had joined in expressing the very limited power of Congress under the Commerce Clause earlier in 1918.[9] McReynolds was known for conciseness and brevity in his opinions. Taft, and probably also Van Devanter, bristled at the prickly McReynolds, however. McReynolds was hard to predict or control, factors Taft would not have liked. Taft felt little respect for Justice McReynolds, finding him "selfish," "prejudiced," "a continual grouch, [who] is always offended because the court is doing something that he regards as undignified."[10] Taft also disliked McReynolds' temperament, characterizing him as selfish, prejudiced, "and one who seems to delight in making others uncomfortable...."[11] As years went by, Taft found McReynolds "the most irresponsible member of the Court," and that things "went smoothly" when McReynolds was gone. Although Taft found McReynolds able,[12] he was put off by McReynolds' selfish and prejudiced demeanor.[13]

There is no record that Van Devanter circulated his draft opinion in *Wyoming v. Colorado* to McReynolds. If he had done so, McReynolds probably would have concurred in the result, and may not have been alarmed by Van Devanter's bias.

Associate Justices Oliver Wendell Holmes and Louis Brandeis, also on the Court during the 1921 term, were more independent thinkers, were not subscribed to the Taft loyalty group, and would logically have better questioned Van Devanter's action. Chief Justice Taft's June 3, 1922, note to Van Devanter mentions Justices Holmes and Brandeis, dismissing their knowledge or interest in "what you say," suggesting that both may have preferred to simply defer to Van Devanter due to their lack of interest in the subject matter with which Van Devanter had expertise. This would explain why neither of them wrote to concur or dissent from Van Devanter's opinion in *Wyoming v. Colorado*. The explanation is unsatisfying, however, due to the intellectual integrity of both justices.

The now greatly regarded and long-serving Oliver Wendell Holmes, Jr., had also been a member of the Court when Van Devanter joined. Originally appointed to the Court by President Roosevelt in 1902,[14] Holmes had served in the Fuller Court, later in the White Court,[15] now in the Taft Court. He would eventually serve until January 12, 1932.[16] In retrospect remembered for his disdain for his colleagues and his "tortuous legalisms,"[17] Holmes is acknowledged for his long judicial service, concise and pithy opinions, and deference to the decisions of elected legislatures. Holmes "believed that the only test of truth for individuals was what they could not help believing, and the only test of truth collectively was what the majority wanted."[18] As an "aristocratic amoral Social Darwinist,"[19] Holmes believed that "only the fittest races, ideas, individuals, and groups would survive in the brutal competition of life."[20] His sense of social Darwinism is today attributed to his life experience, as scholar, soldier and judge. In 1881, Holmes published the first edition of his well-regarded book *The Common Law*, summarizing his views developed over the preceding years. There, Holmes sets forth his view that the only source of law, properly speaking, is a judicial decision. "Judges decide cases on the facts, and then write opinions afterward presenting a rationale for their decision. The true basis of the decision, however, is often an 'inarticulate major premise' outside the law. A judge is obliged to choose between contending legal theories, but the true basis of his decision is necessarily drawn from outside the law."

Unlike some of the rest of the Court, Holmes' was still bright in 1922. Chief Justice Taft observed, "Holmes ... has not lost his mental acumen so far as I can see, and his power of rapid work is still marvelous."[21] But Justice Holmes had been ailing significantly all spring of 1922, had not been present in Washington, and had prostate surgery in the summer.[22] Although he had returned when the Court convened in October 1922, he remained a little slow.

Chief Justice Taft had noticed Holmes' physical problem and commented upon it in April 1922.[23] "'Association with Justice Holmes is a delight,' [Taft] wrote. 'He is feebler physically, but I cannot see that the acuteness of his mind has been affected at all.... In many ways he is the life of the court, and it is a great comfort to have such a well of pure common law undefiled immediately next one so that one can drink and be sure one is getting the pure article.'"[24] Had Holmes' not been distracted with his own prostate surgery, the Chief Justice may have shared with Holmes that he had seen Van Devanter's final draft opinion in *Wyoming v. Colorado*, as they walked to the Court together, a practice engaged in by Holmes and Taft until 1925.[25] But there is no evidence of Van Devanter having circulated the draft himself, nor that Holmes had any independent knowledge of it.

It is difficult to assess what Holmes' view of the Laramie River case may have been, had he been there. Holmes could have had little trouble acquiescing to Van Devanter's view of the necessary outcome in *Wyoming v. Colorado*, as he may have seen Van Devanter's western experience as the basis for his best understanding of the common law that should be determined to be the law of the case. But such acquiescence grants no respect to the jurist that was Holmes, nor to his own western water law knowledge. In another case involving the State of Colorado and an interstate river, the South Platte, which made it through the Supreme Court in 1916, Associate Justice Holmes wrote the opinion. Published on November 20, 1916,[26] Holmes opined that the State of Colorado was justified in using its adjudicative process to quiet claims between competing claimants, based on prior appropriation.

Alternatively, Holmes may have seen the merits in the Laramie River case differently than Van Devanter, Holmes being an independent thinker. The Taft-Van Devanter team was cautious of Holmes' predilection to dissent. Pursuant to this reality, it would be better to keep him uninformed. Certainly Chief Justice Taft viewed Holmes' dissent potential disparagingly.

> "I am very fond of the old gentleman [Holmes], but he is so completely under the control of Brother Brandeis that it gives to Brandeis two votes instead of one. He has more interest in, and gives more attention to, his dissents than he does to the opinions he writes for the court, which are very short and not very helpful," was the faintly despairing observation of the Chief Justice in May, 1928.[27]

On the merits, Holmes probably would have agreed with Van Devanter, due to his basic view that the law is not premised on logic, but experience.[28] Holmes' belief that the common law reflects human experience and life's natural selection[29] would have squared well with Van Devanter's giving deference to the politically powerful and first-vested interests represented by the prior appropriation doctrine, a doctrine closely affiliated with the notion that might makes right.[30] Holmes acquiesced to the imperialist tone of American foreign policy in the Spanish American war cases questioning whether the "Constitution follows the flag."[31] American imperialism of the period was consistent with the doctrine of prior appropriation, a doctrine Wyoming and Justice Van Devanter characterized as an equitable one, which gives legitimacy to the first and strongest. A social Darwinist, Holmes would have been sympathetic to seniority of right based on assertiveness of claim. He likely would have supported the idea of first in time, first in right. Sometimes his deference to authority, particularly if legislative, was so extreme that it "verged on judicial abnegation."[32]

Whatever Holmes' legal view may have been, there is no evidence that Van Devanter sought to enlist his support of the decision in *Wyoming v. Colorado.* Van Devanter did not need Holmes in this case and did not involve him. It was just as well, as Holmes was too preoccupied with his own prostate condition to pay attention.

The last, and most junior member of the Court whose absence must be resolved is Associate Justice Louis Brandeis. He seems strikingly to have been the single member of the Court who would have opposed the injustice of Van Devanter's preference and bias, had he been aware of it. It is unclear where Justice Brandeis may have been in May and June of 1922, when Justice Van Devanter secreted his opinion through the Supreme Court's opinion publication process. But had he known, he probably would have opposed the outcome on principles of bias, if not on the merits. Thirteen years later, Justices Brandeis and Holmes would stand in the liberal minority against the Four Horsemen's (including Van Devanter's) resistance to FDR's New Deal Legislation. There, Brandeis argued that the law should be principled, rather than convenient. Had he asserted the same perspective earlier in 1922, one would certainly expect that he would have opposed Justice Van Devanter's participation in resolving a conflict about which he was so personally involved.

In 1922, Brandeis was clearly not a member of the Taft Court's ruling cabal, Chief Justice Taft being of the opinion that Brandeis intended to diminish the reputation of the Court, through dissent. Brandeis was not a "good fellow," but rather a liberal anomaly in a conservative court. Brandeis had been appointed Associate Justice by President Woodrow Wilson, whom Brandeis had supported in the 1912 election,[33] on June 6, 1916.[34] Brandeis would serve until February 13, 1939—through the long conservative control of the Court, and become a longtime nemesis of Willis Van Devanter.

At this time, Chief Justice Taft was uncertain of Brandeis' intentions or potential effect.[35] Upon Taft's arrival at the Court in 1921, he had found it "badly divided" and "far behind on its calendar."[36] The calendar issue he could deal with through administration and legislation (the Judiciary Act of 1925). But the factional discord, which Taft saw as a "people problem" manifested in dissents, was more difficult to resolve. Throughout his tenure as Chief, Taft would seek to bring harmony, as had been his administrative bent in all his prior governmental service. In the long run, although initially resentful of prior conflict with Brandeis, Taft worked graciously[37] to accommodate Brandeis' service on the Court, and was ultimately won over by Brandeis' "luminous mind and great learning."[38] At the early point in Taft's administration, when Van Devanter's opinion in *Wyoming v. Colorado* was published, Taft's desire to maintain accord in judicial fiat probably counseled that Brandeis simply not be informed.

Brandeis' opinion of Van Devanter was apparently not entirely dismissive, according to his biographer, Melvin Urofsky, quoting Brandeis' remark to his friend Felix Frankfurter, "Van Devanter knows as much about jurisdiction as anyone, more than anyone."[39] And, by April 1922, several months before Van Devanter published his opinion in *Wyoming v. Colorado*, Brandeis appears to have become resolved to Taft's style and leadership on the Court. In a conversation with his ally Felix Frankfurter, Brandeis is reported to have said to Frankfurter that "it's difficult for me to understand why a man who is so good a Chief Justice, in is function as presiding officer could have been so bad a President."[40]

Brandeis' biographer describes Van Devanter's skill as "coordinator and strategist" and stalwart in the "often tedious cases involving public land law, admiralty, and corporation law." Like Taft, Brandeis was known to have sent his draft opinions to Van Devanter before circulating them with the remainder of the Court. Taft may have called Van Devanter the Chancellor due to his working the court on the Chief's behalf, checking with the different justices, sometimes trying to persuade them to change their votes, but Brandeis called him the "cardinal," and in one instance, the "Jesuit general," "the man who really runs the Court." Despite their jurisprudential differences, Brandeis and Van Devanter apparently enjoyed "warm and respectful personal relations,"[41] and that Brandeis had a "guarded affection" for Van Devanter."[42]

The conclusion that one must inevitably reach is that Justice Van Devanter knew the whereabouts, absence, physical condition, and proclivity of all his "brethren" when he submitted his written opinion to the publisher of the Supreme Court reports at the very tail end of the 1921 Supreme Court term. He had awaited the day when the Court's principals were greatly in transition, feeble and distracted, and in the final analysis smoked his personal agenda past the Chief Justice.

30

The Decree and Holding of *Wyoming v. Colorado*

Associate Justice Van Devanter's injunctive Decree in the Laramie River case precluded Coloradans from using any more than 15,500 acre feet per year of Laramie River water if delivered through the Laramie-LaPoudre Tunnel, nor more than 37,750 acre feet per year overall, leaving the rest of the volume of the Laramie River available for use in Wyoming. Estimates of normal flow in the Laramie River presented in the litigation ranged from 188,000 acre-feet to 300,000 acre-feet per year. The Decree thus left 151,000 to 263,000 acre-feet per year for use in Wyoming. The June 6, 1922, Decree provided:

> It is considered, ordered and decreed that the defendants, their officers, agents and servants, be, and they are hereby, severally enjoined from diverting or taking from the Laramie River its tributaries in the State of Colorado more than fifteen thousand five hundred (15,500) acre-feet of water per annum in virtue of or through what is designated in the pleadings and evidence as the Laramie-Poudre Tunnel appropriation in that State, Provided that, this decree shall not prejudice the right of the State of Colorado, or of any one recognized by her as duly entitled thereto, to continue to exercise the right now existing and hereby recognized to divert and take from such stream and its tributaries in that State eighteen thousand (18,000) acre-feet of water per annum in virtue of and through what is designated in the pleadings and evidence in the Skyline Ditch appropriation in that State; nor prejudice the right of that state, or of any one recognized by here as duly entitled thereto, to continue to exercise the right now existing and hereby recognized to divert and take from such stream and its tributaries in that State four thousand two hundred and fifty (4,250) acre feet of water per annum in virtue of and through the meadow-land appropriations in that State which are named in the pleadings and evidence; nor prejudice or affect the right of the State of Colorado or the State of Wyoming or of any one recognized by either State as duly entitled thereto, to continue to exercise the right to divert and use water from Sand Creek, sometimes spoken of as a tributary of the Laramie River in virtue of any existing and lawful appropriation of the waters of such creek.[1]

The Decree was modified later in 1922, again in 1932 and 1940.[2]

Justice Van Devanter's substantive opinion in *Wyoming v. Colorado* was most recently relied upon by the U.S. Supreme Court in 2010 in the case of *State of South Carolina v. State of North Carolina*,[3] a case involving the Catawba River, and in a 2011 case, *Montana v. Wyoming*, a case involving an interstate compact on the Yellowstone River.[4]

In *State of South Carolina v. State of North Carolina*, Chief Justice Roberts, with whom Justices Thomas, Ginsburg, and Sotomayor joined, concurring in the judgment in part and dissenting in part, wrote for the majority:

A State's citizens also need not be made parties to an equitable apportionment action because the Court's judgment in such an action does not determine the water rights of any individual citizen. We made that clear long ago in two decisions arising from the same dispute, *Wyoming v. Colorado*, 298 U.S. 573 (1936), and *Wyoming v. Colorado*, 309 U.S. 572 (1940). In those cases, Wyoming sought to enforce this Court's earlier decree apportioning the Laramie River. See *Wyoming v. Colorado*, 260 U.S. 1 (1922). We held that the decree controlled the allocation of water between Wyoming and Colorado, not within them. As we recognized, our decision apportioning the river did not "withdraw water claims dealt with therein from the operation of local laws relating to their transfer or ... restrict their utilization in ways not affecting the rights of one State and her claimants as against the other State and her claimants." 298 U. S., at 584. Thus, although the decree referred to particular uses of water in Colorado, we held that those individual uses could vary from the terms set out in the decree, so long as the total diversion of water in Colorado was no greater than the decree allowed. See id., at 584–585; 309 U. S., at 579–581. We reiterated the point in *Nebraska v. Wyoming*, 325 U.S. 589, 627 (1945), observing that the apportionment of a waterway between the States has only an "indirect effect" on the rights of individuals within the States.

It is unlikely that Chief Justice Roberts had studied the history of the personal stake of the real parties in interest in the original Laramie River case.

The case of *Wyoming v. Colorado* has been espoused as the basis of the western water law principle that the prior appropriation doctrine (first in time equals first in right) prevails across state lines with respect to common water bodies, notwithstanding that prior appropriation is a state law principle. After consideration of the history surrounding the case, and particularly the bias of the opinion's author, the decision in the case can hardly be sustained as the basis for any legal, or equitable principle, notwithstanding the Court's several references to it in recent cases.

James E. Sherow has argued that Associate Justice Van Devanter's holding in *Wyoming v. Colorado* does not establish a legal principle regarding the interstate application of the prior appropriation doctrine at all, but is rather merely an application of equity by the Supreme Court in a conflict between states.[5] Even that analysis, which is protectionist of the Supreme Court's integrity, does not adequately dismiss the case for what it is: an act of self interest, bias and prejudicial error. It does not call to account the judicial misbehavior which any modern, principled ethicist would regard as beyond acceptable.

The same day that the opinion and decree in *Wyoming v. Colorado* was published, June 5, 1922, another opinion in an interstate water case was published in the Supreme Court's reports. That opinion, *Adelbert A. Weiland, as State Engineer of Colorado, et al. v. Pioneer Irrigation Company*,[6] was published immediately following Justice Van Devanter's opinion in *Wyoming v. Colorado*. But its authorship was attributed to Associate Justice John Hessins Clarke. Justice Van Devanter had learned in March directly from Justice Clarke that he intended to resign from the Court, due in part to the torment he received from Justice McReynolds. In July and August, Justice Clarke corresponded with Justice Van Devanter frequently regarding his frailty, weariness and intention to resign.

On July 31, 1922, Justice Clarke sent a handwritten note to Justice Van Devanter saying,

The truth is, my dear friend, my situation is quite paralyzing me. I mean I find myself without [illegible] or desire to go anywhere or to do anything—all interest in life has gone out of me.

> I am here in my sister's old home, quite alone, with the old servants., and this may contribute to any state of mind although I find my chief satisfaction in thinking of them and being surrounded by things they selected and enjoyed. The neighbors [illegible] are all that could be desired—the change is on me. But no more of this, time the anodyne may help me.

On August 11, 1922, Justice Clarke sent another note to Justice Van Devanter declining Van Devanter's invitation to Parry Sound, premised on issues of settlement of Clarke's sister's estate. But, he said, "There is a matter about which I cannot write which I very much wished to talk over with you." August 23 and August 31, Justice Clark sent two more handwritten notes to Justice Van Devanter. The latter described Clarke's physical condition, frailty, weariness and intention to resign the court. "I have to have time to get acquainted with my own soul before it leaves my body." Earlier in the spring, Clarke had communicated his intention to retire somewhat broadly within the Court, to be effective in the fall of 1922. Clarke would leave the bench permanently on September 17, 1922.

The case that Justice Clarke had ostensibly authored in June, sometimes referred to as *Nebraska v. Colorado*, involved the Republican River which flows from Colorado into Nebraska. The opinion affirmed the Eighth Circuit's decision, and relied, for its determinative authority, upon the controlling "constitutional" rule of law set forth in Van Devanter's own opinion of *Wyoming v. Colorado* published the same day.

> As to the merits of the case. In the discussion of the jurisdictional question it has been sufficiently developed that the essential controversy here involved is whether priority of appropriation of water, from the part of an interstate stream in Colorado, for beneficial use on lands in Nebraska, into which State the stream in a state of nature flows, gives superiority of right over later appropriation also made in Colorado from the same stream, but for use in that State. Both of the lower courts held that the presence of the state line did not affect the superiority of right and enjoined the Colorado state officials from treating the appellee in the distribution of water otherwise than it would be treated if the canal were wholly within the State of Colorado and all the lands irrigated therefrom were in that State. The question thus presented is so fully disposed of on principle and authority in the opinion of the court this day announced in No. 8 Original, Wyoming v. Colorado, ante, 419, that further discussion of it would be superfluous and upon the authority of that decision the decree of the Circuit Court of Appeals is Affirmed.[7]

It is most peculiar that Justice Clarke could have known the decision in *Wyoming v. Colorado*, or have read it prior to Monday, June 5, when Chief Justice Taft had only reviewed it the Saturday before, and there is no record of any broader distribution, especially as Clarke was, at the same time, failing physically and eschewing his judicial responsibilities altogether.

Pioneer Irrigation Company of Nebraska had first sued Colorado's state engineer on August 8, 1913, in U.S. District Court for Colorado, on the basis of that court's diversity jurisdiction. Pioneer claimed an 1890 priority right to water diverted from the North Fork of the Republican River within the State of Colorado. Colorado's state engineer denied Pioneer's claim on the basis that Colorado's constitution and statutes provided that the water in natural streams belonged first to Coloradans and could not by law be appropriated for use in another state, regardless of priority of appropriation, the same argument that had been first made by Colorado's attorney general in the Laramie River case. The U.S. District Court agreed with Pioneer. Colorado's appeal to the U.S. Circuit Court of Appeals for the Eighth Circuit was heard, in 1916, before reargument of the Laramie River case before the Supreme Court in 1918. Colorado was represented by Victor Keyes, Colorado's Attorney General, and Delph Carpenter, the same counsel who were awaiting the opinion in *Wyoming v. Colorado*. Mr. Leslie E. Hubbard, Mr. Fred Farrar and Mr. Charles Roach were also on the briefs for Colorado. Carpenter made the oral argument. Mr. Edwin H. Park represented the appellee Pioneer Irrigation Company. The Eighth Circuit had affirmed the District Court.[8]

Colorado appealed the case to the Supreme Court. Although the Republican River decision was attributed to Clarke in the official report, the better guess is that it was actually authored by Van Devanter, in the same way he ghost-wrote opinions for the Chief Justice. Perhaps not coincidentally, Van Devanter still supervised the Eighth Circuit judges who handled the Republican River case, and remained a long-time acquaintance, if not endearing friend, of Judge Sanborn. Associate Justice Van Devanter had risen from the Eighth Circuit Court of Appeals to the Supreme Court in 1911. This case had reached the appellate court after his departure. Once on the Supreme Court, Van Devanter became the Supreme Court justice with administrative responsibility for matters arising from the Eighth Circuit to the Supreme Court.

Part IV

Implications for Water Law

31

What of the Merits of *Wyoming v. Colorado*?

Bias, prejudice and preference aside, what can be said substantively about Justice Van Devanter's opinion in *Wyoming v. Colorado*? How does it fare as a water law case? First, with respect to its most oft-pronounced legal principle, it is inconsistent. The opinion purports to be an exercise of the Court's equity jurisdiction. Yet the water law principle it espouses is little more than a declaration of federal common law, a practice not foreign to Justice Van Devanter's activist judicial "conservatism." One reconciliation of this anomaly is that the case holds for the proposition that adoption of the principle of prior appropriation by one state estops that state, as a matter of equity, from rebutting the assertion of the principle of prior appropriation by another state. James Sherow puts it this way in his "Latent Influence of Equity in *Wyoming v. Colorado*":

> For some time historians and legal scholars have distorted Justice Van Devanter's decision by interpreting it as recognizing prior appropriation dates along interstate streams as if no state boundary existed. The justice had simply used *one* prior appropriation date in Colorado as the means to divide the stream flow of the Laramie River between the two states in an equitable manner, and thereby denied Colorado's contention of sovereign control over its water by apportioning the Laramie River flow between the two states.[1]

Sherow's proposition is questionable, however, in that Justice Van Devanter had distinguished the "relation back" principle of prior appropriation law, a device he had used in his career in the Department of the Interior to give priority to railroad land claims, thereby affirmatively hacking off seven years of Colorado's priority:

> An appropriation does not take priority by relation as of a time anterior to the existence of such a purpose. [That is, a purpose] to pick up and carry through [on the] primary conception [of development of a water resource.][2]

The effect of Van Devanter's distinguishing the principle was to give preference to some of Wyoming's later claims established in the seven year interval between 1902 and 1909. Colorado had argued that Cache la Poudre use was first established as of August 25, 1902, a date supported by its permit issued by the Colorado State Engineer, whereas the Wheatland use in Wyoming was only established in 1909.[3] Van Devanter admits, without specificity, that some of Wyoming's claims "must be treated as relating to later dates," and therefore as being junior to that appropriation. But he examines the Wyoming claims for uses initiated in the 1902–1909 period no further. Had Van Devanter applied the relation-back principle differently, the outcome, in acre-feet of water, may have differed dramatically. James Sherow observes:

> Notice [that] Justice Van Devanter did not award any Wyoming irrigators the right to divert water before the Greeley-Poudre Irrigation District could through its tunnel. Rather, the Skyline Ditch could divert 18,000 acre feet per year; the hay meadow farmers could divert 4,250 acre feet per year; and the Greeley-Poudre Irrigation District could divert 15,500 acre feet per year *before* Wyoming irrigators could count on receiving any flows from the Laramie River. Prior appropriation, as if state boundaries were absent, would not govern the continued distribution of water between the states, and both remained free to administer water rights according to the laws of each.[4]

If there is a precedent established by the case of *Wyoming v. Colorado*, it should be acknowledged as a precedent in equity, not a legal precedent. The State of Wyoming had argued that prior appropriation is a principle in equity, the Supreme Court declared that its jurisdiction was in equity, and Justice Van Devanter ruled that equity favored Wyoming over Colorado. With respect to the Court's "equity" jurisdiction, however, it doesn't feel much like the opinion "does equity." Wyoming did not come into the controversy with clean hands, and Justice Van Devanter's conflicted and biased position would clearly be regarded an abuse of equity, were it the subject of the judicial enquiry.

And the case should not be included in the Court's "equitable apportionment" jurisprudence. Justice Van Devanter did not apply any of the analysis or consider the important principles of the more modern equitable apportionment cases. Although the Supreme Court's exclusive jurisdiction over equitable apportionment cases between states gave the Wyoming litigants their jurisdictional premise,[5] Wyoming never alleged or proved any injury to the sovereign interest of the State of Wyoming. The jurisdictional premise merely provided the Wyoming litigants the opportunity to seek their own justice and Van Devanter the opportunity to not be overturned in serving them. Only the constructive inference of equitable apportionment jurisdiction was raised by the characterization of the litigants as states, rather than private parties.

In an equitable apportionment case, the plaintiff state must prove injury, at least so sayeth the Supreme Court in 1931,[6] 1936[7] and 1943.[8] Without injury to a plaintiff state, there is no original jurisdiction. In the 1945 case involving competition by the states of Wyoming, Nebraska, and Colorado for water in the Northern Platte River, Justice Douglas does stick up for Justice Van Devanter's finding original jurisdiction on the sole basis that "where there is not enough water in the river to satisfy the claims asserted against it the situation is not basically different from that where two or more persons claim the right to the same parcel of land. The present claimants being States, we think the clash of interests to be of that character and dignity which makes the controversy a justiciable one under our original jurisdiction."[9] Justice Douglas did not point to any finding in *Wyoming v. Colorado* that the lack of Laramie River water to satisfy all claims was any more than a fear.

Rather, in his opinion in *Wyoming v. Colorado*, Justice Van Devanter found, merely and conveniently, that "the interests of the State are indissolubly linked with the rights of the appropriators. To the extent of the appropriation and use of the water in Colorado, a like situation exists there." This conclusion was based on the glossy observation that "as respects Wyoming the welfare, prosperity and happiness of the people of the larger part of the Laramie valley, as also a larger portion of the taxable resources of the two counties, are dependent on the appropriations [of water] in that State."[10] One wonders why it might take eleven years to render a decision in a case where the general welfare of the state was at risk.

The substantive law of equitable apportionment is about the objective of fair allocation of economic opportunity. Each state claiming some portion of a common interstate resource is entitled to some reasonable share of that resource. Justice Douglas pointed out in *Nebraska v. Wyoming*[11] that even as between states both or all of which utilize the prior appropriation scheme, "if an allocation between appropriation States is to be just and equitable, strict adherence to the priority rule may not be possible." In 1907, Justice Brewer had said, in *Kansas v. Colorado*, that in the case of an interstate river, the Court's primary objective is to make an "equitable apportionment of benefits between the ... States resulting from the flow of the river." In 1982, Justice Sandra Day O'Connor said, in *Colorado v. New Mexico* that the Court applies federal common law to determine each state's share.[12] In 1938, Justice Brandeis said, in *Hinderlider v. La Plata River & Cherry Creek Ditch Co.*, that local law is not determinative:

> Fair allocation rather than consistency with locally generated expectations became the touchstone of equitable apportionment. Local law remains, however, central to an equitable apportionment inquiry. Although the Court has never been very precise about the source of the law of equitable apportionment, its early decision makes it clear that the grant of original jurisdiction requires a federal law and a federal law that will not allow one state to use its law to gain an unfair advantage over another.[13]

The idea of superiority of rights, whether by prior appropriation or otherwise, should not be controlling upon the Supreme Court in an equitable apportionment case. Sherow observes that "those who think prior appropriation governs interstate stream use and base their arguments on Justice Van Devanter's decision in *Wyoming* v. *Colorado* (1922), are standing on shaky ground."[14] Nor is the Court bound by the variance between two states' riparian or appropriative water law origins. Rather, "all the factors which create equities in favor of one State or the other must be weighed...."

The Court's more recent equitable apportionment decision, *Colorado v. New Mexico*, indicates that the Court will likely consider the comparison of harm and benefit,[15] the feasibility of means to improve water use efficiency and enhance water supplies, and the protection of existing economies dependent on water.[16] The Court may consider a state's commitment to water conservation and avoidance of waste relevant, because protection of existing, prior wasteful uses at the expense of newer, more conservation-oriented uses would not be equitable. Justice Thurgood Marshall's request of the special master in *Colorado v. New Mexico* to make specific findings on remand illustrates the potentially more expansive concerns of a modern Supreme Court in an equitable apportionment case.[17]

The Court will also likely consider population and economic demand relevant. Justice Van Devanter's opinion in *Wyoming v. Colorado* considered none of these.

Another substantive theme raised by Justice Van Devanter's opinion in *Wyoming v. Colorado* is the question whether the determination of rights to the use of water is a matter of state or national law. This question remains central to any political or legal debate among water law practitioners, and was manifest in the Supreme Court's 2012 consideration of *PPL Montana, LLC v. Montana.*[18] It was central to the history of the development of irrigation projects in the arid west, and to the political debate over Congress' passage of the Reclamation Act in 1902. But Justice Van Devanter's substantive opinion regarding the United States' interest in interstate water seems suspect for two reasons. First, Van Devanter admittedly raised and dismissed the possibility of the United States' interest on his own initiative, without it having been raised by either of the parties. But also, the answer he gave accorded primarily with that of his political principal, Senator Francis Warren, and rebutted that of Warren's political opposition, Senator Francis Newlands. The debate obviously and necessarily involves the Commerce Clause and the Supremacy Clause of the U.S. Constitution, the implication of which western water politicians and lawyers still blithely decline to consider.

32

What of the Effect of the Decision in *Wyoming v. Colorado*?

Notwithstanding the merits of the decision, Justice Van Devanter's opinion in *Wyoming v. Colorado* had a significant effect on the politics, and law, of western water. It, together with Holmes' decision in *Bean v. Morris*, solidified interstate competition for multi-state water supply and drove the formation of the primary interstate device prevalent today in water allocation—interstate compacts developed pursuant to the Constitution's "Compact Clause."

Justice Van Devanter must have been starkly aware of the implications of his decision upon the interstate political discussion then underway on the Colorado River. Negotiation of the Colorado River Compact was fully engaged as he considered the Laramie River case in the spring of 1922. President Harding had named Californian Herbert Hoover, President Wilson's head of the U.S. Food Administration, as Secretary of Commerce on March 5, the year before, and the federal representative to the statutory Colorado River Compact Commission in December. The Commission met at the Department of Commerce in January. It held six public hearings in the West between March 15, 1922, and April 2, 1922, in Phoenix,[1] Los Angeles,[2] Salt Lake City,[3] Denver,[4] and Cheyenne.[5]

Ex parte communications from the parties with Justice Van Devanter, including from counsel from Wyoming, were common. And Van Devanter's long-time contemporary from Wyoming constitutional work in 1880s–1890s, Congressman Mondell, was by this time majority leader of the U.S. House of Representatives. Mondell, the senior congressman from the Colorado River Basin, had corresponded with Frank C. Emerson, Wyoming's compact representative.[6] Dan Tyler notes that Mondell wrote to Wyoming's Emerson on May 22, a mere two weeks before Van Devanter's decision.[7]

Like Van Devanter a dedicated Republican, Mondell had been long involved in the interstate water issues in the West. A mere year younger than Van Devanter, he had for many years been engaged in farming, stock-raising, and railroad construction, interests with which Van Devanter himself was long associated. Mondell had served as assistant commissioner of the General Land Office from November 15, 1897, until March 3, 1899, a term contemporaneous with Van Devanter's service as Assistant Attorney General in the Department of the Interior. Later, Mondell was chairman of the House Committee on Irrigation of Arid Lands in the 58th and 59th Congresses and House Committee on Public Lands in the 60th and 61st Congresses before he became House majority leader in the 66th and 67th Congresses. In 1921 Mondell had opposed HR 582, which would have approved an earlier draft of the Colorado River Compact.[8] Twenty years earlier, during the debate on the 1902 Newlands Act, Mondell had advocated a Tenth Amendment basis for state sovereignty over western streams as soon as they became states.[9] "Mondell points to the acts of 26 July 1866, 9 July 1870 and 3 March 1877 as the definitive congressional recognition of state control over the appropriation and distribution of water."

Contemporaries in Wyoming's state constitutional formation, and serving the Theodore Roosevelt administration regarding lands, waters and the west, Van Devanter and Mondell certainly had a common view and goal with respect to Wyoming's reliance on water resources. Mondell's view of state control over water resources had won the day in Van Devanter's opinion in the Laramie River case.

Congressman Mondell would have cared about the interstate water issues that were involved in the Laramie River case, as they pertained to the Colorado River, of which Wyoming claimed a share. Mondell had opposed the congressional authorization for state negotiation of the Colorado River Compact.[10] Running for the Senate in 1921,[11] Mondell's view of the Colorado River situation (as well as the Laramie River situation) must at least have been privately communicated to Van Devanter. Van Devanter was certainly aware of Mondell's state's rights position regarding control of water,[12] no less Senator Francis Warren's, the two of them now maintaining a thirty-year confidence.

Of course, Van Devanter's holding would have implications to both Colorado's and Wyoming's negotiating posture regarding the Colorado River, as California's claims predated both of the upper basin states' water use. Professor Tyler describes the context of negotiations from the upper basin perspective:

> [In] 1922, when upper basin states of the Colorado River, including Colorado, demanded protection for undeveloped water rights at a time when California's irrigated agriculture was expanding, the upper state's principal concern was the potential for California to establish senior reservoir rights by means of a dam in the lower end of the Colorado River. When the Supreme Court handed down its decision in Wyoming v. Colorado that same year, recognizing the legitimacy of interstate prior appropriation, Carpenter knew that the upper basin's only hope for equity was agreement on a seven-state compact plan that relied on comity, not priority or competition.[13]

Counsel for both Wyoming and Colorado in the Laramie River case were present at the Compact Commission meetings being held in the spring.

> [At the April 2, 1922, Cheyenne public hearing, Carpenter] engaged his old opponent, Wyoming attorney Nellis Corthell, in a disagreement over the potential impact of a Supreme Court decision in Wyoming v. Colorado if that decision were to come during CRCC negotiations. Corthell believed that a ruling would "lighten the burden of this commission." Carpenter replied that, win or lose, the Court's opinion would be entitled to "great respect," but would have no bearing on CRCC negotiations.[14]

However, Tyler relates that,

> speaking for the upper basin in general, Wyoming Commissioner Emerson objected to any suggestion of use limitations on states of origin.[15]

In order to avoid a cataclysmic confrontation with California, Colorado agreed to Carpenter's "equitable apportion by agreement" approach. There was just no way to avoid it. Justice Van Devanter had protected the water Wyoming needed from the Laramie River and exposed the upper basin to the longer-held claim of the Californians to the Colorado River. The Colorado River Compact was signed by representatives of the seven Colorado River Basin states at Bishop's Lodge at Santa Fe, New Mexico, on November 24, 1922.

Van Devanter's opinion in the Laramie River case also had an immediate effect on other western states with claims to interstate water resources. After the opinion was published, attorneys for Kansas, New Mexico, Wyoming, and Nebraska began to announce intentions to litigate their alleged priority rights against neighboring states.[16]

Had Justice Van Devanter done the same as had Justice Brewer, taking the case in equitable apportionment, a different outcome would likely have been produced. And the law following would likely have differed. Equity, equitable apportionment, and reasonable use, all consistent with Justice Joseph Story's opinion in *Tyler v. Wilkinson*,[17] would have guided the future. Instead, might, money, favoritism, paternalism, preferment and patronage would lead development of the American west. Even intestate agreements authorized by the Compact Clause of the U.S. Constitution would be negotiated from an economic and political power perspective, rather than one guided by equity and resource management.

33

The Case for Recusal

Why did Justice Van Devanter not recuse himself in the Laramie River case? Water Law in the west would have been different had he done so. Perhaps the answer is so obvious as to make the question naïve. But modern ethics would dictate that he should have done so. And it is of course also naïve to presume that the U.S. Supreme Court is not, even today, a political institution. Jeffery Rosen's discussion about Justice Sandra Day O'Connor's loyalty to the Republican Party in elective politics in *Bush v. Gore* (2000) illustrates the point well. Justice Van Devanter's decision and opinion in *Wyoming v. Colorado* could hardly be characterized as anything other than political, given his political history, his familial loyalty, and the times.

For the American generation that learned its ethics from the tawdry, but fascinating, Watergate Scandal, governmental ethics matters. In the latter years of the Rehnquist Court, and again in the first years of the Roberts' Court, the public has grown to expect that the Supreme Court will act either as a collegial mass, or at least as a divided court arrayed across a principled spectrum with a swing-voting justice calling the outcome. From today's perspective, it seems unusual that an opinion of the Supreme Court would carry only one justice's signature, that there would be no concurring or dissenting opinions, that the full Court would, in essence, acquiesce in a single justice's sole control of a pending case. In a significant 2009 opinion, the modern Court recognized that judicial bias arises when one litigant "chooses his own judge" without the consent of the opposing party.[1] Judicial recusal has become the respected norm for new associate justices joining the court.[2]

It is difficult to determine whether the Court's leadership or other associate justices knew of Van Devanter's clear conflict of interest as there is little evidence that they knew much about the case at all. Chief Justice White knew the case existed, as he heard argument on it at least once. But he was dead when the decision was published. Chief Justice Taft knew the case existed, but perhaps not until the last minute before it was published. It is probably better merely to conclude that most of the Court just didn't know about the conflict of interest. As we have seen, the Chief's intended collegiality, where members of the Court were expected to get along and go along, suggests his willingness to overlook the conflict. Indeed Taft may have viewed loyalty to family and prior-client interests as an asset.

James MacGregor Burns has said:

> But neither has the Supreme Court been *above* politics. Most justices have been political activists—*party* politicos—before joining the court. Many have owed their elevation to party ties, as

a reward for loyalty, with every expectation that they will not turn coat on the court. Justices might shed party labels when they take their seats on the bench—newspapers don't print the (R) or (D) after their names when reporting decisions—but, with notable exceptions, they do not abandon their party doctrines. Instead they become politicians in robes.[3]

Chief Justice Rehnquist explained in his Supreme Court history that politics is the context in which the Court operates:

[The Supreme Court] has always been beset by temptations to be too timid on the one hand, or too bold on the other, in passing on the constitutionality of laws enacted by Congress or by the state legislatures. The temptation to be too timid comes not only because of attacks from the President and Congress or denunciations in the press. It also arises because judges have often had a background in politics and frequently share many of the same sentiments as possess members of the executive and legislative branches of government.[4]

Judicial abuse of personal interest from the bench is first documented by Herodotus in *The Histories*. Recusal would have been the better course in the Persian courts, as consequences were dire.

He [Darius] also made Otanes the military commander of the coastal peoples. Onate's father Sisamnes had been one of the royal judges, but he had taken a bribe to deliver an unfair verdict, and so King Cambyses slit his throat and flayed off all his skin. He had thongs made out of the flayed skin, and he strung the chair on which Sisamnes had used to sit to deliver his verdicts with these thongs. Then he appointed Sisamnes' son to be a judge instead of the father whom he had killed and flayed, and told him to bear in mind the nature of the chair on which he would sit to deliver his verdicts.

So now Otanes, the one with this chair to sit on, became the successor to Megabazus' command, and captured Byzantium, Chacedon, Antandrus in Troas, and Lamponium. Taking a fleet from the Lesbians, he captured Lemnos and Imbros, both of which were still inhabited by Pelasgians at the time.[5]

The idea that judges who are interested in the outcome of the matters before them should recuse themselves appears again in Roman law, which permitted parties to remove judges where there was any suspicion of their impartiality. In the common-law tradition upon which American practice became based by the middle nineteenth century, the basis for recusal requests was refined from general suspicion to identification of a particular financial stake in the case. But even with the recusal option available, litigant disqualification of judges on the basis of bias was not an option in the English tradition fundamental to American common law.[6]

American ethics codes, legislatures and court rules have variously sought to define bias by enumeration of unique actions compromising judicial objectivity, including hearing cases they have previously tried, cases where they are material witnesses, or cases involving their prior government service.[7] And certain common-sense rationalizations sometimes compromise strict standards of conflict avoidance: small judicial pools, "duty to sit," "someone has got to be the judge" or the conflict will go on. Some argue that too rigid a standard of recusal or disqualification can hamper the elevation of jurists from trial to intermediate or final appellate courts.

Jeffrey Toobin points out that "[c]uriously, there are no formal rules governing when Supreme Court justices must withdraw from cases."[8] There is a Code of Conduct for United States Judges, which applies to U.S. Circuit Judges, U.S. District Judges, Court of International Trade Judges, Court of Federal Claims Judges, Bankruptcy Judges, and Magistrate Judges. Its canons contend that "a judge should uphold the integrity and independence of the judiciary," that "an independent and honorable judiciary is indispensable to justice in our society," that "a judge should avoid impropriety and the appearance of impropriety in all activities," and that "a judge should respect and comply with the law and should act at all times in a manner that promotes public confidence in the integrity and impartiality of the judiciary." The Code doesn't apply to U.S. Supreme Court justices. "[A] Supreme Court justice cannot be replaced in a given case...."[9]

Over its history, the Court has engaged in a collegiality that permits suasion between the justices behind closed doors (curtains). Jeffrey Rosen reminds that Chief Justice John Marshall "insisted that his colleagues room together in the same boardinghouse, so that they could discuss cases over glasses of his excellent Madeira."[10] Chief Justice Rehnquist relates that "Marshall, who throughout his thirty-four years as Chief Justice lived with his colleagues [then five associate justices] in a boardinghouse near the Capitol during the time they were in Washington, probably walked from his own boardinghouse to administer the [presidential] oath to Jefferson."[11] By the early twentieth century, Chief Justice Taft was still walking to the Court with Justice Holmes, and Justices Van Devanter and Day were doing the same (or at least down 16th Street to Pennsylvania Avenue to catch the trolley up to the Capitol). Taft's notion of "good fellows" was at least premised on history if not intellectual integrity.

Even the Court's most famous historic case, honorific *Marbury v. Madison*, about which any constitutional scholar can regale regarding the appropriate role of the Court, called out for Chief Justice Marshall's recusal. He had been the incumbent Secretary of State in the Adams Administration responsible for delivering Marbury's commission. Marshall's successor, James Madison, President Jefferson's Secretary of State, refused to deliver it, giving rise to the litigation. Marshall did not recuse himself and held the authorizing legislation, the Judiciary Act of 1801, unconstitutional notwithstanding his having operated under it as Secretary of State. Rather, as we all know, Marshall took the opportunity to write the seminal opinion on the Supreme Court's role in the American government.

In his latter day, Chief Justice William Rehnquist was a sound proponent of recusal to avoid appearance of extrajudicial preference. As an Associate Justice, Rehnquist had disqualified himself from participating in the Nixon Tapes Case. As a result he was given the task by his colleagues of assigning the seats within the courtroom for those who wished to hear the oral argument. "Although I would like to have heard the arguments just as a matter of interest, I decided that there was no place I could possibly sit in the courtroom and hear them without giving rise to speculation that perhaps I was secretly participating in the case after all, and so I simply remained in my chambers during the argument."[12]

Rehnquist looked back on the behavior of the Court with some better historical perspective on preservation of judicial ethic, recounting the action of Justice John Catron in the Court's consideration of the *Dred Scott* case:

"...the Court made what must be judged to be a serious error by the standards of judicial conduct today, and to me seems inexcusable by even the somewhat laxer standards of that day. Justice John Catron, who did not cease dabbling in Democratic politics at the time he was appointed an associate justice by Andrew Jackson, decided that perhaps [Justice] Grier's fellow Pennsylvanian, newly elected President James Buchanan, might be able to bring Grier around to agreeing that the Missouri Compromise was unconstitutional. It is also interesting to note parenthetically that Grier and Buchanan, like Taney, were alumni of Dickenson College. With the knowledge of Chief Justice Taney, Catron wrote Buchanan and urged the latter to write a letter to Grier as to the desirability of the latter's joining with the majority on this question. Buchanan apparently did so, and Grier's response to Buchanan gives a full chronology of the case within the Court to that date, and indicates that Grier had now been persuaded to join the majority."[13]

In another instance of judicial infidelity, Rehnquist recounts the unfortunate behavior of Associate Justice Stephen J. Field. In 1863 Congress created a tenth circuit to serve the Pacific states. Lincoln appointed Field, an active War Democrat supporter of Lincoln's war effort, to the newly created seat. Field's adventurism and political activity in California were not unlike Willis Van Devanter's in Wyoming thirty years later.

Born in Connecticut, Field was admitted to the New York Bar in 1841. He sailed for California in 1849 by way of Panama, landed in San Francisco and sailed up the Sacramento River to Marysville (a town above Sacramento on the river), where he was elected Alcalde (magistrate) three days later. Elected to the California legislature a year later, he practiced law in Marysville for seven years before his election to the Supreme Court of California.

Field's standards were bared in a case involving the ownership of land just beyond the borders of the City of San Francisco. Title to the land was based upon a Mexican land grant. The U.S. Board of Land Commissioners, which was charged with determining titles to such properties, had refused to confirm title to the City of San Francisco because of what it saw as a flaw in the Mexican title. The City appealed to the district court. The district court declined to hear the case, as the district court judge was interested in the claims himself. Field felt the claims dispute should be resolved and so drafted legislation, shepherded through Congress by Senator Conness of California, providing that in cases where a district judge was interested in a land claim pending before him, the matter should be transferred to the circuit court—in this instance where newly appointed Associate Justice Field now sat as the Tenth Circuit Court. When the case came to him, he held in favor of the City of San Francisco.

When Field got to Washington and began sitting with the U.S. Supreme Court, San Francisco and the private claimants both appealed his earlier decision. Field opposed the Court's hearing the case on appeal but was outpolled. Before the merits could be heard, Field drafted another bill confirming title in San Francisco. The California delegation again moved Field's bill through Congress. The Supreme Court's consideration of the case on the merits was moot. Field's earlier determination of title remained unamended.[14]

In the 1945 case of *Jewell Ridge Coal Corp. v. Local 6167, U.M.W.*[15] the coal company petitioned for rehearing of the majority's opinion on the basis that Justice Black, who had joined with the majority, should have disqualified himself. Local

6167's case had been argued by a Birmingham lawyer who had been Justice Black's law partner for a short period some twenty years before. "Chief Justice Stone, rather than preparing the usual 'order list' denial of the petition, drafted a short opinion stating that the question of disqualification of an individual justice is never open for consideration by the full Court. Justice Black insisted that the petition should be denied without any explanation, as was the custom in orders denying petitions for rehearing." Justices Jackson and Frankfurter concurred that "only a justice to whom a request for disqualification was addressed was empowered to decide that request."[16]

Today's Chief Justice Roberts has not proclaimed his view as to the appropriate behavior of the Court, nor the obligation of justices to declare or recuse themselves. At least in one 2006 instance, *Hamdon v. Rumsfeld*,[17] however, the Chief recused himself on the basis that he had sustained the action of the President who appointed him, George W. Bush, as an appellate judge in the action below. And in a 2010 case, *Stop the Beach Renourishment v. Florida Department of Environmental Protection*[18] Justice Stevens recused himself in a case involving the assertion of unconstitutional taking of Florida beach property, on the basis that he owned such property himself.

A 2009 case, *Caperton v. Massey Coal Co.*, raised the question whether recusal is required when a significantly large campaign donation in a judicial election has been made by a party in a case pending before the court. Hugh Caperton and Harman Development Corp. won a $50 million fraud verdict against A.T. Massey Coal Co. Massey's CEO had donated $3 million to help elect Judge Brent Benjamin to the West Virginia Supreme Court of Appeals, which reversed the lower court's award. Benjamin refused to recuse himself, on the basis that he had no personal financial stake in the outcome of the case, and cast the deciding vote on the three-judge court in Massey's favor.

When Caperton appealed, the Court reversed the West Virginia Court of Appeals, Justice Kennedy saying for the majority that

> there are instances when the introspection that often attends this process may reveal that what the judge had assumed to be a proper, controlling factor is not the real one at work. If the judge discovers that some personal bias or improper consideration seems to be the actuating cause of the decision or to be an influence so difficult to dispel that there is a real possibility of undermining neutrality, the judge may think it necessary to consider withdrawing from the case.[19]
>
> ...there is a serious risk of actual bias ... when a person with a personal stake in a particular case had a significant and disproportionate influence in placing the judge on the case by raising funds or directing the judge's election campaign when the case was pending or imminent.[20]
>
> Just as no man is allowed to be a judge in his own cause, similar fears of bias can arise when—without the consent of the other parties—a man chooses the judge in his own cause.[21]

It seems implausible that Justice Van Devanter could have stood the test laid down by the modern Court. He should have recused himself. Today's western water law might be different had he done so.

Part V

Willis Van Devanter's Justice

34

Van Devanter's Indian Cases (1897–1921)

Willis Van Devanter served as Assistant Attorney General for the Department of the Interior smack in the middle of the U.S.' Indian "assimilation" policy, a policy initiated in 1887 by the passage of the Dawes Act, or General Allotment Act,[1] its objective being to assimilate indigenous people into the mainstream of American culture as middle class farmers. One congressional enactment, in the summer of 1897 shortly before Van Devanter's matriculation to the Department of the Interior, declared the "settled policy of the Government to hereafter make no appropriation whatever for education [of Indians] in any sectarian school" and "that hereafter the Commissioner of Indian Affairs shall employ Indian girls as assistant matrons and Indian boys as farmers and industrial teachers in all Indian schools when practicable to do so."[2]

This was not the first instance in which attorney Van Devanter had shown his mindset regarding America's native peoples. Friedman and Israel specifically mention the "noteworthy case" of *Ward v. Race Horse*[3] that Willis argued before the U.S. Supreme Court in 1895. The case involved elk hunting by one Race Horse, a member of the Bannock Indian Tribe, who had killed seven elk on U.S. property otherwise used for unregulated cattle grazing, thereby ostensibly violating a Wyoming state statute, passed in 1895, prohibiting the same. The United States had treated with the Eastern Shoshone and Bannock Tribe of Indians on February 24, 1869,[4] establishing the Fort Hall Indian Reservation. The Treaty reserved to the Bannock Tribe "the right to hunt upon the unoccupied lands of the United States so long as game may be found thereon and so long as peace subsists among the whites and Indians on the borders of the hunting districts." John Lacey's prior law partner, now Judge Riner of the U.S. District Court for Wyoming, ruled in Race Horse's favor, granting his petition and application for writ of *habeas corpus*, and ordering him released from the Uinta County jail.[5] Among other things, Judge Riner repeated the prosecution's allegation that

> the lands at the place where the alleged offense was committed, and in the country adjacent thereto, which were not then inclosed and fenced by settlers and entrymen thereon, were, at the time of the commission of the offense, used as an open and common grazing ground for the grazing of live stock by the citizens of the state of Wyoming and citizens of other states, who had and owned live stock in large numbers at that time grazing, running, and ranging thereon; that the country adjacent thereto was, in the year 1895, and other years previous

thereto, divided into round-up districts, pursuant to the laws of the state of Wyoming; and that the cattle ranging thereon were, in the year 1895, and in other years previous thereto, rounded up, gathered, and handled, according to the long-established custom prevailing upon such round-ups, and pursuant to the laws of said state.

"Inclosure," as opposed to "enclosure," is the legal determination (either legislated or self-determined by power and wealth) that common land should be converted to private land. In England, "Inclosure Acts" had been prominent in Parliament throughout the period 1845–1882. In this case the common land was that land owned by the United States and not yet conveyed to anyone else.

Notwithstanding the desire of the politically active cattle establishment of Wyoming to utilize the unsettled prairie for its own purpose, without private ownership or other documented right of entry, a desire reflected in the Wyoming anti-hunting statute enacted by the Wyoming legislature in 1895, Judge Riner found that the Supremacy Clause of the U.S. Constitution[6] and a strict reading of the relevant treaty language exonerated Race Horse from Uinta County's prosecution. On appeal of Judge Riner's order to the U.S. Supreme Court, Justice White artfully construed the treaty's language so as to permit the "march of advancing civilization [which] foreshadowed the fact that the wilderness, which lay on all sides of the point selected for the reservation, was destined to be occupied and settled by the white man, hence interfering with the hitherto untrammeled right of occupancy of the Indian."[7] The Bannock Tribe's treaty rights thus conveniently existed only "so long as the necessities of civilization did not require otherwise." Whereas Attorney Van Devanter had apparently argued before the Court that Wyoming state law prevailed over federal treaty, a view directly contrary to the Supremacy Clause, Justice White's opinion rested squarely on the notion of Manifest Destiny. "The right to hunt given by the treaty clearly contemplated the disappearance of the conditions therein specified." Van Devanter was nevertheless accorded credit for his victory.[8]

Justice White's opinion in the *Race Horse* case was published only one week after Justice Henry Billings Brown's opinion in *Plessy v. Ferguson*[9] establishing the notion of "separate but equal" by upholding a Louisiana law requiring the separation of black and white passengers on railway cars , finding that the law did not violate the Thirteenth Amendment. Only Associate Justice Harlan dissented. Attorney Van Devanter had obviously found a sympathetic ear on the Supreme Court.

The American tribes themselves were now conveniently regarded as an interference with the cultural and economic development of individual Indians, a notion not inconsistent with the social Darwinism and moral imperative in which Van Devanter had been trained. The policy also incidentally coincided with the objective of breaking up tribal land masses protected by treaty and congressionally created reservations. The essential effect of the Dawes Act was a highly fractionated and "patchwork" ownership pattern within Indian holdings and an overall decline in the total amount of Indian-held property, dropping from 138 million acres in 1887 to 52 million acres in 1934.[10] The assimilation policy was eventually repudiated in the 1928 Meriam Report, "Problem of Indian Administration,"[11] and statutorily rebuked in the Wheeler-Howard Act, or Indian Reorganization Act of 1934.[12]

Assistant Attorney General Van Devanter's role in implementation of the

Dawes Act is documented in his numerous writings published in the *Decisions of the Department of the Interior Related to Public Lands* ("L.D."). His client Secretary of Interior's interest in reorganization of the administration of Indian affairs much involved him, particularly as Van Devanter was easily identified as the western lawyer from Cheyenne. Assistant Attorney General Van Devanter made decisions regarding which Indians were entitled to allotments, which non–Indians had superior claims due to newly-created settlement rights. In one case, Van Devanter found that three Indian men in Washington State could not garner homestead rights, which they claimed against the Northern Pacific Railroad's claims, because they hadn't "abandoned their tribal relations," a condition imposed by Congress when extending homesteading rights to Indians.[13] In another, he found that "Allotment Indians" could not represent themselves in lawsuits to get their paid taxes back from a state that was not authorized to collect them, but rather must rely on the United States Attorney in all litigation.[14] In another, he found that Indians must pay the government for the lands they were allotted out of proceeds they received from the sale of their prior reservation.[15]

It is not surprising that, once attaining his appointment to the U.S. Supreme Court, Associate Justice Willis Van Devanter would be assigned cases involving issues affecting native Americans. His Western experience, his six years' experience in the Department of the Interior, his seven years on the Eighth Circuit, all positioned him to be the "expert" on Indian cases.

In *Kindred v. Union Pacific R.R.*,[16] Van Devanter reviewed a 1909 Hook decision from the Eighth Circuit. Judges Hook, Sanborn and Phillips had heard the case below. Van Devanter affirmed Hook's opinion, holding for the Union Pacific Railroad, Van Devanter's former client. The case involved the divestiture of Delaware Indian land in Missouri, on a reservation earlier diminished in size by Act of Congress, and recognition of the railroad's continued right of way for construction of its rail line across the divested land. Van Devanter viewed the divestiture and sale of Indian lands, as well as preference for railroads, approvingly.

In a case the following year, however, Van Devanter held in *United States v. Mille de Chippewas*[17] that when Congress had consented to be sued, it became liable when its subsequent congressional action violated existing tribal rights that had vested under an earlier Indian treaty. Later that year, in *United States v. Sandoval*,[18] Van Devanter considered "whether the status of the Pueblo Indians and their lands is such that Congress competently can prohibit the introduction of intoxicating liquor into those lands notwithstanding the admission of New Mexico to statehood." In evaluating the intergovernmental question, essentially about federal priority, Van Devanter revealed his condescension to the native peoples. "The people of the pueblos, although sedentary, rather than nomadic, in their inclinations, and disposed to peace and industry, are nevertheless Indians in race, customs, and domestic government. Always living in separate and isolated communities, adhering to primitive modes of life, largely influenced by superstition and fetishism, and chiefly governed according to the crude customs inherited from their ancestors, they are essentially a simple, uninformed, and inferior people." Their "inferiority" justified federal regulations prohibiting sale of liquor to Indians. "With one accord, the reports of the superintendents charged with guarding their interests show that they are dependent upon the fostering care and protection of the government, like reservation Indians in general; that, although industrially superior, they are intellectually and morally inferior to many of them, and that they are easy victims to the evils and debasing influence of intoxicants." Van Devanter does not mention in any of these cases that he was dry. Nor does he mention his preference for good cigars, a preference revealed by correspondence to his cigar dealer preserved in his Supreme Court era documents now housed in the Library of Congress. Van Devanter echoed his condescension the following year in *Perrin v. United States* and *Pronovost v. United States.*[19]

Five years later, in 1918, in *Alaska Pacific Fisheries v. United States,*[20] Van Devanter found for the Indian tribe, rather than a California fish company, that the Annette Islands, in Alaska, conferred to the tribe by Congress, included the adjacent fishing grounds. In 1919, Van Devanter agreed with the Pueblo of Santa Rosa, in *Lane v. Pueblo of Santa Rosa*[21] that their land was theirs in its entirety under the laws of Spain and Mexico, before annexation of the Gadsden area by treaty in 1853, and title to the land couldn't be transferred at will by the United States. The members of the Pueblo were not "wards" of the U.S., Van Devanter opined. In 1920, in *Ward v. Love County*[22] and *Broadwell v. Carter County,*[23] Justice Van Devanter upheld Justice Lamar's prior (1912) decisions in *Choate v. Trapp,*[24] *Gleason v. Wood,*[25] and *English v. Richardson*[26] holding that Congress had passed title to Indian lands in Oklahoma free of state taxation. The county must return the unlawfully collected taxes.

Justice Van Devanter also addressed the conflict and interaction of laws, both *inter alia* tribal and federal jurisdiction and state and federal jurisdiction with respect to law enforcement on Indian reservations in *Southern Surety Co. v. Oklahoma,*[27] and *United States v. Quiver.*[28] But Indian law issues were not apparently, regarded as Van Devanter's exclusive domain as other members of the White Court wrote for the Court on Indian law questions, to wit: Chief Justice White—*United States v. Anderson*[29]; *Kennedy v. Becker,*[30] Justice Holmes—*Tinker v. Midland Valley Co.*[31]; *Carney v. Chapman*[32]; Justice McKenna—*Mullen v. Simmons*[33]; Justice Brandeis—*Turner v. United States*[34]; Justice Pitney—*United States v. Hutto*[35]; and Justice Clarke—*Ash Sheep Co. v. United States.*[36]

35

Van Devanter's Income Tax Cases (1920–1925)

Two decisions written by Justice Pitney had diminished the application of the income tax laws passed by Congress at the turn of the twentieth century. The first, in 1895, *Pollock v. Farmers' Loan and Trust Company*[1] said that bond interest was not income and could not be taxed. The second, in 1920, *Eisner v. Macomber*[2] said that capital gains were not income and therefore could not be taxed.

Later in 1920, in *Evans v. Gore*[3] Justice Van Devanter wrote for the majority, finding that a law passed by Congress imposing an income tax on judges' salaries violated Art III, § 2 of the Constitution, and that the passage of the Sixteenth Amendment didn't cure it. The Sixteenth Amendment said briefly, "The Congress shall have power to lay and collect taxes on incomes, from whatever source derived, without apportionment among the several States, and without regard to any census or enumeration." Van Devanter argued, as a matter of policy, that judicial salaries existed for the benefit of the public interest, as they establish judicial integrity and independence, rather than benefit the private interest of the judge. The case would be followed by Justice McReynolds in 1925 in *Miles v. Graham*.[4] In the process of reaching his conclusion, Van Devanter quotes Chief Justice John Marshall "whose rich experience as lawyer, legislator, and Chief Justice enabled him to speak as no one else could":

> Advert, sir, to the duties of a judge. He has to pass between the government and the man whom that government is prosecuting; between the most powerful individual in the community and the poorest and most unpopular. It is of the last importance that, in the exercise of these duties, he should observe the utmost fairness. Need I press the necessity of this? Does not every man feel that his own personal security and the security of his property depends on that fairness? The judicial department comes home in its effects to every man's fireside: it passes on his property, his reputation, his life, his all. Is it not to the last degree important that he should be rendered perfectly and completely independent, with nothing to influence or control him but God and his conscience? ... I have always thought, from my earliest youth till now, that the greatest scourge an angry Heaven ever inflicted upon an ungrateful and a sinning people was an ignorant, a corrupt, or a dependent judiciary [Debates Va. Conv. 1829–1831, pp. 616, 619].

Later Van Devanter says:

> It is clear beyond all need of exposition that, for the definite maintenance of constitutional understandings, it is indispensable alike for the preservation of the liberty of the individual and for the preservation of the integrity of the powers of the government, that there should be some

> nonpolitical forum in which those understandings can be impartially debated and determined. That forum our courts supply.

Worthy thoughts indeed, unfortunately in this case fashioned so as to defend the incomes, rather than the integrity, of the bench. When the substantive law issue was reviewed again in 1938, in *O'Malley v. Woodrough*,[5] Justice Frankfurter observed that "*Evans v. Gore* itself was rejected by most of the courts before whom the matter came after that decision." Justice Pittney's decision in the *Pollock* case would be reversed in *South Carolina v. Baker.*[6]

In an April 14, 1924, decision, *Burns Baking Company v. Bryan*,[7] Justices Butler, Taft and Van Devanter superimposed their judgment about what is reasonable to regulate in the interest of health and safety, for that of the state legislature. They held that regulating weights and measures was not necessary to protect against fraud, the setting of maximum weights for loaves was not really necessary to protect consumers against fraud and deception, and therefore that the law doing so was unconstitutional—primarily because it interfered with business freedoms. Brandeis and Holmes dissented.

In a May 4, 1925, case, *Shafer v. Farmers Grain Company*,[8] Justice Van Devanter wrote that North Dakota's grain inspection and grading law, a statute typical of the progressive movement of the middle American states of the early twentieth century, was constitutionally invalid because it affected a product that would be otherwise transacted in interstate commerce. The North Dakota regulatory power was thus divested in favor of federal regulatory power, albeit scantly exercised. The North Dakota law required the inspection of grains by a licensed inspector at the point of delivery into the wholesale market. The grade determined through inspection, essentially a function of size and "dockage" (foreign, non-grain material), would affect the market price. Under the lesser controlling system prevailing under the federal law, the ultimate sellers and purchasers of grains at retail could determine grade and thereby determine market price. The grower, remote from the market, could not review or influence the decision, although the market price determined flowed back to the amount of revenue the grower would receive. The grower had no control of the market. Van Devanter acknowledged that state-interstate conflicts were often soft conflicts difficult to determine but resolved the conflict rather summarily. Brandeis dissented.

Alpheus Thomas Mason observed that by the time Chief Justice Taft retired in 1930, "the Court sat in separate camps. Taft, Butler, McReynolds, Van Devanter, Sutherland and Sanford sat in one camp. Dissenting Justices Holmes, Brandeis and Stone sat in another. The majority construed governmental power narrowly, standing in the face of legislative attempts to address economic and social problems. The minority favored permitting legislative experimentation to address growing awareness of those problems."

36

The Four Horsemen

On May 18, 1937, President Franklin Delano Roosevelt was breakfasting in bed, propped up on pillows reading the morning papers, as was his practice. At 9:45 a.m., a letter was delivered to him which broke a constitutional log-jam and permitted FDR to proceed with adopting a new pattern of national American government that would bring the United States out of the Great Depression. The letter was from Associate Justice Willis Van Devanter. It carried the message that Van Devanter had decided to resign from the Court. A bill sponsored by Congressman Halton Sumner titled "An Act to Provide for Retirement of Justices of the Supreme Court" was attached. Justices sitting on the bench for at least fifteen years could retire with full salaries not subject to the income tax, and could serve as "reserve" judges until their deaths. The retirement provisions of this legislation still prevail for Supreme Court justices. The full blow-by-blow account of the "constitutional conflict" giving rise to this development is laid out in Joseph Alsop and Turner Catledge's book, *The 168 Days,* Leonard Baker's *Back to Back: The Duel Between FDR and the Supreme Court,*[1] Marian C. McKenna's *Franklin Roosevelt and the Great Constitutional War: The Court Packing Crisis of 1937*[2] and numerous others.

Congressman Sumner's bill had been fashioned to resolve a significant constitutional law confrontation between President Roosevelt's more liberal view, that Congress can regulate commerce generally, and the then-Supreme Court majority's more conservative view, that Congress cannot and should not. Upon the end of President Hoover's term, economic conditions in the United States were bleak. Once in office, Roosevelt led an aggressive legislative agenda to create government action addressing the economic condition. The Supreme Court had been conservative for decades, asserting itself as the bastion of preservation of the conservative status quo, standing defiantly against what it regarded a "social revolution"[3] in the making. The conservative court, says Phillip Cooper, "sought to repeal the Progressive era and impose a rigid laissez-faire capitalism on all public policymaking at all levels of government. It was an effort, as Holmes put it, to enact 'Mr. Herbert Spencer's social statics.'"[4]

In the Hughes Court's official photograph for the period 1932–1937, now published in *The Illustrated History of the Supreme Court of the United States,* Chief Justice Hughes sits with Van Devanter to his right and James Clark McReynolds to his left. George Sutherland sits to McReynolds' left; Louis Brandeis sits to Van

Devanter's right. All seem businesslike, with the exception of Brandeis, who appears taciturn. Again, Van Devanter is straight-faced, belying no clear emotion. Clean shaven, unbespectacled, hands draped in front of himself as though becoming ready to play the piano. Behind, stand Owen Roberts, Pierce Butler, Harlan Stone and Benjamin Cardozo, all four as though looking for a fight.

From 1933 through 1937, the Court, through the cohesive and organized front of Associate Justices Van Devanter, McReynolds, Sutherland, and Butler, with Associate Justice Owen Roberts sometimes enlisted to their conservative view, consistently opined to undercut the constitutional validity of Roosevelt's New Deal economic and social programs.[5] Rehnquist described the situation:

> The eight associate justices who sat with Hughes were a varied lot. The four whose legal philosophy was least sympathetic to sustaining New Deal measures were dubbed the "four horsemen": Willis Van Devanter; James C. McReynolds, appointed by Wilson in 1914; George C. Sutherland, appointed by Harding in 1922; and Pierce Butler, appointed by Harding in 1923. All were over seventy years of age [in 1937].[6]

Theodore M. Vestal observed that "using a catch-22 logic, the conservative block found states could not regulate much because of Congress' commerce power, and Congress could not regulate much because of the states' police power."[7] Based on this Quixotic logic, the conservative Court overturned the Railway Pension Act

U.S. Supreme Court, official portrait of the Hughes Court, 1936. Back row, left to right: Associate Justices Owen Roberts, Pierce Butler, Harlan Stone, Benjamin Cardozo. Front row, left to right: Associate Justices Louis Brandeis, Willis Van Devanter, Chief Justice Charles Evans Hughes, Associate Justices James McReynolds, George Sutherland. Van Devanter now leads the "Four Horsemen" as a senior member of the Court sitting to the Chief Justice Hughes' right (courtesy Wyoming State Archives).

in *Railroad Retirement Board v. Alton Railroad*[8] in 1935 on the basis that it violated the commerce clause and condemned the National Industrial Recovery Act[9] on the basis that it violated the tax clause, in *Schechter Poultry v. United States*.[10] There, even Chief Justice Hughes wrote that Congress could not authorize the minimum wage and maximum hour provisions of New York State's live-poultry code through delegation of authority to the National Recovery Administration. Vagueness and generality unconstitutionally spoiled the delegation. The Court went on to void the Agricultural Adjustment Act's processing tax[11] in *United States v. Butler*[12] in 1936, and struck down the New York State minimum wage law in *Morehead v. New York ex rel Tipaldo*[13] on the basis that it violated the due process clause.

A new working environment didn't help. The Supreme Court's new building was now complete, and some of the justices were moving in. Justice Van Devanter was now the most senior associate justice. Hoover's appointee Justice Owen Roberts was the most junior, with just four years on the bench. Seven members of the court had been appointed by Republicans, only two by Democrat Woodrow Wilson.[14] Justice Van Devanter and the conservative Court's members elected to stay in their old offices at home. Rehnquist says:

> When the new building was first opened at the beginning of the October 1935 term, the justices had been used to working in their homes. They would come to the courtroom in the Capitol building to hear oral arguments, and to hold conferences, but they had law libraries in their homes and did their preparation for argument and conference there. The members of the Court were quite reluctant to abandon these arrangements in 1935, and many of them continued to work out of their homes.[15]

Supreme Court historian Bernard Swartz observed:

> Yet many of the Justices were attached to the old courtroom and deemed its location in the Capitol an important plus. The Court may have been barren in physical facilities, but its atmosphere was rich in dignity and tradition. President Taft wanted to initiate construction of a Supreme Court Building. Chief Justice White resisted the idea; he feared that the public would lose interest in the Court if it left the Capitol. Indeed, after the Court finally moved out of its cramped Capitol quarters in 1935 to the marble temple in which it now sits, a Justice was to refer longingly to "that wonderful old courtroom in the Capitol, which I think it was almost a desecration of tradition to leave."[16]

The conservative court trudged on, finding unanimously in *Louisville Joint Stock Land Bank v. Radford*[17] that regardless of the great emergencies created by the farm depression, congressionally modeled regulation could not deprive a mortgage holder of too much of its security without paying just compensation, and finding eight to one in *Humphrey's Executor v. United States*[18] that the President was not empowered to remove a member of the Federal Trade Commission merely because he disagreed with that member's philosophical perspective.

Of the Four Horsemen, conservative Van Devanter was the ringleader, the "man behind the curtain." According to Roger W. Corley, throughout the roughly thirty-six cases generally regarded as within the Roosevelt/Supreme Court conflict, Justice Van Devanter is identified as the primary author or signator of none.[19] Yet his conservative point of view was advocated through the mutual authorship of others. Edward Lazarus observes that "every day of argument or conference, the Four

Horsemen would ride to and from the Court together for the purpose of coordinating their positions."[20]

In a manner now again in vogue in the Supreme Court, Associate Justices Van Devanter, Sutherland, Butler, McReynolds had asserted an "originalist" view that the Constitution's meaning is fixed solely by the words' original meaning and their framers' intentions,[21] a view clearly contradicted by Chief Justice Hughes' 1933 opinion in *Home Building and Loan Association v. Blaisdell.*[22] But "originalism" for the Horsemen was not so straight-jacketed as it might seem, for the framers' "intensions" were subject to compliance with the desired result as well. Thus, although sworn in to the originalist view, the judicial activism of these conservative justices was unbridled when they needed to interpret the Constitution in a manner that served their political objectives.

For Chief Justice Hughes, on the other hand, as Kenneth L. Holland explains, the "vision of our time" as it relates to constitutional language is a relevant guide to the development of Supreme Court law. He dismissed the notion that the words of the Constitution had to mean the same thing when written and now.[23] With Hughes as the Court's Chief Justice, Justice Owen Roberts found enough space to move away from the four ardent conservatives, making their majority insecure.

In the face of the conservative Court's intransigence and President Roosevelt's momentum, Congress recognized it must resolve the tension. Even though the issue at stake was governmental potential in the face of constitutional conservatism, the popular political issue was the age of sitting justices and their staying too long on the Court. Congress approached the problem in its political terms. Marian McKenna explains:

> Under [Texas Congressman Sumners' bill] a justice of the Supreme Court, instead of resigning, could retain his office but retire from active service. This measure is considered one of the oddest sideshows in the entire history of the Supreme Court fight. It had been offered in a previous session of Congress, when Sumners saw the probability that the Court would run into trouble. Sounding out the situation in 1936, he learned that Justices Sutherland and Van Devanter were considering retiring, but uncertainty about salary provisions for justices was holding them back. Although full pensions until death were already in effect, they had reason to fear that Congress might again impose the salary cuts, like Justice Holmes and others had to take under the Economy Act of 1933.[24]

In 1894, the Supreme Court had ruled that a federal income tax, surely a fair device for taxation of the wealthy, was unconstitutional. In 1925, the Supreme Court had held in *Miles v. Graham*[25] that income taxation of a federal judicial salary was an unconstitutional diminution of compensation. Van Devanter had voted with the majority. McKenna continues:

> They did not want to become subject to the income tax, and would have done so under existing law with loss of their judicial status. Sumners designed a bill preserving their judicial status, establishing the new category of "retired justice," which retained minor judicial functions. If they retired, as opposed to resigning, they would in a sense still be members of the Court; thus their compensation could not be reduced by law, nor would they be subject to the income tax.
>
> This earlier bill sailed through committee and on to the House floor, only to have this delicately conceived plan upset by a filibuster lead by Sumners' fellow Texan, Tom Blanton, who insisted that no man, not even a Supreme Court justice, deserved more than his own annual

honorarium of $10,000. That left the matter unresolved at the end of 1936. Sumners revived his bill in January 1937, hoping to get it through both houses with the retirements over and done with before Roosevelt could make his move.[26]

Chairman of the House Judiciary Committee, Congressman Sumners moved his bill out of Committee, where it passed the House without amendment, and was sent on to the Senate. Rehnquist recounts:

> On Friday, February 5, 1937, members of the President's Cabinet, the Democratic leadership of both houses of Congress, and the chairmen of the House and Senate Judiciary Committees were summoned to meet with the President in the Cabinet Room of the White House. When Roosevelt entered the Cabinet Room from the Oval Office, he was followed by a secretary who placed a pile of papers at each seat around the table. The papers contained a message to Congress from the President, recommending that the judicial branch of the government be "reorganized." ... The reorganization was to be accompanied by a draft bill providing that for each member of the Supreme Court who was over seventy years of age, and did not elect to retire, the President would be empowered to appoint an additional justice to the Court and thereby enlarge the Court's membership up to a total of fifteen. Since six of the nine members of the Court were then over seventy years of age, if none of them chose to retire upon the enactment of the bill, the President would immediately be authorized to appoint six additional justices to the Court.[27]

Willis Van Devanter was now 78 years old. Democrats Carl Hatchett of New Mexico, Pat McCarran of Nevada and Joseph Mahoney of Wyoming quickly announced their opposition to Roosevelt's plan. Roosevelt's proposal was quickly dubbed the "Court-packing plan" by its critics. In reaction, Congressman Sumners' judiciary retirement bill quickly passed the Senate on February 26, 1937 and became law on March 1, 1937. The President's proposal, however, hung in the Senate Judiciary Committee,[28] was later reported with disapproval, and then hung further on the Senate calendar. But Roosevelt was undeterred. According to Justice Rehnquist,

> The President [Roosevelt] seized the opportunity in a Democratic victory dinner held at the Mayflower Hotel in Washington on March 4 to shift from the basis of age to the basis of constitutional obstructionism in his attack on the Supreme Court.[29]

Congressman Sumners and Idaho's Senator William Borah were both known to be close friends of Justice Van Devanter.[30] William Borah, who Leonard Baker claims "had lines of communication to the conservative members of the Court," had urged Van Devanter to retire[31] in advance of the President's proposal.[32] Justice Rehnquist says that

> Justice Van Devanter had been considering retirement for some time, and he was a good friend of his fellow westerner in the Senate, William E. Borah of Idaho. Borah suggested to Van Devanter that if he were going to retire, he might as well do it at a time when it would help to defeat the Court bill. Van Devanter accordingly picked the morning of May 18, 1937, to call in a wire service reporter covering the Supreme Court and announce that he had moments earlier sent by messenger a letter of resignation to the President. Coincidentally, May 18 was the day on which the Judiciary Committee was to meet and vote on the President's plan, and as the committee convened, Senator Wheeler made sure that each member was aware of the news of the Van Devanter resignation which had just gone out on the ticker tape. The committee, meeting in closed-door session, quickly voted on six variations of the same proposal, designed to save some part of the President's original plan. Each proposal failed.[33]

Van Devanter's action accepting the retirement proposal, on his negotiated terms, was widely believed to have been the result of counsel from Senators Borah and Burton Wheeler (who now lived in the same apartment house on Connecticut Avenue, as Willis Van Devanter).[34] After Van Devanter retired, Senator Borah even took the position that because Van Devanter had retired under the terms of the newly enacted pension legislation, and had not "resigned." Thus the Van Devanter position was not vacant. Utah's Senator George Sutherland may also have participated in encouraging Van Devanter departure. Sumners' retirement bill was fully suited to Van Devanter's age and situation, as well as his anathema to the income tax. Thus, by May 18, 1937, Van Devanter's retirement letter was ready for delivery to President Roosevelt (in bed). With Van Devanter's willingness to accept a golden parachute in hand, the Senate Judiciary Committee retired Roosevelt's court packing plan the same day with a formal report disapproving the court-packing bill.

While Justice Van Devanter and Congress put the final touches on the arrangement that would permit Van Devanter's retirement, the conservative court was getting its last licks. On March 29, the Court published its opinion in *West Coast Hotel v. Parrish*.[35] The majority opinion written by Chief Justice Hughes upheld Washington State's minimum wage statute. Justice Sutherland dissented on behalf of the conservative bloc including Van Devanter. The conservatives found the state minimum wage statute offended the Due Process Clause.[36]

On April 14, a month before Van Devanter sent his resignation letter to President Roosevelt, the Court published its opinion in *National Labor Relations Board v. Jones and Laughlin Steel Corporation*.[37] Van Devanter, joined by Sutherland and Butler, argued that federal regulation of labor-management relations violated the Commerce Clause because the effect on interstate commerce was too indirect and remote. And on May 24, six days after Roosevelt received his resignation, the Court published its opinion in *Steward Machine Co. v. Davis*.[38] Van Devanter joined the majority opinion written by Justice Cardozo finding that the unemployment insurance system created by Congress must fall as Congress had relied on its taxing power only as a mere pretext.

Van Devanter retired on June 1, 1937. Roosevelt's "court packing plan" was finally abandoned on July 22, 1937, when Roosevelt's proposed legislation was removed from consideration by the full Senate. Leonard Baker summarizes the battle between the Court and the President sublimely: "As the political activities appeared to be writing a finish to the Court duel, those persons most immediately affected—the justices of the Supreme Court—were away from Washington. The 1936–1937 session had ended June 2, and they had left the city almost immediately.... Van Devanter, his resignation in effect, was happily roaming around his 708-acre farm in Ellicott City, Maryland, dressed in a straw hat and old clothes."

Years later, Van Devanter was merely remembered as retired from the court due to "advanced age, enactment of improved judicial retirement statute, realization that further opposition to New Deal would be unsuccessful."[39] He would later serve by designation as U.S. District Judge.[40]

Van Devanter's resignation provided Roosevelt his first Supreme Court appointment opportunity. Roosevelt appointed Senator Hugo L. Black of Alabama to Van Devanter's seat on the Court. As Sutherland also retired, Roosevelt gained a second opportunity to fashion the Court, appointing Stanley Reed to fill Sutherland's seat. The Court gradually began to be reshaped in its more modern view of the role of the Commerce Clause.

From today's perspective, Franklin D. Roosevelt seems to have won the constitutional conflict popularity contest, while Justice Van Devanter lost and is for the most part largely forgotten. Where Roosevelt is regarded one of the greater presidents, in part because of his success in reviving U.S. economic prowess (albeit ultimately through war), Van Devanter is regarded as one of the Court's lesser justices. The range of political conflict exercised through the Supreme Court of course has not been forgotten. Seventy-five years after the aggressive constitutional conflict that played out between Roosevelt and Van Devanter, the same constitutional interpretation issue would manifest itself in liberal and conservative views expressed in majority opinions emanating from the conservative majority in the Roberts Court.[41]

37

The Measure of a Justice

There is no established standard by which to measure the success of a U.S. Supreme Court justice. Longevity and productivity seem to be common themes, but are perhaps not very meaningful standards. "The history of the Court abounds with long tenures, but even three decades does not guarantee that a justice will leave much of a legacy."[1] Only nine justices of the Supreme Court served longer than Willis Van Devanter. Two of those, William O. Douglas and Hugo L. Black, both appointed by Franklin Roosevelt, served longer.[2]

One study by Jeffrey Rosen pairs justices seeking the "most influential and effective justice" utilizing the standard of the greater willingness "to moderate the application of his principles in the name of the broader good of the Court and the country"[3]—a worthy standard indeed. Chief Justice Rehnquist respected a justice's ability and willingness to "cut the intellectual meat" as a sign of judicial leadership, rather than mere leadership by conciliation.[4] Rehnquist also remarked on a justice's ability to approach the cases he was obliged to decide with "total detachment."[5] But Rehnquist's highest regard in judicial attributes seems to have been for the ability of a justice to persuade his colleagues,[6] an attribute for which Justice Van Devanter is often praised.

Generally speaking, Supreme Court historians regard Associate Justice Van Devanter as having been a "failure" as a justice. He is often ranked as "one of the weakest of the justices."[7] Henry J. Abraham finds the "failure" designation too harsh.[8] Court historians most quickly berate Van Devanter for his having written so few opinions. Claire Cushman Johnson totes Van Devanter written opinions at 346 in twenty-seven years on the Court.[9]

Van Devanter is often said to have had "chronic writer's block," Schultz claiming that Van Devanter wrote fewer opinions than any of his brethren.[10] In fact, Van Devanter averaged three written opinions a term during his last decade on the Court, according to Johnson, citing Drew Pearson, including only 22 during the first six years of the 1930s when the Court produced 963 opinions overall.[11] And the counting cannot have included the ghost-writing that Van Devanter did under the auspices of other Justices' names.

Alpheus Mason claimed that Van Devanter "produced practically nothing."[12] Schultz suggests that Van Devanter recognized his own condition as "pen paralysis" and that "he did not do his share of the Court's opinion writing."[13] Van Devanter is remembered by Henry Abraham "for writing fewer opinions not only than any other justice who served with him, but also than any justice appointed between 1853 and 1943. He barely averaged three opinions a year during his last decade on the Court—only one in two years, none in one, and in his entire career on the high bench he penned only four dissenting and one concurring opinion."[14]

But the "writers block" assessment is too facile. Van Devanter did a lot of writing. But he certainly did not like to show his cards if he didn't have to. Van Devanter seemed to have the skill to infuse his thinking into others, to persuade others what to think, to write for others what they might or should say. He expressed himself through the pens and voices of others—a ghostwriter. His meticulous personal correspondence is impressive. His personal correspondence while on the Court, now available in the Library of Congress, was all typed with retained carbon copies. There are no strikeovers, back spaces, sentence fragments, ums or ahs. Van Devanter's signature, even at his later years on the Court was measured, even, meticulous, not scrawled or flourished.

Even as a young Wyoming lawyer, Van Devanter's "comprehensive" law practice was attributed to his manner: what Johnson describes as "thorough, well organized, and meticulous."[15] Van Devanter's grandson said of his grandfather and father that "the training of both Willis Van Devanter [attorney] and his son C.O. Van Devanter [engineer] made for accuracy. In fact both were not only accurate and methodical to the extreme, but both were almost precisionists. Both compiled extensive data...."[16] On the Court, Van Devanter's meticulous approach likely also contributed to a backlog of reported cases. Mason characterizes Van Devanter's problem as perfectionism:

> Van Devanter presented a unique problem. Though the "strongest man on the court" and indispensable in conference, the Associate Justice was "opinion-shy." He was, more-over, a perfectionist, "never content to let an opinion go until he has polished it and worked on it until it is a gem. But he is only able to get out a few opinions during the year on that account." The Chief Justice took every possible step to relieve him. Once when Van Devanter, near collapse due to his backlog of cases, posed "a nerve straining situation," the Chief Justice [Taft] told brother Horace: "...we have all got to unite to help him out." The extra load usually fell to Taft himself. During the eight full terms of the Taft regime, Van Devanter wrote a total of only ninety-one opinions for the Court compared with Taft's two hundred and forty-nine.[17]

Van Devanter's meticulous nature and attention to detail is borne out in review of his total career. The opinion-count approach, however, potentially leads to false conclusions where one justice insinuates his point of view through others, or merely writes an opinion for another justice and signs the other justice's name to it. Substantively, Van Devanter was no lightweight. His powers of persuasion in the conference setting are widely acknowledged by Court historians. Schultz says, "He was influential in group decision-making, because he was extremely intelligent, had a near-photographic memory, and knew a great deal of obscure and arcane federal law."[18]

Historians also acknowledge that Van Devanter was largely responsible for the 1925 "Judges' Bill" that allowed the Supreme Court greater control over its own docket through the certiorari procedure. Van Devanter was the primary spokesman/lobbyist for the Supreme Court before the Congress in advocating the bill.[19]

And Van Devanter was widely respected as an expert on judicial procedure, a knowledge valuable as a basis for declining, as well as electing, to act.

But it does not appear that Justice Van Devanter ever adopted the judicial dispassion that Chief Justice Rehnquist promoted, or that the public, perhaps naively, now expects of Supreme Court Justices. Loyalty to client interest, personal interest and political interest appears to have been Justice Van Devanter's primary motivation throughout his judicial career. His behavior in the Laramie River case differed little from his machinations in defense of the Wyoming cattle barons' crimes in the Johnson County War when practicing law back in Wyoming in the early 1890s. His loyalty to his prior client Union Pacific Railroad never faulted. In the later, 1927, case involving President Harding's Attorney General Henry M. Dougherty, and tangentially the U.S. Navy's petroleum reserves in Wyoming's Teapot Dome oil, *McGrain v. Dougherty*,[20] Justice Van Devanter found that Congress had the power to investigate and issue subpoenas even without an explicitly stated legislative purpose. The decision varies notably from Van Devanter's conservatism regarding the powers of government. It is easy to suppose, however, that Van Devanter's prior knowledge and potential inside track on the case's political implications influenced his choice of outcome. Wallace Johnson observed a bit casually that "Van Devanter supported Congressional power on a matter where he may have had historic background from his time as Assistant Attorney General or because it was located in Wyoming."[21]

Van Devanter's prowess in the conference room is mentioned by most Court historians, particularly referring to Chief Justice Taft's high regard for Van Devanter's argumentative skills. Taft also utilized the strategy of a "rump conference." Walter F. Murphy reports that Taft would convene "Van Devanter and several of his other friends for Sunday afternoon meeting at his home. There the group would thrash over some of the more difficult cases and opinions so that they could present a united front to the rest of the Court."[22] No doubt Van Devanter would become the lead advocate for the rump conference's pre-concluded position in the later full-Court conference. The intended effect was certainly to roll any dissenting justice into joining the now majority. Phillip J. Cooper recounts that Justice Felix Frankfurter later quoted Justice Brandeis, who was sitting in these conferences, that "Van Devanter would not be moved by threats of dissent by Brandeis."[23] Edward G. White says in his biography of Oliver Wendell Holmes

> Brandeis perceived the inner workings of the Supreme Court during Taft's Chief Justiceship as dominated by majority justices, such as Willis Van Devanter, who lobbied successfully with their "conservative" colleagues to ensure larger majorities by suppressing dissents.... The result was that a number of 5–4 decisions became rendered as 6–3 or even 7–2.[24]

Van Devanter had succeeded throughout his career in the context of the "smoke filled room." Wyoming politics, state and national Republican conventions, private correspondence—some of it coded for secrecy—were Van Devanter's practiced venues. And Van Devanter was an inveterate cigar smoker—his personal correspondence while on the U.S. Supreme Court includes monthly cover letters tendering payment to his cigar provider.

Thus, Van Devanter is better remembered for his private suasion than for his public communication. But he is also remembered for his conservatism. Together with Justice Sutherland, who came to the Court in 1922 in the months following Van Devanter's opinion in *Wyoming v. Colorado* and departed shortly after Van Devanter's retirement, Van Devanter is remembered by John M. Ferren as an "unconstructed conservative"[25] and Leonard Baker as a "consistent conservative."[26] Kermit Hall suggests that he be considered the "foremost intellectual conservative on the court during his 26-year tenure. His service was distinguished primarily by his performance in the conference and as a critic of his colleagues' opinions."[27] Schultz says,

> These decisions were unusual in that they did not focus on specific, defective portions of these laws but instead presented policy statements that demonstrated that the Court had, in essence, returned to its 19th century policy of prohibiting Congress from enacting laws that might have even the slightest effect upon interstate commerce.[28]

Peter Irons says,

> [After Taft's appointment of Van Devanter, his] supposed progressivism quickly vanished; during twenty-seven years on the court, he voted so consistently against governmental power that Justice Harlan Fiske Stone dubbed him "Commander in Chief of Judicial Reaction."[29]

Schultz says:

> As an associate justice of the Supreme Court, Van Devanter continued the precedent he established while on the Court of Appeals, disfavoring federal regulation of the economy. He concurred in decisions that established precedents limiting Congress' ability to pass laws concerning issues such as child labor and "yellow dog" contracts that allowed employers to require, as a precondition to employment, that workers sign away their right to unionize. The other salient prejudice that Van Devanter took to the high court was an interpretation of the due process clause of the Fourteenth Amendment that prevented state regulation of maximum work hours and minimum rate of pay.[30]

Peter Hoffer says,

> [Van Devanter] opposed civil rights and First Amendment liberties. Throughout his career, he could be counted on to take the least liberal position possible.[31]

Just as the attribution of Willis Van Devanter's paucity of publication to writer's block is too facile, so is the assessment that Willis Van Devanter was a principled conservative. Even the conservatism he espoused wasn't especially principled. Rather the "conservative" logic of his opinions, and the opinions of those he joined, was often outcome-determined—not unlike his opinion in *Wyoming v. Colorado*. His decisions are premised primarily on a view, consistent with social Darwinism, that the federal government should not be involved as a matter of policy, rather than any particular basis in the Constitution. The strong should not be deterred in their use of the weak. Van Devanter was primarily a politician and an opportunist. Educated in the old school tradition and principle that the educated should govern, elevated in the politics of preferment, trained in the judicial philosophy that the law is that which judges say it is, and comfortable with the social Darwinism of the conservative Court which acceded to the assertion of power as the basis of legal entitlement, Van Devanter was in the end mostly, and tragically, intransigent to change. As Wallace Johnson observed,

Van Devanter, despite his ability, despite his usefulness, seldom has deviated from a viewpoint as outmoded as the law of the six-shooter which governed Wyoming in the days when Van Devanter practiced law there.[32]

And as Stephen C. Halpern and Charles M. Lamb have acknowledged,

As one illustration of how dogmatic decisions amid rapid environmental change can be less than desirable, consider the fates of McReynolds, Sutherland, Butler, and Van Devanter, labeled by some as having been "failures" on the Court. Although it is usually argued with good cause that their being cast into lower echelons of judicial repute reflects their having lost a policy struggle over economic regulation during the 1930s, we can also suggest that whatever their short-term failings might have been, their more fundamental tragic flaw was their inability to adjust their conservative economic ideologies to post–Depression chaos; whatever value their laissez faire dogma had during the first three decades of this [twentieth] century, it was ill-suited to the political system during the fourth. Thus it was not simply the Four Horsemen's laissez faire morality that prompted a dismal appraisal by students of the Court, but their lack of vision as to what the Court's role ought to be during a time of crisis. On the horns of the stability-change dilemma, they held to stability with a vengeance.[33]

All in all, less has been written about Justice Van Devanter's life, and his contribution to Supreme Court jurisprudence, than has been written about some of the Court's more esteemed thinkers and jurists, at least four of whom were present at some point during Justice Van Devanter's tenure on the Court. Justices Harlan, Holmes, Hughes and Brandeis were all on the Court during Van Devanter's term, perhaps diminishing him in the historian's estimation. All have been biographed significantly. Some of the adjectives describing Justice Van Devanter, used by those who wrote about others during the period, are illustrative, however. Lewis Gould, for example, refers to Van Devanter's "limitless ambition" in early life.[34] They suggest an opportunist, a man who could have thrived in the "me generation," a man impressed with wealth and power, a man who understood and benefited from laissez faire economic policies typical of our more modern decades of excess.

The "golden parachute" arranged at his retirement is all too suggestive of the self-serving behavior of some modern CEOs in conflict of interest with their shareholders, and too similar to the self-indulgence of the railroad industry with which Willis Van Devanter had grown up. In retrospect, he appears doctrinaire and uncompromising.

Whatever judicial historians may think of Justice Van Devanter, they cannot discount his loyalty—one might say loyalty to a fault. Professors Bickel and Schmidt summarize it succinctly:

Van Devanter's man in Washington was Francis E. Warren, Civil War veteran, rancher, Senator from Wyoming, a shrewd, energetic, and durable Republican regular. Senator Warren's man in Wyoming, his confidant, counsel, and political manager, was Van Devanter.

Evaluating the Justice's years before he was appointed to the Court, the two professors wrote:

As to Van Devanter himself, the truth is that he had no distinct ideological commitments in these years. Whatever had lodged in him in Wyoming was not yet developed, and he brought no commitments from the Department of the Interior or the Court of Appeals. No doubt William D. Mitchell and Chief Justice Stone were right when, after Van Devanter's death, they located the origins of his attachment to "economic freedom" and to the philosophy that the

> least government is the best in his experience of old Wyoming, where "men were the masters of their fate," and where "industry, character and brains earned success," the fruits of which a man was allowed freely to enjoy. In these conditions of Van Devanter's early career, whether quite realistically perceived or somewhat idealized, we may find, if anywhere, "the seeds of his judgments," as Mitchell said (citing 316 U.S. xxi–xxii, xxxix [1942]). But only a later hindsight enables us to do so."

One must conclude that Van Devanter was the ultimate "inside politician"—he who works the power bases, angles and technicalities inside the system so as to accomplish unseen ends, which can benefit his or his friends' personal agendas. Justice Van Devanter was a man who worked his objectives on the inside of organizations, rather than on the outside—but by the end of his career, the organization within which he worked was committed to a political establishment whose days had passed. There is significant evidence of this conclusion: Van Devanter's early education, his paternal training as a lawyer through apprenticeship with his father, his unseen hand in the instruments of Wyoming statehood, his supposed expertise of judicial behavior and jurisdictional device in the practice of law, his purported expertise in conference in the Supreme Court, his paucity of published opinions, his success at keeping behind the scenes in the constitutional conflict of 1935–1937 (permitting the three other "Four Horsemen" to appear to author the confrontational opinions), his longstanding "friendship" with members of the Congress, and ultimately the political compromise which he crafted with Franklin D. Roosevelt through Senator Borah, both in its sly results and in Van Devanter's personal benefit.

Willis Van Devanter was a man of a lot of mischief. And a secretive man, a man who did not show his cards if he was not required to, a man who covered his tracks, burned his early correspondence, wrote letters in code, and asked others to destroy his correspondence upon reading it.

Looking back to the silver issue in Wyoming politics, Bickel and Schmidt sum it up rather well:

> when the silver issue split Wyoming Republicans in 1897 and the Warren faction found it prudent to favor bimetallism, Van Devanter went along, drafted a resolution on the subject, and discoursed at length to Warren on political strategy and consequence—but never the merits of bimetallism. It was some time before the ideologically committed Justice emerged alongside the skilled political and legal technician—whom, incidentally, the ideologically committed Justice was never to submerge.

Willis Van Devanter was the man of the velvet hand. His signature, placed below the photograph of the Court's sitting of 1933–1937, is even, perpendicular and ultimately legible, reflecting a clear-headed and calculating man. His visage suggests no less. His silent, non-public intervention, his quiet, adept drafting betrayed him not. The ever articulate, ghost writing spinner, he used exaggeration, self aggrandizement, secrecy and manipulation to his benefit. The truth was as he defined it, not as it was put to him by any context other than the political reality. A man who knew how to place his commas, a man behind the scenes, a man behind the curtain, a lifelong Mason, verisimilitude was his friend, the truth a mere acquaintance. Careful, operative, sly, strategic, master of false impression, he stretched the truth and the justification where it was required. Where did this skill come from? Did Van Devanter learn it in Wyoming, or teach it to Wyoming? Did he learn it from his ratiocinative, self-justified schooling? Was his puffing, bloating, aggrandizing, over- and mis-representing mind principled or convenient? Nixonian in style, an artisan of opportunism, Van Devanter could be grudging, clandestine, knavish, brave, self confident, loyal, indirect, patient, judgmental or proud. He was a smart, literate, tight-lipped, perfectionist. Somewhere at school, Machiavelli may certainly have been on his reading list.

38

Finis

Francis E. Warren served in the Senate until his death in Washington, D.C., on November 24, 1929, a tenure longer than any other to that time. He was buried in the Lake View Cemetery in Cheyenne, and is remembered most publicly through the name of the U.S. Air Force Base near Cheyenne, Wyoming.

On May 18, 1937, Willis Van Devanter retired from the Court. President Roosevelt replaced him with Associate Justice Hugo Black, a Democrat hailing from Alabama.

In 1938, U.S. Supreme Court's New Rules of Civil Procedure removed the formal distinction between equity and legal procedures.

In 1939, Associate Justice Brandeis retired from the Court. President Roosevelt replaced him with Associate Justice William O. Douglas.

Willis Van Devanter died in Washington, on February 8, 1941, eight months before Justice Brandeis, who also died in Washington, D.C., October 5, 1941.

It was the end of an era.

Human ethics must be considered within the framework, and times, of the more general society in which the human actor lived and worked. Willis Van Devanter appears the epitome of his age—the Gilded Age—and of the enhancement and protection of wealth and vested interests for which that historical period is known. *Wyoming v. Colorado* is a case about more than water law principles and judicial impropriety. It typifies the Gilded Age: rapid growth, industrialization, perfection and manipulation of the corporate model, rise and control of Republican machine politics primarily in Ohio and New York after the Civil War, Wall Street underwriting, westward expansion, railroad construction and transportation. Although the opinion in the case was not published until 1922, by which time agrarianism, populism, progressivism, recession and World War had tempered Gilded Age enthusiasm, its author seems not to have been similarly tempered by the changing of times. And so it is with today's water law: built in an age of presupposed abundance, but needed to fit within an age of acknowledged scarcity.

Van Devanter's legacy still manifests itself in the water management infrastructure of the American West and impedes providing essential resources to environment and urban populations successfully, while maintaining agricultural prowess, in the coming century. The question becomes whether we can successfully manage limited natural resources, such as water supply the shortage of which the United States and the world will in future endure, under legal principles first established in the Gilded Age. Conflict is certain if the legal paradigm established by that Age's principles and ethics cannot be rescinded or modified in the public good.

Associate Justice Van Devanter played a significant role in setting the firmness of the prior appropriation doctrine in the American West. When the Supreme Court's reliance on that doctrine is considered within the context of the other issues of governmental function *vis a vis* wealth accumulation and control then before the same Supreme Court, the doctrine's place in the panoply of conservative principles protective of aggressive, perhaps overreaching, self help and vested rights, is evident. This alone would perhaps be no problem were it not for the growing paucity of the water resource.

From today's perspective, we should reconsider the notion that first in time should be first in right. We should abandon the notion that claims to water may be unlimited even though water resources are not. We know now that surface waters are limited in volume. Even though we cannot see beneath the ground's surface, we know that the groundwater is likely connected to surface waters in some hydrogeologic way. We know that the water stored in the ground is not itself unlimited. We would be better to put all users, and all holders of right, on a level playing field, perhaps each constrained by the notion of reasonable use.

And we should think about prioritizing needs, rather than just rights. This would be better for sorting out future use, permitting society to help determine the highest and best uses of water based on social priorities. As to existing rights, shifting to a different water distribution paradigm would only diminish existing property rights to the extent of conflict with other important societal uses, and only to the extent that they are unreasonable. Whether that adjustment could be construed as a "taking" of prior rights, in the constitutional, 5th Amendment sense, depends upon the particulars of each case. And whether a legal system which necessarily disenfranchises late comers as a class can survive challenge under the equal protection clause of the Fourteenth Amendment is an open question.

Water is the future's essential shortage commodity, both locally and globally. Competition from multiple jurisdictions for limited water resources is said to be the future context of international warfare. In the United States, states, counties, groundwater basins, river basins all defend their water against foreign incursion. "Not in my backyard!" has become "Not from my backyard." "Trans-basin" is an ugly word. Much has been said about the devices of prior appropriation and interstate compact. But the history of motivations and vested-interest protections which gave birth to those devices belie the reality that they are both false solutions to fundamental problems of water allocation. The question remains whether a more "integrated" planning is necessary to bridge forward from a resource-limited conflict stage to a resource optimized one.

When Willis Van Devanter's life and work is considered in the context of the intellectual environment in which he lived and learned, some may feel his actions somewhat exonerated as typical or normal. But, to accept in retrospect the period in which he lived as a justification for his actions, rather than to indict the period itself, is to abandon the progress that retrospection allows, and to abandon any effort to undo the mistakes of the past.

What can be learned, as it relates to water management, from this rather unfortunate jurisprudential history? First, the predictive wisdom that water is the future's essential shortage commodity is merely an expansion of the past: water has also been history's essential shortage commodity. Second, a legal system that partitions control of this essential resource has the potential to motivate stratagem to manipulate dominance over the apportioned parts. Hopefully, the historical pattern will not manifest itself in future conflict, especially in the international context. And hope is a good thing.

In Willis Van Devanter's 1930 speech to his Marion, Indiana, admirers, reprinted in the *Indiana Law Journal,* he observed, "More modern water conflicts are no different, politics rather than water supply planning. Fear of loss of water resources drives water politics notwithstanding actual future impacts of water development. Water is regarded as a limited resource, regardless of maximization of its availability and use through artificial plumbing." This certainly had been his guiding principle in 1922, when he published the opinion in *Wyoming v. Colorado,* a case that he had surreptitiously husbanded through eleven years of tenure on the Court before publishing it while the Court was at its weakest.

Willis Van Devanter was indeed a man of his times. But the necessary question is whether those times, and the law that was generated of those times, should govern our more modern times, particularly if the retirement of that law raises no constitutional constraints.

In very recent years, more comprehensive water resource management approaches are being explored, usually at the more local stream, tributary or groundwater basin level. These are more dependent on increasingly rigorous hydraulic and hydrologic information, more inclusive of objective, purpose, participant and public interest, and more creative in regulatory approach than the simple interstate compact paradigm generated by the prior appropriation doctrine and the fear of faster development elsewhere. As development has now fully reached the point where water resources are claimed by more rights than there is water supply, a new paradigm is necessary. Regulation-constrained market-like devices utilized in the creative water settlements of recent years will permit some reallocation of rights to needs, and to some extent reconfigure our water use priorities, although doing nothing for the social injustice of apportioning water based on the date of the acquisition of water rights. Water markets depend upon continuance of the partitionment paradigm of prior-appropriation and interstate compact. The better course is to abandon the prior appropriation doctrine, a doctrine so clearly based on the assertion of power, in favor of a new social agreement on the better ways to deliver and use water in the public interest. The last lesson is, however, perhaps the most obvious: the U.S. Supreme Court is no good place to take a matter so important as the best utilization of our important sustenance—water.

Epilogue: That Was Then, This Is Now

What are we to make of the present implementation of the prior appropriation doctrine? Access to water in the American West is still substantially managed through that doctrine. Seventeen states[1] call it out as their "water law." The doctrine, still relying primarily on date of initiation of water use, doesn't consider which uses of water are most valued by a contemporary society. Legislatures and the courts have attempted to address that shortcoming, establishing municipal preferences,[2] environmental rights,[3] and growth management statutes.[4] But none of those inroads provide for the better life of individual humans, whose direct personal right to use water for domestic purposes is recognized only primarily in the rights of municipalities. It is that right, and the right of those humans to live in a healthful environment, which is prejudiced.

The doctrine rests on the assumption that there will always be sufficient water to satisfy most, if not all, the rights, a reckless assumption in the advent of climate change. It makes no consideration of the values of contemporary society. The doctrine relies on a central premise, "*appropriare,*" self help, which is inapposite to limited resource allocation. The doctrine is poor public policy.

The now-fashionable approach to the problem of moving water to need is to establish water "markets," turning rights into commodities that fiscally reward senior water rights holders whose older rights have now lost their utility value. Burdened with the hydrological and environmental consequences of transfer of water's use from one place to another, these markets don't work very well. Transactional costs are huge given the complex administrative Band-Aids implemented by states attempting to make social equity out of a legal regime worthy of Adam Smith.

Why need there be any priority system between rights at all? Under the common law's water law principles, equality of rights, opportunity and use was the prevailing concept, not priority. Premised largely on the ownership of the land on which the water presented itself, every water right was subject to the same use limitation: reasonable" or "correlative" use. This equivalence concept prevails throughout large portions of the United States and the rest of the world. From a global perspective appropriative water rights are the exception rather than the rule.

State courts and legislatures should devise water use allocation systems that are consistent with the U.S. Constitution. Just as local government's police power is exercised to protect the public health and welfare through the enactment of land use ordinances, so may it be used to allocate water in a manner consistent with equal protection of the laws.

What are the alternatives if courts find that prior appropriation laws violate the Equal Protection Clause of the Fourteenth Amendment to the U.S. Constitution? The answer is so conspicuously obvious as to be somewhat embarrassing. Repeal the time element of the prior appropriation doctrine. The question is not whether the legal entitlement to divert and use water has been legally and appropriately created or whether that entitlement should continue. The question, rather, is the extent of the right, whether it should possess the attribute that it may divest the similar later diversion or use of water by others whose entitlement was later established.

Leave existing rights in place. Apply correlative rights limitations on the volume element of existing rights, as had prevailed under the common law. Let new rights be established subject to the correlative rights principle as well. What will be the effect? As populations and demands increase, the society at large will feel the burden. But the burden will be distributed by the reasonable use requirement taking into account the competitive demand. Individual water users will be compelled to exercise conservative water practices. Equality of rights will be restored.

Equivalence of opportunity is a notion generally ensconced in the Equal Protection Clause. Population growth, growth management, interconnectivity of surface and groundwater and limited water supply generally are apt to make the inequivalence worse. Somehow the doctrine does not feel up to the standard by which the U.S. Constitution suggests we should live.

We know now that surface waters are limited in volume. And we also know, even though we cannot see beneath the ground's surface, that the groundwater is likely connected to surface waters in some hydraulic/hydrogeologic way, that the water stored in the ground is not unlimited. We would be better to put all users, and all holders of right, on a level playing field, each constrained by a reasonable use doctrine. This certainly would be better for sorting out future rights, permitting society to help determine the highest and best uses of water based on social priorities.

The appropriative right to use water for economic uses includes the rights to use it remote from source. At the common law,[5] that right was acquired only by the mere act of diversion of water (as personalty) from a surface water body (taking it for one's one own). This means of acquiring the right was later ensconced in statute. "Prior appropriation" is the attribute of such rights created by self action that permits the right's holder to preclude later diverters from diminishing supply. It is this attribute that raises the problems of equal protection.

The Fourteenth Amendment to the U.S. Constitution, Section 1, provides:

> "All persons born or naturalized in the United States, and subject to the jurisdiction thereof, are citizens of the United States and of the state wherein they reside. No state shall make or enforce any law which shall abridge the privileges or immunities of citizens of the United States; nor shall any state deprive any person of life, liberty, or property, without due process of law; nor deny to any person within its jurisdiction the equal protection of the laws."

The Clause is activated through litigation initiated in U.S. District Court pursuant to 42. U.S.C. §1983.[6] Cases brought under that jurisdictional statute have developed along with the sensitivities of American culture.

> "The generations that wrote and ratified the Bill of Rights and the Fourteenth Amendment did not presume to know the extent of freedom in all of its dimensions, and so they entrusted to future generations a charter protecting the right of all persons to enjoy liberty as we learn its meaning. When new insight reveals discord between the Constitution's central protections and a received legal stricture, a claim to liberty must be addressed." *United States v. Windsor*, 570 U.S. 771 (2013).

Under the U.S. Supreme Court's Equal Protection jurisprudence, a law is constitutional if the relationship between the class of persons or rights subject to the law's mandate and the governmental purpose the law is designed to pursue withstands judicial scrutiny. "In considering laws challenged under the Equal Protection Clause, this Court has evolved more than one test, depending upon the interest affected or the classification involved."[7]

Laws typically establish some privilege or prohibition for a particular class of persons. Where the relationship between the classification and the law's purpose are colorable, i.e., doesn't flunk the smell test, judicial scrutiny seeks only that there be a "rational basis" for the classification's definition. If no such basis exists, the classification is "invidious" or "arbitrary," and the Equal Protection Clause is violated.

Where the classification is wholly arbitrary ("suspect") or the right "fundamental," judicial scrutiny is "strict."[8] Where strict scrutiny finds onerous effect on suspect classifications or fundamental rights, the Court evaluates whether the state's interest is not "compelling" and whether a less suspect, or more narrowly drawn (more precise) classification might suffice. If so, discrimination is found. The Equal Protection Clause has been violated.

This two-tiered approach has been variously described in U.S. Supreme Court cases. It's clearest rendition was stated by Justice O'Connor in 1988: "Unless a statute provokes 'strict judicial scrutiny' because it interferes with a 'fundamental right' or discriminates against a 'suspect class,' it will ordinarily survive an equal protection attack so long as the challenged classification is rationally related to a legitimate governmental purpose."[9]

The initial question is whether a classification established by a state's legal infrastructure,[10] either itself or by its effect, is rationally related to that infrastructure's purpose. "Under traditional equal protection analysis, a legislative classification must be sustained if the classification itself is rationally related to a legitimate governmental interest,"[11] or "purpose."[12] "[T]he classification must be reasonable, not arbitrary, and must rest upon some ground of difference having a fair and substantial relation to the object of the legislation, so that all persons similarly circumstanced shall be treated alike."[13] "[A]n arbitrary classification bearing no reasonable relationship to the subject matter of the legislation, and is discriminatory" violates the Equal Protection Clause.[14] A "'classification must be not arbitrary but based on a real and substantial difference having a reasonable relation to the subject of the particular legislation.'"[15]

Can a statute that permits one water user to get water when it is in short supply, but deprives it of another, even though their water needs are the same, their only distinguishing characteristic being when their rights were established, survive muster under rational basis analysis? Is the time factor rationally related to natural resource management in any way at all?[16]

> "The decisive question as presented in almost all cases is whether the classifications drawn in a statute are reasonable in the light of its purpose. This presupposes that one knows or can identify the purpose of a law or ordinance, which ... is a far from simple undertaking. A preliminary point, however, must be made about terminology. At times reasonableness of classification is used as pertaining not only to the desired relationship of the classificatory trait to the purpose of the law but also to the composition and cohesiveness of the class selected for special treatment."[17]

The Supreme Court's "rational basis" analysis causes us to ask for the purpose of prior appropriation statutes. Legislative purpose in the context of equal protection analysis has been described as the goal or objective or aim of a law, in other words what the law principally wishes to bring about. Sometimes the purpose may be expressly stated. Sometimes it must be divined from legislative intent or the law's operation. Sometimes purpose can be divined through etymology (the history and meaning of the words used), through context (how words are used in a sentence or paragraph) or through inclusionary and exclusionary examples.

Unfortunately, no legislature or court has ever clearly identified the interest intended to be served by the prior appropriation doctrine. In considering what that interest may be, we must remember that it is not the means by which water rights may be established that is at issue (although that too is questioned by the cunning history set forth in the previous chapters). Under the common law, they could be established by acquisition of the fee interest in property or by diversion of water adjacent to another's riparian property. Under present statutory law they can be established only by governmentally sanctioned appropriation. Rather, it is the attribute of the statutory right, that timing creates priority of right, that must be justified by compelling state interest.

"The basic rule developed by the Supreme Court in the area of constitutional equality is that 'the Equal Protection Clause does not forbid discrimination with respect to things that are different' but only demands that similar things or persons must be treated similarly. '[W]hat the equal protection of the laws requires is equality of burdens upon those in like situation or condition.'"[18] "The purpose of an act must be found in its natural operation and effect."[19]

The doctrine's first statutory implementation related to arid lands—to "make the deserts green." It permitted diversion of surface water from its natural source and transportation to remote, otherwise dry lands. Because appropriation has been adopted throughout the arid states, but not in the less arid states, it has been called the "arid states doctrine" by some. The purpose of this legislation may thus be to make dry lands arable. The early "codes were limited to dealing with irrigation."[20] More generally, "in the development of the appropriation doctrine in the Western States, diversions of water for mining, domestic and irrigation purposes were commonly made" through appropriation.[21] Addressing aridity may thus be the state's primary interest in the doctrine. It is, in short, a legal convenience through which to enable movement of water from where it is to where it is not. It is difficult to see the nexus between aridity and time.

What might be the purpose of the time priority aspect of the doctrine? A state's most plausible interest may be to establish certainty as between rights, as in the nature of property recordation or lien priorities in commercial law.[22] This is, of course, the popular history of mining rights claims. This purpose is, however, nowhere stated in the judicial or legislative history of the prior appropriation doctrine pertaining to water.

Prior appropriation statutes usually carry the requirement that the appropriated water be used "beneficially." The statutory purpose may therefore be to generate economic benefit from water's use. Western states' statutes generally don't define "beneficial use." Instead, they list examples without stating whether the list is exclusive or merely suggestive of a more general attribute. Reading the early cases (e.g., water used for milling, mining, farming), one clearly discovers that the common attribute of "beneficial" is economic benefit.

In all the early (English Fourteenth Century) riparian use cases, water was used beneficially when it was put to work: grinding flour, turning a wheel, activating other motion in the production of goods, producing energy. In the early (American Nineteenth Century) appropriation cases, beneficial uses included moving earth in mining and farming arid ground. Only later statutory amendments suggest non-economic uses (e.g., water held in-stream for environmental purpose, fishery enhancement, recreation). Domestic and stock watering uses of surface or ground water have been honored since time immemorial, without proof of "beneficial use," recognizing water's life-sustaining properties.[23]

Neither legislatures nor courts have used the word "beneficial" in the water context to mean beneficial to the common good. Don't forget that the prior appropriation doctrine was adopted during the "Gilded Age" where creation of economic opportunity and protection of moneyed interests was the driving force, as the case earlier examined by this book sorely demonstrates. Given the doctrine's protection of vested interests, the state's interest may simply be to protect those moneyed interests.[24]

Because the doctrine's deference to economic benefit may interfere with enhancement of domestic water use, public health cannot be the statutory purpose. Most modern statutory definitions of beneficial use do include domestic use, albeit constrained by prior non-domestic uses. Sustenance of life is the object with domestic use, rather than economic benefit. Unfettered domestic use is more greatly served by common law riparian or groundwater rights, than by common law appropriation rights.

The state's interest (purpose) certainly is not fair and reasonable distribution of public resources nor insuring water availability of water for all citizens, the environment, or traditionally vulnerable groups—rural, low income, tenant populations—most significantly affected without water supply.

Practically applied, the doctrine permits junior rights holders to take water when there is greater water supply. And rights must be used or be lost. The state's interest cannot therefore be preservation of water supply, conservation, or most efficient use, either in surplus or in shortage. As the doctrine maximizes the removal of water from the water body both when water is in surplus and when it is in shortage, the state's interest cannot be protection of the water body. And the state's interest cannot be perpetuation of the common law, which stressed equality of rights of riparian and groundwater rights holders.

Traditional equal protection analysis would ask whether the classification established by the legislation rationally pursues its purpose.[25] Beginning with the proposition that all men should be treated alike except where there are relevant differences between them, "rational basis" analysis requires that such relevance be proved by the legislative authority responsible for the distinction. This required a balancing of the significance of the impact of the difference in treatment and the importance of the distinction in treatment of the bettered and disenfranchised groups.

The Supreme Court has dealt with time-based discrimination before. Its "rational basis" cases sort into three types: those where the state's purpose is unknown or unclear, those where the purpose is legitimate and clear (this type falling into three groups dealing with judicial administration, tax administration and business and commerce administration, respectively), and those dealing with state purposes or interests opprobrious on their face (closely affiliated with the fundamental rights cases).

A classification is likely irrationally related to purpose where no purpose is apparent. *Mayflower Farms v. Ten Eyck*,[26] an early (1936) rational basis case, a seminal one upon which many later cases are based, is particularly apropos. The Court considered a classification directly analogous to the prior appropriation classification. There, a municipal law regulated milk prices. Milk sellers in business before the law took effect could sell their milk at a lower price. A time element differentiated between pre- and post-law milk sellers. The Court found no stated reason for the discrimination,[27] and concluded that the Equal Protection Clause had been violated.

A year later, in *Hartford Steam Boiler Inspection and Ins. Co. v. Harrison*,[28] the Court addressed a statute dealing with mutual insurance companies, but excluding stock insurance companies from the class. The statute permitted corporate action through salaried representatives, but precluded stock insurance companies from so acting. The Court found that this "arbitrary classification bearing no reasonable relationship to the subject matter of the legislation" violated the Equal Protection Clause. Again, the challenged classification served no apparent purpose.[29]

The first group of generally clear purpose equal protection cases involves judicial administration. There the Court's judicial acumen understands viscerally the unequal justice imparted by discriminatory classification.[30] The second group of clear purpose equal protection cases involve state tax administration. These cases clearly illustrate the lack of relationship between device of classification and statutory purpose.[31] "[D]istinctions in the treatment of business entities engaged in the same business activity may be justified by genuinely different characteristics of the business involved."[32] In the case of prior appropriation classifications, business entities engaged in the same business activity have no guarantees of similar water right benefits. Indeed, particularly in agriculture, two farmers growing the same crop for the same market, but with different water rights, one senior to the other, have substantially different benefits. One has the economic advantage over the other. Likewise, citizens of different cities with differently-timed water rights suffer different water conservation limitations.

> "[T]he equal protection clause means that the rights of all persons must rest upon the same rule under similar circumstances, *Kentucky Railroad Tax Cases*, 115 U.S. 321, 337; *Magoun v. Illinois Trust & Savings Bank*, 170 U.S. 283, 293 and that it applies to the exercise of all the powers of the state which can affect the individual or his property, including the power of taxation. *County of Santa Clara v. Southern Pac. R. Co.*, 18 Fed. 385, 388-399; *The Railroad Tax Cases*, 13 Fed. 722, 733. It does not, however, forbid classification; and the power of the state to classify for purposes of taxation is of wide range and flexibility, provided always, that the classification 'must be reasonable, not arbitrary, and must rest upon some ground of difference having a fair and substantial relation to the object of the legislation, so that all persons similarly circumstanced shall be treated alike.' *Royster Guano Co. v. Virginia*, 253 U.S. 412, 415; *Air-way Corp. v. Day*, 266 U.S. 71, 85; *Schlesinger v. Wisconsin*, 270 U.S. 230, 240. That is to say, *mere* difference is not enough: the attempted classification 'must always rest upon some difference which bears a reasonable and just relation to the act in respect to which the classification is proposed, and can never be made arbitrarily and without any such basis.' *Gulf-Colorado & Santa Fe Ry. V. Ellis*, 165 U.S. 150, 155. Discriminations of an unusual character especially suggest careful consideration to determine whether they are obnoxious to the constitutional provision. Compare *Martin v. District of Columbia*, 205 U.S. 135, 139, *Bell's Gap R.R. Co. v. Pennsylvania*, 134 U.S. 232, 237." At pp. 37, 38. Quoted at length in *Hartford v. Harrison*."[33]

In *Schlesinger v. Wisconsin*,[34] the Court found that differentiation of tax treatment on inter vivos transfers (on those performed within 6 years of death and on those performed more than 6 years of death) violated of the Equal Protection Clause. Here, the stated purpose of the statute was the prevention of avoidance of payment of the estate tax. The Court found that the timing of inter vivos transfers of wealth did not indicate an attempt to avoid payment of estate taxes. "A classification for purposes of taxation must rest on some reasonable distinction." Here a time-based classification with much more plausible relationship to a more clearly stated purpose than exists in prior appropriation statutes went down under rational basis analysis.[35]

A third group of this sort of cases involve regulation of commerce. Several cases passing muster under the "rational basis" analysis are informative.

The Supreme Court found in *Connolly v. Union Sewer Pipe Co.*[36] that a statute establishing different applications of the antitrust law (one for goods manufacturers and sellers generally, another for agricultural goods) violated the Equal Protection Clause. And, in *Department of Agriculture v. Moreno*,[37] the Court found that federal food stamp regulations establishing different treatment of two classes of indigent people violated the equal protection aspect of the Fifth Amendment. The class of related people who lived in the same household was qualified to receive food stamps. But the class of unrelated people who lived in the same household was not. The purpose of the program was stimulation of the agricultural economy. "Under traditional equal protection analysis," the Court said, "a legislative classification must be sustained if the classification itself is rationally related to a legitimate governmental interest." "The challenged statutory classification ... is clearly irrelevant to the stated purposes of the Act."[38]

Then there are the opprobrious purpose cases. The Court found in *Shapiro v. Thompson*,[39] that several states' statutes differentiating between classes of applicants for welfare benefits (some being resident within the state for more than one year, others being resident within the state for less) violated the Equal Protection Clause. The states' purposes were to protect the state's fisc, or "to erect a barrier against the movement of indigent persons into the State or to effect their prompt departure after they have gotten there." The Court found that "the interests which appellants assert are promoted by the classification either may not constitutionally be promoted by government or are not compelling governmental interests."[40] Moreover, the classifications interfered with the welfare applicants' right to travel.

In *Romer v. Evans*,[41] another case of this type, the Court struck down a Colorado constitutional amendment preventing local governments from passing discrimination protections for homosexuals on the basis that the classification was designed specifically to preclude that class from otherwise enjoying the laws enjoyed by others. That purpose was sufficiently suspect, i.e., not a legitimate state interest, to despoil the rational relationship between classification and purpose.

> "Even in the ordinary equal protection case calling for the most deferential of standards, we insist on knowing the relation between the classification adopted and the object to be attained. The search for the link between classification and objective gives substance to the Equal Protection Clause; it provides guidance and discipline for the legislature, which is entitled to know what sorts of laws it can pass; and it marks the limits of our own authority."

As Justice Kennedy opined in *Romer v. Evans*, otherwise decided under "fundamental rights/strict scrutiny" analysis, "some statutory classifications are justified where the purpose is clear, and the classification serves the purpose." The Court will uphold them when the classifications are "narrow enough in scope and grounded in a sufficient factual context for us to ascertain some relation between the classification and the purpose it served. A law declaring that in general it shall be more difficult for one group of citizens than for all others to seek aid from the government is itself a denial of equal protection of the laws in the most literal sense."[42]

The classification at issue here is based on time. Earlier established rights holders are in the class. Later established rights holders are excluded from the class. Those not yet included in either class can be denied the opportunity to obtain any water right. Senior v. junior. The classifications do not consider proximity to source water, amount of investment, nature of use or any other particularly described purpose. "The first in time is the first in right." Early is good; late is a problem. It is difficult to reason that timeliness relates causally to the objectives of aridity, beneficial use, or efficiency. Thinking specifically about aridity, the agricultural soil's dryness is just as much moistened by a junior right holder's water as by a senior right holder's water. And about beneficial use, does a junior right holder's farming produce less economic benefit than does a senior right holders' farming? Does the time-based classification of rights serve or rationally relate to these purposes at all?

Some other water rights classifications might be more rational, e.g., "the most arid, the first in right," "the most economic benefit, the first in right," "the most efficient, the first in right," "the most proximate, the first in right," or the "most environmentally salubrious, the first in right." Timeliness would better seem to suggest preference for development of riparian lands, rather than remote arid lands, as they were earlier and easier to develop. Indeed, in ancient arid cultures, ancient cities situated upstream on more advantageous points of water access claimed superior water rights. But timeliness does not indicate whether any use is more or less beneficial, economic, more or less wasteful, or more advantageous to the current whim of society (e.g., environmental use, industrial use). And, timeliness seems to be irrationally related to the purpose of protecting water supply for domestic sustenance. We all need water, notwithstanding when our right to it was established.

Considering the "rational basis" opprobrious purpose cases, the question becomes whether the preservation of existing, vested interests, if that is the purpose of the prior appropriation doctrine, is an opprobrious purpose, one within governmental aegis. This purpose is often promoted by vested interests, albeit masked by legislative device suggesting an appropriate purpose. One can argue, of course, that vested interests make positive contributions to the general economic well-being. But that is logically questionable in the context of the even distribution of natural resources. And then, even accepting that protection of vested interests is a salubrious purpose, is the time classification rational? Not necessarily, as it may have the incidental effect of protecting vested uses that are no longer economically advantageous. Protection of vested interests is in direct contravention of the idea of equal distribution of rights, inherent in the Equal Protection Clause.

Generally, the rational basis cases evaluate whether different classes suffer different economic consequences due to the law in question. Under this thinking, the classifications created under the prior appropriation regime would seem to violate the Equal Protection Clause as they create different economic effects upon otherwise equivalent water users. Both the tax administration cases, and business and economic regulation cases suggest that the Equal Protection Clause guarantees an equal economic playing field. Arbitrary legal classifications interfere with that. The judicial administration cases suggest a rigorous application of the rational basis approach, closer to fundamental rights/strict scrutiny thinking. These cases intimate that the Court would look skeptically upon the validity of the prior appropriation regime's effect of denying new water rights for domestic use.

Six of the cases from all of the three groups of rational basis cases addressed time-based classifications. All were struck down as violations of the Equal Protection Clause. No time-based classification cases were found where the classification was upheld.

The Court in *Mayflower Park v. Ten Eyck* found no possible justification for the time-based discrimination, particularly dismissing statutory "grandfathering" as a legitimate purpose for the time-based classification:

> "We are referred to a host of decisions to the effect that a regulatory law may be prospective in operation and may except from its sweep those presently engaged in the calling or activity to which it is directed. Examples are statutes licensing physicians and dentists which apply only to those entering the profession subsequent to the passage of the act and exempt those then in practice, or zoning laws which exempt existing buildings, or laws forbidding slaughterhouses within certain areas but excepting existing establishments. The challenged provision is unlike such laws, since, on its face, it is not a regulation of a business or an activity in the interest of, or for the protection of, the public, but an attempt to give an economic advantage to those engaged in a given business at an arbitrary date as against all those who enter the industry after

that date. The appellees do not intimate that the classification bears any relation to the public health or welfare generally, that the provision will discourage monopoly, or that it was aimed at any abuse, cognizable by law, in the milk business. In the absence of any such showing, we have no right to conjure up possible situations which might justify the discrimination. The classification is arbitrary and unreasonable, and denies the appellant the equal protection of the law."[43]

Mayflower Park was an unclear purpose case. Its purpose could only be deduced from its statutorily-created classifications. Its purposes and classifications were tautological. They protected income certainty for one group of market participants at the expense of other equivalently based market participants. Certainty enhances the economic benefit derived from exercising a vested right.[44] Traditional equal protection analysis eschewed tautological purpose-classification analysis—where the classification was used to define the purpose. In such cases, rationality can be presumed and not questioned. Any classification would justify its purpose. That the purpose and the classification would coincide would justify all suspicious classifications which might have nefarious, discriminatory, or other undesirable purposes. Protection of vested interests, preference for the social mores of prior generations, preference for the economic conditions of a prior society, or preference for prior invested capital over yet-to-be invested capital can be justified under tautological classifications.

In *Oregon v. Mitchell*,[45] the Court found fault with the distinction between long- and short-term residents' eligibility for voting because they discriminated between classes of people based on time (duration of residence). In *Shapiro v. Thompson*,[46] the unconstitutional classification was residence time. The classification interfered with the welfare applicants' right to travel. In *Dunn v. Blumstein*,[47] the Court found durational residence laws violated the Equal Protection Clause because they divided residents into two classes, old residents and new residents, thereby penalizing those persons who have traveled from one place to another to establish a new residence during the qualifying period. In *Schlesinger v. Wisconsin*,[48] the Court found that differentiation of tax treatment on inter vivos transfers (on those performed within 6 years of death and on those performed more than 6 years of death) violated of the Equal Protection Clause.

Comparison of the classification of timeliness, as implemented by the prior appropriation doctrine, and the classification of reasonable use, as inherent in the common law, illustrates the arbitrariness of the former classification.

In sum, timeliness seems an irrational classification through which to pursue either the irrigation of arid lands or deriving economic benefit from the water resource. And a classification is clearly inconsistent with modern objectives of making the greatest social utility of that resource. It cannot be forgotten that every person, every society, every societal sector must have water for basic human existence. There is a social need for economic interests in natural resources to forego claims in lieu of those held for the public good. Where the resource is unlimited, the legislation may be clearly economic. But when the resource becomes limited and access to the resource is essential to life, then the legislation should be motivated by more than economics.

It is conceivable that the Court would go beyond "rational basis" analysis to consider this time-based classification under its "strict scrutiny" standard, analyzing the classification more scrupulously on the basis that the right to water is "fundamental." That more rigorous analysis is called for when the right at issue is such. State laws injurious to fundamental rights "must be shown to be necessary to the accomplishment of some permissible state objective."[49] "[C]lassifications which might invade or restrain them must be closely scrutinized and carefully confined." *Harper v. Virginia Board of Elections*,[50] *Roe v. Wade*.[51]

The Court's equal protection jurisprudence has recognized a number of fundamental rights, often premised on their nexus to "life, liberty and the pursuit of happiness." These include the right to vote,[52] the right to associate,[53] the right to racial equality,[54] the right to privacy,[55] the right to practice your religion,[56] the right to work for a living,[57] the right to marry,[58] the right to procreate—a "human right" basic to perpetuation of the human race,[59] the right of parents to direct the upbringing of their children,[60] the right to interstate travel,[61] and the right to possess and bear arms for personal self-defense.[62]

You can live without voting (many do). You can live without associating (although we may have found it difficult in "social distancing"). You can live without racial equality (although it has been now forcefully advocated that racial inequality corrupts society). And, you can live without privacy, religion, marriage, procreation and child-rearing. You can live without interstate travel. And you can live without bearing arms. But you cannot live without water. Nothing is more fundamental.[63]

The United Nations International Covenant on Civil and Political Rights recognizes rights to self-determination, to liberty, and to due process of law, freedoms of movement, thought, religion, expression, peaceful assembly, and association.[64] Without water, none of those rights can be exercised.[65] Without water, there is no life. Liberty means nothing. Happiness cannot be pursued. All three are "inalienable" rights according to the Declaration of Independence. Certainly, the right to water, necessary for the availability of all three, is also "inalienable." If inalienable, the right to water is axiomatically fundamental.[66]

Humans need air and water to live. That's pretty fundamental. An average adult human's body is 55 percent to 60 percent water. Going without domestic water for approximately 10 days causes death by dehydration. C. Thomas Dienes wrote that it is "difficult to conceive of any interest of greater importance to the individual and to the viability of a free and democratic society than access to the basic requisites of subsistence." "Whether or not we recognize that a citizen has a constitutional 'right' to subsistence, his interest in such subsistence for the effectuation of all other constitutional guarantees is so fundamental as to demand greater judicial protection than pure economic interests."[67] In his treatise *Equal Protection of the Laws*, Polyvios Polyviou asked, "Should not the interests in food, shelter, medical aid, education and other so-called necessities of life also be brought within the inner circle of fundamental rights? Can one doubt that nothing is of greater importance to the individual and to the viability of a free and democratic society than access to the basic requisites of subsistence?"[68]

In the course of human history, due to heavy reliance on mineralized groundwater or impure surface water, water was not always consumed domestically to the same extent as today. Beer and wine were more greatly consumed, their alcohol content eradicating impurities. By the fourteenth century, water was turned to power in grinding mills. By the eighteenth, it was turned to industrial power as steam locomotion. And at least since Mesopotamia, water has been used for irrigation. These historical uses do not minimize modern consumption of water treated adequately for domestic consumption. The U.S. Supreme Court noted in a 1970 Equal Protection case, "While neither the antiquity of a practice nor the fact of steadfast legislative and judicial adherence to it through the centuries insulates it from constitutional attack, these factors should be weighed in the balance," and "[t]he need to be open to reassessment of ancient practices other than those explicitly mandated by the Constitution."[69]

Today, many western states have domestic use preference statutes: Alaska,[70] Arizona,[71] California,[72] Colorado,[73] Idaho,[74] Kansas,[75] Nebraska,[76] New Mexico,[77] North Dakota,[78] Oklahoma,[79] Oregon,[80] South Dakota,[81] Texas,[82] and Wyoming[83] all have some sort of statutory protection for domestic water use. Rationalizing that preference against senior rights can be difficult. One would think that every person is entitled to consume water. The prior appropriations doctrine, however, suggests a different idea: that older rights can preempt domestic consumption if it is more recently established.

Strict judicial scrutiny requires asking some hard questions: What is the source, nature and status of the right or interest that the regulation allegedly encroaches? What governmental interests and objectives are served by the statutory conditions, provisions or requirements? Are they compelling? How much does the enactment interfere its exercise? Do less drastic means exist by which to accomplish the same state objectives? Has the enactment *illegitimately* affected an individual right, or has it done so in an *arbitrary* fashion? In short, are the statutory distinctions *necessary* to promote a *compelling* state interest?

An interest is compelling if it refers to something necessary or crucial, such as national security, preserving large numbers of lives, or promoting explicit constitutional rights or protections. A law or policy is narrowly tailored if it avoids encompassing in the classification more than those necessary or appropriate to achieve realization of the compelling state interest, i.e., it is "overbroad," and addresses the essential aspects of the compelling interest. There must not be a less restrictive means to effectively achieve the compelling government interest. Equally restrictive means, alternatively available, are not dispositive of narrow tailoring. The question is whether the asserted state interest is so compelling as to justify interference with the fundamental right.

The fact that water may be made available through some other source than one's own water right, e.g., bottled water, municipal supply, captured rain water, is no defense to the equal protection problem. Compare the marriage cases.[84] That a homosexual couple has heterosexual marriage or a governmentally sanctioned partnership agreement available to them does not cure the equal protection problem. The question is whether right to water is fundamental, in which case state interest must be compelling, or whether the classification is alone, on its face, rationally related to a legitimate statutory purpose.

Economic betterment or "beneficial use" alone is not a justification if the classification that accomplishes it is defective in its own right. Beneficial use could have been stated as justification for the classification of slavery, for example, before the Thirteenth and Fourteenth Amendments were adopted. Slavery exacted a labor force that made the production of cotton economic. Water secured by and protected by the doctrine of prior appropriation exacts a natural force, an engine, that generates an economic return, by irrigation, mill, industry, hydropower. The question is whether the state's interest in promoting economic betterment, through protection of vested rights, is so compelling as to justify interference with human right of life, liberty and happiness.

Humans' biological dependence on water seems just as essential as the other emoluments of life strictly analyzed against purported state purposes in the Supreme Court's Equal Protection jurisprudence.[85]

The lack of a clearly stated purpose for prior appropriation's time classifications may cause the Court concern (as it would have under "rational basis" analysis). In *Fisher v. University of Texas*, an affirmative action case, the Court observed that "strict scrutiny requires the university to demonstrate with clarity that its "'purpose or interest is both constitutionally permissible and substantial, and that its use of the classification is necessary ... to the accomplishment of its purpose.'"[86]

Classifications by time have not held up well in "strict scrutiny" cases. Fundamental rights have been upheld against durational residency voting regulations based on time.[87] Other state justifications for voting regulations have also been questioned.[88] Time of residence was an "invidious classification" denying the right to medical care in an indigents case.[89] And the extension of time of incarceration in "work off" payment of fines was found to be "impermissible discrimination.[90] Upholding of tradition is not a sufficiently compelling state interest to justify interference with a fundamental right. The state "interests" asserted in these cases had the consequence of entitling some and disentitling others, just as the prior appropriation doctrine.

Using time as an entitlement test has racial implication. American demographics are changing. "Newcomers," whether they be immigrants, equalized and upwardly mobile "minorities", or exponentially growing ethnicities, will not be able to realize the same water rights through their own self actualization as earlier generation Americans unless they enrich the latter through outright purchase of senior rights. The inequality gets worse with time, as the value of senior water rights increase with scarcity.

Although the Fourteenth Amendment ostensibly addresses state action, nonstate action sanctioned by the state's action can also breach the Amendment. In *Reitman v. Mulkey*,[91] a race case, the United State Supreme Court held that in the case of California's Proposition 14, "the State had taken affirmative action designed to make private discriminations legally possible," thereby violating the Fourteenth Amendment's Equal Protection Clause.[92] The effect of time-priority discrimination may be perpetrated by private parties (i.e., senior water rights holders) rather than the state itself where the state's statutory and judicial actions have permitted and perpetuated a private right.

So that was then. And this is now—time to change our thinking about how water rights are allocated, distributed and used. And time to return to John Locke's prescient and practical distinction between our right to the water we have collected from the community well and now rests in our own urn, and the right to return to the well to fill the urn again.

Chapter Notes

Prologue

1. "The surname van Devanter, meaning of (or from) Deventer, is of Netherland origin, derived from the ancient City of Defenter, in the province of Oeryssel on the River Yssel." Braden Vandevanter, in Van Devanter, Christobelle, *The Van Devanter Family*, E.W. Stephens Company, Columbia, MO (1943) Foreword.

2. Holsinger, M. Paul, "The Appointment of Supreme Court Justice Van Devanter: A Study in Political Preferment." 12 American Journal of Legal History 324 (1968), (hereafter, Holsinger, 1968).

3. 531 U.S. 98 (December 12, 2000).

4. 558 U.S. 310 (January 21, 2010).

5. 567 U.S. 519 (June 28, 2012).

6. 259 U.S. 419.

7. Elwood Mead was reported as Wyoming State Engineer (in charge of water rights and interstate competition for water) in the Session Laws, State of Wyoming, Fifth State Legislature (1899).

8. 259 U.S. 498.

Chapter 1

1. Between 1864 and 1868 the Bozeman Trail ran from the North Platte River to Virginia City, Montana—through the last hunting grounds of the Northern Plains Indians. Beginning in 1866, the Trail was protected by three military posts: Fort Reno; Fort C.F. Smith; Fort Phil Kearny. For two years there was constant freighting along the trail and around the posts. When, in 1868 the Union Pacific Railroad was complete across Wyoming, the Trail was no longer a short cut to Virginia City. The military posts had become a liability to the Government. Negotiations began with Red Cloud and the warring Lakota Sioux and Cheyenne bands in 1866, culminating in the Fort Laramie Treaty of 1868. The Bozeman Trail forts were closed. The Lakota Sioux agencies on the Missouri and a reservation in western South Dakota were established. Over its 2 short years, Fort Kearny was under constant siege by Lakota Sioux, Cheyenne and Arapaho warriors. Two of the West's famous battles were fought near this Fort: The Fetterman Fight on December 21, 1866, in which 80 soldiers under Capt. William Judd Fetterman were annihilated by 2000 combined warriors from various tribes. This battle was followed on August 2, 1867, by the Wagon Box Fight when 32 soldiers and civilians held of 1000 warriors in a day-long battle. The epic of Fort Phil Kearny ended in August of 1767 when the U.S. Military abandoned the Fort. The fort was then burned by Cheyenne warriors.

2. Frederick A. Cleveland, Fred Wilber Powell, *Railroad Promotion and Capitalization in the United States*, Longmans, Green and Co., New York (1909) (hereafter "Cleveland"), 264, 265.

3. Richard White, *Railroaded:* R. Fogel, *Railroads and American Economic Growth* 123 (1964).

4. 27 Cong. Ch. 16; 5 Stat. 453.

5. In 1867, George Francis Train, of the Chicago and Northwestern Railroad, proposed construction of the Denver-Cheyenne spur. The spur line would be complete and delivering supplies to Colorado's Caribou silver strike of 1869 by June 1870. Many Denverites sold their possessions and moved to Cheyenne, believing that Denver would become a ghost town and Cheyenne the great metropolis of the West.

6. Cleveland.

Chapter 2

1. Cf., Richard White, "It's Your Misfortune and None of My Own," *A New History of the American West*, Oklahoma University Press (1991); Morton J. Horwitz, *The Transformation of American Law, 1780–1860*, Oxford University Press (1992) (Cambridge, Mass. 1977); Horwitz, *The Transformation of American Law 1870–1960: The Crisis of Legal Orthodoxy* (New York, 1992).

2. Rehnquist, William H., *The Supreme*

Court: How It Was, How It Is, William Morrow & Co. (1987) (hereafter "Rehnquist").

3. Cf. also, Richard Hofstadter "William Graham Sumner, Social Darwinist," *The New England Quarterly*, Vol. 14, No. 3 (Sep. 1941), 457–477.

Chapter 3

1. Morton J. Horwitz, *The Transformation of American Law 1870–1960: The Crisis of Legal Orthodoxy* (New York, 1992), 99, 100. Morton J. Horwitz, *The Transformation of American Law, 1780–1860*, Oxford University Press (1992) (Cambridge, MA, 1977).

2. Horwitz, 100. Citing A. Hirschman, *The Strategy of Economic Development* 71 (1958); H. Scheiber, *The Ohio Canal Era: A Case Study of Government and Economy 1820–1861* (1969), R. Fogel, *Railroads and American Economic Growth* 208–24 (1964); A Fishlow, *American Railroads and the Transformation of the Ante-Bellum Economy* 57–62 (1965); See also, R. White, *Railroaded.*

3. 17 Stat.424. February 12, 1873.

4. Carlson, W. Bernard, "Technology and America as a Consumer Society, 1870–1900," in Calhoun, Charles W., editor. *The Gilded Age: Perspectives on the Origins of Modern America*, Lanham, MD: Rowman & Littlefield, 2007; Tractenberg, Alan, *The Incorporation of America: Culture and Society in the Gilded Age*, New York: Hill & Wang, 1982.

5. Andrew Carnegie claimed that Spencer was the individual that had influenced him most and had provided the philosophical basis for his pursuit of wealth. Carnegie began investing in American steel when he realized that the steel rails being introduced in England in the early 1870s were superior to the iron rails in America. Utilizing the newest technologies, such as the Bessemer blast furnace and the Siemens-Martin open hearth, he built the largest steel company in America.

6. John Pierpont Morgan, founder of J.P. Morgan & Co., led the merger movement, creating giant industrial corporations. During the Civil War, Morgan purportedly sold defective guns to the Union army at inflated prices. He installed a telegraph line in his office so that he could buy and sell gold based on battle news from the front. After the war, he launched a strategy of monopolizing the railroads. By 1900, his assets included the South Atlantic, Reading, Erie, and Northern Pacific railroads, and major positions in the B&O, the Atchison, Topeka, and Santa Fe. He merged the Edison General and Thompson-Houston Electric companies into General Electric, creating an industrial conglomerate. And he merged Carnegie Steel with several other steel companies to create U.S. Steel. He ultimately established a set of holdings more varied than either Carnegie or Rockefeller.

7. John D. Rockefeller built a monopoly in the oil industry in less than ten years. When competing adventurers glutted the oil market by opening new oilfields, Rockefeller bottlenecked the oil delivery system by gaining control of the distilling industry. In 1868, he formed Standard Oil Company. The company was one of thirty oil refining companies in Cleveland, processing only 5 percent of the nation's total oil. Rockefeller built his monopoly by cultivating preferential treatment from the railroads that hauled his product. He negotiated secret contracts basically securing lower transportation rates in exchange for increased market share. Lower transportation costs enabled him to undercut the competition on price. As market share increased further, the railroads sought his business, enhancing his negotiating power against them, thereby reducing his costs yet further. Horizontal integration soon became the method by which other industrialists would attempt to eliminate their competitors and make their industries more stable and profitable.

Chapter 4

1. "Actions addressing the wrongful disturbance of enjoyment of property where there was no trenching on title, no dispossession of the landowner, nor 'direct' physical or trespassory injury to the land." "In the twelfth and thirteenth centuries *praecipe* writs provided a 'real' action to the freeholder for damage to incidents of his property, as well as for assertion of right or title to the freehold." Joshua Getzler, *A History of Water Rights at Common Law*, Oxford University Press, 2004, 52, 53 (hereafter "Getzler"). These writs stood "mid-way between the indubitably possessory assizes and the indubitably proprietary writ of right." Maitland, *Forms of Action*, 46. The cause of action was formally called the "assize of nuisance." "The initiating writ for recovery of land was the *quod reddat*; the main writ for recovery or defence of incidents was known as *quod permittat*, by which the defendant could be ordered positively to remove a nuisance interfering with the plaintiff's enjoyment of property, or negatively to permit the plaintiff the untrammeled enjoyment of his appurtenant or incidental property rights." Getzler, 44, citing Milsom, "Introduction to *Novae Narrationes*," p. lxxxviii. The notion of *nuisance* was also inherent in the assize of *novel disseisin* created in the reign of Henry II around 1166. It "provided a simple and widely employed

remedial procedure for dispossessions. An assize could require the lord of a tenement to redress wrongful recent interference with a plaintiff freeholder's possession of the tenement, rather than trying and establishing title directly." Getzler, 54. Citing Leongard, "Assize of Nuisance 161–5, Digest of Justinian 43.16.3. 15-16; 43. 17.3.2; and Henry de Glanvill, *Tractatus de Legibus et Consuetudinibus regni Angli qui Glanvilla vocatur* (The Treatise on the laws and customs of the realm of England commonly called Glanville) (c. 1187–9), bk. XII, c. 11–4, bk XIII, c. 32–7; G.D. G. Hall (ed. and trans.), London, 1965, 142–3, 167–8. "The action was brought before royal justices and a local jury. Verdicts under this procedure might carefully set out the details of the parties' respective rights and duties regarding the nuisance, as in a 1213 assize of novel disseisn for diversion of water from a mill, where the nuisance to the mill was abated by specifying the rights of the parties to the water flow for particular times and places along the stream, and assigning duties for the maintenance and repair of the watercourse." Getzler, 54, 55, citing Flower (ed.) Curia Regis Rolls, 326–8; Case 554, "Concord in the King's court," (York, 1184), in English Law Suits from William I to Richard I, Vol. II (R.C. van Caenegam (ed), Selden Society, cvii, 1991), 606. The assize of nuisance was also brought by the writ of *questus est*. Getzler, 55. A writ evolving from the same legislation of Henry II creating the assize of novel disseisin.

2. Time immemorial also became a defense to shield the tenant with an obligation of servitude, but not an affirmative basis upon which to establish title. "Time immemorial" essentially meant outside living memory, beyond a specified point of legal memory. "This period of legal memory was set by the lengthy limitation times for the real or proprietary actions, introduced to replace the vagaries of customary or historical memory. The cut-off date for this period was originally set at the time of the Norman Conquest, as the ultimate historical font of all titles. Later the time was set at Richard I's coronation. The Statute of Merton 1236 then fixed time of memory for the writ of right at the commencement of the reign of Henry II in 1154, some eighty-two years before, with a shorter limitation for *mort d'ancestor* and writs of entry being the last return of King John from Ireland." Getzler, 90.

3. A *praedial servitude* is a service, burden, or charge granted for the benefit of one tract of land which affects or encumbers another, as in the case of an easement. One tract is "dominant" and the other is "servient." While easements generally permitting access are broadly understood as servitudes today, other servitudes were broadly accepted in Roman-Civil and English common law. "Pasturage," for example was another servitude, the right to pasture one's livestock on another's property. Getzler, 83, de Bracton, f. 53b, ii, 60–1. Another servitude, "puture," imposed the customary right to take food for man, horse, and dog from land of various tenants within the forest or hundred to sustain the keepers of forests and some bailiffs or sheriffs of hundreds, all in service of a manorial lord. "The seigniorial monopolies of mill-suit were aggressively defended in the lord's courts and sometimes lords claimed to control all possible uses of a local watercourse, in effect claiming complete seigneurial control of water flow in the manor." Getzler, 19, 20. Such control was, however, ultimately precluded by Parliamentary actions dictating that control of flowing water for milling purposes be compromised in favor of river transport and fishing during the late fourteenth century.

4. "Banalities" or "soke services" imposed by thirteenth century seignors (both secular and monasterial) compelling tenants to use milling services financed or constructed by the overlord. See, Getzler, 19. See: *Legis Henrici*, 9, § 9, in Maitland, Frederic William, *Domesday Book and Beyond*, Norton, 1966, 80. "Soke rights could also extend to the bread oven, the wine press, the brewery, the dye-pan, the breeding bull or boar, and the fulling mill." See also, Marc Bloch, "The Advent and Triumph of the Water Mill," in *Land and Work in Mediaeval Europe* (1935).

5. Occupancy of land over passage of time was, during the feudal period, a successful basis of shield (defense) against dis-seisin (i.e. of possession by tenancy) by affirmative claims of adverse possession, because passage of time gave rise to the assumption of believed and intended title. But passage of time was not successful as a sword for the establishment of positive title based on adverse possession. F. Pollack and F.W. Maitland, *The History of English Law Before the Time of Edward I*, 2 vols. (2d Ed., 1895), ii, 141.

6. Getzler, 91. Parliaments and courts recast the limitation periods for real actions from the sixteenth century onwards.

7. Sir William Blackstone SL KC (1723–1780), English jurist and Tory politician, admitted to Middle Temple, and called to the Bar there in 1747. He gave up his practice as a barrister in 1753 and embarked on lectures on English law, leading to publication of *An Analysis of the Laws of England* in 1756, and published a second treatise, entitled *A Discourse on the Study of Law*. Returning to the bar, he was elected as Tory Member of Parliament for

the "rotten borough" (a parliamentary election district where the population previously justifying the seat in Parliament had dissipated) of Hindon in 1761. In such boroughs, "representation" was artificially maintained by the crown or by an aristocratic patron. More than 140 of 658 parliamentary seats were in rotten boroughs when the Reform Act of 1832 was passed. 50 of them had fewer than 50 voters. Blackstone ultimately gained appointment to the Court of King's Bench in 1770, later leaving to replace Edward Clive as a Justice of the Common Pleas. He remained in this position until his death in 1780.

8. Bernhard Knollenberg, *Origin of the American Revolution 1759–1766*, The Free Press, 1961, 151.

9. Justinian *Institutes*, 2.1., 2, 4.-6., 11. Later followed by de Bracton f. 7b-8, ii, 39–40; f 207; iii, 128.

10. Justinian *Institutes*, 2.1.1: Justinian *Digests* 1.8.2. Pr.-1 (Marcianus).

11. *Dominium* was protected by actions in u*sacapio*, an action for the perfection of purported transfers of *dominium* possessed by an owner in good faith. Gaius, *Justinian's Institutes* 2.6.pr., *Digest of Justinian* 41.3.1; Modestinus, D. 41.3.3; Neratius, D. 41.10.5.1.Pr -1' *Usacapio* was inapplicable to perfection of incorporeal rights over land (like water). Getzler, 91.

12. John Locke, *Second Treatise of Government*, §§ 29 and 33 in *Two Treatises of Government* (P. Laslett (ed.), Cambridge (1960), 331, 333.

13. "By the absolute rights of individuals we mean those which are so in the primary and strictest sense; such as would belong to their persons merely in a state of nature, and which every man is entitled to enjoy, whether out of society or in it." Blackstone, *Commentaries*, i, 123–4.

14. Getzler, 160.

15. In the Roman system "ownership" must be proved as an absolute right, that is, beyond disproof by owner of rival title. Ownership could be defended without possession. Possession could be defended without title.

16. Getzler, 1, 2.

17. "I still lend my counsel and books to such young students as will fix themselves in the neighborhood. Coke's institutes and reports are their first, and Blackstone their last book, after an intermediate course of two or three years. It [Blackstone] is nothing more than an elegant digest of what they will then have learned from the real fountains of the law." *Thomas Jefferson Writings*, Merrill D. Peterson (ed.) Library of America, 1984, 1225, Thomas Jefferson Letter to John Tyler (judge and father of President John Tyler), May 26, 1810. "Blackstone, whose commentaries were canonical to the founding lawyers… "Alan Dershowitz, *The Case Against Impeaching Trump*, Skyhorse Publishing, 2018, 11.

18. Blackstone, Vol. 1 of *Commentaries* (1765).

19. Benjamin Fletcher Wright, *The Federalist by Alexander Hamilton, James Madison and John Jay*, Metro Books 2002, 33. Alexander Hamilton's Federalist 69 distinguishes the proposed American presidential authority from that of England's royal king's authority as had been described by Blackstone, *n*446. In 1800, John Adams defended the Alien and Sedition Acts passed in 1798 by the Federalist-dominated 5th United States Congress as legitimate based upon Blackstone's work. Thomas Jefferson advocated the unalienable right to freedom of conscience. The Sedition act expired, the men punished under that law were pardoned by Jefferson, and the more expansive view of free speech prevailed in America.

20. T.E. Lauer, "The Common Law Background of the Riparian Doctrine," 28 *Missouri Law Review* 60,72 (1963).

21. 4 Mason 397 (1827). 24 Fed. Cas. 472 (No. 14,312) (C.C.D.R.I. 1827). Story's earlier (1816) opinion in *Martin v. Hunter's Lessee* had established the appellate jurisdiction of the United States Supreme Court. See, T.E. Lauer, "The Common Law Background of the Riparian Doctrine," 28 *Missouri Law Review* 60 (1963).

22. Wyoming Supreme Court Interpretive Display, Wyoming State Supreme Court Law Library, 2019.

Chapter 5

1. *Kansas v. Colorado*, 185 U.S. 125 (1902). See also: *Kansas v. Colorado*, 206 U.S. 46 (1907); *Connecticut v. Massachusetts*, 282 U.S. 660 (1931); *New Jersey v. New York*, 283 U.S. 336 (1931); *Washington v. Oregon*, 297 U.S. 517 (1936); *Colorado v. Kansas*, 320 U.S. 383 (1943); *Nebraska v. Wyoming*, 325 U.S. 589 (1945); *Colorado v. New Mexico*, 459 U.S. 176 (1982); 467 U.S. 310 (1984); *Nebraska v. Wyoming*, 515 U.S. 1 (1995).

2. Original 137, 563 U.S. 368 May 2, 2011, 577 U.S. 137 (March 21, 2016). Montana v. Wyoming, 563 U.S. 368 (2011) Montana sued Wyoming, claiming Wyoming breached the Yellowstone River Compact. Wyoming allowed its irrigators to use an efficient irrigation system that increased water usage and decreased the amount of water flowing back to Montana. The U.S. Supreme Court ruled that efficient irrigation systems were allowed as long as the water

was used to irrigate the same number of acres." Wyoming Supreme Court Law Library, Justice Learning Center.

3. *State of South Carolina v. State of North Carolina*, No. 138, Orig. 558 U.S. 138, 175 L. Ed. 2d 713, January 20, 2010) (also 552 U.S. 804, 169 L. Ed. 2d 7, 128 S. Ct. 349).

4. *Arizona v. California*, 283 U.S. 423 (1931); *Washington v. Oregon*, 297 U.S 517 (1936); *Colorado v. Kansas*, 320 U.S. 383 (1943).

5. *Colorado v. New Mexico*, 459 U.S. 176, 183 (1982) (citing *Kansas v. Colorado*, characterizing the body of law as "interstate common law").

6. *See Nebraska v. Wyoming*, 515 U.S. 1, 11–13 (1995); *Nebraska v. Wyoming*, 507 U.S. 584, 593 (1993); *New Jersey v. New York*, 283 U.S. 336, 345–46 (1931); *Kansas v. Colorado*, 206 U.S. 46, 114 (1907).

7. *Colorado v. New Mexico*, 459 U.S. at 187.

Chapter 6

1. See, *Georgia v. U.S. Army Corps of Engineers*, 302 F. 3d 1242, 1247 (11th Cir. 2002); *Georgia v. U.S. Army Corps of Engineers*, 2:01-cv-0026 (N.D. Ga.); *Southeastern Federal Power Customers v. Caldera*, Case no. 1:00-cv-02975 (D.D.C).

2. Article I, Section 10, Clause 3. "No State shall without the Consent of Congress ... enter into any Agreement or Compact with another State, or with a foreign Power...."

3. 42 U.S. Statutes at Large171, see: 61 Congressional Record, 4817–6210 (August 1–24, 1921, HR 6877).

4. 43 USCA § 617l(b), 45 Stat. 1064 (12/21/1928).

Chapter 7

1. *Dred Scott v. Sandford*, 60 U.S. 393 (1857).

2. Rehnquist.

3. Jeffrey Rosen, *The Supreme Court*, Times Books (2006), 78, 96 (hereafter "Rosen")

4. Proceedings of the Twenty Second Annual Meeting of the American Bar Association, Held at Buffalo, New York, August 28, 29, 30, 1899. Dando Printing and Publishing Co., Philadelphia (1899), 679.

5. 27 Cong. Ch. 16; 5 Stat. 453.

6. Mark Warren Bailey, *Guardians of the Moral Order: The Legal Philosophy of the Supreme Court, 1860–1910*, Northern Illinois University Press (2004) (hereafter "Bailey), 25.

7. Bailey, 4. Bickel, Alexander M., Schmidt, Benno C. Jr., *History of the Supreme Court of the United States*, Volume IX, The Judiciary and Responsible Government, 1910–21, Macmillan Publishing Company, New York (1984). Alexander Bickel was a Harvard Law trained, U.S. Supreme Court Law Clerk for Justice Felix Frankfurter, ending his career as Sterling Professor of Law at Yale in 1974 (hereafter "Bickel/Schmidt").

8. Harrison commanded the 1st Brigade of the 1st Division of the XX Corps of the Army of the Cumberland in the battles of Resaca, Cassville, New Hope Church, Lost Mountain, Kennesaw Mountain Marietta, Peachtree Creek and Atlanta.

9. Van Devanter, Willis, "The Supreme Court of the U.S.," 5 *Indiana Law Journal* 553–562 (May 1930).

Chapter 8

1. Leon Friedman & Fred L. Israel (eds.), *The Justices of the United States Supreme Court, 1789–1969, Their Lives and Major Opinions*, R.R. Bowker Company, New York, 1969 (hereafter "Friedman/Israel").

2. During law school, Taft reported the political news for the local Cincinnati newspaper, then later secured a federal appointment with the Internal Revenue Service. "The internal revenue service in 1882 was, like most government agencies, a refuge for politically deserving veterans of the G.A.R. and other hacks. A few trusted employees did the actual work and Taft was promptly informed that these should be replaced by still more hacks [appointed by the Arthur administration]." Pringle, 61.

3. Pringle, 63, 65. The G.O.P. lost the House of Representatives in 1882. Among other victories, the democrats gained heavily in Hamilton County, Ohio. Taft went into law practice with a Major Harlan Page Lloyd, who had been associated with this father. By 1887, William Taft had served as Hamilton County's prosecuting attorney and later secured an appointment from Ohio Governor Foraker, in alliance with Boss Cox, to fill a vacancy on the Ohio Superior Court created by the departure of Judge Judson Harmon, who was returning to private practice.

4. Friedman/Israel.

Chapter 9

1. 60 U.S. 393.
2. 78 U.S. 113 (1871).
3. 83 U.S. 36. (1873).
4. Art IV, § 2, U.S. Constitution.
5. 92 U.S. 214 (1875).
6. 92 U.S. 452 (1875).
7. 95 U.S.487, January 14, 1878.
8. 94 U.S. 113.

Chapter 10

1. Friedman/Israel, Vol. 3, 969. "The twenty-five-year-old Van Devanter, who could have earned a comfortable living in Indiana, preferred the raw and boisterous frontier life and the opportunities it offered him. His quick action, according to a biography of his early years, showed 'how much store he placed in the presence of a friend in power.'" Although this colorful reference to the cowboy life of Wyoming may satisfy some biographers, there is no evidence that the urbane Willis Van Devanter ever shared the rough-and-ready outdoor life.

2. Holsinger (1968), 171.

3. The 1884–1885 *Cheyenne Directory*, showed the Wyoming Stock Growers Association's Officers as J.M. Carey, President, A.H. Swan Executive Committee.

4. Holsinger, 173–175. Citing, Maurice Frink, et al., *When Grass Was King* (Boulder, Colorado: ,University of Colorado Press, 1956), 205, and pp. 166–167, and E. S. Osgood, *The Day* of *the Cattleman* (Chicago: The University of Chicago Press, 1957), 98.

5. Morris, Robert C., *Collections of the Wyoming Historical Society*, Vol. 1, Wyoming Historical Society (1897) (hereafter "Morris").

6. John A. Hawgood, *America's Western Frontiers*, Alfred A. Knopf (1967), 325.

7. Hawgood.

8. Clay later sized up A.H. Swan, whose operation he would inherit after its financial difficulties. See John Clay, *My Life on the Range*, Chapter XXVII. "[A.H. Swan's] failure was a rotten piece of business as one could imagine, and it gave the western cattle business a very black eye. His operations had one and all been of the most reckless character. With his casual hypnotism he had worked his credit to a finish, pyramiding one debt upon another, borrowing from Paul to pay Peter and carrying along with evident success great schemes, skillfully concealing the weak points and boosting the strong ones. But to no avail. Nature outraged claimed its retribution and Swan courted, flattered, gradually drifted downwards, a better man in his decline than in his glory, but he never got on his feet again financially. Leaving Cheyenne, he lived for a while in Ogden fighting an uphill battle, and he died in an asylum almost forgotten."

9. 106 U.S. 629.

10. 109 U.S.3, 3 S. Ct. 18; 27 L. Ed. 835 (1883).

Chapter 11

1. Larson, 177.

2. Johnson, 403, 407, 408.

3. Morris, 111.

4. Johnson, 403, 407, 408.

5. Friedman/Israel, 970.

6. Gould, Lewis L., *Wyoming, a Political History, 1868–1896*, Yale University Press, 1968, 126, citing Lewis L. Gould, "Willis Van Devanter in Wyoming Politics, 1884–1897," unpublished PhD. Thesis, Yale University, 1966, 1–102.

7. Holsinger, 175.

8. Morris, 343.

9. Mr. Nagle came to Cheyenne in 1867 to engage in the grocery business. He had previously been a merchant in the mining towns of the Colorado Rockies. His business in Cheyenne grew to become one of the most extensive in the Wyoming Territory Colorado, western Nebraska, western South Dakota and North Dakota. He was instrumental in expansion into the Black Hills when gold was discovered there.

10. The completed residence cost $50,000, including all details, equipment and furnishings.

11. The 1892 Cheyenne City Directory, shows Francis E. Warren residing at 200 W. 17th St., and John W. Lacey, residing at 23rd and Ferguson Streets; The Alphabetical List of Advertisers, shows advertising by Willis Van Devanter, 17 (that page torn out of directory in the collection of the Wyoming State Library). The 1918 Telephone Directory, Cheyenne District, The Mountain States Telephone and Telegraph Company, shows F.E. Warren, Office, F.E. Warren Merc Co., Warren Live Stock Co., located 116 W. 16th, Tel # 288; F.E. Warren Residence, at 222 E. 17th, Tel. # 243; and F.E. Warren Garage, at 209 E. 19th, Tel # 216 W. It also shows John W. Lacey, at 300 E 17th Street, Cheyenne, Tel # 283 (The Whipple House), and The Carey Farm, Tel # 131W in Wheatland.

12. 118 U.S. 557.

13. Morris, 111.

14. Morris, 244.

15. Christopher Knowlton, *Cattle Kingdom: The Hidden History of the Cowboy West*, Houghton Mifflin Harcourt (2017).

16. Holsinger (1965), 173–175.

17. Lester C. Hunt, *Wyoming: A Guide to Its History, Highways and People*, Works Projects Administration, American Guide Series, Oxford University Press, 1940, 100–101.

18. Holsinger, 173–175.

19. Hawgood, 325.

20. Holsinger, 173–175.

21. Friedman/Israel.

22. The first trolley passengers were legislators who were taken from the Union Pacific Depot to the Capitol. Trolleys were brightly painted for three routes: the Red line ran to the Fairgrounds, Yellow ran east on 19th to Russell Avenue, and the Green from the Capitol to the Lake View Cemetery where Warren would ulti-

mately lie In 1884, Warren would also built the Mercantile Building, much of which would be leased to the Burlington Railroad for use as a depot (1887–1932).

23. A situation otherwise occurring several times in the west. See, Timothy Egan, *The Worst Hard Time: The Untold Story of Those Who Survived the Great American Dust Bowl*, Houghton Mifflin (2006).

24. Friedman/Israel, Vol. 3, 970.

25. Friedman/Israel, Vol. 3, 970. The Burlington Railroad (with route from Chicago to Omaha) would ultimately be merged with the Union Pacific. The Burlington Routes 1887-Presemt. Incorporated as the Cheyenne & Burlington Railroad in March 1887, the 30 mile long Wyoming segment was a part of the larger 145 mile long Chicago, Burlington & Quincy (CB&Q) Railroad line that ran from Midland Nebraska, westward to Sterling, Colorado, and then northwestward into Cheyenne, Wyoming. Completed and opened to traffic to Cheyenne on December 11, 1887. The Wyoming portion, now vacated, ran from the Colorado-Wyoming state border in the vicinity of Carpenter, Wyoming into downtown Cheyenne with stations established in Carpenter, Arcola, Camp Stool, and Altvan. This line constructed of 'light rail' was designed to haul agricultural products, some passengers, and industrial products needed in the growing west. In 1887, Burlington purchased the Warren Emporium (Mercantile) Building which had been originally constructed by F.E. Warren, to be their Burlington Depot.

26. Johnson, 403, 407.

27. News item in the *Cheyenne Weekly Leader*, January 19, 1888, quoted in Holsinger, 179.

28. Editorial in the *Cheyenne Weekly Leader*, January 19, 1888, quoted in Holsinger, 178, 179.

29. Bickel/Schmidt, *n*159, 44.

30. Larson, 178, 179.

31. News item in the *Cheyenne Weekly Leader*, February 2, 1888, cited in Holsinger, 180.

32. Lorah B. Chaffee, *Sons of the West: Biographical Account of Early Day Wyoming*, Caxton Printers (1941).

33. Morris, 344. Van Devanter was not a delegate to the First Constitutional Convention in 1887.

34. Morris, 111.

35. Indiana's Democratic legiślature had defeated Harrison's re-election to the U.S. Senate. His presidential nomination must certainly have felt like a vindication.

36. News item in the *Cheyenne Weekly Leader*, December 23, 1888, cited in M. Paul Holsinger, "Willis Van Devanter: Wyoming Leader, 1884, 1897," *Wyoming State Historical Society*, Annals of Wyoming, Lola M. Homsher (ed), Wyoming State Archives and Historical Department, Volume 37, October, 1965, Number 2, 182.

37. Charles W. Calhoun, *Benjamin Harrison*, Times Books (2005), 2.

38. 233 to 168.

39. Melville Fuller was nominated for the Chief Justice position by President Cleveland when Chief Justice Morrison Waite died in 1888. He was confirmed by a vote of 41 to 20, with nine Republicans voting with the Democrats to confirm him.

40. Holsinger, 181, 182.

41. Laurence H. Tribe, *God Save This Honorable Court: How the Choice of Supreme Court Justice Shapes Our History*, Random House, New York, 1985.

42. Van Devanter letter to Alfred A. Bright, April 4, 1889, quoted in Holsinger, 182.

43. Charles W. Calhoun, *Benjamin Harrison*, Times Books (2005), 38.

44. Friedman/Israel.

45. Larson, 233. "At the time Wyoming was becoming a state, Van Devanter was serving as a criminal judge."

46. Holsinger. (1965), 185.

47. Van Devanter letter to Francis E. Warren, January 21, 1897, quoted in Holsinger, 182.

48. Holsinger, 185.

49. Gould, 126, citing Gould, unpublished PhD. Thesis, 1–102.

50. Gould, 128.

51. At the 1890 general election for Justices of the Supreme Court, Van Devanter got 8013 votes, Ashbury B. Conaway got 8597, Herman V.S. Groesbeck got 8267, all 3 Republicans. Van Devanter got the most votes from Laramie County.

52. David Schutz (ed), *Encyclopedia of the Supreme Court*, Facts on File Library of American History (2005), 496.

53. Bickel/Schmidt.

54. Morris, 111.

55. Holsinger, 185.

56. Gould, 126, citing Gould, unpublished PhD. Thesis, 1–102.

57. Holsinger, 194; Kermit L. Hall (Ed), *Oxford Companion to the Supreme Court of the United States*, 2d Edition (2005), 1045 (hereafter "Hall").

58. Johnson, 403, 407.

59. The 1884–1885 *Cheyenne Directory*, showed J.W. Lacey, Chief Justice of Wyoming, residing at 420 20th.Street. F.E. Warren, Merchant and stockman is shown residing at 420 17th, N.E. (at the corner of Warren Avenue);

and Van Devanter, Willis, attorney-at-law, at the West Corner 18th and House streets.

60. Judge Riner would serve as Wyoming's lead District Judge until October 31, 1921, and as a Senior Judge until March 4, 1923. Riner took his oath of office before Van Devanter, who was at that time chief justice of the Supreme Court of the state of Wyoming. Judge Riner's name appears in the roster of Masons on the Masonic temple on 16th Street in Washington, D.C., a block toward the White House from later Associate Justice Van Devanter's Washington, D.C., home and office.

61. Holsinger, 189, *n*92.

62. Hall, 1045.

63. Friedman/ Israel.

64. Morris, 199.

65. 29 P. 88 (1892).

66. 29 P. 741 (1892).

67. 30 P. 953 (1892).

68. 45 P. 508 (1896).

69. Friedman/Israel.

Chapter 12

1. Holsinger, 192.

2. The "Johnson County War" is sometimes also referred to as the "Invasion of Powder River." The basic facts of this episode of Wyoming history are well known by Western historians, and are retold in several contemporary and later accounts, like Mercer, et al., the *Riders of Judgment*, D.F. Barber, *The Longest Rope* (biography of Will Walker, witness to Champion/Ray killings), John Clay, *My Life on the Range*; Frank Canton, *Frontier Trails*; Charles A. Guernsey, *Wyoming Cowboy Days*; Wayne Gard, *Frontier Justice*; John W. Davis, *Wyoming Range War: The Infamous Invasion of Johnson County*; Bill O'Neal, *The Johnson County War*; Helena Huntindon Smith, *The War on Powder River*, some of them movies.

3. Wyoming's statehood two years earlier put no end to the changing social dynamic driven by economic insecurity of the cattle industry, western settlement pursuant to congressional homestead policy and the general aridity of the western plains. Wyoming's population had become 60,705 by 1890. Conflicts over land ownership or use were a somewhat common occurrence throughout the late 1800s and early 1900s. "Rustling" was increasing due to harsh grazing conditions.

4. William H. Kittrel, Foreword in: A.S. Mercer, *The Banditti of the Plains or The Cattlemen's Invasion of Wyoming in 1892 [The Crowning Infamy of the Ages]*, University of Oklahoma Press, 1954, xli (hereafter "Kittrell").

5. Born on June 6, 1839, Mercer was a member of one of the founding families in Seattle, Washington. Asa's brother Thomas was a major landholder in early Seattle, after whom Mercer Island and Mercer Street are still named. In 1861, Asa assisted his brothers in clearing land north of Seattle on which to establish a new territorial university, now the University of Washington. Mercer, the only college graduate in Seattle at the time, was hired as the university's sole instructor. A member of the Washington State Senate, Mercer became well-known throughout the West as a publisher. He eventually went to Cheyenne to publish the Northwestern Livestock Journal, a publication financed by the WSGA.

6. Woods, Lawrence Milton, *Asa Shinn Mercer: Western Promoter and Newspaperman, 1839–1917*, Arthur H. Clark Co., Spokane, 2003. U. of Wyoming Library # F594.M52/ W66 2003). Woods' study of Mercer reveals Asa Mercer first as a publicist, an advocate, a journalist, a colorful and prolific writer. He was competitive and indefatigable as a capitalist, entrepreneur, salesman, speculator par excellence, and frustrated fortune seeker. Emotionally, he was romantic and possessed boundless enthusiasm, exuberance, and energy. But he was also footloose, vacillating and frequently alone—an absentee parent and spouse spending long days in transit on near-quixotic business ventures. Oft the debtor, sometimes the judgment debtor, Mercer was seldom the creditor, never the judgment creditor. Through it all, the common thread was Mercer's savvy sense of the light of opportunity. When he spotted it, he fashioned his location, his business ventures, and his political suasion, to take advantage of it, unfortunately leaving him in the end saddened and merely situational. Indeed, the pragmatist and survivor, he lived a long life of 78 years. But in doing so he embittered himself with numerous people, including one of his longest acquaintances and truest supporters, Rev. Daniel Bagley, with whom Asa's elder brothers Thomas and Aaron had originally come to Seattle. All in all, Woods' summary that Asa Mercer was "not dull" rings as an apposite understatement.

7. Initiation of the plan to divest the "rustlers" of their lives and wealth is attributed to one H.B. Ijams, then secretary of the Wyoming Board of Livestock Commissioners. Ijams contended that the first Wyoming legislature, which had convened the year before, had authorized the Board to seize and sell the cattle of those characterizable as "rustlers," with the proceeds of sale to be extra-judicially remitted to the Board. Some $100,000 in funds were raised by this device. Mercer, 29–31.

8. E.S. Osgood, *The Day of the Cattlemen*, University of Chicago Press (1957).

9. Ten men rode up to the establishment of "Cattle Kate" (Ellen Liddy Watson) and Jim Averill, roped them and, "dragged them out to a near-by gulch, tied their hands behind them, and fastening one end of each rope to the limb of a tree that extended over the gulch, pushed them off to choke and die." Kittrell, xxxvii–xxxix. See also, George W. Huffsmith, *The Wyoming Lynching of Cattle Kate*, High Plains Press.

10. "The *Casper Weekly Mail* of July 26, 1889, said that prominent land owners had been guilty of the hanging and the Grand Jury of Carbon County was informed of the event, but no witnesses could be found, so the suspects were not arrested." Kittrell.

11. First, one Waggoner on June 4, 1891, and one Orley E. "Ranger Jones on November 28, 1891. On November 30, one J. A. Tisdale was ambushed in his wagon returning to his home sixty miles from Buffalo. The assailant, who Tisdale had overheard and recognized as Frank M. Canton, prior sheriff of Johnson County, before he left Buffalo the day before, drove Tisdale's wagon out of sight and shot his horses. A passing, unseen witness, a Charles Basch, identified Canton to Johnson County Sheriff W.B. Angus, who sent a posse to recover Tisdale's body. They found it and that of Ranger Jones, both murdered. Canton was arrested but later released after a two-day trial. When later evidence further incriminated Canton, according to Mercer, he fled Wyoming to the state of Illinois, from which Acting Governor Barber refused to extradite him. Mercer, 25, 26. Frank Canton returned to Cheyenne in March 1892 and was given a hearing before Judge Blake. He was set free on bond, for which sureties, members of the Stock Growers' Association, appeared on his behalf on April 4. According to Mercer, sureties for the $30,000 bond were Hubert E. Teschemacher, Wm. C. Irvine, E.S. Rouse Boughton, Fred G.S. Hesse, Lafayette H. Parker, A.R. Powers, Joseph G. Pratt, Elias W. Whitcomb, Arthur B. Clarke, John N. Tisdale, David R. Tisdale, James W. Hammond, Charles S. Ford, Henry W. Davis, George P. Bissel, William E. Guthrie, Ralph M. Friend, George W. Baxter, Hiram B. Ijams, Frank H. Laberteaux and Ranslaer S. Van Tassel. Mercer, 26, 27.

12. Holsinger, 185, citing March 19, 1892, correspondence from Francis E. Warren to Willis Van Devanter.

13. A group of small Johnson County ranchers led by a local rancher named Nate Champion had formed the Northern Wyoming Farmers and Stock Growers' Association (NWFSGA) to compete with the WSGA. The WSGA "blacklisted" the NWFSGA and told them to stop all operations, but the NWFSGA refused the WSGA's order to disband and instead made public their plans to hold their own roundup in the spring of 1892. The WSGA's claim was that the open range was theirs to be used because of prior use, notwithstanding the official policy of the United States implemented by the homestead acts.

14. J.W. Hammond, W.C. Irvine and Charles Hecht.

15. "Confession of George Dunning," in: A.S. Mercer, *The Banditti of the Plains or The Cattlemen's Invasion of Wyoming in 1892 [The Crowning Infamy of the Ages]*, University of Oklahoma Press (1954), 190 (hereafter "Dunning").

16. Mercer, 40.

17. General Order No. 4, Cheyenne, Wyoming, See, Mercer, 40.

18. Section 33, Chapter 85, Wyoming Session Laws, 1890, See, Mercer, 41.

19. Mercer, 42.

20. See, Mercer, 45, S. McGreavy, "Amos Barber, Charles Penrose and the War on the Powder River," *Surgery, Gynecology and Obstetrics*, April 1973 136(4), 632–8.

21. Two men, who had evidently been spending the night at Champion's ranch, were captured as they emerged from the cabin early Saturday morning to collect water at the nearby Powder River. A third, Nick Ray, was shot standing in the doorway of the cabin. He died a few hours later. The hired mob besieged Champion inside the log cabin.

22. Someone in the mob later pinned a note to Champion's corpse reading "Cattle Thieves Beware."

23. Mercer, 36.

24. A first-hand account of the siege at the TA ranch also appeared in *The Times*, the *Chicago Herald* and other papers at the same time.

25. Dunning, 189, 191.

26. The Sixth Cavalry disarmed Walcott and 45 other men and took possession of 45 rifles, 41 revolvers and some 5,000 rounds of ammunition.

27. Johnson, 403, 407.

28. Clay later denied that he was involved in planning the armed incursion.

29. Johnson, 403, 407.

30. Dunning, 183.

31. Larson, 275.

32. Dunning, 172, 173.

33. Dunning, 175.

34. Dunning, 177.

35. Morris, 350.

36. Holsinger, 185, citing March 19, 1892, correspondence from Francis E. Warren to Willis Van Devanter.

37. Dunning, 176. "On the 5th day of April I helped to load the three wagons and the three carloads of horses, and the baggage that belonged to the mob; a man by the name of Van Tassal bossed the job. I saw Ijams [Director of WSGA] again in the afternoon of the 5th of April."
38. Johnson, 403, 407.
39. Holsinger, citing Francis E. Warren correspondence to Willis Van Devanter, April 15, 1892 (Warren Papers).
40. Kittrel, xxxix.
41. Dunning.
42. Holsinger, 189–192, citing Van Devanter letter to Francis E. Warren, April 20, 1892.
43. Struthers Burt, *The Powder River: Let'er Buck*, Rinehart & Co., Rivers of America series, 1938, 296.
44. Holsinger, 189–192, quoting Van Devanter letter to Joseph M. Carey, June 27, 1892.
45. Holsinger, 189–192.
46. Johnson, 403, 410.
47. Holsinger, 195–196. The executive committee of Wyoming's Republican party consisted of Van Devanter as chairman, Senator Joseph Carey, Otto Gramm, Benjamin Fowler, and Frank M. Foote.
48. Holsinger, 189–192, quoting Edward Stanwood, *A History of the Presidency*, Houghton Mifflin Company, New York (1912), 509.
49. Friedman/Israel.
50. Holsinger, 196.
51. Friedman/Israel.
52. Holsinger, 197, 198.
53. Warren was awarded a congressional medal of honor on September 30, 1893, for action on June 15, 1863, during the siege of Port Hudson, LA. Young F.E. Warren had "volunteered" to carry timber forward in the face of heavy fire, so as to fill a ditch in front of the earthworks of a fort so artillery and other groups could advance. "Warren to Pass on All Appropriations Bills of Government Hereafter," *Wyoming State Tribune*, March 8, 1922, Courtesy of Wyoming State Archives. Coincidentally, this was the same battle in which the later Chief Justice Edward Douglas White, then a young Confederate lieutenant and aide to the confederate commander, had surrendered with his fellow officers and their commands to the commander of the Nineteenth Army Corps of the Union forces. "Senator Warren, Medal of Honor Man, Is Only Citizen to Receive Two Invitations to be a Mourner." *Wyoming State Tribune*, November 7 (post WWI year undated in clipping), Courtesy of Wyoming State Archives. Justice White's ascension to the Chief Justiceship later in 1922, and Warren's opposition to it, would opportune Warren's advocacy of Willis Van Devanter's appointment to the Court. See also, Bryant Irey, "Frank E. Warren's Life Reflects Work and Fame," *Billings Gazette*, July 21, 1929. At Wyoming State Archives.

Chapter 13

1. October 12, 1923 letter from Philip A. Rollins to Princeton University Library published in Mercer, xiii–xv.
2. Holsinger, 189–192.
3. Holsinger, 189–192.

Chapter 14

1. Holsinger, 199.
2. Holsinger, 199, 200.
3. Larson, 293.
4. Ch. 301, Sec. 4, 28 Stat. 422.
5. Van Devanter letter to M.C. Barrow, September 4, 1894, quoted in Holsinger, 199.

Chapter 15

1. He refused to send the Hawaii Treaty, intended to lead to Hawaii's statehood, to the U.S. Senate.
2. U.S. Attorney General Opinions, 21 Op. Att'y Gen. 274 (1895).
3. Holsinger, 199, 200, citing News item in the *Rocky Mountain* (Denver, Colorado) *News*, July 8, 1897.
4. Holsinger, 201–203. Citing Warren letter to Mark A. Hanna, April 24, 1896.
5. Holsinger, 201–203. Citing Herbert Croly, *Marcus Alonzo Hanna: His Life and Work*, Macmillan Co., 1923, 185–186, and Senator Warren's May 15, 1896 correspondence to Mark Hanna, McKinley's campaign manager.
6. Holsinger, 189, citing Van Devanter letter to Warren, March 11, 1897, and Van Devanter letter to Warren, January 21, 1897.
7. Gould, unpublished PhD. Thesis, 268–93.
8. Holsinger, 203–206. Citing Warren correspondence to William McKinley, January 21, 1897, U.S. Department of Justice, Appointment Papers—Willis Van Devanter, MSS in National Archives, Washington, D.C. "Letters of recommendation for Van Devanter came to President elect McKinley from Senator Clarence Clark and Representative Mondell." Citing Clarence D. Clark and Frank Mondell correspondence to William McKinley, January 28, 1897, U.S. Department of Justice, Appointment Papers—Willis Van Devanter, MSS in National Archives, Washington, D.C. "Another letter bore the signatures of 'all the Senators and members of Congress from Wyoming, Colorado, Utah, and

Idaho who were true to the Republican Party during the last campaign.' Wyoming Republican officials from Governor W. A. Richards to the state and federal judges also added their names to the requests."

9. Friedman/Israel.
10. Friedman/Israel.
11. Morris, 199.
12. Holsinger, 189, *n*92.

Chapter 16

1. Bickel/Schmidt (citing Van Devanter letter to Warren January 31, 1897, Van Devanter to Warren, March 11, 1897, Van Devanter Papers.
2. Friedman/Israel.
3. Born on September 19, 1835, in Mobile, Alabama, Hotchkiss was the grandson of Revolutionary War hero Ethan Allen. He served in the Seminole War in Florida, in the Pacific Northwest, and in the Mexican-American War, where he served as Gen. Wilfield Scott's inspector general in the march on Mexico City. In 1862, he served as the chairman of the War Board, the organization that assisted President Lincoln and Secretary of War Edwin M. Stanton in management of the War Department and the command of the Union armies while there was no general-in-chief, after Lincoln relieved Maj. Gen. George B. McClellan of his responsibilities as general-in-chief and before Maj. Gen. Henry W. Halleck replaced him.
4. Bickel/Schmidt.
5. Referred to simply as "Land Decisions" (L.D.).
6. 24 L.D. 305 (1897).
7. 24 L.D. 372 (1897).
8. 24 L.D. 404 (1897).
9. 24 L.D. 562. (1897).
10. Donald E. Cooke, *Atlas of the Presidents*, Hammond, 4th Ed. (1975).
11. Abraham, 129–130. "His reputation as a progressive during his stint in the U.S. Department of the Interior, where he served as an attorney specializing in matters involving public lands and Indian affairs, had been a real factor in his appointment to the circuit court by TR."
12. David, McCullough, *The Path Between the Seas: The Creation of the Panama Canal 1870–1914*, Simon & Schuster, 1977, 249.
13. 26 Stat. 826.
14. Rehnquist, 138.
15. Rehnquist, 155–157.
16. Rehnquist, 268.
17. Ch. 349, 32 Stat. 791.
18. New York Times, March 9, 1903. "Acts of the 57th Congress: More than 1200 Private Acts Went Through and Were Approved by the President."
19. There is no record that Roosevelt paid any heed to the notorious affairs of Tom Horn, who had worked for the WSGA in the Johnson County War and was now sitting in the Laramie County Courthouse Jail, awaiting his hanging for the murder of thirteen year-old Willie Nickel at his family's small ranch near Iron Mountain Wyoming. No doubt the conviction was known to Roosevelt on the ride, if not before (the October 1902 trial being a fanfare), as Deputy Marshall Joe LaFors, who had educed Horn's confession through inebriation (causation unspecified) and therefore conviction (see, *Horn v. State*, 73 P. 705 (1903)) rode along with Warren and Roosevelt from Laramie to Cheyenne that day.

Chapter 17

1. Friedman/Israel.
2. *Musser-Sauntry Co. v. Brown*, 126 Fed. 141 (8th Cir. 1903).
3. *Chicago M. & St, Ry Co. v. Voelker*, 129 Fed. 522, 527 (8th Cir. 1904).
4. *Chicago & N.W. Ry. Co. v. Andrews*, 130 Fed. 65 (8th Cir. 1904).
5. *Chicago Great Western Ry. Co. v. Crotty*, 141 Fed. 913 (8th Cir. 1905).
6. *Chicago Great Western Ry. Co. v. Smith*, 141 Fed. 930 (8th Cir. 1905).
7. *St. Louis & S.F. R.R. v. Dewees*, 153 Fed. 56 (8th Cir. 1907).
8. *Great Northern Ry. Co. v. United States*, 155 Fed. 945 (8th Cir. 1907).
9. 208 U.S. 452 (1908).
10. *Denver City Tramway Co. v. Cobb*. 164 Fed. 41 (8th Cir. 1908).
11. *Portland Gold Mining Co. v. Duke*, 164 Fed. 180 (8th Cir. 1908).
12. *Great Northern Ry. Co. v. Hooker*, 170 Fed. 154 (8th Cir. 1909).

Chapter 18

1. 54 U.S. 362 (May 26, 1894).
2. 169 U.S. 466, modified 171 U.S. 361 (May 9, 1898).
3. 320 U.S. 521 (1944).
4. 156 U.S. 1 (1895).
5. 166 U.S. 290 (March 22, 1897).
6. 53 F. 440.
7. 19 U.S. App. 36.

Chapter 19

1. Financiers of a scheme to corner the market in the stock of the United Copper Company, traded "on the curb.," realized that the banks upon which they were relying to support their

borrowing to cover short sales weren't as liquid as they thought. The New York Stock Exchange ultimately lost 50 % from the year before, and a wave of unconfidence spread across the nation, causing many state and local banks to declare bankruptcy. Confidence was not fully restored until the creation of the Federal Reserve System in 1913.

2. Born in Cincinnati in 1857, Taft was the son of a prosperous Cincinnati lawyer, Alphonso Taft. He graduated from Cincinnati Law School in 1880 and was admitted to the Ohio Bar the same year. He became Hamilton County, Ohio prosecutor the next year. The year following, 1882, he began law practice in Cincinnati, the same year Willis Van Devanter graduated from the same Cincinnati Law School. Taft served in the Arthur administration and was later appointed U.S. Solicitor General, while Willis Van Devanter was advising the Union Pacific and Cheyenne cattlemen plotting their crimes in anticipation of the Johnson County War. On March 21, 1892, Taft resigned his position as Solicitor General in order to become appointed as a United States Circuit Court Judge for the Sixth Circuit (Ohio, Kentucky, Michigan and Tennessee) where he served until 1900.

3. It was well known that Taft had long aspired for such an appointment, but that he repeatedly declined the appointment in deference to the importance of the jobs in which he then served. Roosevelt now endorsed Taft for President in the 1908 Republican Party convention in Chicago.

4. Bryan had been defeated twice, in 1896 and 1900, by William McKinley. This time, Bryan ran against the establishment and the nation's business elite. Taft, the conservative wolf in progressive sheep's clothing, undermined Bryan's significant liberal support by adopting some of Roosevelt's progressive planks as well as Bryan's reformist ideas.

5. Pringle, 196, 269.

6. Pringle, 96.

7. Pringle, 262. Taft said: "Since the birth of the Republican party it has stood for the affirmative of every proposition ... which involved doing something for the country. The Democratic party has generally stood for negation.... The Republican party dates back to 1854, when it was organized to resist the encroachments of the slave power and ultimately to save the Union and to eradicate the cancer of slavery from the body politic. It carried on a four years' war of proportions never before and never since exceeded. It fought the way of the government back to the resumption of specie payments from the sea of ... depreciated currency. It built the Pacific railroads, which united the East and the West and brought into close contract with the markets of the world the vast expanse of territory between the Mississippi and the Rocky Mountains. A hundred other great governmental policies it has carried out since 1861 ... policies in all of which it has been opposed by the Democratic party." *Id*, 263, 264.

8. "Taft rarely worried when the Republican Party was in power; he was nearly always uneasy when it was not. He rarely fought the Republican bosses, however corrupt. After an occasion when he had launched a vigorous attack on one of them ... he modified it." Pringle, 58.

9. Pringle, 57, 58.

10. Pringle, 60.

11. Pringle, 529, 530, quoting from Taft letter to Lurton, May 22, 1909.

12. Pringle, 266. Taft had had earlier experience with the Court and the single-handedness of individual justices. Justice David J. Brewer replied to Secretary of War Taft, in response to Taft indignation regarding a Supreme Court decision(Warner, Barnes and Co.) affecting the Philippines, that he [Brewer] and his colleagues who had differed on the insular question had "paid no attention to the case at all and let the other five run it." Justice Holmes was the author of the opinion.

13. 206 U.S. 46 (1907). Brewer's decision was joined by then Associate Justice White. Brewer was later remembered for his judicial objectivity in the case, ruling in a manner antithetical to his home state's interest. The prior opinion in the case was authored by Chief Justice Fuller in 1902, Kansas v. Colorado, 185 U.S. 125 (1902).

14. Lurton was born in Newport, Kentucky, on February 26, 1844, the son of a physician turned clergyman. He was a sergeant major in the Confederate Army during the Civil War, serving in the 5th Tennessee Infantry, 2nd Kentucky Infantry, and 3rd Kentucky Cavalry. Twice captured by Union forces, the second time sent as a prisoner of war to Johnson's Island Prison Camp in Sandusky Bay, Ohio, he was later paroled by President Lincoln. Lurton was the oldest justice appointed to the Court, aged 65 when appointed in 1910.

15. Pringle, 530. Taft was criticized by the bar associations and labor of appointing his friend, motivated by personal loyalty, rather than his best interest in rebuilding a vital Supreme Court.

16. George Washington, who appointed the entire Supreme Court, and Franklin D. Roosevelt, who served as president for just over twelve years, appointed more Supreme Court justices than William Howard Taft, who appointed six. Andrew Jackson appointed five. Abraham Lincoln appointed five. Four of Taft's

appointees were relatively young at ages 48, 51, 53 and 54.

17. Willis Van Devanter and Francis E. Warren often wrote to each other in "ciphered" correspondence—a code that would not permit others to understand the writing. The "ciphered" letter was first composed, then the words in the letter transferred to a table in which the words in the sentences were set out left to right in four or five columns. The words were then copied into the ciphered correspondence by reading down the columns. In this form, the finished "ciphered" correspondence made no sense, unless it was first set back into the columns (unciphered) by the reader who knew the method.

18. Van Devanter Papers, Box 8, item 19, Correspondence with Hon. Charles Nagel, Department of Commerce and Labor, Washington, D.C., 418–422, April 19, 1910, "Dear Mr. Secretary" "[Your note] says that the statement is made that the number of opinions written by me is not in fair proportion to the work done by my associates and that I do not participate in the hearing of cases as fully as I should. The statement is a grave one and it gives me no little pain because it does me an injustice." Letter goes on to argue the complexity and hard work of Van Devanter's cases. Correspondence to F.E. Warren, 423, April 19, 1910, forwarding copy of letter to Nagel, attributing smear to Judge Sanborn.

Van Devanter also touted the geographic expanse of jurisdiction of the Eighth Circuit Court of appeals on which he served. The Eighth Circuit "embraces twelve states and one territory, has a population of five million in excess of any other circuit and has a still greater relative proportion of railroad mileage," he argued.

19. Van Devanter Papers, Box 8, item 19, Correspondence to F.E. Warren, 317, April 7, 1910, 321–324, April 10, 326, 327, April 10.

20. Van Devanter Papers, Box 8, item 19, Correspondence to Mr. N.L. Loomis, General Solicitor, Union Pacific R.R. Co., Omaha, Nebraska, from Cheyenne, February 12, 1910.

21. Van Devanter Papers, Box 8, item 19, correspondence to F. E. Warren, 377, April 13, 1910; correspondence to F.E. Warren, April 16, 1910. "Mr. Severance was here the other day to present a matter before me" [does not mention that it was the UP antitrust case] "and afterwards said to me that he thought Judge Sanborn's chances were not at all good even if the appointment came to this circuit." [An ex parte communication regarding the judge's interest from counsel arguing a case before him.] Personal letters have gone to the president from all the Judges, state officers, ex-judges, ex-state officers and others of prominence from Wyoming, many have gone and are going from Denver, some have gone and others are going from Utah. Others in lesser number have gone from other sections. Still others will follow from the conference of Judge Lacey and his friends. Mr. Burdick is in Denver to-day and Judge Riner will be there Monday.... Judge Lacey just received a cipher message from Loomis which repeats a message from Washington somewhat as follows: 'New York is very much in earnest and is vigorously pushing for appointment irrespective of Hughes, and it is now believed in close administration circles that President is inclined to accede to claims of new Yorkers in filling this vacancy. Am just informed in very reliable way that President regards Van Devanter very highly, and if appointing from eighth circuit would probably appoint him, and probably contemplates appointing him later on. Close friends of administration says that while New Yorkers are pressing very hard, the western endorsements for Van Devanter are in nature of letters more or less formal, as letters naturally are; that more vigorous endorsement of Van Devanter might win this time, and that appointment will probably not be made for a month or so. Just saw Senator Clark and while he is hopeful for Van Devanter he has no definite idea of President's position.' This telegram was sent to Loomis by a Mr. Clancey, who seems to be a confidential correspondent of his at Washington..."

22. Van Devanter Papers, Box 8, item 19, correspondence to Hon. Dennis T. Flynn, 383, April 13, 1910, regarding Gov. Hughes; correspondence to Hon. Walter H. Sanborn (St. Paul, MN), and Hon. William H. Munger (Omaha, NB) addressed from Cheyenne, Wyoming, 385, April 13, 1910; correspondence to Hon. Elmer B. Adams (St. Louis, MO) (Circuit Court judge), Hon. John E. Carland, Sioux Falls, S.D. (District Court Judge), 388, April 14, 1910.

23. Van Devanter Papers, Box 8, item 19, 406, April 16, 1910 letter to Hon Clarence D. Clark, U.S. Senate, from Cheyenne. "I take this opportunity to express to you my sincere appreciation of your attitude in this matter, and of your earnest commendation of me." Letter suggests forwarding letter of support of Judge Helm, lately Chief Justice of Colorado Supreme Court, to President Taft. Box 8, item 19, letter to Hon. Cornelius N. Bliss, New York City, re: Presidential appointment, 407, April 16, 1910. "It is said that the President is considering my name in connection with the existing vacancy in the Supreme Court caused by the untimely death of Mr. Justice Brewer, who was appointed from this circuit, and that a goodly number of the bench and bar and others in the circuit have written

the President suggesting that I be appointed to the vacancy. Thus far I have refrained from soliciting any action in my behalf, but some of my friends, notably Senator Warren, are rather pronounced in the belief that our very cordial relations justify my doing so in this instance. I yield to their belief, but not without hesitation; first, because it really impinges upon a natural sense of modesty, and, second, because it may prove embarrassing to you in that the names of others with whom you maintain equally cordial relations may also be under consideration. But suffice it to say that if you freely and properly can commend me to the President I will appreciate your doing so. At this long range, I personally know but little about the situation, but my friends entertain the belief that if the appointment comes to this circuit it probably will come to me;..."

24. Van Devanter Papers, Box 8, item 19, correspondence to Major Frederick C. Bryan, 701 Colorado Building, Washington, D.C., 412, April 18, 1910, "Out of an appropriate sense of modesty I have not undertaken to do anything at all for myself, but the bench and bar in this region have very generously endorsed me and have actively sought my appointment." "You probably know that Alfred A. Frazer, one of our class-mates, has been, or is, a Judge of one of the courts at Zanesville, Ohio, and is highly esteemed, as his works in the law school indicated that he would be. It may be that if the present situation were called to his attention, he would be glad to write to the president, but as to that I do not know."

25. Van Devanter Papers, Box 8, item 19, correspondence to F.E. Warren, 413, April 18, 1910, forwarding Frederick C. Bryan letter of reference and regarding "Judge Lacey's" correspondent sending telegrams. Correspondence to A.C. Campbell, Reclamation Service, Interior Department, 414, Aril 18, 1910, re correspondence and conversation with General Michener. Correspondence with Judge Van Orsdel, 2500 Ontario Rd, Washington, D.C., p 415, April 18, 1910, re: acquaintance with Mr. Needham, President of George Washington University, and suggesting encouragement of letter of recommendation. Correspondence to F.E. Warren, 428, April 24, 1910, regarding machinations of lobbying President Taft. Correspondence to F.E. Warren, 432, April 25, 1910 forwarding copy of letter from Secretary Nagel. "I have shown the Nagel correspondence to Judge Lacey..."

26. Van Devanter Papers, Box 8, item 19, telegram to F. E. Warren, from Cheyenne, 436, April 27, 1910, "I deeply appreciate and sincerely thank you for what you have done and am well satisfied with outcome. I leave for Chicago Thursday morning and must leave there for Saint Paul not later than six o'clock Sunday evening. Will stop at Congress hotel in Chicago. If you reach Chicago before I leave will be glad to meet you any time or place, but do not want you to change your plans or be put to any inconvenience. Willis Van Devanter."

27. Associate Justice Charles Evans Hughes, Sr., was born on April 11, 1862, in the midst of the Civil War. He attended Madison University (now Colgate University) then transferred to Brown University, where he graduated in 1881 at age 19, youngest in his class, receiving second-highest honors. For the next two years he worked at Stevens Institute Academy in Davenport, Florida, where he taught Japanese, Latin, and Calculus in order to earn money for law school. He entered Columbia Law School in 1882, and graduated in 1884 with highest honors. Hughes was elected Governor of New York in 1906, defeating Democrat William Randolph Hearst, where he served until 1911 when offered his Supreme Court seat. He resigned his position on the Court, as associate justice, to become the candidate of the Republican and Progressive Parties in the 1916 U.S. Presidential election, which he lost to Woodrow Wilson (by 23 electoral votes and 594,188 popular votes). The election hinged on California, where Wilson managed to win by 3,800 votes and its 13 electoral votes and thus Wilson was returned for a second term. He served as United States Secretary of State during the Warren G. Harding and Calvin Coolidge administrations. (1921–1925). Herbert Hoover, who had appointed Hughes' son as the Solicitor General in 1929, appointed Hughes as the Chief Justice of the United States in 1930, succeeding Chief Justice Taft, He served as Chief Justice until 1941. He died on August 27, 1948.

28. Pringle, 532.

29. Hughes was sworn in as Associate Justice on Sunday, October 9, 1910.

30. On July 4, 1910.

31. White was the first Associate Justice to be appointed Chief Justice since President George Washington appointed John Rutledge to be Chief Justice in 1795. Some historians believe that President Taft appointed White, who was 65 years old at the time and overweight, in the hope that White would serve a short period after which Taft might someday be appointed to the same post—which in fact happened eleven years later.

32. In 1878, White was appointed to the Louisiana Supreme Court, at age 33; in 1891 the Louisiana state legislature elected him to represent Louisiana in the U.S. Senate.

33. Pringle, 535, citing letter to Helen Taft,

February 21, 1894. Born November 3, 1845, Justice White had been raised in Louisiana, the son of a slaveholding sugar planter. He attended Mount St. Mary's College in Emmitsburg, Maryland and Georgetown College (now Georgetown University) in Washington D.C., after which he enlisted in the Confederate Army. He was captured in 1863 and held as a prisoner of war until the war's end.

34. Moody had originally gained his notoriety by having been U.S. Attorney for Eastern Massachusetts and junior prosecutor in the Lizzie Borden murder case. He was a protégé of Henry Cabot Lodge and Theodore Roosevelt's progressive attorney general trust buster, targeting Standard Oil. See, James McGregor Burns, *Packing the Court*, Penguin (2009), 118.

35. Moody's last day sitting with the Court had been May 7, 1909.

36. Larson, 318.

37. Irons, 260. "Taft chose [Van Devanter] largely to fill a 'western seat' on the Court and to satisfy Republicans who grumbled that two of the president's three nominees—Lurton and White—were Democrats."

38. Peter Charles Hoffer, Williamjames Hull Hoffer, N.E. Hull, *The Supreme Court, An Essential History*. University Press of Kansas (2007), 192. "When Fuller died and White was elevated, Taft tapped Wyoming Republican Willis Van Devanter for the vacant seat. A former senator and power in his state and an able craftsman as both lawyer and federal circuit judge, he lobbied for the seat and then occupied it for twenty-six years." (hereafter "Hoffer").

39. Pringle, 533.

40. Holsinger, 175, 176.

41. Johnson, 403, 409, *n*19.

42. Johnson, 403, 410.

43. Abraham, 129–130. "White's promotion left his own associate justiceship to be filled. This time Taft turned to his own party, selecting the urbane Willis Van Devanter of Wyoming, a 51-year-old judge of the U.S. Court of Appeals for the Eighth Circuit."

44. Larson, 318. Like White, Joseph Rucker Lamar was a southern Democrat, making his confirmation by a Republican Senate somewhat doubtful. Nevertheless, Larmar's confirmation went through smoothly and Lamar was confirmed five days after his nomination. On the bench, Lamar reportedly lacked imagination or creativity. He died after five years of service, in 1916. During Lamar's short tenure on the Court, it is likely that Lamar and Van Devanter agreed on many things, as both had, in private practice, represented railroads and many other large corporations. Associate Justice Lamar was the cousin of former Associate Justice Lucius Lamar. He was born on October 15, 1857, two years before Justice Van Devanter. Lamar spent most of his life in a socially prominent family in Georgia. He attended the University of Georgia and Bethany College. Lamar studied law briefly at Washington and Lee University and passed the Georgia bar in 1880. While in private practice, Lamar served two terms in the Georgia legislature. Lamar was appointed to the Georgia Supreme Court in 1903 but served only two years.

45. Harlan sat longer than most justices. He was among the last of the tobacco-chewing justices. He was reportedly always within spitting distance of a spittoon. John Marshall Harlan, the more liberal of the Court Justice Van Devanter joined, and the lone dissenter in *Plessy v. Ferguson*, died on October 14, 1911, leaving the Court within nine months of Van Devanter's arrival. Harlan, a Kentucky Republican (a Whig until that party's dissolution), was born June 1, 1833 to a southern aristocratic, civic-minded family, slaveholding but loyal to the Union (rising to the rank of colonel in the Union Army during the Civil War) whose members played active roles in public life. Harlan studied law at Transylvania University and finished his legal education in his father's law office. Harlan was named to the Court in 1877 by President Rutherford B. Hayes, whom he had helped nominate as head of the Kentucky delegation to the 1876 Republican national convention.

46. Not "conservative" in the modern sense that it necessarily construed the Constitution as the framers would have intended, nor in the modern sense that the Court should not "legislate from the bench," but "conservative" in the political sense: protective of wealth, vested interests, corporate structure, societal framework as handed down from prior generations, etc. For example, according to some accounts, Justice Oliver Wendell Holmes had assured Roosevelt, in order to secure Holmes' nomination to the Court, that he would vote to sustain the administration's position that not all the provisions of the United States Constitution applied to possessions acquired from Spain, an important question on which the Court was then evenly divided.

47. Chief Justice White, Associate Justice Lurton.

48. Associate Justices Harlan and Holmes. Holmes graduated from Harvard, as class poet, in 1861. Holmes enlisted in the fourth battalion, Massachusetts militia, and then received a commission as first lieutenant in the Twentieth Regiment of Massachusetts Volunteer Infantry. He saw much action, from the Peninsula Campaign to the Wilderness, suffering wounds at the

Battle of Ball's Bluff, Antietam, and Fredericksburg. He is also said to have shouted at Lincoln during the Battle of Fort Stevens He carried a bullet in his body until his death.

49. 163 U.S. 537 (5/18/1896).

50. Then Associate Justice White had signed on to the majority opinion in the *Plessy* case written by Associate Justice Henry B. Brown.

51. Edward G. White, *Justice Oliver Wendell Holmes*, Oxford University Press, 1993, 311, citing Van Devanter Papers.

52. Mason, 56. "President Taft, rating Supreme Court appointments among his most important functions, had the good fortune to appoint five Associate Justices [including Van Devanter] and a Chief Justice.... Each appointment was a source of pride. All, including the Southern Democrat White, entertained views closely akin to Taft's."

53. Jeffrey Toobin, *The Nine*, Anchor Books (2008), 6, 24, 299 (hereafter "Toobin").

54. Bailey, 5. "During the seventy-two-year period from 1860 until 1932, only two Democrats had been elected president of the United States: Grover Cleveland and Woodrow Wilson." Rehnquist, 215. Indeed, the Wilson years suggested some intercession, but it was not until later broken by Franklin Delano Roosevelt in 1935, in the face of opposition from Van Devanter as leader of the Four Horsemen, that the Court's conservatism calmed.

55. Bailey, 113, 114.

56. Bailey, 142.

Chapter 20

1. 161 F. 324 (8th Cir., Sanborn, April 17, 1908).

2. Eighth Circuit citation unavailable. On review: 219 U.S. 426 (1911).

3. "[A] construction which would deprive the railroad company of its substantial right to select, and would render nugatory the exertion of power of the Secretary of the Interior to approve lawful selections when made, would destroy the right which it was the purpose of Congress to confer. That the effect of holding that lands lawfully embraced in a list of selections duly filed and awaiting the approval of the Secretary of the Interior could, in the interim, be appropriated at will by others would be destructive of the right of selection is not only theoretically apparent from the mere statement of the proposition, but has, moreover, in actual experience, been found to be the practical result of carrying that doctrine into effect. *See* 25 Opin.Atty.Gen. 632. The power to approve was judicial in its nature. Possessing that attribute, the authority therefore involved not only the power, but implied the duty, to determine the lawfulness of the selections as of the time when the exertion of the authority was invoked by the lawful filing of the list of selections ... the elementary principle of relation, repeatedly sanctioned by this Court and uniformly applied by the Land Department from the beginning up to this time, under similar circumstances, in the practical execution of the land laws of the United States." 219 U.S. 380.

4. 173 Fed. 177.

5. *Standard Oil Co. v. United States*, 221 U.S. 1 (1911).

6. *United States v. American Tobacco Co.*, 221 U.S. 106, 142–155 (1911).

7. Bickel/Schmidt.

8. 221 U.S. 106. (1911).

9. Bickel/Schmidt, 671, 672.

10. 223 U.S. 683 (1912).

11. See *Bailey v. Sanders*, 228 U.S. 603 (1913), *Logan v. Davis*, 233 U.S. 613 (1914).

Chapter 21

1. Van Devanter Papers, U.S. Library of Congress (hereafter "Van Devanter Papers") May 13, 1921, typewritten note from Chief Justice E. D. White to Van Devanter: "My dear Judge, I have written Mr. Justice McKenna that I will not be at the next conference and probably not at the final one. By way of explanation I say that this is due to an indisposition which I am sure is of no moment, but which may keep me in for the time stated.

2. Stephen C. Halpern, Charles M. Lamb, *Supreme Court Activism and Restraint*, Lexington Books (1982), 307.

3. Peter Irons, *A People's History of the Supreme Court*, Viking (1999), 286 (hereafter "Irons").

4. Irons, 245.

5. Irons, 273.

6. Irons, 282.

7. Irons, 325. By 1909, Republican's needed the support of southern Blacks in order to be nominated to the presidency. Irons, 323.

8. Irons, 282.

9. Irons, 276.

10. Pringle, Henry F., *The Life and Times of William Howard Taft*, Farrar & Rinehart, Inc. (1939) (hereafter "Pringle"), 4–7.

11. Pringle, 40.

12. Pringle, 49, 50.

13. Van Devanter Papers, July 6, 1921 handwritten letter from W.H. Taft to Justice Van Devanter.

14. Van Devanter Papers, September 30, 1921, CJ Taft notice of meeting.

15. Van Devanter Papers, October 17, 1921,

copy of Gardiner Lathrop correspondence to chief justice Taft re: Judge Pollack, October 19, 1921, copy of correspondence from N.H. (Union Pacific, General Solicitor) to Sen. Charles Curtis re appointment of District Judge Pollack, Kansas City, to Eighth Circuit, Wm. H. Taft's letter to Gardiner Lathrop, The Railway Exchange, Chicago—all found in Van Devanter's personal files. Copy sent by Loomis to Van Devanter, October 29, 1921. "After leaving you [VDV] in Washington, I had in mind Gardiner Lathrop of Chicago and D. W. Mulvane of Topeka as the proper persons to handle the matter we talked about."

16. Pringle, 99, 100.

17. Van Devanter Papers, December 7, 1921, typewritten note, Wm. Taft to Van Devanter.

18. 257 U.S. 312.

Chapter 22

1. The case was docketed as No. 7 Original. That number appeared on the October Term 1916, Transcript of Record. The cause number of the case changed, for some unknown reason, to No. 8 Original. The 1916 Transcript of Record bears the No. 7. Justice Van Devanter's 1922 Opinion bears No. 8 Original.

2. Today the reservoirs are designated as WID Reservoirs No. 1 and No. 2, constructed in 1895 and 1901, respectively. Reservoir No. 2 was enlarged in the late 1950s. Reservoir No. 1 was enlarged more recently. Water is diverted from the Laramie River at the Laramie River Diversion Dam through the Wheatland Tunnel and into Bluegrass and Sybille Creeks. District Canals No. 1 and No. 2 deliver water to district irrigators from Sybille Creek and WID No. 2 Reservoir, respectively. Canal No. 3 flows from Sybille Creek into WID No. 1 Reservoir. The district currently serves 850 users with approximately 54,000 irrigated acres.

3. James E. Sherow, "The Latent Influence of Equity in Wyoming v. Colorado (1922)," *Great Plains Research* 2(1) 1992, 7–26, Center for Great Plains Studies (1992) (hereafter "Sherow").

4. "[Carpenter] believed the case was politically motivated and it had been initiated by two men who planned to turn Laramie River water into Lake Hattie near Woods Landing, Wyoming. Knowing their planned project was "junior" in priority to the Greeley-Poudre Project, they 'started a series of agitations around Laramie City to the effect that the Colorado diverters were about to take *all* of the water of the Laramie River in Colorado and divert it to the Cache la Poudre Valley.' According to Carpenter, they used this threat to gain votes during the most recent political campaign." Daniel Tyler, *Silver Fox of the Rockies, Delphus E. Carpenter and Western Water Compacts*, University of Oklahoma Press, 2003, 317, *n*6, citing Delph Carpenter letter to C.W. Crouter, Wheatland, Wyoming, 20 July 1911, Delph Carpenter Papers.

5. Tyler, 7–12.

6. Tyler, 7–12.

7. 135 Fed. 411 (1905).

8. 141 Fed. 64 (1905).

9. Act of February 21, 1911, ch. 141, 36 Stat. 925, 43 USC 523–525.

10. Tyler, 89, 324, *n*17, Carpenter Papers, Box 86, folder 23. "In a letter to Judge Evan A. Evans, Chicago, Carpenter wrote that $2.8 million of $5.1 million bonds were sold as of 1911 when Wyoming sued Colorado. Outstanding bonds had depreciated to approximately 25 percent of their value and lands that were supposed to benefit from this project had depreciated to a "nominal value" due to the fact that the project was only 54 percent complete."

11. A Brief accompanied the Demurrer. University of Colorado law school library, dated December 28, 1911. Charles F. Tew entered his appearance as Attorney General for Colorado on January 24, 1912.

12. 259 U.S. 419, 483.

13. 259 U.S. 419, 469.

14. 259 U.S. 419, 456.

Chapter 23

1. *Wilson v. New*, 243 U.S. 332 (March 19, 1917).

2. Act of September 3, 5, 1916, 39 Stat. 721, c. 436.

3. 243 U.S. 332 (March 19, 1917).

4. The Ku'e Petitions, containing 38,000 signatures, were submitted opposing approval of the treaty.

5. Rowley, William D. *Reclaiming the Arid West: The Career of Francis G. Newlands.* Bloomington: Indiana University Press, 1996, (hereafter, "Rowley").

6. Rowley, 100.

7. Rowley, 100.

8. Rowley, 51. "Newlands' business interests ran contrary to his public ambitions. He regretted the suit [brought by Union Mill and Mining against ranchers in the upper Carson regarding the Water Law of 1889], but the company pressed it. Newlands' solution was a comprehensive storage system on the Carson to guarantee water both to ranchers and to mill men.... Agriculture now challenged the preeminency of industry in the state and would eventually win the suit in 1897. Newlands could not concede

to agricultural interests all the water of a river whose power for years had turned mills that ground out the riches of the Comstock.... He insisted that he did not stand against the agricultural interests, but rather against the 'large landed proprietors' who constantly expanded their acreage. Cattle ranching did not represent the type of agricultural development he envisioned.... He noted that in the previous two years before the filing [of the lawsuit] (1887–1888) ranchers had appropriated all the Carson River waters from July 4 to January, forcing the mills to close. Small farmers downstream, who had prior rights to water, were also adversely affected by the upstream ranchers, he asserted. Thus Newlands cast himself in the role of champion of the small farmer, not simply as a defender of the milling monopoly. Farmers represented a forward looking group for Nevada, while ranching interests seemed wedded to Nevada's frontier past."

9. Rowley, 67.
10. Rowley, 16.
11. Rowley, 76.
12. Act of June 17, 1902, 32 Stat. 388.
13. Rowley, 101, citing *Washington Times*, December 29, 1901.
14. Rowley, 102.
15. Rowley, 103.
16. Rowley, 102.
17. Ch. 349, 32 Stat. 791.

Chapter 24

1. Rowley, 1.
2. 30 L.D. 382.
3. 143 U.S. 389.
4. File folder L5000.73 "Laramie River," Drawer 11, Denver: Colorado State Engineer's Office.
5. Van Devanter Papers, February13, 1922, typewritten cover letter from Edwin S. Booth, Solicitor, Department of the Interior to Justice Van Devanter.
6. 259 U.S. 419, 456.
7. 42 U.S. Statutes at Large171. See Congressional Record 67th Congress, 1st Sess. (August 19, 1921). 61 Congressional Record, 4817–6210 (August 1–24, HR 6877).
8. 259 U.S. 419, 461.
9. 259 U.S. 419, 463.

Chapter 25

1. Van Devanter Papers, Personal Correspondence, January 10, 1922, typewritten note from Wm. H. Taft reminding Van Devanter of their private meeting, 11:15 "tomorrow morning" at "Clinedinst's."
2. Van Devanter Papers, Personal Correspondence, January 16, 1922, note from Wm. H. Taft to Justice Van Devanter.
3. Van Devanter Papers, Personal Correspondence, January 25, 1922, note from Wm. H. Taft to Justice Van Devanter.
4. 259 U.S. 20 (1922).
5. The first important prohibition case of the Taft court was argued in December, 1921. Taft needed Van Devanter's vote in order to uphold the Volstead Act, imposing prohibition, and the Eighteenth Amendment, and he corresponded with Van Devanter securing it. Pringle, 984. See cases *Corneli v. Moore*, 257 U.S. 491 (1/20/1922); *Grogan v. Hiram Walker & Sons*, 257 U.S. 80 (5/15/1922).
6. Van Devanter Papers, Personal Correspondence, December 26, 1921 handwritten note from C.J. William H. Taft to justice Van Devanter, "My Dear Justice, I handed your memorandum of the North Dakota decision to Day for his digestion. I suppose the case you mention is on its way up here—I would hand the mem' to Pitney just to enable him to see the great advantage other court of dissents. Most dissents, elaborated, are a form of egotism. They don't do any good, and only weaken the prestige of the Court. It is much more important what the Court thinks than what anyone thinks, not that sense of proportion is not present in the minds of some of our brethren. As to B, that sense is not lacking but his ultimate purpose is to break down the prestige of the Court. Merry Xmas and a Happy New year too you and yours, Sincerely yours, Wm. H. Taft." In 1920, before Taft was appointed to the Court by Harding, a full 30 percent of cases were published with dissenting views, with a full 21 percent in 1921. Drew Noble Lanier, *Of Time and Judicial Behavior: United States Supreme Court Agenda-Setting and Decision-Making, 1888–1997*, Selinsgrove: Susquehanna University Press (2003), 118, (hereafter "Lanier").
7. Lanier, 118.
8. Pringle, 1049.
9. Pringle, 125, 126. "In 1896, also, Taft became dean and professor of property at his legal alma mater, the Cincinnati Law School. He did this, of course, because of his devotion to the institution and because of his deep interest in legal education."
10. Pringle, 100.
11. Pringle, 46.
12. Willis Van Devanter letter to M.C. Barrow, September 4, 1894, quoted in Holsinger, 199.
13. Henry J. Abraham, *Justices, Presidents and Senators*, Rowman & Littlefield (1999), 129–130 (hereafter "Abraham").
14. Pringle, 129.

15. Pringle, 343.
16. Pringle, 341, citing War Secretary Diaries.
17. Pringle, 361.
18. Pringle, 381, quoting from Taft letter to W.R. Nelson, Feb. 23, 1909.
19. Alphons Thomas Mason, "William Howard Taft: President by Chance, Chief Justice by Choice," 55 ABA Journal 35 (January 1969), (hereafter "Mason").
20. Van Devanter Papers, Personal Correspondence, February 3, 1922, typewritten note from Justice Mahlon Pitney to Justice Van Devanter, and February 10, 1922, and undated handwritten notes from Justice Oliver Wendell Holmes to Justice Van Devanter critiquing jurisdictional bill and referring to correspondence between the Chief Justice and Justices McReynolds and Day. March 7, 1922, copy of Wm. H. Taft note to Justice Day forwarding sent jurisdiction bill for comment. March 27, 1922, Wm. H. Taft personal handwritten note to Justice Van Devanter regarding House Judiciary Bill.
21. Pringle, 998–1000, citing letter from Taft to TR.A. Taft, February 8, 1925.
22. A "writ of certiorari" was, at common law, a written order of a reviewing court to a lower court asking that the record of the court below be certified to the reviewing court as complete and accurate. Based on that certification, the reviewing court would take jurisdiction. In today's appellate practice, a motion (or petition) for writ of certiorari is made as a means to ask a reviewing court to seek the record of the lower court and assume jurisdiction.
23. File folder L5000.73 "Laramie River," Drawer 11, Denver: Colorado State Engineer's Office.

Chapter 26

24. 262 U.S. 553, 623; 263 U.S. 350 (1923).
25. 263 U.S. 365 (1923).
26. Bernard Schwartz, *A History of the Supreme Court*, Oxford University Press, N.Y., Oxford, 1993 (hereafter "Schwartz").

Chapter 27

1. Van Devanter Papers, March 7, 1922, handwritten note from Justice Clarke to Justice Van Devanter.
2. A strong progressive Democrat, Clarke was born in New Lisbon, Ohio on September 18, 1857. He attended Western Reserve College and Case Western Reserve University. Clarke practiced law with his father after law school, in Youngstown and Cleveland representing corporate and railroad interests. He ran twice unsuccessfully for the U.S. Senate as a Democratic Progressive. President Woodrow Wilson appointed Clarke to the U.S. District Court for the Northern District of Ohio in 1914. When Charles Evans Hughes resigned his position on the U.S. Supreme Court in 1916 to run against Wilson for the Presidency, Wilson nominated Clarke to replace Hughes.

Although Clarke's departure from the Court is often attributed to his desire to advocate the League of Nations, his exceedingly unpleasant relationship with Justice James Clark McReynolds was more likely the cause of his resignation. Clarke resigned from the Court in just under six years. Clarke's support for progressive causes never reached fruition on the Court. Clarke died on March 22, 1945.

3. Van Devanter Papers, March 7, 1922, March 20, 1922, letter from A.C. Campbell, Atty., Cheyenne, to Justice Van Devanter.
4. Van Devanter Papers, Letterbooks, Vol. 33, 17, April 12 letter to Hon. A.C. Campbell (State Bar Association) Cheyenne, Wyoming, "Likewise, see April 12, 1922 letter to Aven Nelson, President, University of Wyoming, Laramie, Wyoming to same effect. Mr. Campbell stayed in contact. See May 8, 1922, letter from A.C. Campbell to Justice Van Devanter regarding the Justice's opinion in *Oklahoma v. Texas* and expressing disappointment with the Justice's having declined the State Bar's invitation.
5. 258 U.S. 574.
6. 24 L.D. 372.
7. Van Devanter Papers, Letterbooks, Vol. 33, 49, May 3, 1922, letter to Funk and Wagnalls, Co., New York City.
8. Van Devanter Papers, Letterbooks, Vol. 33, 14, April 10, 1922, letter from Justice Van Devanter to Herbert V. Lacey, Cheyenne, Wyoming.
9. Van Devanter Papers, April 13, 1922, letter from Herbert V. Lacey to Justice Van Devanter.
10. Van Devanter Papers, May 2, 1922, letter from John W. Lacey.
11. Van Devanter Papers, Letterbooks, Vol. 33, 79–87, June 5, 1922.
12. Van Devanter Papers, Letterbooks, Vol. 33, 72, May 15, 1922, letter to John W. Lacey, Cheyenne, Wyoming, "My dear Brother, Your letter of the 2d instant, with its several enclosures all relating to my law books, was duly received. It was not convenient to look over it at the time, but that has now been done. I am too much engrossed and too tired to give the matter much consideration, attention or to write you at length. Shortly stated, my ideas are as follows: I do not want you and Herbert, or either of you, to take the books unless you want them, or to pay more for them than you should pay...."

13. Tyler, 104, citing Diary of Delph Carpenter, 5, 11 January 1918, Delph Carpenter Papers.

Chapter 28

1. "Warren to Pass on All Appropriations Bills of Government Hereafter," *Wyoming State Tribune*, March 8, 1922, Courtesy of Wyoming State Archives.

2. Van Devanter Papers, Letterbooks, Personal Correspondence, April 20, 1922, Wm. H. Taft note to Justice Van Devanter forwarding draft opinion in "Stockyards Law case."

3. Van Devanter Papers, Personal Correspondence, May 12, 1922, note from Wm. H. Taft to Justice Van Devanter.

4. *Bank of Trade of City of Chicago v. Olson*, published a year later as 262 U.S. 1 (1923).

5. *Continental Insurance Co. v. U.S.*, 259 U.S. 156 (May 29, 1922).

6. Van Devanter Papers, Letterbooks, Vol. 33, 75, May 23, 1922 letter from Van Devanterto Chief Justice [Taft].

7. Van Devanter Papers, Personal Correspondence, June 3, 1922, handwritten note from Chief Justice Wm. H. Taft to Justice Van Devanter.

8. Sherow, 18–20.

9. Walter F. Murphy, *Elements of Judicial Strategy*, University of Chicago Press (1964), 42.

10. Mason, 208.

11. Potter was variously Justice and Chief Justice of the Wyoming State Supreme Court from January y, 1895 to December 20, 1927.

12. Van Devanter Papers, Personal Correspondence, September 9, 1922, handwritten note from Charles N. Potter, Chief Justice, Supreme Court of Wyoming. Judge Potter continues: "The date of its mailing was in a week when I had two nurses a day and night nurse and was very sick. But whatever the others may have thought, I had [illegible] that I was carrying through it, though the matter was then more or less one of indifference in my mind.... C.N. Potter." Potter reverts to political discussion of Republican politics in Wyoming. Chief Judge Potter died in 1927 and was succeeded by William A. Riner. Riner arrived in Cheyenne in 1902, affiliated with the Republican Party, and was city attorney of Cheyenne from 1908 until 1911. He was appointed U.S. District Attorney, District of Wyoming, 1911–1912, by President Taft, then appointed by Governor Robert Carey to the First Judicial District Court in 1922. Appointed Justice of the Wyoming Supreme Court by Governor Frank Emerson on January 10, 1928, to fill a vacancy created by the death of Chief Judge Potter, where he served until 1942.

13. Holsinger, 203–206.

14. Sherow, 17, 18, citing Carpenter, D. E. 1931. Letter from Delph E. Carpenter to Clarence L. Ireland, 1 July. File folder L5000.73 "Laramie River," Drawer 11, Denver: Colorado State Engineer's Office.

15. Holsinger, 189, *n*92.

16. Van Devanter Papers, Letterbooks, Vol. 33, 88, June 9, 1922, Justice Van Devanter letter to Mr. Hero Hudgin, Parry Sound, "I expect to leave here about the 19th of June," giving instructions to make the place ready for his arrival. He had had a longstanding invitation out to Judge John Pollock, of Kansas City to join him at Parry Sound, Willis Van Devanter Papers, June 12, 1922 typed letter from Judge John Pollock.

17. Van Devanter Papers, Letterbooks, Vol. 33, 110, June 17, 1922 letter from Justice Van Devanter to Mrs. John W. Lacey, Cheyenne, Wyoming.

18. Van Devanter Papers, Letterbooks, Vol. 33, 117, June 19, 1922 letter from Justice Van Devanter to wife "Dollie," "My very dear wife: ... Herbert Lacey came here yesterday and Winslow asked him to come up and have supper with me. He was looking very well. His mother had reached home before he left and had a pretty sore ankle—considerably swollen; Herbert knew but little about it save that waiter was attending to it. I think Herbert left in an hour or so after his mother arrived. Mr. Loomis [Union Pacific general counsel] had sent for him to come to Omaha and then had sent him on here about some matter that I do not know about. Herbert said that the family were all well save his mother's ankle. He did not say how long he would be here, but I gathered it might be two, three or four days."

19. Van Devanter Papers, Letterbooks, Vol. 33, 459, February 28, 1923 letter to Mr. Nellis E. Corthell, Laramie, Wyoming, "Dear Mr. Corthell: Enclosed is a document which its author thinks is 'profound,' unless perchance he is attempting the perpetration of a joke. It occurs to me that you will be diverted for the moment in looking at it. Doubtless its author will be as happy, if not happier, if he does not know that you have seen it. If he is working for you or about you, its contents and general purport will readily suggest to you the uncertainty of his future course and that some advance in his present direction may affect his responsibility. I merely call the matter to your attention so that, if you are not already accurately informed, you can see what the situation is. Of course, I do not care to have the document returned. Very sincerely, Willis Van Devanter."

Letterbooks, Vol. 33, 500, March 26, 1923, letter to Mr. Nellis E. Corthell, Laramie Wyoming, "Dear Mr. Corthell: Your letter of the 23d instant is along your best lines. To read it is a genuine diversion. I am glad the author of "Profound Analysis," etc., is not capable of any harm beyond appealing to the susceptibilities of the tender hearted, such as the president of the American Express Company. Evidently you understand him and are in no danger of being taken unawares. I merely wondered whether you had about you a smoldering volcano which might take you by surprise some day. Very sincerely, Willis Van Devanter."

Chapter 29

1. Van Devanter Papers, Letterbooks, Vol. 33, 152, October 24, 1922, Justice Van Devanter letter to Justice John H. Clarke, "The Court has convened. Justice Sutherland has taken his place, we have made our call on the president, and the work is now proceeding. You are missed on all hands, and the expressions of regret at your absence are of a character which could not be otherwise than pleasing to you could you only know about them. The brethren all look refreshed after the vacation. Justice McKenna does, and yet he shows the impress of his mature years. Justice Holmes looks very well considering the sever operation which he has undergone. He moves about a little more cautiously than usual, but is as cheerful as ever. My guess is that he is endeavoring to husband it without saying so. H and Mrs. Holmes are at the Powhatan and I understand they are having an elevator put in their house and perhaps some other changes made. Justice Pitney is not with us. During the summer he has improved at times and at others has fallen back to his condition of last spring. Two weeks ago he was being attended by a day nurse and night nurse, and saw no one outside his immediate family. The Chief Justice went over to Morristown to confer with Mrs. Pitney, but was unable to see the justice. The experts are disposed to believe he had a partial stroke last term, and that it would not be advisable for him to assume his judicial work at an early date. At times he needs assistance in rising from the bed and sitting up, etc. He and his wife are considering whether it would not be well to secure an act of Congress permitting him to retire without attaining the age of 70. He has some means, but his income without the salary is not sufficient to cover their reasonable expenses."

2. Van Devanter Papers, Letterbooks, Vol. 33, 402, January 27, 1923, letter to Justice William R. Day, Partridge Inn, Augusta, Georgia, "I was greatly pleased yesterday to learn that you had reached Augusta in good condition, and I hope that ere you get this you are rested from your journey and beginning to realize the advantages of a sojourn in the sunny south. In a climatic way it must be a very agreeable transition." Justice Van Devanter's letter goes on to describe his visit with Justice Pitney, his frailty, inability to speak clearly, emotionalism, and potential replacement by Judge Sanford.

3. Van Devanter Papers, Personal Correspondence, August 21, 1922, handwritten note from Justice Day to Justice Van Devanter, "I again wished I might have accepted your more than kind invitation to visit you in your Island Home. But age, and other things, must be reckoned with." "I cannot tell you, my dear Judge, how much the thought of separation from the Court Bench is one whenever I think of it. My association has been so long and so pleasant that the tie is hard to break." "I have written and get no response from Mrs. Holmes as to the Judge's condition. Have you heard anything?"

4. Van Devanter Papers, Letterbooks, Vol. 33, October 11, 1922 letter to Judge Sanborn, Eighth Circuit, St. Paul. "Please be good enough to let me take up the following matter with you in a confidential way. By so doing we may be able to work out some public good, and in any event, it will not do any harm. Chief Justice White, a southern democrat, has been succeeded by Chief Justice Taft, a northern republican, Justice Clarke, a northern democrat, has been succeeded by Justice Sutherland, a western republican. Justice Day, a northern republican, may retire within two months. Justice Pitney was the latter part of last term and has not improved during the summer. It is a complete nervous breakdown, coupled with a slight stroke of paralysis. His physicians advise that he cannot return to the work, and when Congress convenes an effort will be made to obtain an act permitting him to retire, as in the instance of Justice Moody. Chief Justice White was a Catholic, as is also Justice McKenna, whose age is such that he probably will not be with us many years. While there has been no authoritative announcement about Justice Day and Justice Pitney retiring, there is some speculation about their doing so and about their successors. Some suggestions are being made to the effect that at least one democrat be selected. Others that a southern democrat be selected. It no doubt would be moving along right lines to select from among men otherwise fitted a democrat, or southern democrat, and while church affiliations should not be made a ground of selection, they equally should not be made a ground of objection."

5. Pringle, 1057.

6. McKenna resigned from the Court in 1925 at the suggestion of then Chief Justice William

Howard Taft. McKenna's ability to perform his duties had been diminished significantly by a stroke suffered ten years earlier. By the end of his tenure McKenna could not be counted on to write coherent opinions.

7. Pringle, 1057. "McKenna was already failing by 1921 and the Chief Justice was soon close to despair over the justice's inability to do his work. 'I don't know what course to take with respect to him, or what cases to assign to him,' Taft confided to Brother Horace in April 1922. 'I had to take back a case from him last Saturday because he would not write it in accordance with the vote of the court ... and have taken it over to myself.'"

8. More interested in politics than law, however, McKenna pursued Republican issues. McKenna served as District Attorney for Solano County, California, as an assemblyman in the California State Assembly (1875–1877), as a Congressman from California i (1885–1892), as a U.S. circuit judge in the Ninth Circuit (appointed by President Benjamin Harrison) (1892–1897) and briefly as Attorney General of the United States (appointed by President William McKinley) (1897–1898), throughout acting in a manner consistent with Republican ideals. His loyalty to these principles was probably the basis for his nomination to the Court.

9. William E. Leuchtenburg, *The Supreme Court Reborn, The Constitutional Revolution in the Age of Roosevelt,* Oxford University Press (1995), 214. "Van Devanter and McReynolds had taken part in the notorious 5–4 decision of Hammer v. Dagenhart (1918) striking down the Child Labor Act of 1916 by presuming to pass judgment on the motives of Congress. The Court ruled that Congress could not ban the shipment in interstate commerce of goods produced by children because Congress was seeking to control intrastate activities and be the products were harmless."

10. Pringle, 971 (citing W.H. Taft correspondence with Horace Taft, April 17, 1922).

11. Pringle, 1057.

12. Pringle, McReynolds generally agreed with Taft on his views of the Constitution and law.

13. Associate Justice McReynolds was a blatant racist, anti-Semite and misogynist. He would not accept "Jews, drinkers, blacks, women, smokers, married or engaged individuals as law clerks." McReynolds refused to speak to Louis Brandeis, the first Jew on the Court, for three years following Brandeis's appointment. He left the conference room when Brandeis spoke. McReynolds refused to sit next to Brandeis (where he belonged on the basis of seniority) for the Court photograph in 1924 (no picture was ultimately taken). When Brandeis retired in 1939, McReynolds would not sign the customary retirement letter. Justice Van Devanter was reportedly supportive of McReynolds' anti-Semitism, joining him in opposition to the appointment of Benjamin Cardozo to the Court. McReynolds would mutter, and often leave the bench, when a woman lawyer appeared in the courtroom to present a case. He thought it effeminate for men to wear wrist watches, and vulgar for women to use red fingernail polish. Like Justice Van Devanter, McReynolds was a long-time member of the Chevy Chase Club, where strong racist rules prevailed.

14. President Theodore Roosevelt named Holmes to the United States Supreme Court on August 11, 1902. The Senate unanimously confirmed the appointment on December 4, and Holmes took his seat on the Court on December 8, 1902. President McKinley had been assassinated in September 1901 and Vice President Theodore Roosevelt took his place. Holmes succeeded Justice Horace Gray, whom he had also followed as Chief Justice of the Supreme Judicial Court of Massachusetts in 1889.

15. He served later in the Taft Court and the Hughes Court, not departing his service to the Court until 1932.

16. Holmes died on March 6, 1935 at the age of 93. In 25 of his 29 years, Holmes never missed a session of the Court. He walked from his home to the Court daily, a distance of some 2 1/2 miles.

17. Holmes described his colleagues as "nine scorpions in a bottle." Rosen, 6, 75.

18. Rosen, 77, 88, 89. "Holmes was one of the founders of what became called the 'sociological' school of jurisprudence in Great Britain, and became called the 'legal realist' school in America a generation later. Legal realism posits that the law reflects shifting moral and political realities, that law is only that which judges say it is."

19. Rosen, 109; "Social Darwinism taught that the notion of 'survival of the fittest' enunciated in Charles Darwin's *Origin of Species* as an explanation for the evolution of life on the planet could be transposed to the world of social and political philosophy." Rehnquist, 208; see, Richard Hofstadter, *Social Darwinism in American Thought,* George Braziller, Inc., Rev. Ed. (1959).

20. Rosen, 77, 89.

21. Pringle, 968, citing W.H. Taft correspondence to his brother Horace Taft, April 17, 1922.

22. Van Devanter Papers, Letterbooks, Vol. 33, 152, October 24, 1922, Justice Van Devanter letter to Justice John H. Clarke, "The Court has convened.... Justice Holmes looks very well

considering the sever operation which he has undergone. He moves about a little more cautiously than usual, but is as cheerful as ever. My guess is that he is endeavoring to husband it without saying so. H and Mrs. Holmes are at the Powhatan and I understand they are having an elevator put in their house and perhaps some other changes made."

23. Pringle, 969. "The Chief Justice had momentary qualms regarding Holmes's fitness: '...both Holmes and McKenna ought to retire,' he said in April 1922. As far as Holmes was concerned, this was doubtless due to that jurist's illness at the time." citing W.H. Taft correspondence to his brother Horace Taft, April 17, 1922, and W.H. Taft correspondence to Learned Hand, March 3, 1923.

24. Pringle, 969. (citing W.H. Taft correspondence to his brother Horace Taft, April 17, 1922, and W.H. Taft correspondence to Learned Hand, March 3, 1923.)

25. Pringle, "Taft's relationship with Mr. Justice Holmes was to be a source of unending pleasure, and thus despite their disagreement on many subjects and on the law. Almost daily, they went to court together—until 1925 on foot and after that by motor."

26. *O'Neil v. Northern Colorado Irrigation Company*, 242 U.S. 20 (November 20, 1916). Holmes held for the defendant State of Colorado. The entire Court (White, McKenna, Holmes, Day, Van Devanter, Pitney, McReynolds, Brandeis, Clarke) supported Holmes' opinion. Mr. L. F. Twitchell, with whom Mr. Fred Farrar, Attorney General of the State of Colorado, Mr. Luther M. Goddard and Mr. Paul M. Clark were on the brief, for defendants in error Colorado.

27. Pringle, 969, 970, citing W.H. Taft correspondence to H.L. Stimson, May 18, 1928.

28. Bailey, 15. "American jurists such as Holmes and Louis D. Brandeis looked to the utilitarian and positivistic theories of law suggested by mid-nineteenth century legal thinkers such as J.S. Mill and John Austin and accepted a more pragmatic, or realist, view of the law based upon a system of 'sociological jurisprudence' and critical historical methods."

29. Rosen, 77, 89.

30. "Holmes had a judicial method that was developed to a greater degree than any other judge's of that day. He had already shown this quality on the state court... He had shown an impassioned indifference to the 'hydraulic pressures' that converge on 'great cases,' a meticulous regard for the strict legal profile of a case, an inclination to let the legislature have its way, a sophistication that prevented him from projecting his economic philosophy and calling it the Constitution—and that in an era when it would have been easy enough to identify his views with the welfare of the nation." Max Lerner, *Nine Scorpions in a Bottle*, Arcade Publishing (1994), 113.

31. Rosen, 106, see, *Hawaii v. Mankichi*, 190 U.S. 197 (1903).

32. Rosen, 80.

33. Brandeis had been opposed on his appointment to the Court by then ex-President William Howard Taft. Notwithstanding the opposition, Brandeis was confirmed to the Court on June 1, 1916, on a largely party-line 47–22 vote. One Democrat, Senator Francis G. Newlands of Nevada, voted against him.

34. Brandeis, the son of Jewish immigrants, was the first Jewish justice ever appointed to the Court. His family had come to the United States from Prague following the failed revolution of 1848, settling in Louisville, where they soon developed a prosperous grain-merchandising business (though they suffered setbacks during the Long Depression of the 1870s).

35. Pringle, 971. "The doubts that persisted [in Taft's mind about Brandeis] were political, social and legal. Late in 1924, Brandeis had indicated that he would vote with the Chief Justice on an important prohibition opinion. But then, Taft complained, 'He went up to Cambridge and must have communed with Frankfurter and that crowd, and he came back with a notice to me that he was going to change his vote. Brandeis tries as hard as he can to be a good fellow, and in many respects he is.' " citing W.H. Taft correspondence with Helen Manning, June 11, 1923.

36. Pringle, 968.

37. Pringle, 971, 972. "Taft's disapprobation of certain of his colleagues, even his dislike for certain of them, was a minor irritation in a happy life. The years that remained were enormously busy, enormously satisfactory. '... the court ... next to my wife and children, is the nearest thing to my heart in life,' he wrote in the spring of 1923." citing Taft letters to Helen Manning (daughter), June 11, 1923, to James R. Angell, December 2, 1926, and to H.S. Pritchett, April 25, 1923.

38. Pringle, 970. "The most difficult personal problem when confronted Taft when he became chief justice was Associate Justice Brandeis. Deep resentment lingered in his heart. He could not forget the Ballinger case. But it was different when, in the summer of 1921, association with Brandeis on the referred tribunal was an accomplished fact. Taft was never lacking for graciousness. He was realist enough to know that rancor must banish before the necessity of working in peace with his brothers on the court. Brandeis, no less than the Chief Justice,

greatly desired this." "Taft could not fail to be won over by the luminous mind and great learning of Justice Brandeis. After two sessions had passed, he said, 'I have come to like Brandeis very much indeed.' True, they differed in the field of 'social economics ... but withal he is a very hard worker,' concluded the Chief Justice." citing W.H. Taft correspondence with Horace Taft, December 26, 1924.

39. Urofsky, Melvin I., *Louis D. Brandeis, a Life*, Schocken Books, 2009, 488.

40. Urofsky, 572.

41. Urofsky, 575.

42. Urofsky, 577.

Chapter 30

1. *Wyoming v. Colorado*, Decree, 259 U.S. 469 (June 5, 1922).

2. See, 260 U.S. 1 (October 9, 1922); 286 U.S. 494 (5/31/1932); 298 U.S. 573 (6/1/1936); 309 U.S. 572 (4/22/1940).

3. *State of South Carolina v. State of North Carolina*, No. 138, Orig. 558 U.S.256, 175 L. Ed. 2d 713, January 20, 2010) (also 552 U.S. 804, 169 L. Ed. 2d 7, 128 S. Ct. 349).

4. *Montana v. Wyoming*, Original 137, 563 U.S.368 (May 2, 2011), 583 U.S. (February 20, 2018).

5. Sherow.

6. 259 U.S. 498 (1922).

7. 259 U.S. at 502, 503.

8. 151 CCA 455, 238 F. 519 (8th Cir. 1916).

Chapter 31

1. Sherow, 18–20.

2. 259 U.S. 419, 490.

3. 259 U.S. 419, 490.

4. Sherow, 18–20.

5. U.S. Const. art. III § 2, cl. 1 (extending the judicial power of the United States "to Controversies between two or more States"); U.S. Const. art. III, § 2, cl. 2 (stating that the Supreme Court has original jurisdiction "in all Cases ... in which a State shall be Party"); 28 U.S.C. § 1251(a) (2006) (providing the Supreme Court's exclusive jurisdiction over a suit as "between two or more States.").

6. *Arizona v. California*, 283 U.S. 423 (1931).

7. *Washington v. Oregon*, 297 U.S 517 (1936).

8. *Colorado v. Kansas*, 320 U.S. 383 (1943).

9. *Nebraska v. Wyoming*, 325 U.S. 589, 610 (1945). If and when a state relies upon the interests of its residents as the basis of standing in original jurisdiction, the state's *parens patriae* responsibility for the protection of the private interests of its citizens becomes the premise for standing. But where the private interests of its citizens is in the only premise, and *parens patriae* is asserted by the plaintiff state, the defense of the Eleventh Amendment should dispel the assertion of Supreme Court jurisdiction.

10. 259 U.S. 419, 469.

11. *Nebraska v. Wyoming*, 325 U.S. 589, 610 (1945).

12. *Colorado v. New Mexico*, 459 U.S. 176, 183 (1982) (citing *Kansas v. Colorado*, characterizing the body of law as "interstate common law").

13. *Hinderlider v. La Plata River & Cherry Creek Ditch Co.*, 304 U.S. 92 (1938).

14. Sherow, 23.

15. *See Nebraska v. Wyoming*, 515 U.S. 1, 11–13 (1995); *Nebraska v. Wyoming*, 507 U.S. 584, 593 (1993); *New Jersey v. New York*, 283 U.S. 336, 345–46 (1931); *Kansas v. Colorado*, 206 U.S. 46, 114 (1907).

16. *Colorado v. New Mexico*, 459 U.S. at 187.

17. Marshall requested findings regarding: (1) the existing uses of wator [sic] from the Vermejo River, and the extent to which present levels of use reflect current or historical water shortages or the failure of existing users to develop their uses diligently; (2) the available supply of water from the Vermejo River, accounting for factors such as variations in streamflow, the needs of current users for a continuous supply, the possibilities of equalizing and enhancing the water supply through water storage and conservation, and the availability of substitute sources of water to relieve the demand for water from the Vermejo River; (3) the extent to which reasonable conservation measures in both States might eliminate waste and inefficiency in the use of water from the Vermejo River; (4) the precise nature of the proposed interim and ultimate use in Colorado of water from the Vermejo River, and the benefits that would result from a diversion to Colorado; and (5) the injury, if any, that New Mexico would likely suffer as a result of any such diversion, taking into account the extent to which reasonable conservation measures could offset the diversion. *Colorado v. Kansas*, 320 U.S. 383, 394 (1943).

18. 80 *U.S. Law Week* 4177.

Chapter 32

1. March 15–17, 1922.

2. March 20, 1922.

3. March 27–28, 1922.

4. March 31, April 1, 1922.

5. April 2, 1922, Tyler, 166, 330, *n*19.

6. Frank Emerson's tombstone today lies near that of John W. Lacey in the Lake View Cemetery in Cheyenne, Wyoming.

7. Tyler, 171, 331, *n*35, citing, January–

May Correspondence File, RG 0037, Colorado River Compact Commission, State Engineer Records, Wyoming State Archives, Cheyenne Wyoming.

8. Serial 6, June 4, 1921, Washington, GPO, 1921), Granting the Consent of Congress to Certain Compacts and Agreements between the States of Arizona, California, Colorado, Nevada, New Mexico, Utah and Wyoming, Hearing before the Committee on the Judiciary of the House of Representatives. Congressional Record, 67th Cong. 1st Sess. (1921), 2271, 2773–74, 5864.

9. Congressional Record, vol. 35, 1902, 6679.

10. Tyler, 133.

11. Biographical Directory of the United States Congress, 1774 to Present, http://bioguide.congress.gov/ scripts/biodisplay.pl?index=M000852.

12. Tyler, 148, 328, *n*76, citing Congressional Record, vol. 35, 1902, 6679. "Mondell points to the acts of 26 July 1866, 9 July 1870 and 3 March 1877 as the definitive congressional recognition of state control over the appropriation and distribution of water."

13. Tyler, 84.

14. Tyler, 171, 331, *n*33. "Carpenter reasoned that if the Supreme Court ruling would have to apply, 'these states could not enter into an agreement as we are trying to do.'"

15. Tyler, 166, 330, *n*19.

16. Tyler, 172.

17. 4 Mason 397 (1827). 24 Fed. Cas. 472 (No. 14,312) (C.C.D.R.I. 1827). Story's earlier (1816) opinion in *Martin v. Hunter's Lessee* had established the appellate jurisdiction of the United States Supreme Court. See, T.E. Lauer, "The Common Law Background of the Riparian Doctrine," 28 *Missouri Law Review* 60 (1963).

Chapter 33

1. "Just as no man is allowed to be a judge in his own cause, similar fears of bias can arise when—without the consent of the other parties—a man chooses the judge in his own cause." *Caperton v. A.T. Massey Coal Co.*, 556 U.S.868 (2009).

2. Associate Justice Elena Kagan recused herself in twenty-one of the cases which would be heard by the Court in its 2010 term, even though no Supreme Court rule requires it. She claimed to have been involved in them in some way as Solicitor General of the United States immediately preceding her appointment.

3. James MacGregor Burns, *Packing the Court*, Penguin Press (2009), 3.

4. Rehnquist, 312.

5. Herodotus, *The Histories*, Oxford University Press, Oxford World's Classics, Robin Waterfield (Tr.) (1998), 312.

6. John Gibeaut, "Caperton 's Coal," ABA Journal (February 2009), 52.

7. Recusal or disqualification for conflict of interest or bias do present certain problems in jurisdictions with small judicial pools. Some claim there is a "duty to sit" in small jurisdictions, as someone has got to be the judge or resolution of conflict will go undone. Too rigid a standard of recusal or disqualification can also hamper the elevation of jurists from trial to intermediate or final appellate courts.

8. Jeffrey Toobin, *The Nine*, Anchor Books (2008), 236.

9. Toobin, 236.

10. Rosen, 12, 34.

11. Rehnquist, 102.

12. Rehnquist, 89, 90.

13. Rehnquist, 141.

14. Rehnquist, 155–157.

15. 325 U.S.161 (1945).

16. Rehnquist, 65, 66.

17. 548 U.S. 557, 126 S. Ct. 2749 (2006).

18. 560 U.S. 702 (June 2010).

19. Id., Slip opinion at p. 13.

20. Id., Slip opinion at p. 14.

21. Id., Slip opinion at p. 16.

Chapter 34

1. 28 Stat. 388.

2. 55th Congress, Sess. I, Ch. 3, 1897, 30 Stat 62, Act of June 7, 1897. (Sometimes also the "Indian Appropriation Act of June 7, 1897.")

3. *Ward v. Race Horse*, 163 U.S. 504 (1896).

4. 15 Stat. 673.

5. *In re Race Horse*, 70 F. 598 (1895).

6. Art. 6, § 2.

7. *Ward v. Race Horse*, 163 U.S. 504 (1896).

8. Holsinger, 193.

9. 163 U.S. 537 (May 18, 1896).

10. Wilkinson, Charles, F., American Indians, Time and the Law, Yale University Press (1987), 8; William C. Canby Jr., *American Indian Law 2d*, West Publishing (1981), 21.

11. Meriam, *The Problem of Indian Administration*, Institute for Government Research (1928).

12. 25 U.S.C. § 461 et seq.

13. 25 L.D. 478, likewise 25 L.D. 95.

14. 25 L.D. 426.

15. 25 L.D. 97.

16. 225 U.S. 582 (1912).

17. 229 U.S. 498(1913).

18. 231 U.S. 28 (1913).

19. 232 U.S. 487 (1914).

20. 248 U.S. 78 (1918).

21. 249 U.S. 110 (1919).

22. 253 U.S. 17 (1920).
23. 253 U.S. 25 (1920).
24. 224 U.S. 665(1912).
25. 224 U.S. 679 (1912).
26. 224 U.S. 680 (1912).
27. 241 U.S. 582 (1916).
28. 241 U.S. 602 (1916).
29. 228 U.S. 52 (1913).
30. 241 U.S. 556 (1916).
31. 231 U.S. 681 (1914).
32. 247 U.S. 102 (1918).
33. 234 U.S. 192 (1914).
34. 248 U.S. 354 (1919).
35. 256 U.S. 524, 530 (1921).
36. 252 U.S. 159 (1920).

Chapter 35

1. 157 U.S. 429 (1895).
2. 252 U.S. 189 (1920).
3. 253 U.S. 245 (1920).
4. 268 U.S. 501(1925).
5. 307 U.S. 277 (1938).
6. 485 U.S. 505 (1988).
7. 264 U.S. 504 (1924).
8. 268 U.S. 189 (1925).

Chapter 36

1. Joseph Alsop and Turner Catledge, *The 168 Days,* Doubleday, 1938, 206. See, full blow-by-blow account of the "constitutional conflict" between President Roosevelt and the Supreme Court in Leonard Baker, *Back to Back, the Duel Between FDR and the Supreme Court,* MacMillan (1967), (hereafter "Baker").

2. Marian C. McKenna, *Franklin Roosevelt and the Great Constitutional War, The Court Packing Crisis of 1937,* Fordham University Press (2002), 454–457 The retirement provisions of this legislation still prevail for Supreme Court justices. See, Toobin, 284.

3. Milton R. Konvitz, "Value of Judgments," *The Saturday Review of Literature,* September 18, 1946, 15.

4. Phillip J. Cooper, *Battles on the Bench: Conflict Inside the Supreme Court,* University Press of Kansas (1995), 57.

5. A period sometimes called "Constitution in Exile." See, Toobin, 25, 97, 117.

6. Rehnquist, 222. Edward Lazarus describes the same situation in *Closed Chambers.* Times Books (1998), (hereafter "Lazarus").

> On one side massed the Four Horsemen, the octogenarian Justice Pierce Butler, James McReynolds, George Sutherland, and Willis Van Devanter, who together with William H. Taft and others deceased had held sway at the Court for a generation. Usually hostile to claims of civil rights or civil liberties, this old order had as its true hallmark a limitless devotion to the right of free contract and the protection of private property from government. For the Four Horsemen, the principles of laissez-faire economics were not merely preferred but part of the natural order 'beyond the right of official control.' Although they swore allegiance to a brand of constitutional fundamentalism that required judges to 'declare the law as written,' with no textual mandate whatsoever, they freely read into the Constitution their own Darwinist notions of social policy. Using the protean doctrine of substantive due process as their sword, they ventured forth to defend the country against all manner of social and economic legislation—minimum wage laws, maximum hours laws, price controls, regulations of interstate commerce—and, thus, set themselves four-square against Roosevelt's New Deal efforts to lift the nation from depression [Lazarus, 283].

During the 1932–1937 Supreme Court terms, the faction of the Court highly supportive of President Roosevelt's New Deal programs, including Justices Brandeis, Cardozo and Stone, were dubbed the "Three Musketeers." Justice George Sutherland was appointed by President Harding to the Court in September 1922 to fill Justice Clark's seat. Justice Pierce Butler was likewise appointed to the Court in November 1922 to fill Justice Day's seat. Both Justices were therefore not present at the completion of the 1921 term, when the Wyoming v. Colorado decision was rendered.

7. Theodore M. Vestal "Harlan Fiske Stone: New Deal Prudence" in William D. Pederson, Norman W. Provizer (eds.), *Leaders of the Pack, Polls & Case Studies of Great Supreme Court Justices,* Peter Lang (2003), 194.

8. 295 U.S. 330.
9. 40 U.S.C. §§ 401–444.
10. 295 U.S. 495 (1935).
11. 7 U.S.C. §§ 601–640.
12. 297 U.S. 1 (1936).
13. 298 U.S. 587(1937).
14. Rehnquist, 216.
15. Rehnquist, 259, 260. This would have likely included justice Van Devanter.
16. Schwartz.
17. 295 U.S. 555 (1935).
18. 295 U.S. 602 (1935).
19. Roger W. Corley, "Was there a Constitutional Revolution in 1937? in, Stephen K. Shaw, William D. Pederson, and Frank J. Williams (eds.), *Franklin D. Roosevelt and the Transformation of the Supreme Court,* M.E. Sharpe (2004), 53.

20. Lazarus, 283.

21. Conservatism of the Four Horsemen style did not repeat until Associate Justice Clarence Thomas joined the Court. See, Toobin, 117.

22. 290 U.S. 398 (1933).

23. Kenneth M. Holland, "FDR and Charles Evans Hughes," in Stephen K. Shaw, William D. Pederson, and Frank J. Williams (eds.), *Franklin D. Roosevelt and the Transformation of the Supreme Court*, M.E. Sharpe (2004), 103. Although sworn into the originalist view, the judicial activism of these conservative justices was unbridled, when they needed to interpret the Constitution in a manner that served their political objectives.

24. McKenna, 454–457.

25. 268 U.S. 501 (1925).

26. McKenna, 335, 336.

27. Rehnquist, 219, 220.

28. U.S. Senate Report 711, 75/1.

29. Rehnquist, 225.

30. Senator Warren was now deceased, upon having left the Senate in 1929, the last member of the U.S. Congress to have fought in the Civil War.

31. Baker, 239. William Borah "had lines of communication to the conservative members of the Court."

32. McKenna, 454–457.

33. Rehnquist, 230.

34. William E. Leuchtenburg, *The Supreme Court Reborn, The Constitutional Revolution in the Age of Roosevelt*, Oxford University Press (1995), 144.

35. 300 U.S. 379 (1937).

36. 300 U.S. 379, 400 (1937). See, Hall, 1045.

37. 301 U.S. 1 (1937).

38. 301 U.S. 548 (1937). Van Devanter joined the majority opinion written by Justice Cardozo.

39. Epstein, et al, 424, Table 5–7.

40. Epstein, et al, 441, Table 5–9.

41. See, e.g., *National Federation of Independent Business, et al, v. Sebilius*, 567 U.S. 519 (2012).

Chapter 37

1. Toobin, 28.

2. In order, they arrange thus: William O. Douglas, 4/04/1939, 11/12/1975 (F. D. Roosevelt) 36 years, 6 months; Stephen Johnson Field, 3/11/1863, 12/01/1897 (Lincoln), 34 years, 6 months; John Marshall, 1/29/1801, 7/06/1835 (Adams), 34 years, 5 months; Hugo L. Black, 8/17/1937, 9/17/1971 (FDR), 34 years; John N. Harlan, 11/29/1863, 12/01/1897 (Hayes), 33 years, 10 months; Joseph Storey, 11/18/1811, 9/20/1845 (Madison), 33 years, 7 months; James M. Wayne, 1/09/1835, 7/05/1867 (Jackson) 32 years; Bushrod Washington, 12/20/1798, 11/26/1829 (Adams) 31 years; William Johnson, 3/24/1804, 8/04/1834 (Jefferson), 30 years; Willis Van Devanter, 12/15/1910, 6/2/1937 (Taft), 26 years, 6 months.

3. Rosen, 21.

4. Rehnquist, 69. Commenting regarding Chief Justice Vinson, Rehnquist says: "The work of the Supreme Court has enough intellectual meat to it that a justice who is either unable or unwilling to do a certain amount of the cutting of that meat is not apt to emerge as a leader simply on the strength of his abilities as a conciliator."

5. Rehnquist., 87.

6. Writing of Chief Justice John Marshall, Rehnquist observed: "Finally, there must have been a strong measure of the ability to persuade his colleagues in Marshall. Obviously Marshall's one month of law studies before his admission to the bar did not give him the tools to overawe his colleagues with learning, but perhaps his experience in dealing with his fellow human beings in such positions as the command of an artillery company during the winter at Valley Forge was a more than adequate substitute for book learning. The conviviality of the boardinghouse life to which he and his colleagues submitted themselves during the short time each year they were in Washington seems to have been made for someone who could capitalize on his abilities as "team leader." Rehnquist, 122.

7. Professors Albert P. Blaustein's and Roy M. Mersky's 1970 poll of 65 law school deans and professors found eight U.S. Supreme Court justices as "failures." They included, chronologically: Willis Van Devanter, James C. McReynolds, Pierce Butler, James F. Byrnes, Harold H. Burton, Fred M. Vinson, Sherman Minton and Charles Whittaker. Abraham, Appendix A.

8. "Although he apparently made significant oral contributions in the justices' conferences and, with Taft, was coauthor of the seminal Judges Bill of 1925, the dearth of his opinions and his doctrinaire rigidity prompted the Court experts to rate Justice Willis Van Devanter a 'failure'—arguably much too harsh a judgment." Abraham, 129–130.

9. Johnson, Claire Cushman (ed.), *The Supreme Court Justices*, 312.

10. Quote Schultz, 496.

11. Johnson., Citing Drew Pearson, The Nine Old Men, 186 (1936).

12. Mason, 195.

13. Hoffer, 192.

14. Abraham, 129–130.

15. Johnson, 403, 407, 408.

16. Braden Vandevanter, in Van Devanter, Christobelle, *The Van Devanter Family*," E.W.

Stephens Company, Columbia, MO (1943) Foreword.

17. Mason, 209, citations omitted. The author makes no attempt to evaluate who wrote Taft's decisions for him.

18. Schultz, 496.

19. Mason, 127.

20. 273 U.S. 135(1927).

21. Johnson, 403, *n*8.

22. Walter F. Murphy, *Elements of Judicial Strategy*, University of Chicago Press (1964), 79.

23. Phillip J. Cooper, *Battles on the Bench, Conflict Inside the Supreme Court*, University Press of Kansas (1995), 57.

24. Edward G. White, *Justice Oliver Wendell Holmes*, Oxford University Press, 1993, 321–2.

25. John M. Ferren, *Salt of the Earth, Conscience of the Court, the Story of Justice Wiley Rutledge*, University of North Carolina Press, 2004, 137. "With ... the retirements of Justices Van Devanter and Sutherland, only two unreconstructed conservative justices remained on the Court, McReynolds and Butler."

26. Baker, 121.

27. Hall, 1045.

28. Schultz, 496.

29. Irons, 260.

30. Schultz, 496.

31. Hoffer, 192.

32. Johnson, 403, 407.

33. Stephen C. Halpern, Charles M. Lamb, *Supreme Court Activism and Restraint*, Lexington Books (1982), 357.

34. Gould, unpublished PhD. Thesis, 1–102.

Epilogue

1. Arizona, California, Colorado, Idaho, Montana, Kansas, Nebraska, Nevada, New Mexico, North Dakota, Oklahoma, Oregon, South Dakota, Texas, Utah, Washington, Wyoming.

2. E.g., RCW 90.03. 550–600, 2003 1st sp.s. c 5.

3. E.g., Ch. 90.22 RCW.

4. E.g., Ch. 36.70A RCW.

5. California's dual water rights system, that recognizes both appropriative and riparian rights, imposes a reasonable use standard on all rights notwithstanding how they were established. Rights are "correlative." California voters adopted a constitutional amendment in 1928 that placed riparian and appropriative rights on an equal footing. The amendment established a universal requirement of "reasonable and beneficial use." Roderick E. Walston, "California Water Law: Historical Origins to the Present," 29 Whittier Law Review 765, 769 (2008). California Constitution, Article X, Section 2; Joslin v. Marin Mun. Water Dist., 429 P. 2ed 889, 893 (Cal;. 1967) (quoting Peabody v. City of Vallejo, 40 P. 2d 486, 498 (Cal. 1935). National Audubon Society v. Superior Court of Alpine County, 658 P. 2d 709, 725 (Cal. 1983).

6. Act of Apr. 20, 1871, ch. 22, § 1, 17 Stat. 13. "Every person who, under color of any statute, ordinance, regulation, custom, or usage, of any State or Territory or the District of Columbia, subjects, or causes to be subjected, any citizen of the United States or other person within the jurisdiction thereof to the deprivation of any rights, privileges, or immunities secured by the Constitution and laws, shall be liable to the party injured in an action at law, suit in equity, or other proper proceeding for redress, except that in any action brought against a judicial officer for an act or omission taken in such officer's judicial capacity, injunctive relief shall not be granted unless a declaratory decree was violated or declaratory relief was unavailable. For the purposes of this section, any Act of Congress applicable exclusively to the District of Columbia shall be considered to be a statute of the District of Columbia."

7. *Dunn v. Blumstein*, 405 U.S. 330 (1972).

8. *Adarand Constructors v. Peña*, 515 U.S. 200 (1995).

9. *Kadrmas v. Dickinson Public Schools*, 487 U.S. 450 (1988).

10. Tribal legislative infrastructure is not subject to the Equal Protection Clause, as tribes are not "states." Although tribal water rights are said to have been created in "time immemorial," a phrase meaning "beyond the memory of living persons" since at least the Thirteenth Century, see, Joshua Getzler, A History of Water Rights at Common Law, Oxford University Press (2004), the tribal water right is neither created by state legislation, nor based in the appropriation (diversion) of water from the source. Tribes don't rest on state law to protect their water rights. They rest on their treaty entitlements with the United States and on the "Winters Doctrine" implying rights granted by Congress in federal statutes creating Indian reservations.

11. *Department of Agriculture v. Moreno*, 413 U.S. 528, 534 (1973).

12. *Kadrmas v. Dickinson Public Schools.*487 U.S. 450 (1988).

13. *F.S. Royster Guano Co. v. Virginia*. 253 U.S. 412 (1920).

14. *Hartford Steam Boiler Inspection and Ins. Co. v. Harrison*, 301 U.S. 459 (1937).

15. *Quaker City Cab Co., v. Pennsylvania.*, 277 U.S. 389 (1928), quoting *Power Co. v. Saunders*, 274 U.S. 490, 493.

16. The state's exercise of the police power

is not germane to the equal protection question. In an early Twentieth Century decision, authored by Justice Harlan, it was made clear that a state's exercise of its police power is inapposite to equal protection analysis. While proper exercise of the police power is an appropriate defense to unconstitutional takings of property under the Due Process Clause, it is no defense to violation of the Equal Protection Clause. In *Connolly v. Union Sewer Pipe Co.*, 184 U.S. 540 (1902), antitrust law applied to goods manufacturers and sellers generally, but not to agricultural goods. Finding the antitrust statute unconstitutional in this regard violative of equal protection, Justice Harlan said "[A] statute of a state, even when avowedly enacted in the exercise of its police powers, must yield" to the Constitution. [T]he guaranty of the equal protection of the laws means 'that no person or class of persons shall be denied the same protection of the laws which is enjoyed by other persons or other classes in the same place and under like circumstances.' *Missouri v. Lewis*, 101 U.S. 22, 31." A state defense relying on the "police power" is no defense against unconstitutionality under the equal protection clause. Police power may be justification in takings analysis but is not in equal protection analysis.

17. Polyvios Polyviou, *Equal Protection of the Laws*, 54.

18. Polyvios Polyviou, *Equal Protection of the Laws*, 681 (quoting respectively, Stone, J., *Puget Sound Power & Light Co. v. Seattle*, 291 U.S. 619, 624, and Day, J., *South Carolina ex rel. Phoenix Mut. Life Ins. Co. v. McMaster*, 237 U.S. 643, 72–3).

19. *Truax v. Raich*, 239 U.S. 33 (1915).

20. Beck, Robert E., et al., *Waters and Water Rights*, Lexis-Nexis, §11.01 (2008).

21. Hutchins, Wells A., *Water Rights Laws in the Nineteen Western States*, U.S. Department of Agriculture, Vol. 1, 227 (1971).

22. When the prior appropriation doctrine was adopted by Washington's legislature in 1917, for example, the doctrine was essentially analogous to Article 9 of the Uniform Commercial Code. Under the UCC, first-filed liens ("security interests") take priority over later filed liens. This filing/notice system gives the later lien holder the opportunity to evaluate his risk, taking into account the total value of the underlying security. In water, a later ("junior") appropriator could evaluate whether the investment in project development was wise given the prior claims and the total amount of water available. But, in 1917, there was little information about the hydrographic limitations of the water supply. So as this became known the courts over the years fashioned legal limitations on the rights established before 1917 under the common law, as well as those rights established by appropriation, hoping to extend the limited water supply. Today, there is generally consensus is that there isn't enough water to go around. State protection the senior water rights holders by closing off new entrants is inconsistent with the UCC purpose analogy.

23. The historical deference to life-sustaining stock watering has been corrupted with the expansion of commercial stock-feeding operations, so that a "beneficial use" test is now likely appropriate.

24. See, e.g., Wash. Laws 1891, Ch. 142, § 7 at 328.

25. Purposes outlawed by the Constitution fail notwithstanding the relationship between purpose and classification. Taking of property without compensation, for example is an outlawed purpose whatever the means adopted. A classification which takes one class of property, but not another is a suspect classification.

26. 297 U.S. 266 (1936).

27. Rather, the Court found: "a discrimination which has no foundation in the circumstances of those engaging in the milk business in New York City, and is therefore so unreasonable as to deny appellant the equal protection of the laws in violation of the Fourteenth Amendment." "The record discloses no reason for the discrimination. The report of the committee, pursuant to which the Milk Control Act was adopted, is silent on the subject. While the legislative history indicates that the differential provision was intended to preserve competitive conditions affecting the store trade in milk, it affords no clue to the genesis of the clause denying the benefit of the differential to those entering the business after April 10, 1933."297 U.S. 266, 272.

28. 301 U.S. 459 (1937).

29. "Despite the broad range of the state's discretion, it has a limit which must be maintained if the constitutional safeguard is not to be overthrown. Discriminations are not to be supported by mere fanciful conjecture. *Borden's Co. v. Baldwin*, 293 U.S. 194, 209. They cannot stand as reasonable if they offend the plain standards of common sense.... "It is idle to elaborate the differences between mutual and stock companies. These are manifest and admitted. But the statutory discrimination has no reasonable relation to these differences. We can discover no reasonable basis for permitting mutual insurance companies to act through salaried resident employees and exclude stock companies from the same privilege. If there were any such basis, it would have been discovered by the state courts. The trial court said there was

none. Two Justices of the Supreme Court were of the same opinion. The prevailing opinion in that court fails to disclose any good reason for the discrimination. The diligence of counsel for appellee has not been more successful. Thus, the efforts in the state courts, and here, to find support for the statute have conspicuously failed." 301 U.S. 459, 462–463.

30. In *Kentucky Finance Corp. v. Paramount Auto Exchange*, 262 U.S. 544 (1923) and *Power Manufacturing Co. v. Saunders*, 274 U.S. 490 (1927), the Court struck down statutes establishing different treatment in the judicial process (one for domestic corporation litigants, another for foreign corporation litigants). In *Levy v. Louisiana*, 391 U.S. 68 (1968), the Court found that differentiating plaintiffs in wrongful death actions (legitimate children could recover for wrongful death of their mother, but illegitimate children could not) violated the Equal Protection Clause. "Legitimacy or illegitimacy of birth has no relation to the nature of the wrong allegedly inflicted on the mother." And in *Glona v. American Guarantee and Liability Ins. Co.*, 391 U.S. 73 (1968), the Court found that differentiating parental plaintiffs in wrongful death actions (parents of legitimate children authorized to sue, but parents of illegitimate children not authorized to sue) violated the Equal Protection Clause. A classification based on the legitimacy of a deceased child had no rational relationship to the statute's stated purpose (discouragement of illegitimacy). In *Rinaldi v. Yeager*, 384 U.S. 305 (1966), the Court found that a statute differentiating between various parties' duty to pay for trial transcripts (unsuccessful criminal appellants who were in jail required to pay costs of trial transcript, but unsuccessful appellants given suspended sentence not required to pay such costs) violated the Equal Protection Clause. "A state statute requiring an unsuccessful appellant to repay the cost of a transcript used in preparing his appeal which applies only to one incarcerated, but not to others, constitutes invidious discrimination in violation of the Equal Protection Clause of the Fourteenth Amendment." In *Baxstrom v. Herold*, 383 U.S. 107 (1966), the Court found that a New York statute differentiating between various parties' right to jury in civil commitments to mental institutions (persons civilly committed generally entitled to jury, but persons civilly committed at the expiration of penal sentence not entitled to jury) violated the Equal Protection Clause. In *Douglas v. California*, 372 U.S. 353 (1963), the Court found that a rule of criminal procedure that differentiated between rich and poor (granting the right of initial appeal with counsel to rich, but granting the right of initial appeal without counsel to the indigent) violated the Equal Protection Clause. In *Gulf, Colorado & Santa Fe Railway Co. v. Ellis*, 165 U.S. 150 (1891); the Court found that a law which required that railroad, but not other, liable defendants pay attorney fees violated the Equal Protection Clause. The classification was not reasonably related to the state's purpose in providing judicial redress of loss. See also, *Atchison, Topeka & Santa Fe Railway Co. v. Vosburg*, 238 U.S. 56 (1915).

31. In *Southern Railway Co. v. Greene*, 215 U.S. 400 (1910), for example, the Court found that taxing statutes establishing different tax obligations for businesses doing business of the same character (a "franchise tax" for foreign corporations, but no "franchise tax" for domestic corporations) violated of the Equal Protection Clause. "The equal protection of the laws means subjection to equal laws, applying alike to all in the same situation." 215 U.S. 400. 412. Physical location of incorporation was the distinguishing attribute between the several taxing classifications. Just as the time attribute of prior appropriation has little or nothing to do with reasonably supposable purposes of the water law, physical location of incorporation had nothing to do with the state's tax solvency.

In 1957, the Court struck down a licensing statute for currency exchange companies in *Morey v. Dowd*, 354 U.S. 457 (1957). The law specifically exempted named existing businesses otherwise fitting the statutory description, e.g., American Express, USPO, Western Union. Finding that the statute violated the Equal Protection Clause, the Court said that "a statutory discrimination must be based on differences that are reasonably related to the purposes of the Act in which it is found," citing *F. S. Royster Guano Co. v. Virginia*, 253 U.S. 412, 415 (1920). *F.S. Royster Guano Co. v. Virginia* was a discriminatory tax case. Virginia's business revenue tax regime taxed all the revenue of domestic corporations with both in-state revenue and out-of- state revenue but did not tax domestic corporations with only out-of-state revenue. Finding that the taxing regime violated the Equal Protection Clause, the Court observed that "the classification must be reasonable, not arbitrary, and must rest upon some ground of difference having a fair and substantial relation to the object of the legislation, so that all persons similarly circumstanced shall be treated alike." *Louisville Gas Co. v. Coleman* was another discriminatory tax case. The law at issue established differential tax rates for recording of deeds, deeds of trust and mortgages depending upon classifications of different mortgage holders. 277 U.S. 32, 37.

32. *Morey v. Dowd*, 354 U.S. 457, 466.

33. *Morey v. Dowd,* 354 U.S. 457 (1957). See also, *Sioux City Bridge v. Dakota County,* 260 U.S. 441 (1923) (different tax assessment valuation methodologies for similar properties violated the Equal Protection Clause); *Hanover Fire Ins. Co. v. Harding,* 272 U.S. 494 (1926) (different tax rates on domestic and foreign insurance corporations violated the Clause). In neither case was there a rational relationship between the classification and the primary taxing objective.

In *Quaker City Cab Co., v. Pennsylvania,* 277 U.S. 389 (1928), the Court had found that a tax assessed only on foreign corporations, but not domestic corporations, violated the Equal Protection Clause. A "classification must be not arbitrary but based on a real and substantial difference having a reasonable relation to the subject of the particular legislation."

34. 270 U.S. 230 (1926).

35. See also, *Cumberland Coal Co. v. Board of Revision,* 284 U.S. 23 (1931) (intentional, systematic undervaluation for tax purposes of one group of owners owning the same class of property as another group violated the Equal Protection Clause). *Iowa-Des Moines Bank v. Bennett,* 284 U.S. 239 (1931) (a statute establishing different tax rates for domestic persons than for national banks to be an "intentional, systematic discrimination" violates the Equal Protection Clause). Likewise, in *Concordia Insurance Co. v. Illinois,* 292 U.S. 535 (1934) (differential tax rates for domestic and foreign corporations violate the Equal Protection Clause, as there was no reasonable basis to differentiate them).

36. 184 U.S. 540 (1902).

37. 413 U.S. 528 (1973).

38. 413 U.S. 528, 534. On the other hand, In *Kadrmas v. Dickinson Public Schools,* 487 U.S. 450 (1988), the statute at issue differentiated between organized and reorganized school districts. There was no Equal Protection Clause violation due to the distinction's relationship to the statute's purpose—encouragement of reorganization of thinly populated school districts. In *Lalli v. Lalli,* 439 U.S. 259 (1978), the statute at issue differentiated between legitimate and illegitimate children. "Two state interests were proposed which the statute was said to foster: encouragement of legitimate family relationships and the maintenance of an accurate and efficient method of disposing of an intestate decedent's property." The Court found these purposes worthy and rationally related to the classification.

39. 394 U.S. 618 (1969).

40. 394 U.S. 618, 627.

41. 517 U.S. 620 (1996).

42. 517 U.S. 620, 633. See, *New Orleans v. Dukes,* 427 U.S. 297 (1976) (tourism benefits justified classification favoring pushcart vendors of certain longevity);*Williamson v. Lee Optical of Okla, Inc.,* 348 U.S. 483 (1955) (assumed health concerns justified law favoring optometrists over opticians); *Railway Express Agency, Inc. v. New York,* 336 U.S. 106 (1949) (potential traffic hazards justified exemption of vehicles advertising the owner's products from general advertising ban); *Kotch v. Board of Port Pilot Comm'rs for Port of New Orleans,* 330 U.S. 552 (1947) (licensing scheme that disfavored persons unrelated to current river boat pilots justified by possible efficiency and safety benefits of a closely knit pilotage system).

43. 297 U.S. 266 (1936), 272–274.

44. See, Davenport, J.H., *Nevada Water Law,* Colorado River Commission of Nevada (2003), 226, 227. "This need for certainty upon which to base capital investment is either expressed or implied in the older water cases, perhaps more in the 'first in time' element than the nature of use element of prior appropriation."

45. 400 U.S. 112 (1970).

46. 394 U.S. 618 (1969).

47. 405 U.S. 330 (1972).

48. 270 U.S. 230 (1926).

49. Fundamentality of rights is sometimes raised in Due Process Clause cases, as well as in Equal Protection Clause cases. The Bill of Rights' Fifth Amendment has been judicially determined to contain an equal protection element. "The test usually articulated for determining fundamentality under the Due Process Clause is that the putative right must be 'implicit in the concept of ordered liberty,' or 'deeply rooted in this Nation's history and tradition.'" *Loving v. Virginia,* 388 U.S. 1 (1967); *United States v. Windsor,* 191 U.S.771 (2013).

50. 383 U.S. 663, 670.

51. 410 U.S. 113 (1973).

52. *Kotch v. Board of River Port Pilots,* 330 U.S. 552 (1947), *Reynolds v. Sims,* 377 U.S. 533 (1964), *Carrington v. Rash,* 380 U.S. 89 (1965), *Williams v. Rhodes,* 393 U.S. 23 (1968), *Kramer v. Union Free School District No. 15,* 395 U.S. 621 (1969), *Cipriani v. City of Houma,* 395 U.S. 701 (1969), *Hadley v. Junior College District,* 397 U.S. 50 (1970), *Evans v. Cornman,* 398 U.S. 419 (1970); *City of Phoenix v. Kolodziejski,* 399 U.S. 204 (1970), *Oregon v. Mitchell,* 400 U.S. 112 (1970), *Dunn v. Blumstein,* 405 U.S. 330 (1972).

53. *Williams v. Rhodes,* 393 U.S. 23 (1968).

54. *Loving v. Virginia,* 388 U.S. 1 (1967); *Richmond v. J. A. Croson Co.,*488 U.S. 469 (1989), *Adarand Constructors v. Peña,* 515 U.S. 200 (1995).

55. *Griswold v. Connecticut,* 381 U.S. 479 (1965); *Roe v. Wade,* 410 U.S. 113 (1973); *Union Pacific R. Co. v. Botsford,* 141 U.S. 250 (1891).

56. *Wisconsin v. Yoder*, 406 U.S. 205 (1972); *Sherbert v. Verner*, 374 U.S. 398 (1963).
57. *Truax v. Raich*, 239 U.S. 33 (1915).
58. *Loving v. Virginia*, 388 U.S. 1 (1967). "The freedom to marry has long been recognized as one of the vital personal rights essential to the orderly pursuit of happiness by free men." at 12, *Skinner v. Oklahoma*, 316 U.S. 535, 541 (1942), *United States v. Windsor*, 191 U.S. 771 (2013), *Obergefell v. Hodges*, 576 U.S., 135 S. Ct. 2071 (2015).
59. *Skinner v. Oklahoma*, 316 U.S. 535 (1942).
60. *Troxel v. Granville*, 530 U.S. 57 (2000).
61. *Dunn v. Blumstein*, 405 U.S. 330 (1972), *Memorial Hospital v. Maricopa County*, 415 U.S. 250 (1974); *United States v. Guest*, 383 U.S. 745 (1966).
62. *McDonald v. Chicago*, 561 U.S. 742 (2010).
63. This does not argue, of course, that the right to use water for non-domestic, purely economic purposes only is also fundamental.
64. *United Nations International Covenant on Civil and Political Rights*, Articles 1, 9, 9, 12, 18, 18, 19, 21, 21, respectively.
65. The Pacific Institute, a non-governmental organization, puts it correctly: "Governments, international aid agencies, non-governmental organizations, and local communities should work to provide all humans with a basic water requirement—and to guarantee that water as a human right. By acknowledging a human right to water and expressing the willingness to meet this right for those currently deprived of it, the water community would have a useful tool for addressing one of the most fundamental failures of 20th century development." http://pacinst.org/issues/the-human-right-to-water/recognizing-the-human-right-to-water/.
66. It may be argued that the right to use water solely for economic purposes is also fundamental. It is certainly advantageous to wealth, perhaps even economic subsistence, but does not necessarily raise the essential relevance to life. Indeed, it may have substantial relevance to liberty and pursuit of happiness. Basic liberty is the unfettered exercise of self-interest. Life itself is essential to that. But economic sustenance, perhaps wealth accumulation, may also be important, if not essential, to that. Certainly, the unfettered exercise of self interest is constrained without water. The meaning of happiness is more difficult to capture, as one person's happiness may not be another's. But the realization of economic liberty and economic wealth through the use of water (at least to the level of sustenance) cannot be gainsaid not to be happiness.
67. C. Thomas Dienes, 'To Feed the Hungry: Judicial Retrenchment in Welfare Adjudication," 58 Calif. L. Rev. 555, 598, 599 (1970).
68. Polyios Polyviou, *Equal Protection of the Laws*, Duckworth (1980), 202.
69. *William v. Illinois*, 399 U.S. 235, 239 (1970).
70. AS §46.15.035 (c)(3), but see AS §46.15.090, 150.
71. ARS § 45–157(B)(1), 251(1).
72. Cal. Water Code §§106, 106.3, 1228.1 (b)(1), 1228.2.
73. Colorado Constitution, Art. XVI, 5 and 6.
74. Idaho Constitution, Art. XV, §§ 3, 4; ICA §42–111.
75. KSA § 82a-701(c), 82a-705.
76. NRS § 46–204 (natural streams).
77. W. Peter Balleau & Steven E. Silver, "Hydrology and Administration of Domestic Wells in New Mexico," 45 Natural Resources Journal 807, 833 (2005).
78. No, NDCC §§ 61–01–01.2, 61–04–01.1 (4), 61–04–06.1 (applies when there is insufficient water supply).
79. Okla. Stat. tit. 82, §§ 1020–1 (2), 1020–3.
80. ORS §§ 536.310 (12), 537.525 (5).
81. SDLC § 46–1-5, 46–1-9 (2).
82. Tex. Water Code § 11.024 (1).
83. WSA § 41–3-102 (b), 41–3-103, 41–3-907.
84. *Loving v. Virginia*, 388 U.S. 1 (1967). "The freedom to marry has long been recognized as one of the vital personal rights essential to the orderly pursuit of happiness by free men." at 12, *Skinner v. Oklahoma*, 316 U.S. 535, 541 (1942), *United States v. Windsor*, 191 U.S. 771 (2013), *Obergefell v. Hodges*, 576 U.S. 135 S. Ct. 2071 (2015).
85. The Supreme Court held in *Obergefell v. Hodges*, 576 U.S. 644, 135 S. Ct. 2071 (2015), that there could be no state interest so compelling as to justify a legal structure that did not accord respect to fundamental rights "central to individual dignity and autonomy," "The fundamental liberties protected by the Fourteenth Amendment's Due Process Clause extend to certain personal choices central to individual dignity and autonomy, including intimate choices defining personal identity and beliefs. See, *e.g.*, *Eisenstadt* v. *Baird*, 405 U.S. 438, 453, 92 S.Ct. 1029, 31 L.Ed.2d 349; *Griswold* v. *Connecticut*, 381 U.S. 479, 484–486, 85 S. Ct. 1678, 14 L.Ed.2d 510. Courts must exercise reasoned judgment in identifying interests of the person so fundamental that the State must accord them its respect. History and tradition guide and discipline the inquiry but do not set its outer boundaries. When new insight reveals discord between the Constitution's central protections and a received legal stricture, a claim to liberty

must be addressed." 576 U.S. The right to water would seem, if anything, more central to dignity and autonomy than the right to marry.

In *J.E.B. v. Alabama ex rel T.B.*, 511 U.S. 127 (1994), the Court found that Alabama's "legitimate interest in achieving a fair and impartial trial," was not sufficiently compelling to justify discrimination in selection of jurors based on gender. The Court, affording "gender-based classifications" "heightened equal protection scrutiny," found that even the right to fair trial did not justify this discrimination, a violation of the Equal Protection Clause. The right to water seems more basic than the right to fair trial, and the purpose of a time-based discrimination regime, whatever that may be, seems far less compelling than the interest in achieving a fair and impartial trial.

In *United States v. Windsor*, 191 U.S. 771 (2013), the Court found that a law having the "purpose and effect of disapproval of [a] class" particularly when the "avowed purpose and practical effect of the law in question are to impose a disadvantage, a separate status and so a stigma," in this case as a homosexual, violated the equal protection element of the Fifth Amendment. The Court's reasoning was "careful consideration" of the effect of a federal statute, finding that the classification at issue was "inconsisten[t] with the central meaning of the fundamental right. The same might be said of prior appropriation's time-based classifications. These and other marriage/gender cases evolve out of *Loving v. Virginia*, a race case. There, the Court found that "marriage is one of the 'basic civil rights of man,' fundamental to our very existence and survival. *Skinner v. Oklahoma*, 316 U.S. 535, 316 U.S. 541 (1942). *See also Maynard v. Hill*, 125 U.S. 190 (1888). To deny this fundamental freedom on so unsupportable a basis as the racial classifications embodied in these statutes, classifications so directly subversive of the principle of equality at the heart of the Fourteenth Amendment, is surely to deprive all the State's citizens of liberty without due process of law. The Fourteenth Amendment requires that the freedom of choice to marry not be restricted by invidious racial discriminations. Under our Constitution, the freedom to marry, or not marry, a person of another race resides with the individual, and cannot be infringed by the State." 388 U.S. 1, 12 (1967) Access to water is even more "fundamental to our very existence and survival" than is marriage. "The freedom to marry has long been recognized as one of the vital personal rights essential to the orderly pursuit of happiness by free men." *Id.* Cannot the same be said for water?

In *Truax v. Raich*, 239 U.S. 33 (1915), accord, *Takahashi v. Fish & Game Commission*, 334 U.S. U.S. 410 (1948), the Court found that the State of Arizona's interest in protecting the employment of U.S. citizens against that of noncitizens was not sufficiently compelling, indeed was not an interest within the purview of States, but rather to the United States, to justify establishing classifications of "qualified electors or native born citizens" and noncitizens which deprived them of their fundamental right to earn a livelihood.

In *Roe v. Wade*, 410 U.S. 113 (1973), the Court balanced Texas' state interests against the right of personal privacy in marriage and procreation, determining that in some instances where the state's interest was "narrowly drawn to express only the legitimate state interests at stake," that interest was sufficiently compelling to justify limited interference with the right. In the water right context, considering the Court's admonition that the state's interest must be narrowly drawn, and that interference with rights must be limited, any broad rights-apportionment approach, which itself pursues no clearly stated purpose, interferes grossly with the fundamental right to use water. In an early race case, a precursor of the fundamental rights/suspect class cases, *Skinner v. State of Oklahoma, ex. rel. Williamson*, 316 U.S. 535 (1942),. the Court found a law authorizing sterilization applied to felons who were "habitual criminals" but not all other felons (including violators of prohibitory laws, revenue acts, embezzlement or political offenses) violated the Equal Protection Clause. "Oklahoma had made no attempt to show that he who committed larceny by trespass or fraud had biologically inheritable traits which he who committed embezzlement lacked." No compelling state interest was alleged or evaluated, perhaps because the implied purpose of eugenic purity was patently uncompelling. The Court, rather, utilized a rational basis analysis, evaluating the distinguishing attributes of the legislative classifications, causing one to ask what might be the reason for establishing different rights for water users who use the water for the same purpose.

In *Oyama v. California*, 332 U.S. 633 (1948), the Court found that a California statutory escheatment process which differentiated between citizens and noncitizen Japanese, establishing different burdens of proof of parentage for each, violated the Equal Protection Clause. Although the statute did not expressly establish unequal conditions for the different classes, its effects did so. The question was not just "whether those rights have been denied in express terms, but also whether they have been denied in substance and effect."

In *Loving v. Virginia*, 388 U.S. 1 (1967) the Court found that Virginia's purposes as defined by Virginia's Supreme Court of Appeals " 'to preserve the racial integrity of its citizens,' and to prevent 'the corruption of blood,' 'a mongrel breed of citizens,' and 'the obliteration of racial pride,' obviously an endorsement of the doctrine of White Supremacy" were not sufficiently compelling to justify discrimination in criminal statutes based on a racial classification. "At the very least, the Equal Protection Clause demands that racial classifications, especially suspect in criminal statutes, be subjected to the 'most rigid scrutiny,' *Korematsu v. United States*, 323 U.S. 214, 216 (1944), and, if they are ever to be upheld, they must be shown to be necessary to the accomplishment of some permissible state objective, independent of the racial discrimination which it was the object of the Fourteenth Amendment to eliminate." Washington's prior appropriation regime must be premised upon a permissible objective other than the discrimination that its prioritized classification system creates. Protection of statutorily vested rights, even if regarded as a permissible state objective, is not independent of the discrimination, but in fact tautologically connected to the discrimination.

In *Brown v. Board of Education*, 347 U.S. 483 (1954), the Court found the racial classification inherent in "separate but equal" education clearly a deprivation of the right to educational opportunity and a violation of the Equal Protection Clause. The Court was so certain of the violation that it didn't even question whether the state interest was compelling. Whether it be educational opportunity, economic opportunity or opportunity of sustenance, can there be any compelling interest that would justify deprivation of the right to the domestic use of water? To the economic use of water?

In *McLaughlin v. Florida*, 379 U.S. 184 (1964), for example, the Court found that Florida's interest "to prevent breaches of the basic concepts of sexual decency" was not sufficiently compelling to justify a classification of crimes that would apply to multiple race couples but not single race couples.

In *Turner v. Fouche*, 396 U.S. 346 (1970) no compelling state interest could be found to support Georgia's informal system of selecting school board members which systematically selected persons of one race but not those of another.

86. *Fisher v. University of Texas*, 579 U.S. (*Fisher I*); *Fisher v. University of Texas*, 579 U.S. (*Fisher II*), 136 S. Ct. 2198 (June 23, 2016).

87. *Oregon v. Mitchell*, 400 U.S. 112 (1970) (state-laws distinguished between long- and short-term residents' eligibility to vote, discriminating between classes of people based on time (duration of residence)). *Dunn v. Blumstein*, 405 U.S. 330 (1972) (Kentucky's purposes of "purity of the ballot box" (protecting it against dual voting and colonization) and insuring knowledgeable voters were not sufficiently compelling to justify durational residence laws dividing residents into two classes, old residents and new residents.

88. *Reynolds v. Sims*. 377 U.S. 533 (1964) (Protection of established culture was found an insufficiently compelling state interest to justify interference with a fundamental right.). *Carrington v. Rash*. 380 U.S. 89 (1965) ("Remote administrative benefit" is not a sufficiently compelling purpose to justify a discriminatory voting right law. *Harper v. Virginia Board of Elections*, 383 U.S. 663 (1966) (Virginia's interest in generating revenue through a poll tax was not sufficiently compelling to justify a classification of voters excluding those who could not pay the tax.) *Williams v. Rhodes*, 393 U.S. 23 (1968) (Ohio's requirement for an established party as a prerequisite to register for elective office burdens the right to vote and associate, violating the Equal Protection Clause.) *Cipriani v. City of Houma*, 395 U.S. 701 (1969). (City of Houma's justification that "property owners have a 'special pecuniary interest' " in utility system elections, "because the efficiency of the utility system directly affects 'property and property values,' and thus, 'the basic security of their investment in [their] property [is] at stake' " was not sufficiently compelling to justify a classification of voters that excluded non-property owners.) Compare, *Gordon v. Lance*, 403 U.S. 1 (1971). *Kramer v. Union Free School District No. 15*, 395 U.S. 621 (1969) (School District's claim of "a legitimate interest in limiting the franchise in school district elections to 'members of the community of interest'—those 'primarily interested in such elections' and "that 'property taxpayers' (including lessees of taxable property who share the tax burden through rent payments) and parents of the children enrolled in the district's schools are those 'primarily interested' in school affairs" was not sufficiently compelling to justify classifications of eligible voters that excluded non-property owners). *Evans v. Cornman*, 398 U.S. 419 (1970) (Maryland's purpose of insuring that voters were "primarily or substantially interested in or affected by electoral decisions" was not sufficiently compelling to justify a residency classification that excluded persons residing within federal reservations within the state.) *City of Phoenix v. Kolodziejski*, 399 U.S. 204 (1970) (Phoenix' stated interest of preferring voters that are more interested in the

issuance of securities insufficiently compelling to justify a classification of qualified voters that excluded non-property owners from qualification vote in an election approving the issuance of general obligation bonds. "The differences between the interests of property owners and the interests of nonproperty owners are not sufficiently substantial to justify excluding the latter from the franchise." Id at 209). *Parish School Board of St. Charles* v. *Stewart,* 310 F. Supp. 1172 (1970), aff'd, 400 U.S. 884 (1970) (Louisiana's interest in fixing the qualifications of voters in school bond elections so as to delegate to the voters in each school district the authority to improve public education in their district was not sufficiently compelling to justify a classification of voters excluding non-property taxpayers and weighting the votes of property taxpayers in accordance with the assessments of their properties.)

89. *Memorial Hospital v. Maricopa County,* 415 U.S. 250 (1974) (Maricopa County's interest in maintaining the fiscal integrity of its free medical care program by discouraging the influx of immigrants, and in inhibiting the immigration of indigents generally, was not sufficiently compelling to justify a classification excluding new residents (those later in arriving within the County) from eligibility for medical care.)

90. In *William v. Illinois,* 399 U.S. 235, 239 (1970). (Illinois' "interest in the collection of revenues produced by payment of fines, through a 'work-off' system," which could extend the term of incarceration beyond statutorily prescribed terms, was traditional, "substantial and legitimate." But that did not justify the "impermissible discrimination" "when the aggregate imprisonment exceeds the maximum period fixed by the statute and results directly from an involuntary nonpayment of a fine or court costs." The general classification of imprisoned persons excluded those persons who had not worked off their fine and court costs.)

91. 387 U.S. 368 (1967).

92. See also, *McCabe v. Atchison, Topeka & Santa Fe R. Co.,* 235 U.S.715 (1914). *Nixon v. Condon,* 286 U.S. 73 (1932).

Bibliography

Abraham, Henry J., *Justices, Presidents and Senators*, Rowman & Littlefield, Lanham, MD (1999).

Abrams, Harry N., *The Illustrated History of the Supreme Court of the United States*, Harry N. Abrams, Inc., New York (1986).

Alabama-Coosa-Tallapoosa River System Compact

Alsop, Joseph, and Turner Catledge, *The 168 Days*, Doubleday, New York (1938), 206.

Antieu, Chester James, *Over Two Centuries of Law and Life, 1775–1975*, F.B. Rothman, Littleton, CO (2001).

Apalachicola-Chattahoochee-Flint River Compact

Bailey, Mark Warren, *Guardians of the Moral Order: The Legal Philosophy of the Supreme Court, 1860–1910*, Northern Illinois University Press, DeKalb (2004)

Baker, Leonard, *Back to Back: The Duel Between FDR and the Supreme Court*, MacMillan, New York (1967).

Bickel, Alexander M., and Benno C. Schmidt, Jr., *History of the Supreme Court of the United States*, Vol. IX, "The Judiciary and Responsible Government, 1910–21," Macmillan, New York (1984).

Burns, James McGregor, *Packing the Court*, Penguin, London (2009).

Burt, M. Struthers, *The Powder River: Let'er Buck*, Rinehart & Co., Inc., "Rivers of America" series, 1938.

Burton, David H., Taft, *Holmes and the 1920s Court: An Appraisal*, Fairleigh Dickenson University Press, Madison, NJ (1988)

Calhoun, Charles W., *Benjamin Harrison*, Times Books, New York (2005).

Canby, William C. Jr., *American Indian Law*, West Academic Publishing, St. Paul (1981)

Carlson, W. Bernard, "Technology and America as a Consumer Society, 1870–1900," in Charles W. Calhoun (ed.), *The Gilded Age: Perspectives on the Origins of Modern America*, Rowman & Littlefield, Lanham, MD (2007).

Cheyenne Weekly Leader (January 19, 1888).

Cleveland, Frederick A., and Fred Wilber Powell, *Railroad Promotion and Capitalization in the United States*, Longmans, Green & Co., New York (1909).

Cooke, Donald E., *Atlas of the Presidents*, Hammond, 4th Ed. (1975).

Cooper, Phillip J., *Battles on the Bench: Conflict Inside the Supreme Court*, University Press of Kansas Lawrence (1995), 57

Corley, Roger W. "Was there a Constitutional Revolution in 1937?" in, Stephen K. Shaw, William D. Pederson, and Frank J. Williams (eds), *Franklin D. Roosevelt and the Transformation of the Supreme Court*, M.E. Sharpe, Armonk, NY (2004), 53.

Croly, Herbert, Marcus Alonzo Hanna, His Life and Work, Macmillan Co., New York (1923).

Cushman, Barry, "The Clerks of the Four Horsemen (Part I)," *Journal of Supreme Court History*, Vol. 39, issue 3 (November 2014), 386–424. ISSN: 1059–4329 DOI: 10.1111/j.1540–5818.2014.12055.x.

Davenport, J.H., et al., "Governmental Interference with the Use of Water: When Do Unconstitutional 'Takings' Occur?" 9 *University of Denver Water Law Review* (2005).

Dunning, George, "Confession of George Dunning," in *A.S. Mercer, The Banditti of the Plains or The Cattlemen's Invasion of Wyoming in 1892* [The Crowning Infamy of the Ages], Norman: University of Oklahoma Press (1954).

Duram, James C. "The Battle to Save the Court," in Stephen K. Shaw, William D. Pederson, and Frank J. Williams (eds.), *Franklin D. Roosevelt and the Transformation of the Supreme Court*, M.E. Sharpe, Armonk, NY (2004), 71.

Egan, Timothy, *Lasso the Wind: Away to the New West*, Alfred A. Knopf, New York, (1998)

Egan, Timothy, *The Worst Hard Time: The Untold Story of Those Who Survived the Great American Dust Bowl*, Houghton Mifflin, New York (2006).

Epstein, Lee, Jeffrey A. Segal, Harold J. Spaeth,

and Thomas G. Walker, "The Supreme Court Compendium, Data, Decisions and Developments," CQ Press, *Congressional Quarterly*, Washington, D.C. (2007).

Ferren, John M., *Salt of the Earth, Conscience of the Court: The Story of Justice Wiley Rutledge*, University of North Carolina Press, Chapel Hill (2004)

Friedman, Leon, and Fred L. Israel (eds), *The Justices of the United States Supreme Court, 1789–1969: Their Lives and Major Opinions*, R.R. Bowker Co., New York (1969).

Frink, Maurice, *When Grass Was King*, University of Colorado Press, Boulder (1956).

Georgia v. U.S. Army Corps of Engineers, 302 F. 3d 1242, 1247 (11th Cir. 2002); *Georgia v. U.S. Army Corps of Engineers*, 2:01-cv-0026 (N.D. Ga.); *Southeastern Federal Power Customers v. Caldera*, Case no. 1:00-cv-02975 (D.D.C).

Gibeaut, John, "Caperton's Coal," *ABA Journal* (February 2009), 52.

Goodwin, Doris Kearns, *The Bully Pulpit: Theodore Roosevelt, William Howard Taft and the Golden Age of Journalism*, Simon & Schuster, New York (2013).

Gould, Lewis L. "Francis E. Warren and the Johnson County War," *Arizona and the West*, 9:2, Summer 1967.

Gould, Lewis L. "Willis Van Devanter in Wyoming Politics, 1884–1897," Unpublished doctoral dissertation Yale University (1966).

Gould, Lewis L., *Wyoming: A Political History, 1868–1896*, Yale University Press, New Haven, CT, 1968.

Hall, Kermit L. (ed), *Oxford Companion to the Supreme Court of the United States*, 2d edition (2005), 1045.

Halpern, Stephen C., *Charles M. Lamb: Supreme Court Activism and Restraint*, Lexington Books, Lexington, MA (1982).

Hawgood, John A., *America's Western Frontiers*, Alfred A. Knopf, New York, (1967).

Herodotus, *The Histories*, Oxford University Press, Oxford World's Classics, Robin Waterfield (Tr.) (1998), 312.

Hoffer, Peter Charles, Williamjames Hoffer, and N.E. Hull, *The Supreme Court: An Essential History*, University Press of Kansas, Lawrence (2007).

Hofstadter, Richard, *Social Darwinism in American Thought*, George Braziller, Inc., Rev. Ed. (1959).

Hofstadter, Richard, "William Graham Sumner, Social Darwinist," *The New England Quarterly*, Vol. 14, No. 3 (Sep. 1941), pp. 457–477.

Holland, Kenneth M., "FDR and Charles Evans Hughes," in Stephen K. Shaw, William D. Pederson, and Frank J. Williams (eds), *Franklin D. Roosevelt and the Transformation of the Supreme Court*, M.E. Sharpe, Armonk, NY (2004).

Holsinger, M. Paul "The Appointment of Supreme Court Justice Van Devanter: A Study in Political Preferment." 12 *American Journal of Legal History* 324 (1968).

Holsinger, M. Paul, "Willis Van Devanter, The Early Years: 1859–1911," unpublished doctoral dissertation, University of Denver (1964).

Holsinger, M. Paul, "Willis Van Devanter: Wyoming Leader, 1884, 1897," Wyoming State Historical Society, *Annals of Wyoming*, Lola M. Homsher (ed), Wyoming State Archives and Historical Department, Vol. 37, No. 2 (October, 1965).

Horowitz, Charles, "Riparian and Appropriation Rights to the Use of Water in Washington, 7 Washington Law Review 197 (1932).

Horwitz, Morton J., *The Transformation of American Law 1870–1960: The Crisis of Legal Orthodoxy*, Oxford University Press, New York (1992).

Horwitz, Morton J., *The Transformation of American Law, 1780–1860*, Oxford University Press, New York (1992)

Howard, James O'Brien, "Constitutional Doctrines of Mr. Justice Van Devanter," State University of Iowa (1937).

Hughes, Charles Evans, *The Supreme Court of the United States: Its Foundations, Methods and Achievements, an Interpretation*, Garden City Publishing Co., New York (1936).

Hunt, Lester C., *Wyoming: A Guide to Its History, Highways and People, Works Projects Administration*, "American Guide Series," Oxford University Press, New York 1940.

Hutchins Wells A., "Water Rights Laws in the Nineteen Western States," U.S. Department of Agriculture Publication No. 1206 (1971),

Irons, Peter, *A People's History of the Supreme Court*, Viking, New York (1999).

Jackson, Robert H., "The Judicial Career of Chief Justice Charles Evans Hughes," 27 *ABA Journal* 408 (July 1941).

Johnson, Claire Cushman (ed.), *The Supreme Court Justices: Illustrated biographies, 1789–2012*, CQ Press, Thousand Oaks, CA (2013).

Johnson, Wallace H., "Willis Van Devanter: A 'Re-examination,'" 2001 *Wyoming Law Review*, 403.

Kittrel, William H., Foreword in A.S. Mercer, *The Banditti of the Plains or The Cattlemen's Invasion of Wyoming in 1892* [The Crowning Infamy of the Ages], University of Oklahoma Press, Norman (1954).

Lanier, Drew Noble, *Of Time and Judicial Behavior: United States Supreme Court Agenda-Setting and Decision-Making, 1888–*

1997, Susquehanna University Press, Selinsgrove, PA (2003).
Larson, T.A., *History of Wyoming*, 2d ed., University of Nebraska Press, Lincoln (1978).
Lazarus, Edward, *Closed Chambers*, Times Books, New York (1998),
Lerner, Max, *Nine Scorpions in a Bottle: Great Judges and Cases of the Supreme Court*, Arcade Publishing, New York (1994).
Leuchtenburg, William E., *The Supreme Court Reborn: The Constitutional Revolution in the Age of Roosevelt*, Oxford University Press, New York (1995).
Mason, Alpheus Thomas, "William Howard Taft: President by Chance, Chief Justice by Choice," 55 *ABA Journal* 35 (January 1969).
Mason, Alpheus Thomas, *The Supreme Court: Palladium of Freedom*, University of Michigan Press, Ann Arbor (1963).
Mason, Alpheus Thomas, *William Howard Taft: Chief Justice*, Simon & Schuster, New York (1964).
McCullough, David, *The Path Between the Seas: The Creation of the Panama Canal 1870–1914*, Simon & Schuster, New York (1977).
McGreavy, P.S., "Amos Barber, Charles Penrose and the War on the Powder River," *Surgery, Gynecology and Obstetrics*, April 1973 136(4), 632–8.
McKenna, Marian C., *Franklin Roosevelt and the Great Constitutional War: The Court Packing Crisis of 1937*, Fordham University Press, New York (2002), 454–457 (See photograph of Justice Van Devanter on June 1, 1937, p. 456).
McKinnon, Harold R., "The Secret of Mr. Justice Holmes," 36 *ABA Journal* 261 (April 1950).
Mercer, Asa Shinn, *The Banditti of the Plains or The Cattlemen's Invasion of Wyoming in 1892* [The Crowning Infamy of the Ages], University of Oklahoma Press, Norman (1954).
Meyer, Michael C., *Water in the Hispanic Southwest: A Social and Legal History, 1550–1850*, University of Arizona Press, Tucson (1984).
Millard, Candice, *The River of Doubt: Theodore Roosevelt's Darkest Journey*, Broadway Books, New York (2005).
Morris, Robert C., *Collections of the Wyoming Historical Society*, Vol. 1, Wyoming Historical Society (1897).
Murphy, Walter F., Elements of Judicial Strategy, University of Chicago Press (1964).
Novick, Sheldon M., *Honorable Justice: The Life of Oliver Wendell Holmes*, Little Brown & Co., Boston (1989).
Osgood, E.S., *The Day of the Cattlemen*, University of Chicago Press (1957).
Pearson, Drew, *The Nine Old Men*, Doubleday, New York (1936).
Pfeffer, Leo, *This Honorable Court: A History of the United States Supreme Court*, Beacon Press, Boston (1965).
Powe, Lucas A., Jr., *The Supreme Court and the American Elite, 1789–2008*, Harvard University Press, Cambridge, MA (2009).
Pratt, Walter F., *The Supreme Court Under Edward Douglass White, 1910–1921*, University of South Carolina Press, Columbus (1999).
Pringle, Henry F., *The Life and Times of William Howard Taft*, Farrar & Rinehart, New York (1939).
Proceedings in Memory of Justice Van Devanter, 316 U.S. v-xlii (1941).
"Proceedings of the Twenty-Second Annual Meeting of the American Bar Association, Held at Buffalo, New York, August 28, 29, 30, 1899," Dando Printing and Publishing Co., Philadelphia (1899), 679.
Rehnquist, William H., *The Supreme Court: How It Was, How It Is*, William Morrow & Co., New York (1987).
Rivera, José, *Acequia Culture: Water, Land and Community in the Southwest*, University of New Mexico Press, Albequerque (1998).
Rosen, Jeffrey, *Louis D. Brandeis: American Prophet*, Yale University Press, New Haven, CT (2016).
Rosen, Jeffrey, *The Supreme Court*, Times Books, New York (2006).
Rowley, William D., *Reclaiming the Arid West: The Career of Francis G. Newlands*, Indiana University Press, Bloomington (1996).
Sarasohn, David, "The Insurgent Republicans: Insurgent Image and Republican Reality," 3 *Social Science History*, No. 3 / 4, 245–261, Cambridge University Press (1979).
Schriver, Harry C., "Oliver Wendel Holmes: The Lawyer," 24 *ABA Journal* 157 (Feb. 1938).
Schutz, David (ed), *Encyclopedia of the Supreme Court*, Facts on File Library of American History (2005).
Schwartz, Bernard, *A History of the Supreme Court*, Oxford University Press, New York (1993).
Sherow, James E., "The Latent Influence of Equity in Wyoming v. Colorado (1922)," *Great Plains Research* 2(1) 1992, 7–26, Center for Great Plains Studies (1992).
Shinn, C.H., "Mining Camps: A Study in American Frontier Government (1885, 1948); William E. Colby, "The Freedom of the Miner and Its Influence on Water Law," in Legal Essays, in Tribute to Orrin Kipp McMurray, 24 *Georgetown Law Journal* 794 (1936).
Summers, Mark Wahlgren, *The Gilded Age, or the Hazard of New Functions*, Prentice Hall, Upper Saddle River, NJ (1997).

Toobin, Jeffrey, *The Nine*, Anchor Books, New York (2008).

Tractenberg, Alan, *The Incorporation of America: Culture and Society in the Gilded Age*, Hill & Wang, New York (1982).

Tribe, Laurence H., *God Save This Honorable Court: How the Choice of Supreme Court Justice Shapes Our History*, Random House, New York (1985).

Triggs, J.H., *History of Cheyenne and Northern Wyoming Embracing the Gold Fields of the Black Hills, Powder River and Big Horn Countries*, The Herald Steam Book and Job Printing House, Omaha, NE (1876).

Tyler, Daniel, *Silver Fox of the Rockies: Delphus E. Carpenter and Western Water Compacts*, University of Oklahoma Press, Norman (2003)

Urofsky, Melvin I., *Louis D. Brandeis: A Life*, Schocken Books, New York (2009).

Van Devanter, Christobelle, *The Van Devanter Family*, E.W. Stephens Co., Columbia, MO (1943).

Van Devanter, Willis, "The Supreme Court of the U.S.," 5 *Indiana Law Journal*, 553–562 (May 1930).

Vestal, Theodore M., "Harlan Fiske Stone: New Deal Prudence," in William D. Pederson, Norman W. Provizer (eds), *Leaders of the Pack: Polls & Case Studies of Great Supreme Court Justices*, Peter Lang, New York (2003), 194.

Walker, Albert H., *History of the Sherman Law*, Beard Books, New York (1910, 2000).

White, Edward G., *Justice Oliver Wendell Holmes*, Oxford University Press, New York (1993).

White, Richard, *"It's Your Misfortune and None of My Own": A New History of the American West*, Oklahoma University Press, Norman (1991).

Wilkinson, Charles, F., *American Indians: Time and the Law*, Yale University Press, New Haven, CT (1987).

Willis Van Devanter Papers, Manuscript Division, Library of Congress, Washington, D.C.

Woods, Lawrence Milton, *Asa Shinn Mercer: Western Promoter and Newspaperman, 1839–1917*, Arthur H. Clark Co., Spokane, WA (2003).

Wyoming v. Colorado, 259 U.S. 419 (1922).

Index

www.ingramcontent.com/pod-product-compliance
Ingram Content Group UK Ltd.
Pitfield, Milton Keynes, MK11 3LW, UK
UKHW051929100926
8556IPUK00022B/1458

9 781476 681207